The Career Change Resume

KIM ISAACS, MA, NCRW, CPRW
KAREN HOFFERBER, M.Ed., CPRW

McGraw-Hill

New York   Chicago   San Francisco
Lisbon   London   Madrid   Mexico City   Milan
New Delhi   San Juan   Seoul   Singapore
Sydney   Toronto

The McGraw·Hill Companies

1 2 3 4 5 6 7 8 9 0   QPD/QPD   0 9 8 7 6 5 4 3

ISBN 0-07-141186-0

McGraw-Hill books are available at special quantity discounts to use as premiums and sales promotions, or for use in corporate training sessions. For more information, please write to the Director of Special Sales, Professional Publishing, McGraw-Hill, Two Penn Plaza, New York, NY 10121-2298. Or contact your local bookstore.

 This book is printed on recycled, acid-free paper containing a minimum of 50% recycled, de-inked fiber.

Library of Congress Cataloging-in-Publication Data

Hofferber, Karen.
   The career change resume / by Karen Hofferber and Kim Isaacs.
     p. cm.
Includes index.
   ISBN 0-07-141186-0 (alk. paper)
  1. Resumes (Employment) 2. Career changes. I. Isaacs, Kim. II. Title
   HF5383.H63 2003
    650.14'2--dc21
              2003002234

To Our Families

**Mom, Neil, Dad, Craig, Nana, and PopPop
Mom and Dad, Carey and Kaylee, Bill and
Victoria, Dixie and Ray**

Contents

v

8 Executives   95

9 Sales/New Business Development   103

10 Technology/Web/Telecommunications   115

Acknowledgments

This book would not have been possible if not for our colleagues within the resume and career organizations of NRWA, PARW, and CMI. Their camaraderie and generous sharing of ideas were key to the development of our skills. Thanks to Deb Dib, Susan Whitcomb, Judy Friedler, Sally Macintosh, Peter Newfield, Michelle Dumas, Marty Weitzman, Jolene Elliott, Murray Mann, Pat Kendall, Kevin Skarritt (Web designer extraordinaire), Betty Geller, Wendy Enelow, Louise Kursmark, Christine Edick, Ann Klint, Phyllis Shabad, John Thorn, Janice Worthington, Kristy Meghreblian, Dan Miller, Judy Hernandez, Doug Hardy, Carole Martin, and Kim Teter.

At McGraw-Hill, we are indebted to our editor, Barry Neville, for believing in the project and promoting the book idea, and senior editing supervisor Sally Glover, whose expert editorial assistance contributed to the quality of this book.

Steve Oskie and Dan Dorotik, your writing talents are surpassed only by your willingness to meet often crazy deadlines, and we are deeply in your debt. Jodie Thompson, this book would still be sitting on the hard drive if it weren't for your unselfish dedication to and support of its completion. Liz Murphy, your dynamic approach gives our clients hope that their career goals will be fulfilled.

Thanks to our clients and all workers brave enough to pursue a career change. Your vision to pursue your life's calling was the inspiration behind this book, and may you always follow and achieve your dreams.

KIM ISAACS THANKS...

To my brilliant coauthor and friend, Karen Hofferber, your talents have no bounds, and I am honored to have authored this work with you. Mom and Neil, thank you for your unending support and everything you've done for me. You are my motivation to accomplish my goals. Dad, your ability to think "out-of-the-box" and never follow the crowd has inspired me always. You came home with that TRS-80 and a computer junkie was born—I haven't looked back since. Nana and Pop Pop, you believed in me and gave me the tools to make something of myself; I am forever grateful for the sacrifices you have made so that your grandchildren could lead better lives.

To my brother Craig, you are my best friend and my rock. You stood by me when others told me not to quit my "day job" to start a resume writing company. Fiona MacLeod, Liz Sunners, Tony Jacobs, Janet Zokites, Cindy Wood, Gertrudis Reigondeaux, Angel and Adriana Pacheco, and Dina Schulman, I'm amazed that you put up with me, but I thank you for always being there no matter what. Finally, special thanks to Laura Ketron—you motivated me to stay on track and take care of business before anything else.

KAREN HOFFERBER THANKS...

Mentor, friend, and boss-extraordinaire, Kim Isaacs, who believed in me from the start, gave me my dream career, and generously (and oh-so-patiently) continues to provide me with her time and limitless talents to guide me through "all things resume." Mom and Dad, you are my inspiration, my example to live up to, and my teachers in life; your unfaltering love, support, and encouragement make anything possible. Bill and Victoria Fairleigh, and Dixie and Ray Hofferber, I am blessed to have you in my life. Stephanie Missun, your loving care of precious Kaylee gave me countless worry-free hours of writing time. And lastly, all my undying love and gratitude to Carey (world's finest husband and daddy), who made "I do" the best two words I've ever spoken—thank you, "Stud," for never failing to support, love, and encourage me; I love you.

Introduction:
Is It Time for a Career Change?

"When you're finished changing, you're finished."
—Benjamin Franklin

For most of her adult life, Maryann had been a college music instructor. Living in Massachusetts, she loved the work and excelled in her field. But when her husband was offered a music department deanship at a university in Alabama, her excitement for him quickly turned to concern when she learned of the Alabama state law prohibiting a husband and wife from working in the same university department. There wasn't another college within 150 miles of the town where they'd be living, and offering private piano lessons would only generate about one-quarter of the income she was used to.

Across the country, in California's Silicone Valley, Robert just learned that his software programming job was being eliminated along with 150 other positions in the company. The news marked his fifth layoff in four years due to the increasing number of IT company mergers, dissolutions, and downsizings. Although highly skilled in his field, Robert was becoming increasingly anxious about remaining in the technology industry with all of its short-term uncertainty and upheaval.

Beverly's job as an accountant for a major insurance company was secure, but she was bored beyond description. Feeling unchallenged and unmotivated, she literally had to drag herself to the office to do what felt to her like the exact same thing she'd done every day for the past nine years.

Conversely, Jeff, employed as a secretary, was passionate about the world of "number-crunching" and liked nothing better than reviewing volumes of financial data and scores of spreadsheets. But he seldom got the opportunity to do accounting work and felt trapped behind the receptionist desk and chained to the switchboard.

The answer for each of these individuals was a new resume, an aggressive job search, and a total career change.

Perhaps you recognize yourself in one of these scenarios, or your reasons for considering a career change may be quite different:

- You may be transitioning from military to civilian life.
- You may be preparing to reenter the workforce after raising your children, recovering from a disability, or caring for an ill or aging loved one.

- You may be longing to return to an earlier career that you abandoned some time ago.
- You may have been repeatedly passed over for promotions at your present company with no immediate prospects of future career advancement.
- You may be looking to join the corporate ranks to rid yourself of the administrative headaches, financial burdens, or long hours associated with owning your own business.
- You may be feeling unrecognized, overworked, undervalued, or totally miserable in your present job.
- You may be happy in your chosen profession, but looking to change industries (say, from technology sales to pharmaceutical sales).
- You may be wishing that you could find employment that would better fit your personality, talents, or passions.
- You may be yearning for a career that would enable you to strike a better work/life balance.
- You may be wishing that your career included more fulfilling work or was more closely aligned with a cause or purpose that you truly care about.
- You may have always dreamed of becoming a ... (teacher, HR rep, counselor, network administrator, etc.)
- Or you may just be feeling professionally restless, without knowing precisely why or what to do about it.

There are a variety of motives that prompt people from all fields, all industries, and all walks of life to change career paths. First, know this—you are not alone.

Millions of working Americans will change careers this year. And next year. And the year after that.

In fact, most U.S. employees will completely change professional directions several times in their lives. Estimates range from two to seven *career* changes (not just *job* changes) for the typical employee, regardless of industry, profession, or educational background. And while there used to be an almost shameful stigma associated with someone repeatedly altering the course of his or her career, now there's often imprudence associated with *not* doing so.

Why? There are a multitude of reasons, first and foremost among them, *survival*.

Corporate downsizing, massive layoffs, and the dot-com downfall have displaced millions of adults in the past few years. In the first three weeks following the tragic events of September 11, over 1000 mass layoff events occurred, impacting almost 118,000 workers. But even before this, a serious market slowdown was already taking place. According to the U.S. Department of Labor's Bureau of Labor Statistics, mass layoff events were up 40.6 percent in 2001 compared to 2000. Preliminary numbers from the first two quarters of 2001 (more than two months before the terrorist attacks) show a 92-percent increase in manufacturing industry mass layoffs, a 29-percent increase in nonmanufacturing industry mass layoffs, and double the amount of mass layoffs due to corporate bankruptcy, compared to the first two quarters of 2000.

To avoid joining the ranks of the unemployed, professionals are changing careers in record numbers.

Technology and changing consumer demand are other factors forcing workers to reinvent themselves professionally. Just ask any former dot-com magnate, keypunch operator, or typesetter.

But in addition to these external forces driving career change, internal influences also come into play. These include a fundamental shift in the thinking of working Americans, many of whom have been on the receiving end of the dreaded pink slip in recent years. Since so many have seen first-hand just how short-lived the employee/employer relationship can be, "company loyalty" has been replaced with "personal fulfillment." Call it skepticism or realism, but the majority of today's working professionals see a 45-year career with a single employer as a thing of the past. New professional challenges, a good career/personality "fit," work/life balance, and opportunities for personal and professional growth have replaced career stability as employment must-haves for many workers. This often means repeated career changes.

The Bureau of Labor Statistics reports that 67 percent of American workers don't like their jobs, and 41 percent of them are not employed in the fields they studied in school. It projects the following degree of career change (with workers either entering these careers or leaving them):

Industry	Percent of Employment Change (1992–2005)
Health services industry	43.4%
Educational services industry	28.4%
Restaurant/food and beverage industry	33.0%
Social services industry	93.1%
Personnel supply services industry	56.6%
Computer and data processing services industry	95.7%
Hotels and lodging industry	40.5%
Amusement and recreation services industry	39.1%
Management and public relations services industry	69.5%
Child care services industry	73.0%
Agricultural services industry	40.5%
Securities and commodities industry	29.9%
Motion picture production and distribution industries	60.8%
Advertising industry	27.5%
Construction industry	26.0%
Wholesale trade industry	19.0%
State and local government work	16.2%
Grocery industry	22.3%
Insurance industry	23.4%
Trucking and warehousing industries	25.7%
Printing and publishing industries	16.4%
Automotive dealership industry	16.3%
Pharmaceutical manufacturing	15.9%

In addition, the Bureau of Labor Statistics estimates in its *2002-2003 Occupational Outlook Handbook* that between 2000 and 2010, there will be a 100-percent increase in the number of computer software engineers, a 53-percent increase in the number of physician assistants, a 62-percent increase in the number of personal and home care aids, a 40-percent increase in the number of fitness trainers/instructors, and a 66-percent increase in the number of database administrators nationwide. This translates into a surge in these career opportunities.

If you are among the millions of professionals who, either through your own choice or through external circumstances, have decided to begin the "recareering" process, this book is for you.

Like any significant change that is undertaken, it's crucial to have the right tools and an effective strategy in order to be successful. Dieters need revised nutrition and exercise plans to shed pounds effectively. Smokers need strategies and/or cessation aids to help them quit. And career changers need compelling resumes and winning action plans to achieve their new professional goals.

A resume is crucial to winning any new job, but it is even more crucial if you are trying to change careers. You will be competing for positions with other professionals possessing more precise matches to the qualifications, credentials, and experience that employers are seeking for any given opening. If your resume does not powerfully communicate the unique advantages and benefits that you offer, you won't receive many interview invitations, regardless of how many ads you respond to or companies you contact.

You may be feeling nervousness, anxiety, or even hopelessness or fear when you think about changing careers. But armed with the strategies, solutions, resume samples, cover letter examples, and "insider tips" you find in this book, you *can* succeed in shifting careers. By redesigning your resume based on the proven techniques you find in the following chapters, you can:

- Position yourself to make a successful career change.
- Target your resume to win more interviews.
- Effectively compete against job seekers with more directly relevant experience.
- Learn to avoid the top 10 mistakes that career changers make.
- Discover how to identify and leverage your most marketable skills and accomplishments to enable you to transition from virtually any career or industry.
- Find dozens of resumes prepared by certified, professional resume writers that resulted in career change success stories.
- Equip yourself with a masterpiece resume, high-octane cover letter, and triumphant job-search strategy to land your dream job!

ARE YOU DISPLAYING CLASSIC CAREER CHANGE SYMPTOMS?

If your job prevents you from spending quality time with your family, prohibits your ability to enjoy outside pursuits, leaves you impossibly stressed at the end of the day, consumes your every waking moment, bores you completely, challenges you less and less, feels out of synch with your interests and abilities, or presents little opportunity for growth, a career change could be in order. If you answer "true" to one or more of the following questions, you're probably ready (and perhaps overdue) for a leap to a new career.

1. Faced with a choice between going to work and submitting to a triple root canal, you'd be hardpressed to pick the least painful option. ❏ True ❏ False

2. You pride yourself on your in-depth knowledge of every brand of aspirin, migraine remedy, and antacid under the sun. ❏ True ❏ False

3. You've got hair loss of epic proportions, not from premature balding, but from repeated friction caused by that glass ceiling you keep bumping your head against. ❏ True ❏ False

4. You recently filled out a volunteer firefighter application, convinced that your years of experience battling burnout could be put to good use. ❏ True ❏ False

5. When talk turns to current television programs at parties, you contribute by discussing who shot J.R. ❏ True ❏ False

6. Your Monopoly game is missing all of its "get out of jail free" cards. (You keep handing them to your boss in the hope of escaping from your cubicle.) ❏ True ❏ False

7. The last time you and your significant other had a night out was at the premier of *Jaws*. ❏ True ❏ False

8. The literary figure you most closely relate to is Dilbert. ❏ True ❏ False

9. Your leisure reading consists of your company's financial statements and training manuals. ❏ True ❏ False

10. If asked by friends or family what you enjoy about your job, the only response you can truthfully offer is cashing your paycheck. ❏ True ❏ False

HOW TO USE THIS BOOK

While it might be tempting to jump right to the samples and try to find a resume that resembles your background, you will do better first to read about resume strategy in Part One and Part Two. As every career changer presents a different resume challenge, arm yourself with knowledge of the strategy behind your resume's development to produce the most compelling document. When viewing the resumes in Part Four, be sure to look at *all* of the samples. Every resume in this book demonstrates an effective way to position yourself for a career change, and you may find a design that you like or wording that appeals to you in samples outside of your specific career target.

Part One: Planning the Attack on Your Resume helps you understand your strengths before you write your resume. Learn about transferable skills—what they are, how to find them, and how to bring them out in the resume. Find out how keywords are powerful marketing tools for your career transition. You will also learn which resume format is right for you, a crucial consideration that can make or break your introduction to a potential employer. Learn about the pros and cons of different resume types, including chronological, functional, and combination formats. Included are tips to select the best format for your needs.

Part Two: Writing a Resume that Opens Doors to a New Career will teach you how to reinvent your resume for a career change. Discover the nuts and bolts of writing a resume for a career change. Understand the value of strategic resume components such as summary, skills, experience, and education sections. Learn to write a resume objective or summary to target your resume effectively for a career change. Get the inside track on how to avoid the top 10 resume blunders made by career changers. Find answers to the most commonly asked questions regarding special circumstances, including employment gaps, unemployment, layoffs, job hopping, military-to-civilian career changers, transition from the corporate to the nonprofit sector (and vice versa), and homemakers returning to the workforce.

Part Three: Maximize Your Resume's Exposure explains how the cover letter is a vital marketing tool for the career changer's arsenal. You will learn how to write an employer-focused letter that prompts hiring managers to call you for job interviews, and the four different types of cover letters (ad response, "cold," networking, and recruiters). After your resume and cover letter are ready to go, find out what to do with your new documents, including how to land employment and informational interviews. Find resources for generating leads, such as participation in trade associations, online networking, targeted-mail or e-mail campaigns, and response to job ads. Learn about strategies that worked in the real world with stories from the job-search trenches—resume writing, resume design, and job search strategies that worked for career changers. You will also find a handy job search contact log to help track your job search progress.

Part Four: Resume Samples by Career Goal provides career change resume examples across numerous fields, levels, and industries. The samples are real resumes that were used in successful job search campaigns, with names and identifying information changed to protect the job seekers' identities.

The end of the book includes resources for career changers, including career counselors, Web sites, and resume writers/contributors. If you find that you need help developing your interview-generating resume, consider contacting one of the talented resume writers listed in the back of the book.

Part 1

PLANNING THE ATTACK ON YOUR RESUME

"Take a chance! All life is chance. The man or woman who goes far-
thest is generally the one who is willing to do and dare. The 'sure
thing' boat never gets far from shore."

—DALE CARNEGIE

1

What Do You Offer?

Brian Simms was on the verge of giving up his dream of finding a job in sales, a career he decided to pursue after 10 years of teaching high school math. His job search was at a standstill because his resume simply listed his teaching experience and credentials, so hiring managers immediately pigeonholed him as a teacher rather than a salesperson. After three months of unsuccessful searching, Brian realized that his resume was holding him back. He restrategized the document to draw out what he would offer as a salesperson, and immediately started receiving calls for interviews.

YOUR RESUME AS A MARKETING TOOL

Competition for the best jobs is fierce, and even more difficult for the career changer. You've got to convince hiring managers that you've "got what it takes" to succeed despite your new career direction. Your resume, then, is not an outline of everything you've done in your career, but a marketing document designed to sell your most compelling credentials. To market yourself effectively, you need a strong handle on the top qualifications for your career goal and your matching qualifications. You need first to understand why you are suited for this transition before you can convince hiring managers that you are worthy of job interviews. This requires occupational research and a good look inside yourself to assess honestly what you offer.

IDENTIFY YOUR TRANSFERABLE SKILLS

Transferable skills are skills that you developed in one career that can be applied to your new career. For example, a teacher possesses excellent presentation, persuasive, human relations, communication, and leadership skills. Your transferable skills do not have to be skills that were formally required in your position. If you assumed additional responsibilities (most likely because you were passionate about the tasks and they relate to your new career goal), the skills you developed may be touted on your resume.

Start by reviewing job advertisements and descriptions for your ideal position. Use online job sites such as *Monster* and *FlipDog.com*, newspaper advertisements, career opportunities posted on company Web sites, and ads listed in trade journals. Carefully review the job descriptions and determine what skills, abilities, training, and experience employers find desirable in the ideal candidate. Compare advertisements and look for frequently requested experience, skills, education, and work traits.

Use the following worksheet (Figure 1-1a) to write a list of the credentials most valued by employers, whether or not you have the desired credentials. Then think about how your qualifications are a close match. This is not the time to fret about your lack of related experience. Stretch your imagination and free-write ideas on why you should be considered for your dream job. Think about transferable skills, personal attributes, and accomplishments that relate to your goal. Review Figure 1-1b to see how a teacher identified transferable skills and experience for her sales career goal.

Figure 1-1a: Identify Your Transferable Skills

Top Eight Credentials Requested in Job Ads	Your Matching Credentials, Accomplishments, and Transferable Skills
1.	
2.	
3.	
4.	
5.	
6.	
7.	
8.	

Figure 1-1b: Teacher Transitioning to Sales

Top Eight Credentials Requested in Job Ads	Your Matching Credentials, Accomplishments, and Transferable Skills
1. New business development skills/ proven sales performer	Achieved consensus and buy-in from administrators and staff to support new fund-raising initiative for United Way; garnered publicity for fund-raising event by alerting media and securing front-page coverage in local newspaper.
	"Sold" students on the importance and value of subject matter.
2. Organizational skills	Integrally involved in the successful creation, launch, and ongoing management of Teacher Induction Program, designed to improve teacher retention in urban schools.
	Praised by local government officials, school teachers/administrators, and parents for direction of "Partners in Education" program aimed at encouraging students to pursue careers in science.
3. Strong interpersonal and communication skills	Expert interpersonal, communication, and morale-building skills, with demonstrated ability to build crucial partnerships with key stakeholders, interface effortlessly with all organizational levels and cultural/socioeconomic backgrounds, unite fractionalized groups, and win enthusiastic support.
	Frequent leader of in-service workshops and educational seminars. Leverage strengths in interpersonal skills to model best practices, reward improvements, and coach weaker areas.
	Work one-on-one with teachers to augment lesson plans, strengthen classroom management, share resource ideas, and pinpoint problems.
4. Bachelor's degree	Master's degree in educational leadership.
5. Excellent presentation, negotiation, customer service, and follow-up skills	Skilled negotiator and relationship builder, with demonstrated ability to facilitate cross-departmental cooperation, ultimately benefiting program quality.
	Effectively manage parent/community relations; tactfully resolve complaints/

Figure 1-1b: Teacher Transitioning to Sales (cont.)

Top Eight Credentials Requested in Job Ads	*Your Matching Credentials, Accomplishments, and Transferable Skills*
	disputes, and seek win-win outcomes to assist special-needs children and their families.
	Jointly directed after-school minicourse program with fellow teacher. Solicited and secured numerous activity sponsors, organized transportation, and developed lively programs that resulted in attendance far surpassing original projections.
6. Computer proficiency	Advanced computer skills, including Word, Excel, PowerPoint, Access, Outlook, and WordPerfect.
7. Team player	Collaborated extensively with superintendents, school administrators, and teachers to pinpoint challenges, strategize program content, and ensure full state compliance.
	Eased frustrations and anxieties of novice teachers struggling to succeed in their new careers. Implemented upward communication mechanisms, open-door policy, and mentorships between beginning and veteran teachers that succeeded in increasing new-teacher retention rates.
	Voluntarily assumed expanded role teaching Spanish to accommodate staffing/budget shortages. Collaborated with school's Spanish teacher to develop grade-level-appropriate instruction, and successfully prepared students to enter next-year Spanish classes at year-end.
8. Goal oriented and highly motivated	Elevated student learning performance and skills mastery beyond initial targets by continuously seeking ways to connect with each student and instilling a shared sense of pride, ownership, and accomplishment throughout their progress.
	Utilized a variety of methods (teacher mentoring program, videos, workshops) to achieve repeated turnaround success and elevate student scores on state-mandated tests.

Figure 1-1b: Teacher Transitioning to Sales (cont.)

Top Eight Credentials Requested in Job Ads	Your Matching Credentials, Accomplishments, and Transferable Skills
	Commended for teaching excellence, with formal recognition as "Teacher of the Month." Consistently achieved excellent student behavior indicating cognitive improvements across critical-thinking and problem-solving areas.
	Outperformed project goals, delivering an increase in participating schools' instructor retention and teacher education program enrollment.

RESEARCH INDUSTRY KEYWORDS

Keywords are industry "buzzwords," terms used by employers to identify candidates with suitable skills for job openings. Due to the widespread use of electronic resume tracking systems in recent years, the inclusion of keywords has become crucial to getting your resume noticed. This is often an area where career changers' resumes fall short—because they don't yet have the specific experience, important keywords are omitted from the resume.

Commonly used keywords include job titles, job skills, computer programs, educational credentials, and personality traits. To start considering the right keywords for your occupation, look at the job advertisements for your ideal position. Study the ads and look for keywords or buzzwords that are frequently mentioned. Incorporate any matching keywords into your resume.

HOW DO I INCORPORATE KEYWORDS IF I DON'T HAVE THE EXPERIENCE?

Keywords may appear anywhere on the document, so you should be able to include important keywords in your resume. For example, an artist who is transitioning to pharmaceutical sales can include the "pharmaceutical sales representative" keyword in the "Objective" section of the resume. Be creative (but not dishonest) when incorporating keywords into your resume so that you achieve maximum exposure. The keyword examples (organized by career category) on the following pages will give you some ideas of important terms for various fields.

Keywords are constantly changing, and the best way to determine keywords is to review employer requirements in job ads. As you review the keyword examples, keep in mind that you will only incorporate job titles and skills that are relevant to your objective.

KEYWORD EXAMPLES

Managers/Executives

Sample Job Titles: CEO, chief executive officer, COO, chief operations officer, VP, vice president, vice president of operations, executive vice president, department head, department manager, president, director of operations, operations manager, executive director, director, assistant director, program manager, senior operations manager, general manager, GM, managing director, manager, assistant manager, plant manager, production manager, line manager, business analyst, engineering manager, product manager, project manager, quality manager

Sample Skills/Credentials: P&L management, margin improvement, strategic planning, executive leadership and supervision, cross-functional team leadership, staff training and mentoring, corporate vision, corporate image enhancement, relationship management, value-added services, vendor and contract negotiations, deal structuring, partnership and alliance building, expansion strategies, business development, facilities planning and management, program development, conflict resolution, marketing, communications, upward communication, employee development, cost control, cost reduction and avoidance, cost containment, competitive market positioning, continuous process improvement, business process reengineering, BPR, restructuring, project management, team building and training, change management, crisis management, turnaround management, start-up operations, manufacturing operations, business plans, fiscal management, financial management, resource allocation and management, budgeting, budget management, supply chain management, EVA, labor relations, M&A, due diligence, TQM, Six Sigma, productivity/output improvement, JIT systems, policy development, board relations, shareholder relations, vendor relations, customer relations, safety programs, materials replenishment systems, plant operations, plant layout, production flow, general operations, ISO, asset management, risk management, materials management, financial planning and analysis, regulatory compliance, product development and market launch, product management, product design, go-to-market launch, new product introduction, e-commerce initiatives and strategy, trend and needs analysis, production supervision, quality control, quality assurance, research and development, R&D, M.B.A., B.S. in management, B.A. in business administration

Technology/Web/Telecommunications

Sample Job Titles: CIO, chief information officer, CTO, chief technology officer, information technology vice president, IT manager, information technology manager, IT director, information technology director, director of system architecture, director of MIS, director of technology, senior network administrator, senior network engineer, senior network manager, network administrator, network engineer, network manager, network designer, senior database administrator, database administrator, DBA, database designer, senior programmer, senior network analyst, programmer, junior programmer, network analyst, junior analyst, network engineering manager, e-commerce director, systems analyst, senior systems analyst, systems engineer, systems administrator, communications technician, telecommunications director, director of application development, LAN manager, WAN manager, software engineer, senior software engineer, software designer, software developer, applications developer, Web developer, Web designer, director of Web site services, Internet manager, QA engineer, software test engineer, helpdesk manager, helpdesk, technical support, desktop support, support specialist, director of system security, staff engineer, senior staff engineer, technical trainer, software trainer, technician, project manager, computer hardware technician, data analyst, technical installer

Sample Skills/Credentials: quality assurance, QA, quality control, technical infrastructure, networking, network administration, systems administration, testing/scripting/documentation, project management, project lifecycle management, software development, technical solutions, solutions engineering, OOA, OOAD, client/server, DNS, distributed systems, embedded systems, GUIs, PKI, code generation, end-user training and support, systems integration/migration/implementation/configuration, troubleshooting, systems design, systems engineering, LAN/WAN administration, LAN/WAN setup and optimization, cross-functional team leadership, IT team leadership, team building, programming, debugging, CRM, technology planning, system security, business continuity, disaster recovery, strategic planning, database management, applications (e.g., MS Office, Visio, Access, Oracle), systems (e.g., Windows, UNIX, Linux), cross-platform expertise, languages (e.g., C, C++, Java, HTML), hardware (e.g., workstations, PCs, USB, monitors, modems), protocols (e.g., TCP/IP, DHCP, NetBEUI, FTP), MCSE, CCNA, CNA, MCT, CTT, A+, server integration, desktop support, technical support, user permission policies, performance enhancement, uptime improvement, systems architecture, information systems, Web site development, Web design, content development, e-commerce business systems and strategies, customer service, memory/RAM, supporting input/output devices, peripherals, computer maintenance, backup/recovery procedures, 3-D modeling, data modeling and analysis, problem solving, technical manuals, technical writing, test reports, business case development, business requirements definition, needs analysis, data warehouse technology, systems analysis, B.S. in computer science, B.S. in computer information systems, A.A. in computer science/computer technology, query analysis, technical and business strategies, dial-in configuration, equipment routing

Education/Training

Sample Job Titles: learning and development specialist, motivational speaker, software training and development manager, organizational development manager, software trainer, corporate training and development specialist, corporate training and development manager, instructor, teacher, program administrator, principal, assistant principal, school administrator, corporate trainer, trainer, e-learning curriculum developer, curriculum designer, teacher's aid, instructional designer, school counselor, superintendent, assistant superintendent, professor, assistant professor, associate professor, department head, dean, assistant dean, associate dean, college administrator, university administrator, university president, university vice president, director of distance learning, distance education coordinator, financial aid advisor, financial aid counselor, guidance counselor, student advisor, admissions director

Sample Skills/Credentials: curriculum design, curriculum development, course development, teaching and learning, e-learning, distance education, distance learning, employee development programs, training program development and delivery, instruction and training, leadership development, staff development and training, classroom management and instruction, student evaluation and assessment, school administration, leadership and supervision, facilities planning and management, diversity training, adult learning, alliance and partnership building, parent/teacher/student/alumni/faculty/staff relations, grant writing, grant management, budgeting, budget administration, facilitation, persuasive communication, school security, coaching, team building and motivation, staff evaluation, budgeting, strategic planning, lesson planning, lesson preparation, training manuals, job aids, computer training, certified trainer, MCT, student counseling, student advising, mentoring, accreditation processes, scheduling, in-service leadership, community service program management, team building and supervision, staff motivation, morale building, public speaking, professional presentations, at-risk populations, atypical learners, textbook evaluation, academics, online training programs, computer-based training, CBT, training module design, learning program evaluation, regulatory compliance, project management, program development and management, needs analysis, competency models, continuous quality/process improvement, organizational development, testing, instructional/program support, learning technologies, instructional technology, written/verbal communication, Macintosh OS, Windows, B.A. in education, B.S. in education, M.A. in education, M.Ed., Ed.D., Ph.D.

HEALTHCARE/MEDICAL

Sample Job Titles: physician, doctor, physician's assistant, nurse, nurse's aid, home healthcare nurse, rehabilitation specialist, counselor, mental health counselor, psychologist, psychiatrist, hospital/medical administrator, medical consultant, medical director, clinical director, medical administrator, healthcare administrator, pharmacist, pharmacy technician, emergency medical technician, EMT, occupational therapist, intern, child life specialist, phlebotomist

Sample Skills/Credentials: medical administration, patient care, hospital operations, clinical operations, strategic planning, relationship management, patient/staff relations, staff supervision, continuity of care, budgeting, budget administration, quality improvement, internal medicine, patient counseling, scheduling, HMOs, outpatient and inpatient treatment/care, healthcare, preventive medicine, chart review, medication disbursement, medication administration, drug safety, case management, quality control, pharmacology, drug therapy, physical assessment, medical-surgical nursing, clinical practices and protocols, quality care, substance abuse counseling, behavior modification strategies, program planning and development, crisis and emergency response, socioeconomic and psychosocial issues, crisis intervention, clinical/medical evaluations, B.S.N., R.N., M.D.

Skilled Trades

Sample Job Titles: plumber, electrician, junior electrician, carpenter, bricklayer, builder, construction worker, architect, junior architect, architectural intern, interior designer, gardener, janitor, maintenance engineer, waste engineer, technician, construction supervisor, construction manager, landscaper, landscape architect, housepainter, mason, machinist, mechanic, automotive painter, hairstylist, horticulturist, fitter, woodworker, mould maker, pattern maker, printer, tool and die maker, crane operator, ironworker, lineworker, painter, decorator, sheet metal worker, refrigeration and heating technician, steamfitter, apprentice, draftsperson

Sample Skills/Credentials: HVAC, refrigeration/heating/cooling systems, circuits, fabrication, repair, installation and maintenance, design, rigging, waste disposal, wastewater disposal, construction, remodeling, renovation, equipment handling, inspection and diagnosis, testing and troubleshooting, preventive maintenance programs, systems and components, electrical systems, fuel systems, assembly, landscaping, land clearing, overhauling, system design, building, gauges, prototypes, jigs, fixtures, switches and relays, circuit breakers, signaling devices, refractory materials, models and templates, model building, interior and commercial design, space planning, spatial planning, color texture and theory, furnishing and fabric selection, lighting design, architectural design, design concepts, drafting, AutoCAD, DataCAD, CAD, drawings, blueprints, urban renewal, building codes, UBC, axonometrics, schematics, feasibility studies, color rendering

Legal/Law Enforcement

Sample Job Titles: attorney, lawyer, counsel, general counsel, corporate counsel, associate counsel, police officer, police supervisor, paralegal, security specialist, security officer, loss prevention manager, security supervisor, director of security and safety, risk analyst, legal secretary, law clerk, legal assistant, deputy, detective, sheriff, marshal, investigator, judge, court reporter, district attorney, DA, prosecutor, partner, senior partner, managing partner, junior partner, security guard, security specialist, security officer, inspector, lieutenant, deputy inspector, sergeant, dispatcher

Sample Skills/Credentials: intellectual property, IP, criminal investigations, administrative support, executive-level reports, investigative research and analysis, database management, leadership and supervision, team building and training, criminal justice, legal issues/legal matters, risk assessment and management, background investigative work, policy and procedure development, undercover investigations and operations, loss control, loss mitigation, loss prevention, risk assessment and analysis, asset protection, workplace and employee safety, law enforcement, planning and managing investigations, crisis response, public safety and administration, emergency planning, tactical field operations, budgeting, project scheduling, project management, community outreach, public/media/employee/customer relations, regulatory and legal compliance, counterterrorism tactics and strategies, workflow planning and scheduling, crime prevention, crime reduction, index crimes, police-community relations, dispatch operations, intelligence gathering, forensics, crime scene analysis, personal protection services, arbitration and mediation, alternative dispute resolution, ADR, interviewing and interrogation, legal research, proposal/memoranda/brief writing, advocacy, anticorruption, criminology, Juris Doctorate, JD, MA in security management, security services, security operations, casework methods, aggression management, inspection procedures, criminal apprehension, court testifying, arrest procedures, traffic enforcement, escort procedures, drug and alcohol testing, firearms/weaponry safety and handling, shrink reduction, surveillance, defensive and take-down tactics, security audits, fraud prevention, hate crimes investigation, workplace violence prevention, hazardous materials handling, HAZMAT, torts, criminal/civil law, trusts and estates, family law, product liability law, evidence, litigation, real property, mergers and acquisitions, real estate purchases and leases, trademark/patent licensing, workers' compensation, employment law, software licensing, P&L enhancement, debt collection, bankruptcy law, contract negotiation/structure/review, federal court litigation, tax assessment strategies, public speaking, guardianships, document preparation, legal documentation, settlement negotiations, structured settlements, transactional law, trial management, case management, B.S./B.A. in political science, B.S./B.A. in criminal justice, certified paralegal

Writing/Editing

Sample Job Titles: reporter, journalist, writer, copywriter, editor, managing editor, researcher, Web content writer, Web content developer, Web content manager, Internet/intranet gatekeeper, editor in chief, editor at large, contributing author, freelance writer/reporter, news writer, copyeditor, editorial assistant, screenwriter, playwright, poet

Sample Skills/Credentials: travelogues, promotional copy, research and analysis, field research, story research, project research, investigative research, reporting, field reporting, copy editing, proofreading, print/Web/broadcast writing, journalism, staff supervision, creative team leadership, ad writing, organization and follow-through, ethics and integrity, interpersonal skills, interviewing, marketing materials, collateral development, novels, poetry, fiction, nonfiction, short stories, Web site concept, Web writing, gatekeeping, content development, AP style, press releases, public service announcements, PSAs, information collection/analysis/dissemination, articles, presentations, review and revision, caption writing, manuals, data collection, creative writing, communication skills, project management, B.A./B.S. in English/communications/journalism

Hospitality/Tourism/Travel

Sample Job Titles: food and beverage manager, F&B manager, food service manager, waiter, waitress, host, maitre d', bar manager, sommelier, bartender, hotel manager, chef, executive chef, restaurant manager, cook, dishwasher, bus person, front desk clerk, front desk manager, maid, housekeeping manager, concierge, travel agent, chamber of commerce director, tourism director, travel coordinator, travel consultant, conference manager, trade show manager, tour leader, resort manager, catering manager, banquet manager

Sample Skills/Credentials: trade show/event/conference/meeting planning and managing, event marketing and coordination, project management, destination/travel planning and promotions, customer and vendor relationship management, budgeting and cost containment, leadership, team building and training, B2B/B2C sales, sales and marketing, strategic planning, food preparation, menu development and pricing, front- and back-of-house supervision, guest relations, customer relations, public relations, complaint handling, conflict resolution, staffing, tour group leadership, start-up operations, restaurant operations, hotel operations, bilingual/ multilingual skills, service orientation, travel coordination, banqueting, reservation systems, travel agency operations, fares and ticketing, retail/corporate/commercial travel administration, VIP guest service, interpersonal and communication skills, customer service, POS systems, hospitality management, P&L management/enhancement, service and quality enhancement, average daily rate, ADR, occupancy increase, business planning and implementation, multisite/multioutlet operations, purchasing program strategies, menu research and development, menu concepts, five-star dining, fiscal management, loss control, catering sales and operations, F&B services, cost controls, training manuals, facility layout, inventory control, employee retention, quality control, sanitation, food/labor costs

Real Estate/Property Management

Sample Job Titles: property manager, assistant property manager, real estate agent, realtor, broker, property rental agent, property rental assistant, construction project manager, developer, civil engineer, structural engineer, estimator, mortgage broker, mortgage processor, home inspector, appraiser

Sample Skills/Credentials: commercial/residential construction, residential/commercial real estate, construction project management, property management, regulatory compliance (OSHA, UBC), bidding, planning, staffing, workflow scheduling/planning/ prioritization, budgeting, quality assurance, code/safety compliance, property maintenance and repair, basic carpentry/construction, vendor/contractor/subcontractor partnerships and relations, customer relations, tenant relations, complaint handling, conflict resolution, property rental and upkeep, B2C sales, real estate sales, tenant dispute mediation, antidiscrimination laws, contract preparation, apartment rental operations, appointment setting, showing properties, property listing and showing, serving eviction notices, new business development, presentations and negotiations, market research, collections, closings, capital improvements, land development, competitive bid packages, equity and debt financing, equipment acquisition, site supervision, government and community relations, project oversight, civil/structural engineering, real estate appraisals, zoning compliance, vendor selection, prospect qualification, new construction presales, revenue generation, repeat/referral business, property valuation

Nonprofit/Social Services/Government

Sample Job Titles: community relations director, community relations coordinator, outreach coordinator, caseworker, case manager, social worker, government agent (e.g., FBI, DEA, FDA, ATF, CIA, IRS), public policy researcher/analyst, minister, church worker, church associate, pastor, rabbi, priest, nun, nonprofit agency director, nonprofit foundation director, program director, program coordinator, fundraising coordinator, director of development, elected official (e.g., senator, congresswoman, mayor), city manager, campaign manager, volunteer coordinator, clinical assistant

Sample Skills/Credentials: casework management, community/ government/ media relations, coalition and consensus building, leadership and supervision, client advocacy, diverse populations, event and program management, volunteer coordination/ motivation/supervision, problem solving, conflict and problem resolution, tact and diplomacy, interpersonal and communication skills, community outreach programs and initiatives, legislation tracking, polling and poll coverage, nonprofit operations, security clearance, public policy research and analysis, geopolitical studies, cultural protocols and issues, public speaking, reports and presentations, document preparation, budgeting, budget administration, cost containment, team building, project management, strategic planning, staff supervision, policy development, public service

WHAT IF I DON'T HAVE WHAT IT TAKES?

For some career changers, it will be difficult to break into their ideal careers without first receiving additional training or accepting an entry-level position to learn the trade. If you find that your career change won't be possible without further training, you need to consider obtaining the necessary training. You might be able to continue in your current profession and enroll in courses for your "dream job" after work hours. You might be able to take on part-time or volunteer work in your field of interest to "get your feet wet" (and be able to add related experience to your resume). The transitionary period between your current situation and achievement of your career change goal is usually fraught with hard work and numerous hours dedicated to career planning, but the end result—career fulfillment—is a worthy objective.

2

Which Resume Format Is Right for You?

The resume format you select can make or break your introduction to a potential employer. As a career changer, your format needs to amplify your qualifications while downplaying your unrelated experience. An employer should immediately see the value that you offer and realize that your credentials are easily transferable to your new goal. Here is a rundown of the various resume formats.

REVERSE CHRONOLOGICAL RESUMES

This format has long been preferred by hiring managers because the career history is easily seen. A chronological resume format presents a sequential employment history in reverse chronological (most recent first) order. A strictly chronological resume leads with experience or education and does not include a career summary section. Because of the emphasis on work history, a chronological resume format is not the best choice for career changers and is not recommended in this book.

FUNCTIONAL RESUMES

A functional resume downplays employment history while emphasizing other credentials that are important to the career goal. Functional resumes will often lead with skills headings to highlight what the job seeker has to offer, while leaving employment history for the end of the resume.

Functional resumes have been the format of choice for job seekers who want to hide information about their backgrounds. Workers with employment gaps, a history of job-hopping, no related work history, and yes, career changers have long used the functional resume to play up their related skills while de-emphasizing specific work experience.

The problem is that hiring managers have become savvy to the strategies used in functional resumes. When a functional resume arrives on a hiring manager's desk, it will likely be met with the question: "What is wrong with this candidate?" Since it's best not to be viewed with suspicion immediately when you're hoping for a job interview, use the functional format with caution. Your resume will need to be well-written and strategized to use a functional format successfully. Only use a functional resume if you have no work history at all, an extremely sketchy work history, or are undergoing a drastic career change.

COMBINATION CHRONOLOGICAL (A.K.A. "HYBRID" AND "COMBINATION") RESUMES

A combination chronological resume presents a reverse chronological work history, but is preceded by a career summary or outline of functional skills that relate to the job target. This format gives employers what they want to see (the reverse chronological work history), while allowing the job seeker to tout key skills and qualifications at the beginning of the resume. This format has been tested by career changers and has proven to be effective, so it is the format most recommended for transitionary job seekers. In fact, the majority of career change resumes featured in this book are in a combination chronological format.

If you decide to use a combination chronological format, you may reorder your employment history so that your most relevant experience is at the forefront. For example, if you are returning to an earlier career, you may label your experience section "Related Experience" and include all of your pertinent jobs, no matter when they were held. Your other work experience can be grouped in a section called "Additional Experience," "Current Position," or "Other Experience." You may also reference your career goal in the section names (such as "Human Resources Administration Experience"). See Craig Star's resume in Chapter 18 to see how to reorder employment to market yourself for a career change.

ALTERNATIVE RESUMES: BROCHURES AND NARRATIVE BIOGRAPHIES (A.K.A. "BIOS")

Some job seekers promote themselves in brochure-style resumes that resemble corporate marketing brochures. This style is suitable for consultants, independent contractors, or professionals who would like to demonstrate their marketing or graphic design skills. Free agents might also use a narrative bio (usually a page in length) to sum up their top qualifications. The nontraditional format gives the job seeker leeway to include the information most pertinent to the job or assignment, while omitting or downplaying unrelated experiences. Refer to Yolanda Percy's resume in Chapter 11 and Joe Smythe's resumes in Chapter 19 to see alternative resume styles.

Part 2

WRITING A RESUME THAT OPENS NEW CAREER DOORS

"Change should be a friend. It should happen by plan, not by accident."

—PHILIP CROSBY

3

Reinventing Your Resume for a Career Change

CAREER DREAM OR "PIPE DREAM?"

When John began his search for a new career, his resume started off like this:

John G. Reynolds
125 Arbor Circle, Apt. # 57
Miami, FL 23476
(555) 555-5555

EDUCATION

1997   B.A. in Secondary Education, Florida State University
Activities: DECA Club, Speech and Debate Team, Kappa Sigma Fraternity

EXPERIENCE

1997–Present   Teacher (Grades 9–12)
ABC School District; Miami VocTech High School—Miami, FL

Responsible for teaching various business and computer classes to high school students covering topics including hardware, software, business management, business writing, and marketing. Responsible for developing lesson plans, creating classroom handouts, teaching freshman- through senior-level computer and business classes, evaluating text books, preparing exams, monitoring the classroom, and evaluating student performance. Support the school board in upcoming bond issues, serve on a variety of school committees such as the curriculum committee and diversity committee, and serve as faculty advisor for the school's DECA Club and Web site. Awarded "Teacher of the Year" in 1999.

Notice anything missing? How about, for starters, what John wants to do for a living? Right now, his resume screams, "I'm a teacher!" You'd never guess that his goal is to break into the completely different field of software sales. Furthermore, you aren't given many hints about the key strengths John brings to the table that would equip him to make the transition successfully from teaching to sales. Put yourself in the shoes of a hiring manager. If you received John's resume along with dozens (or even hundreds) of other resumes from candidates with more closely related sales backgrounds, would you be very likely to select John for an interview?

Here's another example:

KENDRA WOODS

918 Richmond St. ▪ Cedar City, IA 97564
Kendra@resumepower.com ▪ (555) 555-5555

Objective:	*To secure a challenging position with a growing company that would allow for advancement and professional development.*
Career History:	
5/97–2/98	Delphonic, Inc. (Cedar City, IA)—Bookkeeper
1/97–4/97	Quantam Corp. (Cedar City, IA)—Office Assistant
3/96–12/96	PediaCare Medical Office (Cedar City, IA)—Receptionist
5/93–2/96	Barn Dinner Theater (Cedar City, IA)—Co-Owner
8/89–5/93	Three Oaks Inn (Omaha, NE)—Food & Beverage Manager; Bar Manager
5/87–8/89	Walco (Omaha, NE)—Assistant Store Manager; Toy Department Manager; Sales Associate

---

Kendra certainly has a diverse background, and it's clear that she's already made a number of transitions throughout her career. But her vaguely worded and cliche-ridden objective gives no clue to her current career target. Is she seeking an administrative assistant position? Is she interested in returning to the food service industry? Or is she trying to reestablish herself in retail management? Surprise—it's none of the above. Kendra's new career goal is to become a corporate or non-profit special event planner.

A career change isn't the only challenge that Kendra is facing. Just look at her job history. Each of her last three positions lasted for less than a year, including one that was only four months long. (In fact, Kendra was working part-time for several temp agencies following the birth of her son.) And it appears that she's been out of work since the beginning of 1998. (Kendra became a full-time, stay-at-home mom when her second child was born, balancing this role with active volunteer work that isn't even mentioned in the above resume.)

Are John and Kendra's career dreams hopeless? Hardly, but their professional backgrounds could be presented in a much stronger and more compelling way. Like any career changer, John and Kendra need to revamp their resumes completely so that strategic sections are included, relevant strengths are highlighted, major accomplishments are showcased, keywords are emphasized, and potential weaknesses are minimized.

THE NUTS AND BOLTS OF A CAREER CHANGE RESUME

Regardless of your background or career target, you will need to include strategic sections in your resume to communicate clearly your goals, key strengths, transferable skills, and relevant achievements. Whether you select a functional or combination chronological format (see Chapter 2), your resume should include the following elements.

1. A Resume Title or Objective

Found right below your name and contact information on the resume, the resume title or objective is the first thing employers will see, so it's crucial that this section be clearly written.

A resume title is similar to the headline in an advertisement—it boldly announces your career goal and provides focus for all of the content on your resume that will follow.

An objective is a statement identifying what it is that you want to do. It should be specific, targeting a definite job/industry goal, and written with a focus on what you can do for an employer, not what you want from them.

Career changers can use both a title and an objective on their resumes, or they can simply choose one or the other.

An objective or resume title is especially crucial for career changers. Unlike professionals who are sticking with the same career track, career changers can't rely on their past job titles to convey what they now want to do. You must tell hiring managers up front what kinds of jobs you are targeting to avoid being pigeonholed in your former career. You also need to eliminate guesswork or confusion on the part of readers by explaining clearly at the outset the kinds of positions you are seeking and qualified to perform. If hiring managers can't figure out what you're applying for or how you are uniquely suited to their needs within the first few seconds of skimming your resume, chances are your phone won't be ringing for interviews.

A common mistake made by career changers is writing an objective that is too general or vague. Consider this "before" example:

OBJECTIVE   *Seeking a challenging position offering opportunity for advancement within a growth-oriented company.*

The author of this objective could be trying to break into pharmaceutical sales, information technology, public relations, or accounting—it's anybody's guess. You're writing a resume, not a mystery novel, so if your objective resembles the above example, scratch it and start over. Remember that hiring managers are busy folks, and they simply don't have the time to ponder the career goals of the hundreds of job seekers who contact them about openings. Be clear and provide needed focus to your resume from the start.

Vague verbiage isn't the only problem with the sample "before" objective. It's also much too focused on what the job seeker wants ("a challenging position," "opportunity for advancement"). Instead, it should explain how this candidate meets employers' needs. In addition, phrases like "growth-oriented company" (or derivations on this theme) have been used over and over by job seekers to the point where they have become meaningless. To pack maximum "punch," your objective must be free of cliches, clearly explain your job target, and convey how you will add benefit and value to an employer's operation.

If you have more than one career change goal, don't fall into the trap of thinking that your resume should be as general as possible for the broadest appeal. This "one-size-fits-all" approach is bound to backfire. Your resume is not a muumuu; if it's a formless, shapeless document lacking a custom-tailored focus, it won't fit employers' needs any better than one of those baggy, sacklike garments. Career changers with diverse job interests should develop different versions of their resumes targeting each of their career goals and highlighting strengths relevant to each.

Here are a few good "after" examples of well-written objectives and resume titles:

OBJECTIVE   *Seeking to leverage a six-year history of superior-rated performance, persuasive public speaking, and creative problem solving to secure an entry-level sales representative position.*

OBJECTIVE   Executive assistant position *providing the opportunity to demonstrate strong computer expertise and acquired skills in organization, customer service, and communication, proven by 12 years of successful self-employment.*

CAREER GOAL   *Desktop Support Specialist/Helpdesk Professional*

2. A Qualifications Profile

The "Qualifications Profile" (or "Career Summary") goes directly below the objective or resume title. This brief section consists of one or two short paragraphs or several bulleted statements condensing for employers your breadth of experience, major areas of strength, and relevant highlights from your background. This is the perfect place to "sell" yourself, and if done well, this section can often be enough all by itself to convince an employer to contact you for an interview.

Your profile should explain how an employer would benefit by hiring you. It should encapsulate the key strengths you bring to the table and convincingly address why you should be called for an interview versus your competition. Keep your profile concise. You're not telling your life story here. Just hit on whatever elements from your background are most compelling in terms of your new career target. You will expound upon these strengths later in the resume, but in the profile, your goal is to summarize your most marketable traits, experience, and credentials.

Before you begin your profile section, make sure that you have a solid grasp of what employers are looking for in your targeted field. Research job ads on the Web or in the newspaper that are similar to what you are looking for in order to identify the key skills and credentials you offer that match employers' needs. Compare the job ads you find and take note of similarities between your background and frequently requested or required skills mentioned in these ads.

Draw up a list of your top 5 to 10 marketable skills and accomplishments, and use this as the basis for your qualifications summary. Keep in mind that employers particularly value candidates who can prove that they have helped to save time, cut costs, generate revenue, improve service, solve problems, or further company goals. These traits are universally valued, regardless of the industry or field you are pursuing, so detail your most standout accomplishments in these areas in your qualifications profile.

3. A Synopsis of Your Key Transferable Skills

After you've identified your transferable skills, you'll want to address them prominently in your resume. Regardless of whether you select a functional or combination chronological style, you can work many of these skills into your objective and opening qualifications profile, since both resume formats utilize these two sections.

For instance, let's say you are currently the manager of a Domino's Pizza franchise but are seeking to become a customer service manager. For both the functional or combination chronological formats, your resume might begin like this:

Yolanda Dominguez

8756 Oak Lane ▪ Philadelphia, PA 02367 ▪ 555.555.5555
yolanda@resumepower.com

Career Objective ———————————————————————

CUSTOMER SERVICE MANAGEMENT

Seeking to leverage strong customer service management background gained from the food service industry to secure a career shift to customer service program management.

Profile ——————————————————————————————

Resourceful, customer-focused management professional with over seven years of experience managing top-performing teams (staffs of up to 18), customer service programs, call center operations, and turnaround initiatives. Proven success catapulting customer satisfaction by 57% (record high) in under two months while simultaneously improving team productivity and morale. Skilled communicator and strategist of service solutions, able to instill a shared vision among all team members of service as the means to driving increased revenue and profits. Adept in building relationships, resolving complaints, and designing win-win solutions benefiting all parties concerned.

If you have selected a functional resume format (see Chapter 2), which relies on skill-based categories to demonstrate your qualifications, your major transferable skills will also serve as topic headings. Below these headings, you will expound on your strengths in each area.

Still using the pizza manager to customer service manager career change scenario, let's say that after conducting research on your new career target, you decide that your skill topic headings will be "Problem Solving," "Communication," and "Team Building and Supervision." Below these categories, you can include skill subsets along with a bulleted list of accomplishments to back your claims further. Here's an example:

Key Qualifications

Problem Solving (*Complaint Handling...Mediation...Creative Solutions*)

- Diffused volatile situations and calmed angry customers upset by delivery delays caused by staff shortages. Won back the loyalty and trust of clients, elevating repeat orders by an average of 15% per month.

- Salvaged the threatened loss of over $56K monthly in key corporate accounts following the opening of primary competitor one block away. Overcame challenge presented by rival's offering of deep discounts to retain 90% of all commercial business.

- Devised cost-effective solution to reverse downward customer-satisfaction spiral. Surveyed existing customer base to identify and correct quality, service, and efficiency issues, lifting store's customer-satisfaction ratings by 57% in less than two months.

If you select a combination chronological resume format (see Chapter 2), which merges elements from both the functional and chronological resume styles, you can incorporate your key transferable skills into an "Areas of Expertise" or "Key Skills" section, as well as the "Experience" section. Here's an example of how this might look:

Key Skills

- Relationship Management (Customers/Vendors/Employees)
- Customer-Service Enhancement
- Complaint Handling & Mediation
- Process Improvement

- Team Building & Supervision
- Call-Center Operations
- Survey Design & Analysis
- Quality Control
- Creative Problem Solving

Experience

Domino's Pizza—Philadelphia, PA

STORE MANAGER, 1997 to Present; ASSISTANT MANAGER, 1995 to 1997

Wholly responsible for daily operations of high-volume pizza franchise location, including customer-relationship management, complaint handling, dispute mediation, staffing, training, P&L, advertising/promotions, and quality assurance. Challenged to correct customer-service issues and maintain store's sales lead despite fierce competition.

- Diffused volatile situations and calmed angry customers upset by delivery delays caused by staff shortages. Won back the loyalty and trust of clients, elevating repeat orders by an average of 15% per month.

- Repaired damaged relationship between franchise owner and corporate headquarters as the primary liaison connecting both parties.

- Salvaged the threatened loss of over $56K monthly in key corporate accounts following the opening of Domino's primary competitor one block away. Overcame challenge presented by rival's offering of deep discounts to retain 90% of all commercial business.

- Devised cost-effective, creative solution to reverse downward customer-satisfaction spiral.
  - Affixed customer surveys directly to pizza boxes and installed automated telephone voice-response system to record customer comments.
  - Encouraged customer feedback (and future repeat business) by offering discounts to all survey participants.
  - Analyzed data collected to identify and correct quality, service, and efficiency issues, skyrocketing store's average customer-satisfaction ratings by 57% in less than two months.

4. A Career History or Chronology

Employers want to know details of where you gained your experience and how long you held each position. If you are using a combination chronological format, you will include company names, job titles, and the dates you held each position in reverse chronological order, starting with your most recent (or current) position and working backwards. If you are using a functional format, you still need to include this information somewhere on the resume in a "Career History" section. Place the most emphasis on your recent career, providing significant detail as far back as 15 years. Spend less time on earlier positions, unless they directly relate or are more relevant to your current career goal.

If your earlier work experience is more closely tied to what you now want to do than your more recent experience, then set up two different "Experience" sections of your resume: a detailed "Relevant Experience" section (where you will highlight responsibilities and achievements of jobs you have held that relate to your new career goal) and a briefer "Additional Experience" section below that (where you can simply list other jobs you have held that are less relevant to what you now want to do). This will allow you to lead your experience section with what is most germane to your professional target, despite the fact that it occurred earlier in your career.

5. Evidence of Your Standout Accomplishments

Many career changers make the mistake of only including their day-to-day responsibilities on their resumes, with no mention of the *outcomes and results* of their efforts. But if you simply rehash job descriptions from the various positions you have held, your resume will only describe *what* you have done instead of *how well* you have done it. (And it will also be about as exciting to read as a "career obituary.") Employers are looking for doers and achievers, so no matter what format you choose for your resume, you must include details of your key accomplishments.

For each of the jobs you have held, think about ways that you have streamlined processes, reduced overhead, generated sales, innovated creative solutions, enhanced customer service, expanded company visibility, or improved morale. Wherever possible, quantify your accomplishments by using dollar amounts, percentages, numbers, before/after comparisons, or other key descriptors. (But take care not to disclose proprietary company information. Some companies prohibit disclosing actual dollar amounts or other information, so make sure you comply with your employers' policies. Information that is published in an annual report or on a Web site is certainly fair game to include in a resume, however.)

If you are using a functional resume style, your accomplishments should be listed below corresponding skill categories (as in the example earlier in this chapter). If you are using a combination chronological style, your accomplishments should appear in a bulleted series below a general overview of your everyday responsibilities.

In case you have trouble differentiating your "responsibilities" from your "accomplishments," keep in mind that responsibilities are duties and job tasks that were expected of you in your position. (Formal job descriptions are a good place to find details of daily responsibilities.) Examples of responsibilities might include the budget amount you were responsible for, the number and types of positions you supervised, and the kinds of daily tasks you were accountable for completing.

Accomplishments are achievements, awards, recognitions, special projects, and promotions. These are specific examples of how you went "above and beyond" in performing your job duties. When thinking about your accomplishments, it is often helpful to use the Problem-Action-Result (PAR) technique. What problems or challenges did you face? What actions did you take to overcome the problems? What was the result or benefit to the company?

To illustrate the power of accomplishments on a resume, consider these before and after examples:

Before—Ho-Hum Responsibility Statement:

- Handled all contract negotiations with telecommunications providers.

After—High-Impact Accomplishment Statement:

- Reduced monthly telecommunication charges 15% (five-figure savings) by renegotiating local and long-distance service agreements.

Before—Ho-Hum Responsibility Statement:

- Served as technical lead of a major systems integration project involving three acquired companies.

After—High-Impact Accomplishment Statement:

- Completed the most extensive IT integration project in company history, serving as technical lead over a $10 million project. Fused complex, multiplatform systems from three acquired companies into a single, cohesive framework, finishing project on schedule, 19% under budget, and with zero business interrupts.

> **Before—Ho-Hum Responsibility Statement:**
> - Wrote and distributed press releases and PSAs promoting the university nationwide.
>
> **After—High-Impact Accomplishment Statement:**
> - Achieved a record-setting 72% media-usage rate by writing powerful press releases and PSAs. Won media "hits" nationwide in publications such as *The Wall Street Journal, The Chicago Sun Times,* and *USA Today.*

Accomplishments are best described by using powerful action verbs, and your resume should be packed with a variety of them. Don't begin each of your accomplishment statements with the same, tired verb. Take pity on hiring managers who, bleary eyed, actually have to *read* all those stacks of resumes piled in their in-baskets. "Managed" is a favorite resume verb, for example, and it's a perfectly good word. But if used more than once or twice, its effectiveness will rapidly diminish. "Oversaw," "directed," "led," and "supervised" are all viable stand-ins for "managed." If you really want to get fancy, try "orchestrated," "engineered," or "designed." You can probably think of a number of other equally good if not better synonyms. The point is, vary your verb choice. Make a loyal friend of your thesaurus. It will keep your resume (and its readers) fresh and alive.

6. Highlights of Your Education or Training

This section details degrees you have earned, academic honors and scholarships you have received, and/or training you have completed (either sponsored by your employers or pursued after hours on your own time). In this section, you can list formal coursework and degrees as well as continuing education programs, seminars, workshops, or self-directed study that you have completed.

Most workers with five or more years of experience place the "Education" section at the bottom of the resume. But as a career changer, you shouldn't be afraid to break the rules. If you have a degree or special training that is highly relevant to your new career goal, you may want to move your Education section to a more prominent position on the resume.

In addition to the preceding six sections, your resume might also include one or more of the following components, if relevant to your circumstances.

7. Computer Skills and/or Foreign Languages

Technology expertise is common in performing a wide variety of job functions, and most working adults have proficiency in at least one or two software applications. Don't assume that employers will consider your computer skills a given, however. Spell them out in your resume in a "Technology Summary" or "Computer Skills" section. Computer programs, platforms, and tools (e.g., PowerPoint, Excel, Windows, TCP/IP) are often used as keyword terms by employers when searching resume databases, so maximize the number of hits your resume receives by including your technology skills.

Foreign language proficiency is also a sought-after skill in today's global economy. Even if you do not consider yourself fluent in another language, you can still accurately reflect your skills with a notation like, "Proficient in basic conversational Spanish" or "Intermediate skills in verbal/written Japanese."

8. Publications, Presentations, or Patents

Are you a published author? Do you have public speaking experience? Have you contributed to patent-holding innovations? Even if the subject matter of these efforts is not related to your new career goal, possessing skills in written and verbal communication and inventive thinking will be valued by virtually all fields. If you have a background in any of these areas, it probably deserves mention in your resume.

9. Awards, Honors, or Special Recognition You Have Received

If your professional or academic career has been chronicled by numerous awards, citations, or special recognition, you may want to showcase your top-ranked performance in a separate "Honors and Awards" section on your resume. Professionals transitioning from the armed services into civilian life are often good candidates for this kind of special resume section, since the military has an extensive recognition program. Keep in mind that you don't need to note each item separately if space is a concern; you can simply summarize the honors you have received by grouping like awards together:

- Six Commendations for Leadership (U.S. Army), 1997–2000
- 12 Meritorious Awards for Acts of Integrity or Perseverance (U.S. Army/National Guard), 1996–2003
- Eight Ribbons for Outstanding Performance (U.S. Army/National Guard), 1996–2003
- 22 Citations for Creditable Accomplishments (U.S. Army/National Guard), 1994–2003

10. Certifications or Licensure

This is the place to list any special industry credentials you have earned through continuing education. Many industries offer professional-development programs culminating in an exam that, if passed, conveys special licensure or certification. In the insurance industry, these certifications include a CPCU (Chartered Property Casualty Underwriter) and CLU (Chartered Life Underwriter). Career changers seeking entry into the finance world can obtain a CPA (Certified Public Accountant) or CFA (Chartered Financial Analyst) credential. And information technology professionals can achieve a variety of certifications such as a CNA (Certified Network Administrator) or MCSE (Microsoft Certified System Engineer).

11. Professional Memberships and Affiliations

A vast assortment of professional organizations exists for virtually any career you can name. Examples include the Society for Human Resource Management (SHRM), the Society of Manufacturing Engineers (SME), The HTML Writers Guild (IWA-HWG), and the International Association of Administrative Professionals (IAAP). Membership requirements and fees vary, but you can sometimes join these organizations based solely on your interest (with little or no formal experience in the field). Listing professional affiliations that support your job target helps to show your seriousness in and commitment to achieving your career change goal, and it also adds more keywords to your resume. In addition, these groups can provide excellent networking opportunities to propel your job search, so it's worth your time to research professional organizations in your targeted field.

12. Testimonials or Endorsements

Capitalize on stellar reviews or praise you have received by featuring quoted passages in a "Testimonials" or "Endorsements" segment on your resume. In this section, you can include excerpts from past performance evaluations, thank-you letters from customers, commendation letters, or recommendation letters. These "sound bites" help to give readers another perspective on your performance and can be powerful additions to a career change resume. You can group these excerpts together or sprinkle them throughout your document.

13. Community Involvement

Chronicling your volunteer experience, civic group or club memberships, or leadership positions you have held on boards or committees is a good way to reflect your civic-mindedness. If your volunteer experience is more relevant to your new career goal than your paid work experience, you will want to expound on this section and move it to a prominent place on your resume.

14. Special Interests or Hobbies

Are you involved in extracurricular pursuits that bear some relevance to your career goal? If so, consider setting up an "Of Note" section, and detail highlights below this heading.

HOW DO I DETERMINE THE ORDER OF RESUME SECTIONS?

Whatever resume format you choose, you will begin with your name prominently displayed at the top of page one, followed by your contact information. (Don't forget to include your e-mail address and cell phone number, if applicable.) Below this comes your resume title and/or objective, immediately followed by your qualifications profile.

After that, the order of your materials will depend upon your unique circumstances. Organize your material so that your strongest credentials, skills, or accomplishments come first. Do you have a degree or special training in the field you are targeting? If so, you may want to place your "Education" section right below your profile. Do you offer a number of transferable skills that are highly relevant to the new career you are targeting? In that case, follow the profile with your "Expertise" section. Are you seeking to return to a career that you abandoned some years ago? If so, create a "Relevant Experience" section and put that right below your profile. Is your strongest qualification your history of top performance? Then include a testimonial excerpt at the end of your profile. Are you trying to gain entry into a career where computer or Web skills are a must? Then place your "Technology Summary" in a prominent position on page one.

Use this same strategy when writing about your accomplishments for the jobs you have held. Lead with "gee whiz" achievements that are most relevant to your career goal. If you are trying to become a corporate trainer, for example, then prominently highlight any achievements from your background that demonstrate your proficiencies in instructional design, public speaking, and team motivation. If you want to break into administrative support, highlight accomplishments that demonstrate computer, organizational, communication, or customer service skills.

Let your career goal dictate the order and amount of detail you give your material. Don't waste valuable space and premium "real estate" on the page describing details from your background that don't directly contribute to your new career goal. Although it's usually not a good idea to eliminate jobs completely from your resume if doing so will create a time gap, you should minimize the particulars from positions you have held that don't somehow contribute to your new professional objective.

RESUME MAKEOVERS: PUTTING IT ALL TOGETHER

At the beginning of the chapter, you met John and Kendra, two career changers with very different job goals and backgrounds but sharing the same problem—lackluster resumes producing zero results. The following excerpts from their new and improved resumes show how they successfully "reinvented" themselves to win multiple interviews and ultimately land their dream jobs.

JOHN G. REYNOLDS

125 Arbor Circle, Apt. # 57 • Miami, FL 23476 • (555) 555-5555 • jgr@resumepower.com

Uniquely Qualified for Position as

SOFTWARE SALES REPRESENTATIVE

- *Award-winning computer instructor* seeking to leverage strong combination of expert technical knowledge and highly regarded presentation/public speaking skills to secure entry-level software sales position.
- *Polished, dynamic communicator*, adept in articulating software features/benefits, translating "techno-speak" into easily understood terms, and quickly diffusing user anxiety/frustration.
- *Well-versed in closing strategies and solution-selling tactics* as a long-time DECA Club faculty advisor and competitive-sales event judge.
- *Skilled persuader and relationship builder*, twice appointed by school board as a primary spokesperson for hotly contested, multimillion-dollar bond issues (both passed).
- *Fast learner*, with passion for new technology and ability to master complex concepts rapidly.
- *Solidly credentialed*, with bachelor's degree, cross-platform expertise (Windows, UNIX, Mac OS), fluency in six programming languages, and proficiency in multiple software/Web tools.

KEY SKILLS

- High-Impact Sales Presentations
- Persuasive Public Speaking
- Advanced Computer Literacy
- End-User Training & Support

- Closing & Negotiations
- Technical Troubleshooting
- Strategic Relationships & Partnerships
- Organization/Follow-Up

PROFESSIONAL EXPERIENCE

Computer/Business Teacher—1997 to Present

MIAMI VOCTECH HIGH SCHOOL—Miami, FL

Accountable for the design and delivery of effective instruction to an average of 175 students in grades 9–12 each semester. Challenged to instill an enthusiasm and competency for various business and computer topics (e.g., Web development, MS Office suite, AutoCAD, networking essentials, business management, business writing, marketing). Develop lesson plans, create learning tools, teach beginning- through advanced-level classes, and continually monitor/evaluate student performance. Fulfill leadership, advisory, or active participation roles on a variety of school committees, student clubs, fund-raisers, and high-profile school board initiatives. *Selected Accomplishments:*

- Honored for outstanding communication/instructional skills as ABC School District's 1999 "Teacher of the Year" (selected from 275 faculty).
- Played a key role in "selling" strongly divided constituency on the merits of two mission-critical bond issues that successfully passed to fund a $2.8 million facility upgrade/expansion. Hand-selected by school board to conduct 50+ persuasive presentations to diverse audience groups and overcame objections to win crucial retiree and corporate community vote.

KENDRA WOODS

918 Richmond St.   Cedar City, IA 97564   Kendra@resumepower.com   555-555-5555

Value Proposition

Offering extensive expertise in special-event planning for mid-sized, Fortune 500, and nonprofit firms, with proven success outperforming revenue/attendance/profit goals by up to 300%.

Achievement Highlights

Special-Event Management:

- Jointly planned and executed hundreds of successful special events for groups ranging from 20 to 250+. (Barn Dinner Theater, Three Oaks Inn)
  - Orchestrated widely praised black-tie dinners, silent auctions, corporate meetings, workshops/seminars, parties, receptions, and theatrical productions.
  - Supervised on-site event staff (up to 25) and oversaw pricing; menu planning/preparation; vendor negotiations; guest relations; and facility setup/teardown.
- Became the de facto corporate-event planner for a wide range of small to mid-size companies across diverse industries (e.g., banking, insurance, manufacturing, high-tech, telecommunications). Earned a reputation for flawless organization, attention to detail, and premium service delivery. (Three Oaks Inn)
- Comanaged major fundraisers for the American Cancer Society, Salvation Army, and ASPCA that resulted in sell-out attendance and generated revenues surpassing targets by 120%, 225%, and 300%, respectively. (Barn Dinner Theater)
- Handpicked by Sal Stockwell, Walco founder and former CEO, to serve on 18-member team responsible for planning all logistics (food, entertainment, travel, agenda, site selection) of two consecutive annual shareholder meetings. (Walco)
- Chaired three large-scale membership drives that strengthened community arts support and doubled "Platinum" corporate sponsorships. (Cedar City Arts Society)

Contingency Planning:

- Commended by key corporate client for proactive planning that salvaged Hawaiian-style luau/barbecue for 125 during torrential downpour. Choreographed a seamless, last-minute change of venue and main course that was transparent to guests and led to $100K in subsequent repeat/referral business. (Three Oaks Inn)
- Repeatedly leveraged quick-thinking skills to overcome event management challenges spanning staff shortages, delivery delays, standing-room-only crowds, power outages, and guests with special needs. (Barn Dinner Theater, Three Oaks Inn)

Marketing, Sales, & Promotions:

- Wrote and supervised the design/production of sales-driving collateral (direct mailers, brochures, print/radio/TV ads) that tripled per-annum revenues in a single year. (Barn Dinner Theater)
- Conceptualized and led store sales rallies (including selection of guest speakers) that lifted revenues in targeted departments by as much as 87%. (Walco)

Team Building, Motivation, & Supervision:

- Demonstrated the ability to lead and motivate both paid and volunteer staffs, with experience supervising teams of up to 65. (All positions)

Career History

CEDAR CITY ARTS SOCIETY—Cedar City, IA
Membership Chair (Volunteer position concurrent with full-time family management/care of now-school-age children), 1996 to present

PERSONNEL POWER, INC./STAFFING SOLUTIONS CORP.—Cedar City, IA
Bookkeeper/Office Assistant/Receptionist (Temp agency assignments), 1996 to 1997

BARN DINNER THEATER—Cedar City, IA
Co-Owner (Year-round, full-time position managing 250-seat venue), 1993 to 1996

TOP TEN RESUME BLUNDERS MADE BY CAREER CHANGERS (...AND HOW TO AVOID THEM!)

1. Failure to convey a specific career goal.

   Solution: Include a clearly stated career objective and/or resume title.

2. Lack of emphasis on employer needs.

   Solution: Rework your resume so that it focuses on how you will benefit an employer.

3. Minimal or zero inclusion of relevant accomplishments.

   Solution: Explain in your resume not only what you have done, but also how well you have done it. Emphasize ways you have saved time, cut costs, generated revenue, or solved problems.

4. Failure to conduct ample research on your new career target.

   Solution: Make sure your resume hits the mark with hiring managers by thoroughly researching your career goal. Identify relevant skills from your background that meet employers' needs, and bring these out prominently in your resume.

5. Lack of keyword density.

   Solution: Maximize keywords on your resume by including essential terms, phrases, and acronyms used in the profession or industry you are targeting where you have like skills and credentials.

6. Too little information.

   Solution: Add details of your accomplishments and the significance of your achievements, and spell out for employers how you can leverage your prior career experience to meet their needs specifically.

7. Too much (or irrelevant) information.

   Solution: Be ruthless in editing your resume. Only expound on skills and achievements that help to prove your capabilities for the specific types of jobs you are targeting. Highlight "universally valued" skills from your background (e.g., ways you have helped to improve sales, profits, or service).

8. Burying the most compelling or relevant information.

   Solution: Prioritize your strengths and lead your resume with your most powerful and relevant qualifications. Write your accomplishment statements so that the outcomes of your efforts are highlighted.

9. Use of the wrong resume format.

   Solution: Determine how your background can best be showcased to make your career change goal a reality. Avoid the chronological format and select either a combination chronological or functional style. (See Chapter 2.)

10. Use of an old, overly general, or ill-fitting resume.

    Solution: Market yourself for your career change by writing a highly focused, targeted document that communicates your strengths and downplays any weaknesses.

4

Career Change Resume FAQs

Q: What can I do about gaps in employment?

A: There isn't much you can do about your work chronology—what's done is done. However, there are a few ways to present your work history so that the gaps are less apparent:

- Consider including only years worked (rather than months and years).
- Place employment dates next to job titles in parentheses.
- Never showcase employment dates around large areas of white space—this draws attention to your chronology.
- Think about other activities that you pursued during your employment gaps. You might be able to "fill in" your gaps with volunteer activities, training, travel, or development of a new skill.

Q: My recent work history makes me look like a job-hopper. What can I do?

A: Try to take a positive spin on your work history. If you've moved around a lot, you demonstrate an ability to work in diverse industries or environments and to step into a role and immediately make a positive impact on the organization. Also, in some industries (such as technology and construction), it's common for employees to move from position to position to take on new projects. Sometimes, *not* moving around is a sign of stagnation. However, if you would like to minimize the appearance of job-hopping, you might be able to group similar positions under one employment heading. For example:

TEACHER, 1999 to 2002
Served as Spanish teacher for ABC School, DEF School, and GHI School...

Q: How should I approach my resume if I'm transitioning from a military to civilian position?

A: Many civilian employers are unfamiliar with military terminology, so try to minimize military jargon, and replace it with terms used in the corporate world. If you achieved a long military career, some of these terms might be so ingrained that you don't even realize that you're using them. If that's the case, show your resume to colleagues and friends with no military background and see if they understand your document.

Military experience offers great opportunities for training, advancement, and performance awards, and you should certainly highlight these on your resume.

Q: How do I transition from a corporate position to the nonprofit sector?

A: Your passion for the nonprofit sector of your choice should shine through on your resume and cover letter. Be clear on why you are making this transition and show how your skills developed in the corporate world would be valuable to a nonprofit organization. Nonprofits are organizational structures that need dedicated workers just like corporate structures, so demonstrate that you have what it takes to make an immediate and enduring contribution to a nonprofit organization.

Q: How do I transition from the nonprofit to the corporate sector?

A: You will find that your achievements and skills developed in the nonprofit sector are transferable to the corporate world. When describing your work history, focus on results, achievements, and contributions that would be desirable to a bottom-line-oriented company. For example, if you worked as a nonprofit program administrator, describe how you increased enrollment, reduced costs, generated donations, elevated staff morale, and attracted volunteers.

Q: I've been out of the workforce raising a family. How do I explain this time on my resume?

A: There's nothing wrong with stepping away from your career to raise a family, so don't feel that you've got to apologize for or hide your choice. Your cover letter can mention that you were raising a family and are now ready to return to full-time employment. You might have other activities to add to the resume to fill this time period, including community and volunteer activities, involvement in professional associations or conferences, travel, etc. Think about any activities or skills you developed during this time period that can be included on your resume.

Q: How do I handle self-employment on my resume?

A: Self-employment might work for or against you when you start searching for a job. Depending on your industry and the types of companies you are pursuing, an entrepreneurial spirit might be favorably received. It shows initiative, dedication, business know-how, and a strong work ethic. However, some employers are cautious about hiring previously self-employed workers. You might be suspected of looking for work to tide you over while you start another venture, or worse, as someone who might steal company ideas and/or clients.

The best way to approach your period of self-employment is to focus on achievements and skills that would be in demand in the business world. If you were self-employed as an accountant, highlight your accounting achievements, key projects, and skills developed during the course of your self-employment.

Q: My experience is unrelated to my career goal, but I've been pursuing training in pursuit of my new objective. How do I handle this on my resume?

A: Lead with a "Career Summary" that sums up your educational foundation and other key skills for your new objective. Follow your summary section with your "Education," and expand upon any courses, special projects, or activities that relate to your objective. When you develop your "Experience" section, do not include unrelated duties or accomplishments—keep this section focused on transferable skills and achievements. If you are completely changing careers, your "Experience" section may just list your employer names, job titles, and dates, without going into descriptions.

Part 3

MAXIMIZING YOUR RESUME'S EXPOSURE

"If we don't change direction soon, we'll end up where we're going."
—Prof. Irwin Corey

5

The Cover Letter

DO I REALLY NEED A COVER LETTER?

Yes, you really do. The cover letter introduces you to potential employers and should prompt them to take the next step—reviewing your accompanying resume. Here are five reasons why your resume should *always* be partnered with a cover letter.

1. It's Proper Business Etiquette.

Your resume should not arrive unannounced, like some unwelcome visitor. Sending a cover letter with your resume, regardless of the type of position you are seeking, shows your business-protocol savvy. Even if your letter isn't read word for word on the first go-round, it will indicate to hiring managers that you understand the importance of traditional courtesy.

2. It Gives You Yet Another Opportunity to "Sell" Yourself to Decision Makers.

This is particularly crucial for career changers, who must work harder to convince hiring managers of the relevance and fit of their backgrounds to employers' needs. The cover letter is a vital marketing tool in your job search arsenal. It gives you the chance to articulate why you are a well-qualified candidate, why you are interested in employment with the particular company or organization to which you are applying, and why you should be selected for an interview. Cover letters give you the advantage of pulling out all of the qualifications, credentials, and strengths you offer in a customized and concise presentation. Forgo the cover letter, and you miss out on a golden opportunity to market yourself.

3. It Allows You to Explain Details or Circumstances Not Covered on Your Resume.

Are you preparing to relocate? Are you available for extensive travel or evening and weekend hours? Are you returning to the workforce after an extended absence due to raising your family, caring for an aging loved one, recuperating from an illness or injury, or some other reason? The cover letter gives you the opportunity to explain these factors. Career changers can also use the cover letter to expound on why they have decided to pursue a new professional direction.

4. It Ensures Your Consideration for the Position(s) of Interest to You.

During any given week, a company may receive hundreds of resumes for scores of different job openings. If your resume arrives without an accompanying cover letter specifying what you are applying for, it makes the job of the hiring manager or human resource professional much more difficult. This is an especially important concern for career changers, whose resumes will likely feature job titles bearing little resemblance to their current professional goals.

5. It Provides Employers with an Example of Your Business-Writing Prowess.

Anybody can claim that they possess "outstanding communication skills," but a well-written cover letter gives you the chance to prove it. Use your letter to showcase your ability to construct clear, error-free sentences and convey your thoughts persuasively.

WHAT IF I'M SENDING MY RESUME VIA E-MAIL?

You still need a cover letter. Send your resume online, on paper, or on a courier pigeon for that matter, but don't forget or neglect the cover letter.

Technology is a beautiful thing, providing instantaneous transport of your materials worldwide. It's a wonderful convenience and a time-saving shortcut, but it's not an excuse to bypass the cover letter. No matter what method you select to submit your documents—fax, Internet, e-mail, or "snail-mail," send a cover letter with your resume.

If you are using e-mail, your cover letter should be pasted directly into the message (not sent as an attachment). If you are replying to an online posting that does not provide a separate cover letter option on the Web site, paste your letter into the message window first, and then follow that with your resume.

THE FOUR TYPES OF COVER LETTERS

Career changers have at their disposal four different kinds of cover letters, and the most successful job seekers take advantage of all these options to maximize the potential for interview invitations.

1. Direct Response to an Advertised Opening

You are probably most familiar with this kind of letter, which replies to a job advertisement placed by an employer in a newspaper or publication, on their company homepage, or on a Web site like Monster. When responding to position announcements, make sure that you include the exact job title (and job reference and ID number, if applicable) somewhere in your letter. Your direct response letter should address how your background meets all (or a majority) of the skills, qualifications, and requirements mentioned in the ad. (*See samples at the end of this chapter.*)

2. Broadcast Letter

Also known as a "cold" cover letter, a broadcast letter is used to contact employers you are interested in working for that have not advertised a specific opening. Since the overwhelming majority (70% or more) of positions that are filled are never advertised, sending broadcast letters is an excellent way for career changers to tap into this "hidden" job market. You will need to do your homework before constructing these letters by researching the companies you are targeting to figure out how your skills can add to the attainment of their missions and goals. Many companies post press releases, annual reports, and "about us" features on their Web sites, so this is a good place to start. The time you invest in this research can pay big dividends in your job search. It will enable you to write a powerful letter linking your abilities with employer-announced initiatives like new product or service launches, or planned expansions or mergers. (*See samples at the end of this chapter.*)

3. Recruiter Letter

Many employers seeking to fill vacancies use search firms, temporary or employment agencies, or placement offices. Professional recruiters (or "headhunters") may function on either a retained or contingency basis. Retained recruiters are hired by a company to find viable candidates for specific openings. Contingency recruiters "shop" promising resumes they receive to a variety of employers in the hope of finding an employment match. In most cases, the recruiter's fees are paid by the company (not you, as the job seeker). Put another way, the recruiter is working for the employer, not for you. It's a mistake to send your resume to just one recruiter and expect him or her to do all of the work and find you a job.

Rather, send your resume and cover letter to as many recruiters as possible to widen your resume's exposure. Your letter to recruiters should explain what kinds of positions you are interested in and how you can help them fulfill their corporate clients' needs. The letter to the recruiter is the *only* instance where you should disclose your salary requirements. For more information on how to handle salary issues in the cover letter, see "Five Things That Don't Belong in a Cover Letter" later in this chapter. (*See samples at the end of this chapter.*)

4. Networking Letter

The goal of a networking letter is to produce job leads rather than job offers. These letters should be sent to individuals who may be able to assist you in your career change by passing your resume along to others, giving you suggestions on who to contact, or providing you with feedback on ways to strengthen your resume. Use networking letters to let personal and professional acquaintances know about your career change and to ask for their help in making the transition. Most people will take it as a compliment that you value their opinion and will be very willing to help you if asked in the right way. Prime candidates for this kind of letter include friends or colleagues you may have lost touch with; representatives from your school's alumni association or career placement office; former teachers, professors, or supervisors; and professionals whose services you currently employ or have used in the past (e.g., your former realtor or current insurance agent can often be the first to hear about new businesses coming into your community, giving you an inside track to as-yet-unpublicized employment opportunities). (*See sample at the end of this chapter.*)

COVER LETTER COMPONENTS (DIRECT RESPONSE, BROADCAST, AND RECRUITER LETTERS)

1. The Salutation

Begin your cover letter with a formal address (e.g., "Dear Ms. Smith") followed by a colon (not a comma). If you don't know the name of the person who will be reading your letter (many ads don't give you a contact name), use "Dear Hiring Manager:" or "Dear Recruiting Professional:" instead of "Dear Sir or Madam:" (which sounds dated and stuffy) or "To Whom it May Concern:" (which sounds cold and impersonal).

2. The Opener

Many career changers find the opening section of the cover letter the hardest to write, partly because of conflicting advice on this subject. Should you try to start your letter with a "bang" by coming up with some clever or unique opening? (And if so, what should you write?) Or should you stick with the tried and true "Please consider me for your <job title> position..." approach?

The answer depends on the type of position you are applying for, how conservative or progressive the company you are targeting is, and your personal communication style. If you are switching to a field like advertising, marketing, or public relations, you can afford to be more creative in your opener. If your career change goal is in a conservative field, like banking, insurance, or finance, then you're safer to begin your letter more traditionally.

Listed below are eight different openers that may give you some new ideas. You should customize them to fit your own unique circumstances, and only select ones that "sound" like you and make the most sense based on your career change goals and situation.

- The "If/Then" Opener:

  "If you are seeking to augment your management staff with a professional who has repeatedly proven the ability to increase profits, customer satisfaction, and employee retention to record highs, then my credentials will be of interest..."

- The Conservative Opener (Emphasizing Employer Needs):

  "Your need for a customer-focused, technically skilled administrative assistant is an excellent fit to my qualifications and career aspirations, and I hope to be considered as a serious applicant..."

- The Conservative Opener (Emphasizing Benefits):

  "In my candidacy for your accountant opening, you will find solid credentials (including recent CPA attainment), technical aptitude (including proficiency in Excel, Peachtree, and QuickBooks), and a highly regarded reputation for attention to detail..."

- The Numbers Opener (sentence fragment intended):

  "Quota-surpassing performance (225% above goal) ... $2.8 million in new-account wins last year ... a 75% same-day close rate. These are the results that I produced for my most recent employer as the #2-ranked sales representative (out of a 95-member team). Given the opportunity, I'm confident in my ability to transition these sales skills from the telecommunications industry to the pharmaceutical industry to deliver similar outcomes for you..."

- The Testimonial Opener:

  " '...a creative problem solver...dedicated and enthusiastic...highly respected leader...delivers projects on time or before deadline...consistently produces high-quality work.' These are a few of the ways my performance has consistently been described on annual performance reviews by my current employer. In my candidacy for your project manager position, you will find all of these traits, as well as the following demonstrated results..."

- The Confident Opener:

  "As your next marketing coordinator, my complete focus will be directed toward achieving the same pace-setting results for you that I have delivered to clients in my private consulting practice. These include a direct-mail response rate of 55%, a customer increase of

The Cover Letter

49

250%, and a recurring annual revenue stream of $1.8 million—all while simultaneously cutting previous company marketing spending between 20% and 50%..."

- The Story Opener:

"Several years ago, I was between dental assistant positions following my relocation to California and was in need of a job. Since my dental technician credentials weren't compatible with California's requirements, I decided to pursue a career in sales. Within 30 days (and after about 15 minutes of training) I became the #1 department sales representative for a Fortune 500 retailer. I now find myself at a new career crossroads, and am eager to combine my earlier sales success with my six-year background in the healthcare industry to become your next record-setting pharmaceutical sales representative..."

- The Company News Opener:

"As a long-time supporter of the high-quality performances sponsored by the Chicago Arts Guild, I was pleased to read of your plans to expand your season year-round next year. Toward that end, I believe that I can help in ensuring the continued financial health of CAG as your new director of development. Although all of my prior fundraising experience has been on a volunteer basis, I have proven the ability to single-handedly raise hundreds of thousands of dollars from corporate and individual donors..."

3. The Body

This is the meat of your cover letter, and it contains the majority of your "sales pitch." The body of your letter should be heavily focused on what you can do for an employer, not what you want from them. Minimize your use of the word "I" (especially at the beginning of sentences) for a more employer-focused tone. You should call prominent attention to the aspects from your background that are most closely related to what the employer is seeking (or what you perceive an employer needs). Avoid word-for-word duplication of what is in your resume. Find new ways to present your standout achievements and credentials. For example, consider condensing similar accomplishments from various positions you have held into one sentence. ("You will find a consistent record of cost-cutting in my background that saved ABC Company $145K annually, slashed DEF Company's overhead by 10%, and reduced XYZ Company's spending by $78K per annum.")

The body of the letter is also where you can explain special circumstances, such as an upcoming move, a return to a former career, or reentry into the workforce. Keep your writing crisp and concise; most cover letters should not exceed one page.

4. The Promise of or Call to Action

Toward the end of your letter, include the next steps you will take or are hoping for. For broadcast or direct-response letters, you should promise to follow up whenever possible. This puts you in control and gives you an excellent "excuse" to contact the company both to ensure that they received your materials, and to establish rapport with a company representative to help increase the odds that your resume gets a first (or second) look. Here's an example of an action promise: "I will follow up with you in a few days to answer any preliminary questions you may have. In the meantime, I can be reached at 555-555-5555."

For recruiter letters (or for situations where you do not have company contact information or have been directed in the ad not to call), it's best to wind up the letter by suggesting what you want the reader to do: "If, after reviewing my enclosed resume, you agree that a meeting to discuss employment further could be to our mutual interest, please contact me at 555-555-5555."

5. The Closing

Always end your cover letter with a thank you to readers for their time. Always. It's one of the few hard-and-fast rules when it comes to cover-letter writing. Follow this with a polite closing.

FIVE THINGS THAT DON'T BELONG IN A COVER LETTER (OR A RESUME)

1. Salary Details

Disclosing details of your past earnings or salary expectations before an employer has expressed strong interest in your candidacy can seriously weaken your negotiating power down the road. As you begin your job search, you are bound to see position ads that warn, "Candidates who do not send salary requirements will not be considered." But research has shown that the vast number of employers will still consider an otherwise qualified applicant who does not include this salary information. This doesn't mean that you should simply ignore the request, however. When you see ads that ask for salary requirements or a "salary history" (which is a separate document, apart from the resume or cover letter) it's best to acknowledge the request with a statement such as, "I would be happy to discuss salary requirements once a mutual interest has been established in my candidacy."

If you really feel pressured, provide a broad salary range instead of a hard number. For example, "My salary requirements are flexible (ranging between $50K and $75K), depending upon the total scope of responsibility." The only exception to this rule is the cover letter addressing recruiters, where it is appropriate to indicate your most recent salary and the minimum compensation you are willing to accept.

2. References

References should be set up as a separate document apart from the resume or cover letter. Don't send your references with your resume and cover letter unless you are specifically requested to do so to avoid inundating employers with volumes of paperwork. If an employer is interested, they will ask for your references.

3. Informality

Your cover letter is professional business correspondence. Don't begin it with "Hi!," "How are you?," or even "Good morning." Don't address the recipient by his or her first name. Don't use stationery with butterflies, flowers, rainbows, or kittens on it. Your cover letter should be printed on the same high-quality paper as your resume, with a matching heading for a cohesive, professional presentation.

4. Personal Photo and Personal Information

Unless you are changing careers to break into the entertainment, broadcast, or fashion industry (e.g., acting, television reporting, or modeling), you should not include a photo of yourself on the cover letter or resume. Although this used to be standard practice several decades ago, it's a definite "don't" today. Many employers will automatically discount applicants who include personal photos to avoid the potential for allegations of discriminatory interviewing practices. Save the photos for your holiday family newsletter.

For similar reasons, don't mention personal details in your cover letter that aren't relevant to your candidacy. Your marital status, age, and ethnicity don't belong on your resume or cover letter.

5. Negativity

Your former boss may have been pompous and irritating. Your last job may have ended in an unfair termination. Your personal finances may be in a shambles if you don't find a job (any job) soon. But your cover letter is not the place for these kinds of accusations, brutal truth telling, or confessions. Negativity about your career (or your life in general) has no place in your cover letter. Don't bad-mouth your previous employer, don't appear desperate, don't narrate a sob story, and don't sound angry or bitter. Keep your tone positive, focus on your strengths, and convey how you will positively impact the organization or company to which you are writing.

Direct response to an advertised opening (business graduate transitioning to human resources):

Lucy Chen

24 Eaton Place, Apt. #5 ▪ Cleveland, OH 34855
555-555-5555 ▪ lchen@resumepower.com

\<Date\>

Shoreline Industries, Inc.
P.O. Box 55
Cleveland, OH 34897

Re: Human Resources Assistant Opening (Job ID#: HR876), advertised on Monster

Dear Hiring Manager:

Your advertised opening for a human resources assistant is a perfect match to my strong desire to begin a career dedicated to human resources. In my candidacy, you will find an eager and enthusiastic recent college graduate offering:

- **A track record of excellent performance** as a part-time/summer employee and intern concurrent with my full-time college enrollment.
- **The proven ability to build genuine rapport** with individuals from all cultural and socio-economic backgrounds, with well-honed skills in diffusing potentially explosive situations. This talent has been repeatedly praised by employers, who have commended me for my interpersonal skills, tact, and diplomacy.
- **Technical proficiency in Windows platforms,** including Microsoft Office Suite.
- **Dean's list performance** at Ohio State College, where I completed my B.S. in business this May.
- **A passion for people and learning, as well as a tireless work ethic**—demonstrated by volunteering many evenings/weekends in an unpaid capacity to help my former employer complete a major facility renovation.

I have recently joined SHRM and am currently enrolled in a human resources development program to further enhance my qualifications in the field.

Your review of my enclosed resume to explore a possible match between your needs and my skills is much appreciated. I would welcome the opportunity to meet with you in person to learn more about your business and provide you with more details of my abilities. I will follow up with you in one week to answer any preliminary questions you may have. In the meantime, I can be reached at (555) 555-5555.

Thank you for your time and consideration, and I look forward to our conversation.

Sincerely,

Lucy Chen

Enclosure

Michael Whitler

14 Central Drive
San Francisco, CA 94117

(415) 123-4567
michael@resumepower.com

<date>

Mr. Robert Peterson
Human Resources Director
ABC Company
33 North 63rd
San Francisco, CA 94117

Re: Executive Assistant to the Vice President opening, advertised in the *San Francisco Chronicle*

Dear Mr. Peterson:

Your need for an executive assistant to the vice president is a precise fit to my qualifications and career aspirations, and if you are seeking a dedicated administrative professional skilled in business computer applications, office leadership, and detailed project management, we should meet. I offer this precise combination of skills, with a 14-year track record of exemplary performance for my employers.

Although my career within the healthcare and rehabilitation field has been rewarding, I am seeking to transition into an office setting where I can maximize my organizational, customer service, and management skills to further business goals and bottom-line objectives. In my candidacy, you will find:

- **A tactful and effective communicator**, experienced in resolving disputes and diffusing difficult situations for win-win outcomes. I have extensive experience working with individuals from diverse backgrounds, and am backed by solid credentials, with a B.A. in psychology.

- **Advanced technical and report-writing skills**, with expertise in MS Office, database management, computer troubleshooting, software training, and data entry/analysis, as well as the proven ability to synthesize complex information into concise, insightful executive summaries and government reports.

- **A team-oriented professional** with a positive work ethic and deep commitment to providing optimal customer service.

- **A well-respected leader**, experienced in supervising office staff.

- **A P&L mindset**, with a history of ensuring maximum levels of government funding through meticulous attention to detail when preparing health department reports.

If you agree that my background, further detailed in my enclosed resume, is well suited to your needs, I would welcome the opportunity to meet with you in person to explore employment possibilities. You may reach me at (415) 123-4567 or via e-mail at michael@resumepower.com. Thank you for your time, and I look forward to hearing from you soon.

Sincerely,

Michael Whitler

Enclosure

Direct response to an advertised opening (farmer/nonprofit foundation supervisor transitioning to sales):

Marcus R. Reeves

| 57 Bridge Lane | Tyler, NE 57986 | m_reeves@resumepower.com | 555-555-5555 |

\<Date\>

Re: Account Manager (Job Reference Code: 23Z8), advertised on HotJobs.com

Dear Hiring Manager:

A cursory review of my career history as a farmer and regional supervisor of a government foundation (the Nebraska Beetle and Worm Eradication Foundation) might at first lead you to question the relevance of my qualifications for your account manager opening. But as I hope to demonstrate below, I have a strong and pertinent sales skill set directly relevant to your needs.

Listed below are verifiable examples that illustrate the abilities you seek:

YOUR REQUIREMENTS:	MY ACCOMPLISHMENTS:
Advancing Financial Gains	I built a start-up farming organization from the ground up, to $750,000 in net valuation, maintaining steady crop sales and business growth within this highly volatile industry characterized by frequent profit losses and subsequent foreclosures.
Communicating Persuasively	Since 1989, when I first won $150,000 in seed money to launch start-up operations of my 1,200-acre independent farming organization, I have used effective sales, communication, and proposal-development skills to close six-figure financing deals with banking institutions every year, securing funding commitments of up to $327,000.
Overcoming Objections	For the foundation, I have repeatedly proven the ability to articulate value/benefits with conviction, overcoming vocal opposition to crop spraying from various environmental/public interest groups as well as from segments of the farming community. To accomplish this feat, I have developed well-honed listening and consensus-building skills and have delivered persuasive presentations through many speaking engagements.
Managing Relationships, Territories, and Operations	As district supervisor for the foundation, I manage 14 full-time employees and 50 seasonal workers throughout a 150K-acre region. This position requires me to be able to cultivate strong relationships with a wide variety of key stakeholders, and I have been successful in building cooperative partnerships with government agencies, hundreds of farmers, civic/community groups, and the media.

My ability to use a solution-centered approach has furthered the primary aim of the foundation to eliminate crop-damaging parasites, preserve farmlands, and sustain profitable enterprises. In fact, it has been so successful that I am, in effect, "working my way out of a job." The foundation's success in eradicating beetles and worms means that soon this operation will scale back to a maintenance-only function. Although my performance has won superior evaluations, it is unclear whether or not the regional supervisor role will still be needed. Beyond that, having accomplished the majority of my objectives, I am ready and eager to assume new challenges. Your opening presents the precise opportunity I am seeking, and would allow me to focus full-time on my proven sales abilities and strong interest in this career.

I will follow up with you in a few days to answer any questions you may have. In the meantime, I can be reached at (555) 555-5555. Thank you for your time and consideration, and I look forward to our conversation.
Sincerely,

Marcus R. Reeves

Enclosure: Resume

SERENA KEMPER

37 Berkestone Ave.   (555) 555-5555
New Haven, CT 02567   serena@resumepower.com

<Date>

Ms. Marcia Whitfield
Marketing and Public Relations Director
DelTech, Inc.
5700 Forest St.
New Haven, CT 02567

Dear Ms. Whitfield:

When time and money are no object, it's easy to direct winning marketing campaigns, manage successful projects, and coordinate filled-to-capacity events. I've done all three—but under Spandex-tight budgets and deadline pressure—for employers as diverse as the Fortune 5, nonprofit sector, and U.S. government.

I can do the same for you.

Allow me to intoduce myself; most recently I was an analyst and project manager for a consulting firm serving U.S. government agencies. I've recently relocated to the New Haven area to begin my scholarship to Yale University's evening master's degree program in technology. I'm pursuing a full-time position in the high-tech/new media industry where I can leverage my unique combination of skills in both analytical research and creative campaign/event management.

Perhaps you have an opening for someone whose career highlights include:

- B.A. in mass communication.
- Creation and implementation of public-relations campaigns, marketing strategies, and special projects/events, widely praised for increasing market share, maximizing sales/profits, and enhancing customer satisfaction.
- Recognition by senior management for slashing travel expenditures and using technology to increase efficiency by 20%.
- Award-winning public-speaking/sales-presentation skills, with demonstrated ease networking with White House staff, senior CIA and FBI officials, university presidents, and Fortune 100 company executives and directors.
- Ability to research, analyze, and communicate highly technical, complex information.
- "Exceptional" performance-review ratings in all categories, including imagination and creativity, oral and written communication, and ability to work independently and in team environments.

Details of these accomplishments are contained in my enclosed resume. I will follow up with you in a few days to introduce myself and answer any questions you may have. In the meantime, I can be reached at (555) 555-5555 or via e-mail at serena@resumepower.com. Thank you for your consideration, and I hope to meet with you soon.

Sincerely,

Serena Kemper

Enclosure

Frank E. Adler

4700 West Acorn Ave. Seattle Message Phone: (555) 555-5555
Dallas, TX 78903 Home: (555) 555-5551
bpadler@resumepower.com Cellular: (555) 555-5552

<Date>

Mr. Roberto Alvarez
Manager of Information Technology
XYZ Corporation
987 Ocean Ave.
Seattle, WA 89054

Dear Mr. Alvarez:

Rhonda Peterson, one of your network administrators and a long-time associate of mine, suggested I contact you regarding my strong interest in joining your IT staff. Toward that end, I am enclosing my resume for your review.

Having recently earned **MCSE, CCNA**, and **CCDA** certifications, I am seeking to transition to the IT field following five years of superior-rated performance as an investment advisor. Specifically, I am pursuing an analyst position, specializing in Cisco routers and switches, within your Solution Center. I am preparing to relocate to Seattle (at my own expense) to join my fiancée and expect to complete the move next month.

Throughout the past year, I have completed a comprehensive program of training in network administration at the Computer Information Technology Institute in Dallas, and am now eager to apply and build upon the skills I have acquired through this intensive training program.

My financial background has provided me with an exceptional work ethic, discipline, focus on customer relationships, and problem-solving skills necessary to succeed in a technical position. I am comfortable in a service-oriented environment and skilled in translating technical information to end users at all levels. The maturity I bring to the table, along with sound judgment and decision-making abilities, will be of value to your IT team.

XYZ Corp. has long led the market in innovative business solutions, and I am very interested in contributing to your continued success. I will follow up with you in a few days to explore the possibility of an interview. In the meantime, I can be reached at the following local Seattle phone number, which I regularly check for messages: 555-555-5555. Thank you in advance for your consideration, and I look forward to discussing my possible professional affiliation with XYZ.

Sincerely,

Frank E. Adler

Enclosure: Resume

Matthew Tobias, M.D.

5600 West Silver Ridge Rd.   *Available for Relocation*   Office: (555) 555-5555
Boston, MA 02127   Home: (555) 555-5551
mt_md@resumepower.com   *and Extensive Travel*   Cellular: (555) 555-5552

<Date>

Ms. Chris Thompson
Chief Hospital Administrator
Rhode Island General Hospital
5500 Hwy 287
Providence, RI 02498

Dear Ms. Thompson:

If your organization has a need for a medical administrative leader skilled in cross-departmental team building, situational analysis, and efficiency/productivity improvements fueling enhanced patient care and organizational profitability, then my credentials will be of interest. Allow me to introduce myself: a dedicated M.D. and medical director with 13 years of experience in both clinical and healthcare operations management.

Last year, I made the decision to begin preparing for a career shift into medical administration/consulting, and toward that end I have completed the first year of an M.B.A. program.

In my desire to join your operation in an administrative or consulting capacity, you will find:

- **A respected leader,** with demonstrated success organizing and managing patient-oriented teams. My background includes operational leadership within both medical teaching clinic and group practice settings, with the proven ability to realize six-figure net income increases and maximize HMO incentive-payment reimbursement. In addition, I have successfully led all aspects of negotiations and medical-practice transitions throughout several ownership transfers.
- **Highly regarded interpersonal skills,** with an approachable, inclusive management style, bilingual fluency (Spanish), and the ability to instill a shared sense of purpose and optimum communication/cooperation between physicians, nurses, and staff. I've had repeated success cultivating mutually beneficial relationships with vendors, corporate management, and throughout the medical and insurance community.
- **An executive-level understanding of fiscal management and budgeting,** with hospital medical executive committee experience and a history of P&L performance enhancement.
- **Solid credentials:** Fellow of the American College of Medical Practice Management, board-certified in internal medicine, and member of the American College of Physician Executives, the American College of Medical Practice Management, and the Boston General medical staff.

If these credentials and achievements, further detailed in my enclosed resume, appear to be a close fit to your needs, a meeting to further discuss your business goals could be to our mutual benefit. I will follow up with you in a few days to answer any preliminary questions you may have and to explore the possibility of a get-acquainted discussion. In the meantime, feel free to call me at (555) 555-5555 (daytime) or (555) 555-5551 (evenings). I look forward to our conversation.

Sincerely,

Matthew Tobias, M.D.

Enclosure: Resume

Darcy Gelmund

987 North Oakleaf Terrace ▪ Indianapolis, IN 47856 ▪ (555) 555-5555 ▪ dygelmund@resumepower.com

<Date>

Ericson Recruiting, Inc.
77 Corporate Dr.
Indianapolis, IN 47856

Re: IT Openings in Software Engineering, Database Administration, or Web Site Development

Dear Recruiting Professional:

Perhaps one of your clients is seeking to augment its IT team with an experienced professional offering triple skills for a single salary. If so, my credentials will be of interest. Allow me to introduce myself: an experienced software engineer, database administrator, and Web developer with strong expertise in full life-cycle project management (from design to launch).

In my background, you will find a record of proven results, with accomplishment highlights including:

- Front-end, back-end, middle-tier, and GUI design of cutting-edge systems that modernized operations, catapulted productivity by as much as 400%, and fused competing business needs into cohesive and elegant solutions.
- Correction of serious IT issues that eliminated prior long-standing histories of daily system crashes.
- Introduction of real-time tracking/reporting technology to turn around lagging product sales and fuel significant gains to operational accuracy and decision-making capabilities.
- Delivery of e-business systems propelling lucrative new revenue streams.
- Architecture of technology innovations key to the capture of new business (six-figure contract wins).

My technology proficiencies include:

- Fluency in multiple programming languages and applications, including Visual Basic, VBScript, Visual InterDev, ASP, FrontPage, HTML, JavaScript, MS Office, Adobe Photoshop, ADO, SQL Server, PL/SQL, and Oracle.
- Strong expertise in client/server architecture, distributed application development, and testing/scripting/documentation.
- Quality assurance know-how, including in-depth experience with defect-tracking systems.
- Lead or sole developer roles on a number of software-application and database build projects.

After spending the past five years as a stay-at-home parent, I am now eager to reenter the workforce full time. I have kept current on my technical skill set, and was recently retained by several local government offices and schools to provide short-term Web and IT consulting services. My minimum salary requirements are in the $40K to $45K range.

I would welcome the chance to speak with you personally about a possible employment match and can be reached at 555-555-5555. Thank you for your time and consideration of my enclosed resume, and I look forward to hearing from you.

Sincerely,

Darcy Gelmund

Enclosure

KIMBERLY BROOKSTONE

505 Evergreen Dr.   Ault, CO 69870   555-555-5555   kimberly@resumepower.com

Ms. Rebecca Tournly, Director
Tempt-To-Hire, Inc.
798 Brazelton Road.
Phoenix, AZ 56897

Re: Administrative Assistant/Office Manager Position Openings

Dear Ms. Tournly:

When you first glance at the employment history section of my enclosed resume, you might wonder, "Why is a Colorado chiropractor contacting me about administrative assistant openings?" It's a fair question, and I hope you will permit me a few moments of your time to explain.

While most small businesses fail within the first three years of start-up, mine has flourished throughout 14 years in multiple locations. The varied skills, self-motivation, and dedication necessary to accomplish this feat seem well matched to the needs of your clients. In my candidacy for employment with your organization, you'll find an accomplished professional whose background includes:

- Hands-on experience with all aspects of the role of an executive assistant, including general office and computer skills, project management, problem resolution, bookkeeping/accounting, confidential records, scheduling, front-office supervision, and follow-through.
- Commitment to life-long learning, exemplified by recent successful completion of Microsoft Office Suite certificate course (encompassing Word, Excel, PowerPoint, and Access).
- Exemplary customer-service skills, proven through a clientele based on 60% referrals.
- Solid background of professional presentation delivery, perfected through years of class instruction to employees, organizations, and the medical community.
- High comfort-level putting professionals and nonprofessionals from all levels at ease, with proven ability to open previously closed doors by converting historically skeptical M.D.s to become primary referral sources as well as loyal chiropractic clients.
- Ability to handle minute details to perfection without losing sight of the "big picture."

I am relocating to Phoenix this fall, and I will be in your area in early September. If your schedule permits, perhaps we can meet during my upcoming visit to Arizona.

My decision to leave my practice has come after careful thought. While it's been tremendously satisfying to build a successful business from the ground up, I've lately found myself restless for new challenges. I'd like to be part of an organization where I can positively impact customer service, operations, and profits, while growing personally and professionally as well.

I will follow up with you in a few days to explore the possibility of an interview. In the meantime, please reach me at 555-555-5555. Thank you for your consideration, and I look forward to speaking with you.

Sincerely,

Kimberly Brookstone

Enclosure

Julie S. Grant

546 Wheaton Way   San Diego, CA 90875   555-555-5555   julie@resumepower.com

---

<Date>

Dr. Joseph Greenberg
Assistant Professor
Northern Arizona University
College of Education
Flagstaff, AZ 57908

Dear Dr. Greenberg:

It's hard to believe that almost three years have passed since you served as my faculty advisor at NAU (back when I was Julie Sullivan), and I hope this letter finds you and your family well. I recall fondly the teaching practicum you led the semester the Learning Center opened, and as you may remember, I was a member of the first student teaching team you accompanied to the Hualapai Indian Reservation during the summer of 1998.

Thanks in large part to your tutelage, I successfully attained an elementary school teaching appointment with the Tucson School District within one week of graduating from NAU in 1999. Now I am once again seeking your kind assistance and knowledgeable advice.

One year after accepting the position with the Tucson School District, I married my husband, a captain in the U.S. Army. A few months later we learned that he would be stationed in Germany, requiring me to regretfully resign from my teaching post.

During the past two years we have moved four times, and this demanding travel schedule has not allowed me to make the minimum 10-month commitment that teaching requires. I've held a variety of positions ranging from retail sales to secretarial work throughout the last two years, and while these have strengthened my skills in a number of areas, they have not been related to education.

Now that my husband's tour of active duty is ending and we are back in the States, I am thrilled to be able to resume my teaching career. We plan to be moving to Flagstaff later this month, and I would consider it a dream come true to be able to teach elementary grades in the same town where I attended school.

I am hoping to tap into your extensive network of contacts as I begin my job search in earnest. Would you be willing to refer me to school administrator colleagues of yours in the Flagstaff or surrounding area who may be in need of an elementary teacher? Any assistance you could provide in terms of suggestions on who to contact would be very much appreciated.

I have enclosed my resume with this letter, and I highly value your opinion. If you have suggestions on how my presentation could be strengthened, I would welcome this advice as well.

Dr. Greenberg, I am deeply indebted to you for your help, and I sincerely thank you for your time. I will follow up with you in a few days and can be reached at (555) 555-5555 or julie@resumepower.com in the meantime.

Gratefully,

Julie (Sullivan) Grant

Enclosure

6

Your Resume's Done—Now What?

You've researched your job target, assessed your qualifications and transferable skills, and developed a compelling resume and cover letter that market you for your career change. Now you can get your job search underway.

While the average job search can take three months, career changers should expect a longer and more arduous search. Your challenge now is to get the word out to hiring managers that you are a strong candidate. Your resume will need exposure to work for you effectively. You've got to approach your career change with a viable plan so that you achieve the best results in the shortest period of time.

As a career changer, you will have the best success if you conduct an aggressive, active job search. This involves contacting employers instead of waiting to be found on online job banks; networking with everyone you know; asking for help from friends, colleagues, and family; and diligently following up on all possible leads. Employ a multifaceted approach to your career change plan to enjoy the best results.

If you feel lost, don't be afraid to seek help. Career coaches are trained to assist job seekers with challenges such as yours. Search the member directory of career coaching and counseling organizations listed in Appendix B, and find a professional who can help you map out a job search strategy that's right for you.

INFORMATIONAL INTERVIEWS

Most job seekers are accustomed to traditional job interviews, to which they are invited after submitting their resumes for advertised openings. Informational interviews, on the other hand, are initiated by the job seeker and are usually not tied into a specific job opening. The purpose of the informational interview is for the job seeker to get information about a company, job, or career, expand his or her network of contacts, and ask for advice and guidance.

The job search is not the time to be shy. To obtain an informational interview, pick up the phone and contact a hiring manager or someone who works in your desired field. Ask for just a few minutes of the person's time to discuss your career. You are not asking for a job, but rather for help and guidance. This is a perfect time to schmooze your contact—make the person feel good, and show a sincere interest in learning about what he or she does for a living. As a career changer, you will find informational interviews to be an excellent opportunity to learn about your new career choice.

When you secure an informational interview, be careful not to capitalize on the person's time, even if he or she is being particularly kind to you. Prepare a list of questions in advance and dress as if you are going to a formal job interview. Be generous with thanking your contact and never forget someone who helped you—that person might need your help in the future. You should stay in touch via phone and letter with all contacts who took time out of their schedules to discuss your career. By keeping them updated on your situation, you might learn about future job leads or about other professionals who can assist you.

NETWORKING

Networking is still the best way to obtain a new position, and this is especially true for the career changer. Networking involves contacting your colleagues, friends, family, and anyone else who can potentially help, and letting them know about your job search. Ask for advice and leads. Identify companies that interest you and contact them to see if they can use someone with your talent. Whenever you send your resume, follow up with a phone call and build rapport with the hiring manager, further expanding your network of contacts. Join trade associations and use the Internet to network.

EMPHASIZING EDUCATION WORKED FOR IMOGEN

Imogen was having little success switching from mechanical design to computer programming until she revamped her resume. Here's what she did:

1. Reordered her materials so that her upcoming degree in computer science was featured prominently toward the top of the resume.

2. Added relevant, in-progress coursework to the resume.

3. Emphasized her training in the opening resume profile.

Results: Imogen's new resume and persistence paid off, and she is now successfully employed as a computer programmer. (See Imogen Kaye's resume in Chapter 10.)

TARGETED RESUME DISTRIBUTION

Conduct research on your ideal employer, and develop a target list of companies where you would like to work. Your search will be more manageable if you limit your list to 50 or so employers. For each company, find out the hiring manager's name (preferably the director of the department where you would be working) and phone number, and establish phone contact before you send your resume. You are building a relationship, not blindly sending your career materials. Once you've spoken with the hiring manager, send a customized cover letter and resume. Keep track of whom you've spoken with, outcomes to date, and what kind of follow-up is necessary. Use the Job Search Contact Log at the end of this chapter to track your progress. (See Figure 6-1.)

AUTOMATED RESUME DISTRIBUTION

A number of services (listed in Appendix A) will e-mail, fax, and/or snail mail your resume to employers, recruiters, and venture capital firms. A great feature of some of these services is the ability to mail merge your resume and letter, so that it looks like you individually wrote to each company. The success of an automated distribution service depends on many factors, including your career field, how "in-demand" you are, job market conditions, and pure luck—landing on the right desk at the right time. It's worth considering because these services are usually inexpensive, fast, and offer a satisfaction guarantee.

> ### HIGHLIGHTING ACHIEVEMENTS WORKED FOR TOM
>
> Tom's desire to break into pharmaceutical sales was realized when he:
>
> 1. Started his resume off with a summary of his previous sales experience.
> 2. Added a colorful graphic to catch readers' attention.
> 3. Made his past sales accomplishments the showpiece of his resume, using specific dollar amounts, percentages, and numbers.
>
> Results: Tom received a job offer in his targeted field almost immediately after sending his resume. (See Tom Fields' resume in Chapter 9.)

RESPONSE TO JOB POSTINGS

Many job seekers use the old "tried and true" way of finding a new position—reviewing job advertisements and sending a resume to positions of interest. If you do respond to job ads, it's usually best to call first (unless the ad specifies that they don't want phone calls). Because the job market is so competitive right now, one job posting might generate thousands of applications, so taking the time to call shows motivation and interest in the position and company. This will set you apart from other job seekers. After you call, send your customized cover letter (addressing and thanking the person to whom you spoke) and resume. You should then follow up with a phone call in a few days to try to arrange an interview.

POUND THE PAVEMENT

In a bygone era, job seekers would physically walk into places of employment and ask for a job. In today's day and age, this method can still be surprisingly effective. Dress in business attire and visit companies on your targeted list. Inquire about job opportunities, see if you can fill out an application, drop off your resume, and/or request an informational interview. There's nothing like an in-person visit to create a great first impression. Be careful not to impose—you're simply inquiring about possible employment with the company.

A FEDERAL-STYLE RESUME WORKED FOR JOHN

John dreamed of working for the Secret Service (or similar government agency) when his active tour of duty in the military ended. Here's his formula for success:

1. Created a detailed, federal-style resume including all information required by the government.
2. Added a high-impact career summary to showcase his passion and suitability for his career goal.
3. Spotlighted his history of awards by including colorful graphics.
4. Emphasized his leadership achievements.

Results: Not only did John win an interview with the Secret Service; he also won interviews with (and is considering several offers from) the CIA, ATF, and DEA. (See John Lawrence's resume in Chapter 24.)

FOLLOW UP

A big mistake that job seekers make is to send out their resumes and wait for the phone to ring. A better strategy is always to follow up on all possible opportunities. Call the companies to which you applied and continue to express your interest in employment. Keep following up until you have a final word from the employer—yes or no. Your dream of achieving your new career goal is not likely to land in your lap without persistent follow-up.

ASK FOR HELP ALONG YOUR JOURNEY

As you embark on your career change journey, realize that you will not be able to achieve your goals without the help of others. Consider having your resume professionally prepared if you think your document is holding you back. Enlist the help of a career counselor or coach if you need career or job-search advice. Ask professionals in your new career field for guidance along the way. Reaching out will help you ease the frustration and insecurities that go hand in hand with a career shift. And know that when you're armed with a powerful resume and a clear job-search plan, your dream of a new career will soon be a reality.

Figure 6-1: Job Search Contact Log

Job Search Contact Log

Date Initiated Job Search [   ]   **Date Hired** [   ]

Instructions: Photocopy this Job Search Contact Log throughout your job search. Keep detailed notes pertaining to each contact and diligently follow up on all leads. When your search is concluded, keep this log for your future reference.

Company name:		Phone number(s):	FAX:
Company address:		URL:	
Contact person(s):		E-mail address:	
Title or position(s) sought:		Where advertised/referral source:	
Date advertised (if applicable):	Date resume mailed:	Date resume e-mailed:	
Date/outcomes of 1st call:	Date/outcomes of 2nd call:	Date/outcomes of 3rd call:	
Notes/follow-up:			

Company name:		Phone number(s):	FAX:
Company address:		URL:	
Contact person(s):		E-mail address:	
Title or position(s) sought:		Where advertised/referral source:	
Date advertised (if applicable):	Date resume mailed:	Date resume e-mailed:	
Date/outcomes of 1st call:	Date/outcomes of 2nd call:	Date/outcomes of 3rd call:	
Notes/follow-up:			

Company name:	Phone number(s):	FAX:
Company address:	URL:	
Contact person(s):	E-mail address:	
Title or position(s) sought:	Where advertised/referral source:	

Date advertised (if applicable):	Date resume mailed:	Date resume e-mailed:
Date/outcomes of 1st call:	Date/outcomes of 2nd call:	Date/outcomes of 3rd call:

Notes/follow-up:

Company name:	Phone number(s):	FAX:
Company address:	URL:	
Contact person(s):	E-mail address:	
Title or position(s) sought:	Where advertised/referral source:	

Date advertised (if applicable):	Date resume mailed:	Date resume e-mailed:
Date/outcomes of 1st call:	Date/outcomes of 2nd call:	Date/outcomes of 3rd call:

Notes/follow-up:

Part 4

RESUME SAMPLES BY CAREER GOAL

"Decide what you want; decide what you are willing to exchange for it. Establish your priorities and go to work."

—H. L. Hunt

7

Managers

Multidivision
Operations
Management

Process-
Improvement
Initiatives

Strategic
Planning &
Budgeting

Training &
Team Building

Business Plans

Contract
Negotiations

Change &
Turnaround
Management

Cost-Control
Strategies

Labor
Relations

Million-Dollar
Sales Growth

Word, Excel,
Windows,
Macintosh

GABRIEL JIMENEZ

(210) 123-4567 • gabriel@resumepower.com • 2 Firth Ave. • San Antonio, TX 78248

Management Professional

Operations Management • Sales Leadership • Business Development

Versatile Fortune 100 management professional with 16-year track record of proven success leading operations, sales, and customer-service divisions. Highly regarded as a creative problem solver, able to assess operational needs and innovate strategies that increase productivity, enhance customer satisfaction, and improve cost-effectiveness. Respected leader, skilled in guiding the turnaround of underperforming divisions.

Career Profile

Demonstrated commitment to meeting and exceeding corporate goals has led to a successful career with Amalgamated Services, with a history of repeated awards and promotions to increasingly responsible positions. Experienced guiding sizable teams of up to 120 in union environments, delivering seven-figure account growth, and facilitating profit-margin improvement. Reputation for organization, integrity, and results.

Experience

AMALGAMATED SERVICES INCORPORATED, 1988 to Present

Senior Account Executive (Sales Department – San Antonio, TX), 1/01 to Present

Promoted to direct account management, retention, and business expansion initiatives for 100 major accounts, valued at $13.9 million total.

- On target to capture over $1 million in additional revenues by year-end.
- Coordinated value-added services such as system integrations linking customers with Amalgamated technology, resulting in account growth with existing customer base.
- Researched, identified, and acted upon shipping and freight trends for all 100 accounts managed. Applied in-depth knowledge of each company's shipping business to negotiate mutually beneficial contracts for new, repeat, and expanded business.
- Selected to attend prestigious leadership-training course designed by Harvard Business School. Serve as area sales manager in supervisor's absence.

Key Account Executive (Sales Department – San Antonio, TX), 7/98 to 1/01

Recruited from operations to play a key role in implementing organizationwide culture shift to a more aggressive, sales-driven focus in order to maintain industry dominance in an increasingly competitive marketplace. Responsible for retention and growth of 350 accounts producing annual revenue ranging from $20K to $100K per client.

- Delivered $650K in new revenues, successfully attaining 100% of business plan.
- Earned 2002 Gold Award (top 5% of companywide sales force).
- Expanded small $15K account into $250K revenue-producer in six months.

Package Operations Supervisor (Delivery Operations – San Antonio, TX), 2/98 to 7/98

Oversaw all aspects of first-shift delivery operations, including supervision, training, and scheduling of 120 hourly and Teamsters Union employees; maintaining on-time performance in a deadline-driven environment; and meeting all production goals.

- Consistently met (and often surpassed) stringent, time-sensitive productivity goals in an industry where even a 2% fluctuation can negatively impact the bottom line.

GABRIEL JIMENEZ

Resume • Page 2

Experience (continued)

Package Operations Supervisor (Business Operations – San Antonio, TX), 9/97 to 2/98

Managed internal dispatch operations, timelines, and supervision of 20 Teamsters Union drivers.

- Became crisis-management expert – adeptly handled unforeseen incidents by adjusting operational plan and resource allocation daily to ensure zero loss in productivity.
- Promoted to supervise delivery operations.

Customer Service Supervisor (Front-Line Operations – San Antonio, TX), 6/90 to 9/97

Led 12-member nonunion team in high-volume customer-service operations.

- Recruited to design and direct complete reorganization of entire operation to enhance effectiveness and efficiency. Reinstilled a commitment to providing optimum customer service, initiated quality standards and training programs, and achieved a profit-margin improvement by reducing six-figure damage penalties 20%.
- Built a more viable organizational structure and a cohesive team of employees.
- Earned companywide recognition for successful turnaround efforts that ultimately enabled location to run seamlessly without a direct supervisor.

Package Operations Supervisor (Reload Operations – San Antonio, TX), 6/88 to 6/90

Oversaw training, scheduling, and performance of eight part-time union employees.

- Developed daily operational plan and achieved all production goals.
- Earned a reputation as an effective trainer and mentor. Fostered the development and subsequent promotions of multiple team members.
- Promoted to customer service supervisor.

Education

UNIVERSITY OF TEXAS AT SAN ANTONIO – San Antonio, TX
BS Degree Program in International Business (in progress; junior status)

SAN ANTONIO COLLEGE – San Antonio, TX
AA Degree in Graphic Design, 1998

Professional Development Highlights

- **Supervisor Leadership** (designed by Harvard Business School) – San Antonio, TX; 2002
- **Situational Sales Negotiations** – San Antonio, TX; 2002
- **SPIN Sales Training** – San Antonio, TX; 1998
- **Account Strategy for Major Sales** – San Antonio, TX; 2001

Available for Relocation

Resume Strategy: *Gabriel's current job title may be "sales account executive," but he makes it clear in the first two paragraphs of his resume that his background includes managing not only sales functions, but also operations and customer-service divisions. His "Career Profile" summarizes his success delivering seven-figure revenues and guiding large unionized teams and he uses bulleted statements in his "Experience" section to show how his contributions improved profits, productivity, and efficiency. In the left-hand column on page one, Gabriel lists his expertise areas of importance to business operations management.*

Samuel Chin

1228 Plank Road
Sunnyvale, CA 94089

samuel@resumepower.com

Home: (408) 123-4567
Cellular: (408) 891-0111

Career Goal: Plant Manager ◆ Manufacturing/Quality Engineering Manager

*Fueling Cutting-Edge Product Development and Providing Strong Organizational,
Financial, and Engineering Leadership within Sophisticated Manufacturing Operations*

Accomplished manufacturing operations manager and engineer with MBA and 13 years of experience driving productivity and profit improvements for multibillion-dollar industry leaders. Skilled manufacturing production analyst with the ability to develop, lead, and introduce revolutionary engineering initiatives that automate production processes, speed products to market, improve features and functionality, enhance revenues, and meet consumer demand. Respected leader, effective in both union and nonunion environments, with the ability to motivate project teams for maximum efficiency and profit gain. Solid project management skills; effectively direct multiple priorities and deliver innovative strategies to exceed corporate objectives. *Areas of Expertise:*

- Manufacturing Operations Management
- High-Level Project Management
- Cost Reduction & Avoidance
- Budget/Financial Management
- Process Reengineering/Research & Development

- Quality Assurance/Regulatory Compliance
- Strategic Planning
- Product Design, Development & Market Launch
- Vendor & Contract Negotiations
- Staff Training & Development/Labor Relations

PROFESSIONAL EXPERIENCE

ABC Motors – Sunnyvale, CA   1997–Present

PROJECT SUPERVISOR, ENGINEERING / MAINTENANCE (2000 – Present)
MAINTENANCE TECHNICAL ADVISOR (1997–1999)

Manage project teams of 10 to 12 engineers and quality/design specialists in the fulfillment of top-priority, sophisticated product-development, engineering, and market-launch activities within an integrated manufacturing environment. Hold full accountability for strategic project planning and management, budget administration, production and facilities management, workforce training and development, quality assurance, and regulatory compliance. Liaise between senior management and engineering/production teams. *Selected Accomplishments:*

- Led teams in the **launch of four new product lines** (representing $40 million in equipment), completing projects under time and budget restrictions; introducing state-of-the-art advancements for minivans, trucks, and SUVs; and meeting high consumer demand for key products. *Successful product launches include*:
  - Three steering components for ABC Truck; second phase of ABC Auto component delivery; and DEF Auto's aluminum truck knuckle.
- Generated **annual labor savings of $750,000** through integration of robots within new production process.
- Directed development of maintenance overtime equalization program that produced **$500,000 in annual savings** by reversing prior history of human errors.
- Reengineered transfer-machine station to reverse repeated, excessive downtime performance, **reducing costs by up to $100,000** annually.
- Resolved safety and environmental concerns, bringing operation into **full compliance with all OSHA and EPA guidelines** and regulations.
- Delivered a $1.2 million annual savings by designing and opening an innovative vibration-analysis test/repair center that improved equipment uptime and measurably enhanced predictive maintenance.

DEF Automotive Company – Sunnyvale, CA   1994 – 1997

TOOL ENGINEER

Recruited as engineer to provide technical support of production and maintenance, quality control, process improvements, project writing, equipment/systems specs and documentation, and cost reductions.

Samuel Chin

DEF Automotive Company (continued), *Selected Accomplishments:*

- Developed tooling designs and equipment improvements for two major production lines that resulted in **over $750,000 annual savings**.
- Spearheaded **$1.1 million in cost savings** through successful design of cold-forming dies that doubled process lifespan and allowed previously outsourced effort to be produced internally.
- Established **two new successful product lines** encompassing transfer machines, dial machining centers, and automated assembly machines.

GHI Electronics – Sunnyvale, CA   1987–1994
Manufacturer of radiators, condensers, evaporators, fuel rails, and compressors for automotive market.

MANUFACTURING ENGINEER, COMPRESSOR (1992–1994)
MANUFACTURING ENGINEER, RADIATOR (1987–1992)
PRODUCTION SUPERVISOR (1987)

Led teams of 40+ in radiator assembly/braze production unit and headed engineer activities for radiator assembly/vacuum braze furnaces and high-volume compressor housing machining process. Managed project writing, quality control, process reengineering, technical support, product design, and production supervision. *Selected Accomplishments:*

- Wrote project specifications for machining station that produced **$275,000 labor savings** and increased statistical process control to a Cpk equivalent of 2.8 (up from below 1).
- Reengineered transfer machining center to produce **highest volume of goods in plant**, exceeding 100% of performance standard and slashing average product completion time from ten hours to seven.
- Worked jointly with vendor to plan, design, and develop **new transfer machining center** housing $9 million in equipment, maximizing efforts of cross-functional team to ensure successful completion.
- Created high-volume manufacturing process for radiators that impressed key figures and secured **$1 million manufacturing contract**, capturing a 40% cost advantage over competition.
- Designed expansion assembly tooling that **eliminated repairs in assembly and braze process** reflecting annual savings of $500,000.
- Conceived and developed repair fixtures/process that yielded **annual scrap savings of $50,000**.
- Co-created new design in drill-head applications that **reduced downtime** from ten hours to one.
- Maintained strong record of **meeting production goals** and motivating staff toward performance gains.

EDUCATION & CREDENTIALS

Master of Business Administration (MBA)   **Bachelor of Science in Mechanical Engineering (BSME)**
University of California, Berkeley, CA (2001)   Institute of Technology, Sunnyvale, CA (1987)

Professional Development:

- Theory of Constraints – Polytechnic Institute, Sunnyvale, CA, 2000
- Root Cause Analysis – Action Company, Sunnyvale, CA, 1995
- Design of Experiments – University of California, Berkeley, CA, 1990
- Statistical Process Control – ABC Motor Co., Sunnyvale, CA, 1987

TECHNICAL SKILLS

Microsoft Office applications, Indramat CNC controls, PLC systems

Resume Strategy: *Samuel's resume profile encapsulates his 13 years of experience driving profit and productivity improvements within manufacturing settings and includes areas of expertise relevant to his plant management career goal. His "Selected Accomplishments" throughout the "Professional Experience" section are quantified with numbers, dollar amounts, and percentages that show his impressive track record, and each begins with a powerful action verb.*

Profile

Skills Summary

Experience

Cliff May

42 Western Drive • Englishtown, NJ 07726 • (732) 123-4567 • cliff@resumepower.com

Resort / Destination Spa Manager

Certified fitness and wellness management professional qualified for leadership positions where business savvy, impeccable client service, and thorough industry knowledge will be of value. Fourteen-year proven track record managing athletic clubs, personal training programs, and massage/wellness services. Commitment to blending mind and body into complete, personalized therapies and programs has earned loyalty of hundreds of customers. Certified as a strength and conditioning coach and massage therapist, with BS in exercise/sport science.

Key Qualifications

- Solid business experience including supervision, inventory, loss prevention, budgeting, accounting, and marketing
- B.S. in exercise and sport science
- Certified strength & conditioning specialist
- Certified bodywork & massage therapist (900-hour certification)
- Expert in health/wellness/fitness/nutrition

Wellness Expertise

- Swedish relaxation
- Sports and deep tissue massage
- Pregnancy/infant/child massage
- Shiatsu and reflexology
- Myofacial release
- Reiki
- Body wraps – mud and seaweed
- Salt glow rubs and facials

WELLNESS GROUP – Englishtown, NJ

Owner, 8/00 to Present

Direct all aspects of successful massage, bodywork therapy, and personal training services business. Apply educational approach to helping clients with mind/body health issues, increasing their cause-and-effect awareness through massage/bodywork therapies and personal-fitness instruction. Take a thorough health history of every client.

- Achieved profitability after three months due to effective management, marketing, budgeting, customer service, client satisfaction, and product quality.
- Built client base from scratch to more than 500 in less than two years. Follow up with all clients to ensure 100% customer satisfaction.
- Work with hundreds of clients, applying expert knowledge of a wide range of therapeutic and training techniques.
- Hired therapist team by third month due to business growth and demand for services.
- Created holiday gift certificate campaign and sold 100 certificates in three weeks.

ACTION GYM – Englishtown, NJ

Personal Trainer/Front Desk, 10/02 to Present

Maintain unsurpassed customer service in fast-paced environment, handling up to 200 clients daily. Provide guidance in proper use of fitness equipment and design customized fitness plans that meet customers' needs. Manage front desk, conduct facility tours, and sell memberships. Train employees on gym policies and procedures.

- Established superior track record of membership sales by using tour presentation skills and broad-based fitness and nutrition knowledge.
- Recognized by management for exceptional ability to listen to customer needs and recommend plans to meet their goals.
- Proved skills in determining motivational tools to use with each individual client.

ACE ATHLETIC CLUBS, INC. – Princeton, NJ

Massage Therapy Director, 9/98 to 7/99; **Personal Fitness Trainer,** 6/98 to 7/99
Evaluated fitness levels, developed motivational personal fitness programs, and delivered massage therapy services. Recruited/hired therapists. Managed scheduling and accounting.

- Promoted to director after proposing massage therapy services, increasing club's efficiency and profits by creating a "found" revenue source for unused rooms.

Cliff May

- Recognized for running successful massage-therapy program, which directly increased company revenues–one-third of club members used the new service.
- Created effective advertising and promotions that increased new memberships during first three months of ad campaign.

NEW JERSEY SCHOOL OF MASSAGE – Newark, NJ

Instructor: Anatomy, Physiology, and Kinesiology I and II, 1997

STATE SWIM AND FITNESS CLUB – Princeton, NJ

Assistant Manager, 1993 to 1997

Provided customers with personalized fitness training, maintained inventory, handled front-desk responsibilities, scheduled and trained new lifeguards, maintained pool, and contributed to revenue growth by increasing membership sales.

- Promoted to assistant manager after first few months.
- Saved club $5,000 a year in maintenance by initiating in-house pool management.

UNITED STATES NAVY – Newark, NJ

Promoted to increasingly responsible positions including **Pharmacy Technician, Head of Pharmacy Compounding, and Contracting Officer,** 1988 to 1992

- Managed annual budget of $1.2 million.
- Reintroduced program to prepackage medicine, significantly enhancing efficiency and customer service by reducing prescription-processing time.
- Honors: Meritorious Unit Commendation, National Defense Award.

Affiliations

- Associated Bodywork and Massage Professionals
- National Strength and Conditioning Association

Education

- **B.S., Exercise and Sport Science,** RUTGERS UNIVERSITY, Camden, NJ, 1997
- Certified Massage Therapist/Chiropractic Assistant, New Jersey School of Massage, Newark, NJ, 1998
- Certified Bodywork Therapist/Strength and Conditioning Specialist, 1998 to Present
- Certified Contracting Officer, 1990
- CPR/First Aid, Current
- Management and sales coursework, Rutgers University, Camden, NJ, 1999

Resume Strategy: *Cliff articulates his goal to move into spa management from massage therapy at the outset, and includes a strong profile in his resume that communicates his thorough industry knowledge and prior management experience. He uses an elegant graphic of sweeping sand dunes and blue sky (in color on the original resume) that reinforces an image of peaceful serenity and distinguishes his resume from the crowd. Cliff's "Skills Summary" is cleverly divided into "Key Qualifications" and "Wellness Expertise" categories, which help to maximize keyword density and enable quick reader skimming. His bulleted accomplishments in the "Experience" section highlight his management and industry acumen.*

Dale Waters

7690 Littleton Trail
Las Vegas, NV 89509

Phone: (775) 555-5555
E-mail: dale@resumepower.com

PROFESSIONAL GOAL: BUSINESS ANALYST

IT Project Implementation ◆ *Project Management* ◆ *Corporate Training* ◆ *Financial Analysis*

Creative and results-oriented manager with diversified experience in competitive business environments. Successful record of conceptualizing and implementing effective strategies for a leading managed health care company. Unique combination of experience in operations, technical, and financial side of business. Recognized for ability to institute quality-assurance programs that optimize customer-satisfaction levels while increasing profits. Well-developed interpersonal skills with proven ability to lead, motivate, and inspire cross-functional teams to meet/surpass objectives. Current scope of responsibility includes overseeing 71 employees and $1.4 million budget. **Expertise includes:**

- Large-Scale Systems Implementation
- Project Management
- Team Building & Leadership
- HMO/POS/PPO Policies
- Contract Negotiations
- Revenue/Profit Management
- Technical Documentation
- Multidimensional Online Analytical Processing
- Turnaround Management
- Training and Development

Professional Experience

HEALTHPARTNERS, INC. (Las Vegas, NV)

Director of Claims Processing — Claims Administration Department, 1999 to present
Oversee 71 staff and $1.4 million budget and institute policies to improve quality and productivity standards. Improve member and provider satisfaction with both HealthPartners and the Claims department. Direct the use of HealthPartners' IT systems, including Amisys, Macess I-MAX and Doc-Flo, ClaimCheck, and EDI clearinghouses, for the effective and efficient processing of provider claims. Strategies and Results:

- **Led conversion of claims processing function from legacy to Amisys system.**
  Reduced inventory from 500,000 to 90,000 within 18 months. Identified and resolved configuration errors, hired temporary staff, and developed crisis log for claims that required immediate attention. Within ten months, processed a record 2.8 million claims on new system and appeased providers, members, and groups.

- **Delivered an 80% auto-adjudicate rate, an increase from 31% with prior system.**
  Reduced claims-processing FTE requirements by 25% within 18 months, translating to $300,000 in annual savings, an increase in quality, and consistent results.

- **Increased receipt of EDI claims from 32% to 50% within 18 months.**
  Set the stage for new processing benchmarks now at 95% of EDI claims within 30 days of receipt, an improvement from 77% prior to system conversion.

- **Retrained and restructured claims-processing team in order to enhance efficiencies.**
  Created a synergistic team cross-trained between different products. Developed a training curriculum with 15 courses for claims analysts and data-entry specialists (providing historical first by enabling data-entry staff to process claims).

- **Developed "source of truth" and "product specialist" roles.**
  Centralized and documented origination of business rules for benefits, fee schedules, authorization requirements, COB rules, and government regulations. Identified uniform resources for business answers, resulting in consistency in claims processing and improved system configuration.

Director Medical Informatics Team — Information Systems Department, 1997 to 1999
Formulated management strategies and custom technical solutions to improve service to HealthPartners' customers. Key player in all aspects of business planning, from strategy through implementation. Produced accurate and timely corporate and ad-hoc reports for both internal and external customers. Redesigned data warehouse for Amisys data structures and new technical platform. Strategies and Results:

- **Evaluated corporate reporting tools and developed new HEDIS reporting infrastructure.**
  Mapped business requirements and developed intranet-based reporting tools. Established formal report-request protocol, set priorities and deadlines, and ensured that customers were kept up-to-date on report status.

Dale Waters

Professional Experience

Director Medical Informatics Team (continued)

♦ **Implemented HR strategies to attract and retain quality staff and build a high-performance team.**
Reevaluated salaries and obtained raises for underpaid staff. Merged and cross-trained IT staff and business-analyst functions. Instituted quality checks in our development process to ensure accurate reporting requirements. Team received the highest scores in the company on job-satisfaction surveys.

♦ **Led two-year, $1.2 million project to redesign data warehouse.**
Introduced concept of multidimensional online analytical processing (MOLAP) via SAS cubes to reduce the number of ad-hoc report requests. The redesign reduced the number of reports and improved usability for end users.

Director, Business Applications Team — Information Systems, 1995 to 1997
Managed $1 million budget and 55 IS personnel. Coordinated all department activities relating to the delivery of business-system services to customers, while ensuring the operational, functional, and data integrity of HealthPartners' business applications. Strategies and Results:

♦ **Took over support for core business system and greatly enhanced its availability and capabilities.**
Eliminated bugs and stabilized the Health Claims Processing System (HCPS). Integrated system enhancements to support rapidly changing business requirements. Improved systems availability from 97% to 99% and completion of core job processes from 85% to 97%.

♦ **Established teams to support specific HealthPartners divisions.**
Improved communications and accountability by providing customers with a key IS contact person. Developed SIR, SAR, and BAR logs and processes for workflow management.

♦ **Designed and implemented the 1997 risk model that was key to regaining profitability.**
Trained company on how risk model affected performance from a system/data-use perspective. Recommended and built a new database and met two-month deadline of being operational with new risk model.

Senior Business Applications Analyst — Information Systems, 1988 to 1995
Financial Analyst — Finance Department, 1988
Promoted to Business Applications Team manager to supervise eight business analysts and foster cooperative teamwork with other IS teams. Coordinated the design, implementation, and ongoing support for all HMO, PPO, and POS products. Trained customers on how to utilize applications to achieve their business-function requirements while leveraging our software investments.

Education and Training

UNIVERSITY OF NEVADA, LAS VEGAS (Las Vegas, NV)
♦ **Master of Science in Professional Accountancy (MSPA),** with honors
♦ **Bachelor of Science in Education**

PROFESSIONAL DEVELOPMENT:
♦ Fundamentals of Successful Project Management — SkillPath, Las Vegas, NV, 1997
♦ Leadership and Team Development for Managerial Success — AMA, Las Vegas, NV, 1995

Technical Summary

Amisys, Macess Imax, Macess Doc-Flo, Novalis/HCPS, Manage 1, ClaimCheck, MS Word/Excel/Access, Oracle

Resume Strategy: *Dale gives his resume focus with his "Professional Goal" resume title, using a tagline below it to further explain his specialty areas in IT project implementation, project management, corporate training, and financial analysis. He groups his top expertise areas in a three-columned, bulleted list within the profile and does explain "Strategies and Results" he has successfully delivered for his various employers in his "Professional Experience" section.*

Blake M. Palmer

578 Crystal Lake Rd.   Home: (651) 555-5555
North Oaks, MN 55127   blake@resumepower.com   Pager: (651) 555-5556

SEEKING POSITION IN SPORTS MANAGEMENT / OPERATIONS

Verifiable Strengths in Communications, Marketing, PR, and Site & Facilities Management

Sports enthusiast with solid operations/facility management experience, strengths in marketing/PR, and a passion for professional and amateur sports. Pursuing a career with a sports team or sports-marketing company. Skilled at building strong team environments and fostering open communications. Accustomed to working in culturally diverse environments, with as many as 26 nationalities represented in the workplace. Adept trainer and motivator with effective interpersonal skills at all organizational levels.

Currently coach football, bowling, and weight training and continually promote concepts of integrity, quality, and teamwork. Served as assistant coach for the North Oaks Youth Organization's 1999 Championship Football Team. Play forward on the North Minnesota Badgers, a USASA soccer team that won the 1999 first-place trophy in Virginia Hills, VA. Credentials include dual bachelor's degrees in physical education and communication fields.

Related Skills

- Operations Management
- Community/Public Relations
- Facilities Planning
- Marketing Communications
- Budget Planning/Management
- Event Planning
- Purchasing and Cost Control
- Staff Supervision, Training, and Development
- Program Development
- Change Management
- Conflict Resolution
- Safety in the Workplace
- Microsoft Word, Excel, Windows 98/95

Career Highlights

JUMP-START, INC. – North Oaks, MN   1998 to present
(Organization serving children and adults with learning disabilities and behavioral disorders.)

Program Director

Maintain oversight for $3.7 million in revenues and operating budget of $1.1 million. Supervise, train, and coordinate 40 employees serving 120 clients. Ensure adherence to agency, federal, state, and local governmental regulations. Monitor and manage all aspects of 11,000 sq. ft. facility. Serve as Chairperson of the Attention Deficit Disorder (ADD) Committee. *Key Contributions:*

- Established strategic alliance with local philanthropic organizations and businesses, providing volunteer and internship opportunities for individuals with disabilities.
- Restructured organizational hierarchy to create a participatory environment for managers, administrators, and staff, which promoted interaction in classroom and program settings.
- Brought program to 94% billing capacity (at top of industry average) after increasing enrollment from 105 to 120. Adjusted staffing levels to accommodate new capacity.
- Developed Therapy Wing to integrate Physical, Occupational, and Speech Therapy specialties in a dedicated wing, which has facilitated quality and continuity of client services.
- Coordinate special events and all volunteer efforts, including the Community Integration Worship for parents and individuals with disabilities.
- Nominated for "1999 Employee of the Year" to the Minnesota Governor's Office for dedication to organizational goals and implementation of effective management and cost controls.

Blake M. Palmer

Resume - Page Two

Career Highlights

LEARNING DISABILITIES FOUNDATION – Minneapolis, MN   1993 to 1998
(Agency serving developmental and learning disabled youth throughout a four-state area.)
Assistant Director
Progressed steadily through the organization culminating in oversight for three homes, $1.8 million budget, and supervision/staffing of 27 managers and support personnel. Oversaw medication administration, development of behavioral support, communication, and speech plans. Directed site-safety and facilities-management processes. Promoted from residence manager, assistant residence manager, and direct care counselor. *Key Contributions:*

- Built strong, cohesive team environment, contributing to company's first "zero site state inspection."
- Created new behavior plans that fostered a sense of accomplishment among residents and staff, instilling a "can-do" mentality among the clients.
- Promoted external recreational activities to ease socialization processes.

Education

CONCORDIA COLLEGE – Moorhead, MN
Master's-Level Rehabilitation Counseling Coursework (24 credits), 1997 to 1998
Bachelor of Science, Physical Education, 1994
Bachelor of Fine Arts, Communication Arts, 1991
Coursework in Public Relations, Advertising, Radio, Magazines, Television, and Communications Law

Internships: **Communication Intern,** 1991 – AGROS, INC. – Mankato, MN

- Contributed to monthly newsletters, assisted with public-relations efforts, and secured cover story on company president in syndicated newspaper.

Public Relations Intern, 1990 - WMIN RADIO STATION – Mankato, MN

Sports

Soccer: NORTH MINNESOTA BADGERS (North Oaks, MN), **Forward**, 1998 to present

- Won tenth annual USASA Amateur Championships, 1999
- Named MVP for the tournament
- Made playoffs, 1998

Football: NORTH OAKS YOUTH ORGANIZATION (North Oaks, MN), **Assistant Coach for Offense**, Season Football, 1999 to present

- Won championship for 9- and 10-Year-Old Division (1999 season: 13 wins, 0 losses)

Bowling: MEN'S BOWLING LEAGUE (White Bear Lake, MN), 1996 to present

- Won League Championship, 1997

Resume Strategy: *Blake gives heavy emphasis to his extracurricular sports/coaching activities in his opening profile, mentioning these qualifications along with his solid background in management and marketing to help employers understand why he is well-suited to a career in sports management. His "Related Skills" section highlights his most relevant expertise and the "Key Contributions" in his "Career Highlights" section provide further evidence of these skills. Since his outside athletic pursuits are relevant to his career goal, Blake also includes a "Sports" section to round out his resume.*

BEN TROUTMAN

Home: 210-123-4567 ◆ Cell: 210-987-6543
14 Water Way ◆ San Antonio, TX 78244 ◆ ben@resumepower.com

Objective	Product Manager ◆ Business Development Strategist ◆ Consultant *Specializing in Technology, Software, and E-business Industries*
Profile	Resourceful, results-driven, and technically skilled professional combining strong background in profitable product/business development with advanced technology expertise. Ten-year history of leading cross-functional teams in the design and deployment of cutting-edge software resolving a myriad of business challenges while simultaneously generating new revenue streams well into the seven figures annually. Solid understanding of business flows/processes, with proven success identifying emerging market opportunities, spotting unmet customer needs, building strong business cases, and effectively bridging market gaps with consumer-driven, cutting-edge solutions. Offer unique perspective; able to respond to challenges from both a technical and business point of view.
Key Knowledge Areas	→ Strategic Planning & Vision → Cross-Functional Team Leadership → Business Development → Go-to-Market Strategy → Full-Lifecycle Product Management → Market, Trend & Needs Analysis → Software Development/E-commerce → Quality Assurance/Security → High-Profile Projects → Digital/Wireless/Internet Technology
Experience	SOFTWARE COMPANY, INC. – San Antonio, TX *Major provider of networking business solutions and leading software company.* **Software Engineer II,** 2/99 to Present Drive new product design by strategizing with cross-functional product development teams. Architect product designs and develop tightly integrated solutions meeting consumer needs across diverse industries (e.g., healthcare, petroleum services, high-tech, network television, retail, and entertainment). Develop proprietary software applications to facilitate provisioning, workflow, reporting, and billing of online applications. Representative Accomplishments: → Augmented VAR's thin-client software with Software Company's ProTech product. Integrated both products into a cohesive solution and presented results to management from both companies. Efforts resulted in executive decision to not only proceed with new product launch, but also acquire second company. Results: Software Company purchased ABC Company in May 2001 and new integrated product has rapidly gained traction in the market, becoming a **top product initiative for 2002** and rising from near zero sales to **$2.5M+** in a single year. → Initiated and led development of Web portal-based user-interface for ProTech (using existing technology), which has become an integral part of the new FutureTech solution. Results: Change in user-interface key to catapulting FutureTech to one of Software Company's top five solutions, anticipated to deliver **$150M** within the next few years. → Conducted technical/market research to recommend best tools for distributed computing. Results: Software Company's vice chairman has announced **major shift in entire company direction to J2EE/EJB technologies**. → Re-architected software for full compliance with Model-View-Controller (MVC) architecture for Web-based applications. Results: Facilitated interface customization ease of use for customers with divergent technical backgrounds. → Voluntarily assumed expanded role as key trainer and "evangelist" for ProTech products. Results: **Heightened corporate visibility and customer awareness** of software as primary spokesperson at technical tradeshows across the U.S.

BEN TROUTMAN

Experience "Ben constantly challenges the status quo by taking a new look at problems and ongoing opportunities… His creative, enthusiastic approach has had a very positive impact on the company… instrumental in convincing management to move the ProTech product to Portal… the results have been great." **– 2002 Annual Review**	ABC COMPANY – San Antonio, TX *Provider of auditing, tax, and consulting services for middle-market companies.* **Consultant,** Business Systems, 5/94 to 12/98 Performed in-depth needs assessments to ascertain project requirements. Created design documents and other written customer deliverables and wrote code (using Visual Basic, SQLBase, SQL Windows, and PowerBuilder) to implement user-driven design. Led debriefing sessions with clients at project conclusion to ensure 100% satisfaction and determine follow-on work potential. Representative Accomplishments: ➔ Integrally involved in large-scale, online-billing-systems project for major health-care provider. Results: **Saved client millions of dollars annually** in billing costs and **generated improved cash flow** through streamlined billing process. ➔ Engaged by international real estate broker to resolve remote-office connectivity issues. Results: **Assisted in architecture of before-its-time intranet-model solution** for enhanced communication flow/knowledge-sharing and marked efficiency gains. ➔ Collaborated with baked-goods distribution company to automate production and reporting. Results: **Decreased business cycle time by 25%.** CONSULTING COMPANY – San Antonio, TX *"Big 5" auditing, tax, and consulting services firm serving large, global corporations.* **Database Analyst** (*Internship*), Tax Technology Group, 5/94 to 5/95 One of two Trinity University students selected for highly competitive internship with Big 5 firm. Challenged to design/program tax-management software. Representative Accomplishments: ➔ **Retained beyond initial four-month internship contract due to superior performance;** continued with Consulting Company for additional eight months (concurrent with full-time college enrollment) as a telecommuting database analyst – a company first.
Education	TRINITY UNIVERSITY – San Antonio, TX **Master of Accountancy,** 1995 [GPA: 3.62/4.0] **Bachelor of Science in Accounting,** 1994 [GPA: 3.59/4.0] Professional Development: Java and Object Design (1999); OOAD (1999); Object-Oriented PowerBuilder Development/Performance/Tuning (1996); Sybase Database Administration (1996)
Technology Summary	**Software:** MS Office, Apache Web server, Tomcat (Web application server) IBM WebSphere, BEA WebLogic, Citrix MetaFrame, Visual SlickEd-it, Visio, MS Visual Studio, Visual SourceSafe, SQL Windows, SQLBase, Paradox **Systems:** Windows NT/2000/XP, NetWare, Windows Terminal Server **Languages:** Java, Enterprise JavaBeans, J2EE, Java Server Pages, C++, UML, LDAP, XML, Netscape Plugins, Internet Explorer (IE), ActiveX Controls **Databases:** Oracle, Sybase, Java Database Connectivity (JDBC)

Resume Strategy: *From the outset, Ben makes his career goal known with his "Objective" section. His "Profile" paragraphs place heavy emphasis on ways he has contributed to product and business development as a software engineer. Ben's "Key Knowledge Areas" section works in keywords important to his career target, and his bulleted "Representative Accomplishments" bring out achievements from his background that are most relevant to product/business development duties. Ben spells out the "Results" of his accomplishments, including the amount of revenue his software products generated in the marketplace.*

Joshua Jacobs

10293 Black Forest Ave.
Toronto, Ontario M6G2N2

Home: 416-555-5555
joshua@resumepower.com

Project Management – Sports Administration

Seeking to leverage skills in strategic planning, product/program development, online business growth, and partner relationship development within the sports event management industry.

Results-driven business development, marketing, event management, and Internet strategist with a proven track record of exceeding corporate revenue and performance-gain goals within highly competitive industries. Fuse cost-conscious approach to project management with innovative, sales-generating marketing and promotional strategies in both online and traditional forums. Able to cultivate contractual agreements and win-win relationships with key external business partners through astute presentation, negotiation, and communication techniques. Skilled in building consensus among partners, teams, and senior management. Impressive career progression with sport and film industry giants (Professional Rodeo Association, NFL, and Miramax Studios).

Areas of Expertise

☐ New Product Introduction	☐ Sports Event Promotions	☐ Business Partnerships
☐ Competitive Market Positioning	☐ Online Marketing Strategies	☐ Resource Management
☐ Exclusive Rights Negotiations	☐ Multimedia Production	☐ Media Relations
☐ B2B/B2C Marketing Tactics	☐ Campaign Leadership	☐ Sports Event Planning
☐ Corporate Image Enhancement	☐ Budget Management	☐ Staff Training & Mentoring

Professional Experience

MIRAMAX FILM CORPORATION – CANADIAN DIVISION – Toronto, Ontario (Canada)
One of five business units for the Miramax Film Corp., a leading film studio.

Associate Manager, Online Marketing Department, 2000 to Present
Co-own responsibility for business development and account management initiatives. Work jointly with Video.com and other business partners to identify Web content and determine pricing models; coordinate efforts with external partners to structure, negotiate, and implement content distribution agreements. *Performance Results:*

- **Designed a road map for the Online Marketing business-expansion strategy** that qualified potential partners and identified significant business developments. Created presentations and produced management reports based on extensive research and analysis of findings.
- **Played key role in negotiations for broadband/Internet content agreements between Miramax and prospective partners,** contributing to closing of distribution deal with Video.com, Amazon.com, and Reel.com. Produced term sheets for potential distribution partnerships and acted as key liaison in dealings.
- **Initiated systematic implementation of Web content distribution agreements** by pinpointing customer needs and developing fulfillment plans, leading to year-over-year advertising and content-syndication revenues of $400,000 per agreement.
- **Synthesized Web site elements to create multimedia sales presentations** that improved online presence and furthered business growth objectives.

PROFESSIONAL RODEO ASSOCIATION – Houston, TX
National sponsor of professional rodeo events attracting millions of viewers around the globe.

Marketing Manager, 1998 to 2000
Led the strategic planning and delivery of a comprehensive Internet marketing campaign that included Web site development and production, online promotional activities, and banner advertising programs. Challenged to heighten online presence of association and pro rodeo events through the inclusion of interactive Web site elements and innovative marketing tactics, all within strict budget limitations. *Performance Results:*

- **Oversaw efforts of 26-member Web development and project teams in redesign and revamp of association Web site.** Emphasized user-interactivity and quality design to maximize ROI for $120,000 project; Web site valued at $500,000 upon completion.

Joshua Jacobs

PROFESSIONAL RODEO ASSOCIATION – (continued)

- □ **Increased sponsorship value of pro rodeo events** through negotiation of agreement with Yahoo! for development of banner advertising program, accomplished at no cost to company and with active participation of seven Pro Rodeo Association sponsors.
- □ **Innovated online marketing strategies** that elicited competitive bids, construction of sweepstakes Web site, and free placement of banner ads on CNN, TNT, and AOL Web sites.
- □ **Developed inexpensive, cost-effective process to update corporate Web site** using CNNi resources; engineered interactive features, including photo gallery, chat rooms, bulletin boards, and video on-demand.

Event Manager, Silver Spurs Division, 1996 to 1998
Coordinated and directed all rodeo championship events within the Silver Spurs Division (TX, OK, NV). Also held responsibility for management of technology, medical, and drug-testing programs, fulfilling budgeting, hiring, and training duties. ***Performance Results:***

- □ **Set the stage for $5 million budget reduction** through creation of integrated operations plan and project-management model that became the standard for future use. Convinced functional managers to produce timelines and deliverables that improved efficiency.
- □ **Solidified reputation of Pro Rodeo Association through implementation of drug-testing program that communicated zero-tolerance policy** and produced no positive drug tests.
- □ **Delivered a $600,000 savings following implementation of technology program** applying project-management principles, cost-containment strategies, and sound hiring decisions.
- □ **Directed successful execution of 18 Silver Spurs Division events, generating positive publicity and producing under-budget events.** Facilitated exhaustive marketing and public-relations efforts to promote event visibility and generate enthusiasm.
- □ **Secured $20,000 donation from Coca-Cola** to establish project management staff certification program.

NATIONAL FOOTBALL LEAGUE – New York, NY
Premier sports organization for professional football teams.

Intern, Publicity Department, 1995 to 1996
Awarded internship among vast pool of candidates vying for position, with primary responsibility for coordinating production for NFL newsletter and 1996 Team Rosters. ***Performance Results:***

- □ **Commended for exceptional performance** in fulfilling organizational goals for production.
- □ **Developed strong, sustainable relationships** with associates and earned respect from committee.

Education

NEW YORK UNIVERSITY – New York, NY

Master's Degree in Sports Administration, 1996
Bachelor's of Commerce Degree, Major: Sports Management, 1993

Technical Skills

- □ Microsoft Project / Microsoft Office Suite
- □ Internet Applications, Research, Navigation
- □ HTML / XML / Dreamweaver / HomeSite
- □ WebSphere / IIS / Site Server

Of Note

- □ Active participant in hiking, inline skating, swimming, running, traveling, and other outdoor/sports activities.

Resume Strategy: *Joshua's goal of entering sports administration as a project manager is clearly displayed in his resume's headline. He reinforces his key qualifications for this very competitive field through a subheading that lists his transferable skills. Joshua includes an "Areas of Expertise" section to add important industry keywords and further show that he possesses the key skills related to his goal. His work history focuses on performance results, showing that he is a top performer in all of his roles. Joshua adds an "Of Note" section to demonstrate his passion for sports.*

Maria Rose Garcia

15 Wellington Drive
Albany, NY 12223

Telephone: (518) 123-4567
maria@resumepower.com

OBJECTIVE: STRATEGIC OPERATIONS POSITION IN AN ORGANIZATION FOCUSED ON MAXIMIZING REVENUE, PROFITABILITY, AND CUSTOMER LOYALTY

Expertise in Fast-Paced and Complex Technical Environments

PROFILE

Well-rounded skillset with proven experience in business operations and customer relations. Expertise in complex technical project management, training, sales, and accounting operations. Known for ability to create environments that position relationships for success, resulting in mutually beneficial and long-term associations.

Results-oriented leader accomplished at improving quality and consistency by building effective processes, teamwork, and structure. Use dynamic leadership and communication skills to establish direction and align, inspire, and develop team members. Demonstrated track record of uniting diverse groups of people to achieve collective goals.

PROFESSIONAL EXPERIENCE

COMMUNICATION SYSTEMS, INC. – Albany, NY   2000 to present
Leading provider of customer care and billing business solutions for the communications industry.

Program Manager, Telephony Customer Implementations
Assigned to manage complex telephony portion of company's first Convergence Express implementation. Project involved voice, video, and high-speed data, and a data conversion to Communication Systems' mainframe and Oracle databases. Core member of knowledge management team; selected to lead telephony knowledge capture effort.

RESULTS: Earned exceptional performance reviews for work on the project and recognized as a primary force for successful project completion. Managed project according to the Project Management Body of Knowledge (PMBOK) process groups:

- *Initiating/Planning* – Enhanced success through rigorous investigation and project planning. Identified and accommodated for previously unknown and crucial tasks, dependencies, and gaps.

- *Executing* – Created a sense of "team" new to Communication Systems. Inspired people to go beyond where they would ordinarily stop. Repaired strained relationship with customer, and maintained positive relationship throughout project. Loaded 99+% of subscriber accounts into the system. Converted over 18,000 service codes to company mainframe with unaccounted variance of less than ten. Converted over $800,000 in customer receivables with unaccounted variance of less than $5.00.

- *Controlling* – Recognized risks and took action to mitigate negative outcomes. Led effort to provide customer with sufficient and clear information about the team's work, resulting in a smoother "go live" because critical issues were addressed before the customer began using the system.

- *Closing* – Generated closure on project phases. Led team to create additional configuration and specification sign-off documents and achieved formal customer endorsement.

ABC TECHNOLOGIES, INC. – Albany, NY   1999 to 2000

Vice President, Consulting Services and Operations
CRM solution provider offering consulting, training, and software. Created, implemented, and managed project management, needs analysis, and client training processes and offerings.

RESULTS: Expanded market by enabling company to successfully compete for and deliver projects of increased complexity. Ensured accounting processes were structured to support business operations. Project management and needs-analysis tools significantly contributed to company's ability to perform work on a fixed-cost basis. Training workshops merited authorized training center status. All three initiatives earned high levels of client satisfaction and resulted in significant additional sales.

Maria Rose Garcia, Resume – Page Two

PROFESSIONAL EXPERIENCE

ABC TECHNOLOGIES, INC. (continued):

- Guided clients' senior managers in defining objectives, scope, deliverables, and deadlines. Needs-analysis and project-management template tools resulted in rapid project ramp-up and progress, yet met the unique needs of each client.
- Employed project-management techniques and tools to organize, present, and manage projects that effectively utilized internal and client personnel. Led internal and client teams to meet objectives.
- Implemented internal time-billing software system that streamlined the billing process, increasing efficiency, improving accuracy, and enhancing cash flow.
- Developed corporate mission and values resulting in a strong foundation for business direction and relationships.

NYNEX – Brooklyn, NY   1988 to 1993

Strategic Account Executive, Voice/Data Account Executive, Data Communication Account Executive
Hired to participate in new company effort expanding offerings to include data communications. Expanded responsibilities to include voice-communications products and services. Chosen for new strategic account executive position involving teaming with systems integration organization.

RESULTS:

- Salvaged relationship with dissatisfied client, resulting in a $670,000 sale.
- Closed $500,000 sale by leading company effort to build relationship with prospective new client.
- Achieved significant new sales by mentoring new sales representative in experimental teaming program. Developed strategy and led team effort to execute strategy.
- Appointed team leader and trainer for an interdepartmental quality improvement team.
- Awarded membership in President's Leadership Council for outstanding sales performance.

TECHNOLOGY COMPANY – New York, NY   1985 to 1988

Installed Base Sales Representative, Major Account Sales Representative
Sold HP3000 and PC-based software and hardware solutions to Fortune 500 client. Worked with multiple customer-management levels, including top EDS management at client locations. Earned position dedicated to expanding business relationships with existing HP clients.

RESULTS:

- Closed $500,000 sale by leading a diverse internal and external team in solving challenging client problem.
- Received Outstanding Performer Award for sales performance and award for best competitive presentation.
- Made significant progress in executive relations at multiple client locations.

EDUCATION

PACE UNIVERSITY – New York, NY
Master of Science in Industrial Administration, 1985
Bachelor of Science in Management, 1985

- Completed two degrees within four years; completed IBM internship, 1984

ADDITIONAL GRADUATE EDUCATION:

- Human Learning and Change, Industrial/Organizational Psychology, Qualitative Methods

Resume Strategy: *Maria's objective clearly states her goal to transition to an operations position, while showing the value she would bring to a company if hired. Her work experience section capitalizes on her managerial experience. The "Results" section for each position demonstrates Maria's ability to achieve positive outcomes and benefit her employer's operations.*

Claire Brady

15-38 47th Street
Astoria, NY 11105

E-mail: claire@resumepower.com

Home: 718-123-4567
Cellular: 917-123-7654

Operations Manager ■ Recruitment Director ■ Call Center / Customer Service Manager

Versatile manager with 12+ years of operational leadership experience and career highlights including:

- **Direction of 200 staff and nationwide operations** for thriving cosmetic surgery practice in 11 U.S. cities;
- **Supervision of 70-team member call center operations;**
- **Startup of new accounting/finance division** for expanding employment agency;
- **Delivery of repeated six-figure cost reductions** enhancing bottom-line performance; and
- **Launch of employee development, upward communication, safety, and incentive programs** that reversed high turnover, reduced injuries, enhanced efficiency, boosted morale, and improved customer satisfaction.

Offer demonstrated cross-functional expertise in areas including recruitment/retention, strategic planning, budgeting, marcom management, P&L management, team building and training, contract negotiations, benefits administration, resource allocation, and OSHA/JCAHO/Title 22 compliance.

Professional Experience

EMPLOYMENT SUCCESS CORPORATION — New York, NY *(Full-service employment agency)*

Division Manager, 2/01 – 11/01

Recruited to build and oversee company's new accounting and finance division. Hired, trained, and supervised staff; strategized and implemented multi-industry corporate marketing program and developed all supporting collateral; built quality pipeline; recruited, coached, and placed accounting and finance professionals from entry- to executive-level; and led salary negotiations with clients and candidates. **Key Accomplishments:**

- **Developed and launched comprehensive recruiter training program** that resulted in expedited deal closures despite "rookie" status of recruiter trainees.
- Designed and implemented direct-mail marketing campaign that **produced steady stream of new business**.
- Built accounting/finance division from the ground up and **generated $40K+ within first few months**.
- **Led well-received, cross-divisional management retreat** that dramatically increased morale and contributed to realization of corporatewide turnaround management initiatives.
- **Orchestrated team-building initiatives** to improve collaboration across multiple locations.

ABC EXECUTIVE SEARCH — Woodside, NY *(Employment agency for temp, temp-to-hire, and permanent placement)*

Executive Recruiter, 7/00 – 1/01

Interviewed, screened, and coached accounting and finance professionals; verified candidate credentials; and matched corporate client needs with applicant pool to close deals and effectively place qualified individuals. Cold-called prospects to win new business and negotiated all aspects of client/candidate contracts. **Key Accomplishments:**

- **Surpassed benchmarks for new recruiters;** achieved $73K in billings in first five months (250% above target).
- **Captured four new corporate clients** as a direct result of personally authored/designed direct-mail campaign.

ACTION MEDICAL INSTITUTE — Jackson Heights, NY *(Nationwide cosmetic surgery center)*

Director of Operations, 10/98 – 7/00; Administrator, 1/96 – 10/98

Rapidly promoted to senior management position directing daily, 200-staff member operations across 27 offices and 11 surgical centers throughout the United States. Managed $6 million annual budget; oversaw HR department, materials management division, and benefits administration; recruited/hired entire New York office (including surgeon); and served as nationwide OSHA coordinator. **Key Accomplishments:**

- **Reduced employee turnover 30%** through leadership of well-received incentive/reward programs, staff/physician open forums, monthly internal communication efforts, and scheduling improvements to maximize efficiency, cost containment, and employee satisfaction.
- **Improved operational safety record** (averting potential for government-mandated shutdown), enhanced workplace ergonomics, minimized staff health risks, and delivered a fault-free OSHA audit (zero citations/penalties) following development and nationwide implementation of safety-training manual and in-service programs, stringent monitoring of procedures/standards, and operation's first mock OSHA survey.

Claire Brady Page Two

ACTION MEDICAL INSTITUTE — (continued)

- **Reduced accounting errors** by developing automated, fully integrated system that flagged batch discrepancies and **improved office manager accountability** through quarterly evaluations of performance/error ratios, and unannounced office visits nationwide.
- **Instituted multitiered cost-saving programs including:** negotiation of $55K reduction in worker's compensation group insurance premium, $283K annual savings in medication costs, six-figure decrease in marketing spend, and $175K in annual payroll expenses.
- Instilled a shared commitment to quality patient care and optimal service, reflected **in steady increase in positive patient satisfaction survey results**.
- Implemented rigorous medication-tracking system for company's 11 surgical offices to comply with federally mandated drug dispensing restrictions, **resulting in zero penalties and reversing prior history of losses**.
- **Expanded operations** through profitable launch of laser hair removal program on both coasts.
- **Right-sized call center operations** by engineering improved systems and upgrading equipment to eliminate patient scheduling errors and increase efficiency of 70-member department.

ASTORIA MEMORIAL MEDICAL CENTER — Astoria, NY (*One of the largest hospitals on the East Coast*)
Nursing Management Assistant, 2/88 – 12/95; **Employment Coordinator**, Human Resources, 7/87 – 2/88

Oversaw administrative and ancillary staff for five nursing units, developed operating budget for eight cost centers, oversaw systems automation, and served as JCAHO/Title 22 coordinator. Functioned as staffing coordinator, responsible for multiple unit/shift scheduling of nursing/clerical staff, including the crucial recruitment of last-minute replacements. **Key Accomplishments:**

- **Trained nursing and ancillary staff on new computer system** and conducted monthly training updates.
- Designed mock JCAHO and Title 22 survey, **key to hospital's successful evaluation**.
- Conducted new-hire orientation for all staff, from entry-level to executive. **Commended by department managers** for thorough, dynamic, and personable orientation programs.
- **Equipped "desperate" hiring managers with qualified nursing candidates** during critical staff shortages.

Education & Training

AS Degree Program in Liberal Arts
New York University — New York, NY (1993 to 1995)
Queens College — Flushing, NY (1982 to 1983)

Professional Development:
Managing in the 21st Century — New York University, 2002; OSHA Preparation, 1997, 1998, 1999; Hospice Volunteer Training — Astoria Memorial Medical Center, 1987

Computer Skills: Windows, Excel, Word, Lotus, QuickBooks

Affiliations

- NAFE — Member, 1998
- SHRM — Member, 1998 to 2000

Resume Strategy: *Claire's resume title makes her career goals clear and her shaded profile section gives a summary of her background leading diverse organizations to produce excellent results. In her "Professional Experience" section, she includes a brief description of her everyday responsibilities and follows this with a bulleted list of her standout accomplishments so that hiring executives can see not only what she has done, but also how well she has performed. Claire bolds key information in these bulleted accomplishments to help her most notable achievements "jump" off the page.*

Thomas Avilla

123 Diamond Head Dr.
Chattanooga, TN 37421   tomav@resumepower.com   Home: (555) 555-5555
     Cell: (555) 555-5115

PLANT MANAGER ▪ PRODUCTION MANAGER ▪ QUALITY MANAGER

Specializing in Multimillion-Dollar Plant Operations ... Paper/Textile Industries

Accomplished plant manager with engineering, management, and production background, highly skilled at restructuring manufacturing facilities to improve the bottom line without sacrificing quality. Considerable expertise in planning and implementing process controls and procedures. Recognize the value of employees and the impact of morale on productivity levels. Continually seek to provide a safe and user-friendly work environment through the adoption of modern technologies. Recipient of several awards for contributions in operations start-up, training and development, cost savings, and commitment to corporate goals.

Skills Offered

- Start-Up Operations
- Project Management
- Budget Administration
- Product Quality Control

- Facilities Planning
- Materials Management
- Purchasing and Vendor Relations
- Equipment Renovation

- Staffing, Training, and Development
- Safety Programs (MSDS, Lockout/Tagout)

Career Highlights

DIXIE GROUP, INC. ▪ Chattanooga, TN
One of America's fastest growing floor-covering companies with 370 employees in two locations.

Vice President, Engineering Department, April 1997 to Present

Manage three engineers, an AutoCAD designer, and ten machinists at a 156,000-square-foot facility that produces $100 million annually for three product groups. Consult with marketing and R&D departments regarding product design and production processes. Design plant layout, monitor production flow, and manage resource allocation with an eye towards quality and bottom-line profitability. Report directly to company president/COO. **Key Contributions:**

- Incurred savings of $2.5 million by designing and building attachment to existing machine, eliminating need for external fabricators. Oversaw concept, feasibility, design, and fabrication stages.

- Increased productivity for the manufacture of self-adhesive rug pads by 25%. Replaced antiquated equipment with cutting-edge machinery, increasing capacity from $15 million to $21 million.

- Added outdoor-carpet production line that increased capacity 100% and generated an additional $12 million in revenue.

- Reduced materials cost and consumption by 20% by decreasing the amount of polymers within product without sacrificing efficacy or quality.

- Standardized equipment and process capability across all locations.

Production Manager, October 1987 to March 1997

Managed production plant with two managers, eight supervisors, four technicians, and 250 production workers operating 24x7. Maintained oversight for budgeting, plant layout, production flow, staffing, training, quality control, and equipment maintenance/replacement. **Key Contributions:**

- Revamped operations at Chattanooga location, improving efficiency from 45% to 75% and reducing waste from 15% to 8.5% within first year.

- Engineered and implemented equipment modifications to enhance process controls, improve product performance, and develop new product features.

Thomas Avilla

Production Manager (continued):

- Developed training program that reduced new-hire training time in half (from eight to four months) by making equipment user-friendly and standardizing operating procedures. Training program was adopted at several facilities domestically and overseas.

- Increased production output by 400% over 12-year period. Expanded from two to ten production lines, and from one product group with three sizes to three product groups with 16 sizes.

- Increased production capacity 30% by introducing 12-hour shift system. Shift conversion accommodated sudden influx of business without requiring acquisition of new equipment (estimated savings: $2.8 million).

- Received award for "Dedication, Loyalty, and Outstanding Performance" for meeting challenge of company growth. Award presented to four recipients out of 400 employees.

Project Manager, November 1986 to September 1987

Selected to manage the construction of a 156,000-square-foot building for corporate office, manufacturing plant, and distribution warehouse. Worked with interior designers, contractors, and architects to monitor progress, evaluate specs, and ensure compliance with building codes. **Key Contributions:**

- Completed project within original time constraints and relocated entire plant within four months, without downtime to shipping and production schedule.

MANZANO CORPORATION ■ Mexico City, Mexico
Wholly owned division of Jonathon Clarke Limited and a licensee of the Procter & Gamble Company.

Plant Manager, August 1981 to October 1986

Oversaw factory start-up and managed 24/7 operations for production of personal-care products in Mexico. Facility was comprised of two production lines and 50 employees working three shifts. Designed plant layout, assessed labor needs, developed job descriptions, and hired new employees. **Key Contributions:**

- Built conversion plant from a vacant warehouse to a fully productive operation within seven months. Project involved equipment procurement, materials acquisition, and employee recruitment.

- Reduced material costs by identifying and qualifying vendors for raw and packaging materials.

Education

UNIVERSIDAD DE MEXICO ■ Mexico City, Mexico
Diploma in Management (*US equivalent* - MBA) ■ **Higher Diploma in Textile Technology** (*US equivalent* - BS)

Computers / Languages

Computer Skills: Word, Excel, Project, Lotus 1-2-3, AutoCAD, Windows 2000
Foreign Languages: Spanish, written and verbal fluency

Resume Strategy: *Because Thomas held the position of plant manager earlier in his career, he is able to begin his resume profile by calling attention to this fact ("Accomplished plant manager..."), a good strategy since this is the position he wants to return to. He spotlights his steady promotional advancement with Dixie Group, Inc., by listing each of his positions held with this company separately, with bulleted "Key Contributions" used to call attention to ways he benefited his employer.*

8

Executives

Suzanne Thick

15 Wateredge Drive
Hollywood, CA 90038

suzanne@resumepower.com

Home: 818-123-4567
Cellular: 818-987-6543

Executive Producer ■ Senior Project Manager

Transitioning from TV commercial production to multimedia/network/entertainment

- **Accomplished executive producer** with 21 years of successful television commercial production experience. Seeking to join a network, studio, multimedia company, or advertising agency to leverage proven skills in strategic planning, creative talent marketing, international business development, and general/financial management.

- **Demonstrated success securing multimillion-dollar, long-term contracts** and producing over 1,500 television commercials for industry giants including Apple Computer, Burger King, Kraft, GM, Sears, and Federated Stores. Superior negotiating and interpersonal skills – able to lead top-performing production teams and liaise between creative talent and corporate/ad agency executives. Flexible and versatile – thrive under tight deadlines and excel in responding to the unexpected.

Qualifications

- Content Development
- Strategic Planning
- Television Production
- High-Profile Project Management
- Brand Development

- Client Relationship Management
- Multimillion-Dollar Budgeting
- Creative Talent Marketing
- Vendor/Contract Negotiations
- Executive Leadership/Supervision
- International Business Development

- Contingency Planning
- Industry Associations: Directors Guild of America (First Assistant Director) and Association of Independent Commercial Producers

Professional Experience

HOLLYWOOD PRODUCTIONS, LLC – Hollywood, CA
Television commercial production company retained by major advertising agencies and brands around the globe for production expertise and film directors' services. Employs five with annual revenue of $2 million.

President/Executive Producer, January 1999 to Present
Manage daily operations – sales, marketing, business development, finance, and strategic planning. Develop partnerships with film directors and ad agencies to generate sales, serve client advertising needs, and capture loyal customers. Supervise all film production and staff and oversee major purchases for TV commercial shoots. Financial responsibility for projects ranging from $100K to $1 million per commercial. *Key Accomplishments:*

- **Built impressive Fortune 500 client list.** Produced commercials for major advertisers, including Apple Computer, Burger King, Kraft, GM, Sears, and Federated Stores. Submitted winning bids to major advertising agencies, including Young & Rubicam, Inc., TBWA CHIAT/Day, Inc., and Deutsch, Inc., and was repeatedly selected from approximately 100 competitors to produce spots. Matched advertisers' needs for specific photography/special effects/product expertise with directors specializing in these fields.

- **Developed proposals for ad agencies,** incorporating in-depth budgeting; location specs; project schedules; and creative, cost-effective recommendations to transform storyboards into feasible realities.

- **Innovated solutions to challenging projects, resulting in strategic contract "wins."** Used vast network of contacts to secure lucrative TV commercial contracts with ad agencies. Enabled agencies to deliver quality campaigns to clients on time and on budget. *Example:*
  - Transformed ABC ad concept despite significant budget limitations set by the manufacturer of the product. Saved an estimated $100K changing location of commercial shoot, meeting client's budget requirements and delivering on ad agency's creative story concept.

- **Successfully introduced European film director to U.S. television commercial market.** Obtained visa for director through skillful negotiations and red-tape maneuvering with multiple entities including INS officials, union representatives, and legal counsel.

COMPANY PRESIDENT TO MULTIMEDIA/NETWORK EXECUTIVE PRODUCER/SENIOR PROJECT MANAGER

Suzanne Thick   Resume, Page Two

HOLLYWOOD PRODUCTIONS, (continued):

- **Produced the most successful television campaign in the history of ABC Foods, Inc.** Convinced corporate vice presidents to accept director's selection of minority talent for ad campaign. Commercial resulted in widening company's market share and setting record-breaking advertising test scores.
- **Forged successful relationship with Japanese advertising agency and client** to produce highly praised commercial. Tactfully overcame language barriers during shoot when Japanese-speaking director discovered musician hired for the commercial spoke only English and French. Sensitive handling of situation resulted in repeat business from ad agency and advertiser.

ACE COMMERCIALS – Hollywood, CA
TV commercial production company serving major advertising agencies with $6 million annual revenue.
Vice President/CFO, May 1988 to November 1998
Oversaw daily operations and managed 10,000-square-foot studio. Spearheaded new business development and client/agency relationship management. Recruited directors and negotiated TV commercial contracts. Oversaw 50 commercial shoots per year, with average project budgets of $250K. *Key Accomplishments:*

- **Tripled gross revenues, generating $5.9 million in new contracts.** Tirelessly recruited new talent and marketed production company/TV director arsenal to advertising agency executives worldwide. Produced over 500 commercials during tenure for industry-leading clients.
- **Maintained net profit levels above 30% for ten years** in an industry where 20% is considered excellent.
- **Proved resourcefulness by procuring hard-to-find resources and enlisting the aid of locals** in remote locations ranging from the middle of the desert to the outer Arctic region.
- **Decreased studio operating expenses 50% by initiating successful office and production facility relocation.** Reduction in overhead allowed company to purchase state-of-the-art production studio and filming equipment. Combated "stigma" of less prestigious location by launching creative PR campaign to leading Hollywood advertising agencies.
- **Secured funding** to finance 25% of company's relocation and studio construction.
- **Selected top-notch team of designers to build special-effects camera.** Researched patent for camera, and used new competitive edge to sign additional directors and agency clients.
- **Built exclusive relationship with DEF International.** Helped client achieve competitive market position for a fraction of the advertising dollars spent by top two competitors, leading to a seven-year relationship and contracts to produce over 800 commercials.

Early Career

ATCO PRODUCTIONS, INC. – Hollywood, CA – **Executive Producer,** 1984 to 1988

THICK & COMPANY – Hollywood, CA – **President,** 1980 to 1984

THICK, BRODERMAN & MARSH – Hollywood, CA – **Producer,** 1973 to 1980 (Earned Silver Industry Award, 1975)

Education & Technical Expertise

HOLLYWOOD COLLEGE – Hollywood, CA – **BS Degree Program:** Completed two years of premed coursework.

Technical Skills: Word, Excel, MediaBid, Windows, 35mm Cameras, Lighting Design, Grip Packages.

Resume Strategy: Suzanne's resume title and tagline communicate her career goal clearly, and her profile shows her extensive production experience and successful record generating seven-figure revenue. Her "Qualifications" section touts her key strengths and credentials and her "Key Accomplishments" are filled with details of her achievements. Suzanne has ample accomplishments relevant to her career goal from her recent positions, so she is able to group her older jobs into a brief "Early Career" section to save space.

BRADLEY JAMES JEFFERSON

7564 Orchard Grove Circle
Cincinnati, OH 47908

E-mail: bjj@resumepower.com
Available for Relocation

Home: 555-555-5555
Office: 555-555-5552

CEO ■ EXECUTIVE DIRECTOR ■ PROGRAM MANAGER

Visionary, dynamic executive, adept in leading corporate, legal, and military operations in startup, turnaround, high-growth, and crisis environments. Achievements include directing manufacturing, mining, and high-tech companies; providing decorated leadership of the military's largest operational theater in the world (U.S., Asia, and the Middle East); and guiding major domestic and international corporations in multimillion-dollar real estate development, M&A, structured settlements, security transactions, limited partnership restructures, and workout strategies.

Proven success right-sizing troubled or underperforming organizations; able to correct profit-draining practices and procedures to attain precedent-setting revenue gains, secure financing well into the seven figures, and implement lucrative global expansion within 12 months of turnaround initiatives. Expert negotiator; lead teams in complex dealings, salvage broken down discussions, and mend adversarial relationships. Reputation for respected leadership and a nonretribution approach to problem solving. Solid credentials – JD; bar admission to the U.S. Supreme Court and multiple states; and licensed real estate broker.

EXECUTIVE SKILLS

- Executive Leadership & Supervision
- Strategic Planning & Profit Enhancement
- Corporate Vision & Mission
- Startup, Turnaround, Crisis & Change Management
- Real Estate Development
- Financing, VC Funding & Workout Strategies

- Mergers & Acquisitions (M&A)
- Security Transactions
- Contract Negotiations & Deal Structuring
- Legal Issues
- Due Diligence/Business & Financial Analysis
- Computers (Windows/MS Office/WordPerfect)

CAREER PROGRESSION

GLADNEY & WHALER – Cincinnati, OH – *Law firm specializing in commercial litigation, risk assessment, and business advice*

Senior Partner, 1995 – Present; **Managing Partner** (Litigation), 1992 – 1994
Wholly responsible for representing client interests as senior litigator in commercial, regulatory, and governmental law environments. Advise corporate/government clients in matters involving security transactions, major real estate acquisitions, corporate and employment issues, financing and workout strategies, leasing, licensing, and contract negotiations. Provide due diligence assessments, proactive risk management, and structured settlements with favorable terms.
Key Accomplishments:

- **Obtained favorable settlement and undisputed title** to crucial service marks for client following successful litigation.
- Negotiated and structured complex security agreement and guaranty with national pension fund legal contingent that **secured $12 million in financing** to propel development of hundreds of real estate units. Adeptly maneuvered throughout legal process to obtain hard-won concessions and limit client liability/exposure.
- Proved the ability to repair fractious relationships, architect creative solutions, navigate bureaucratic red tape, and unite disparate groups to secure win-win outcomes benefiting all parties concerned. Collaborated with citizens, council members, and government officials to **promote and win approval of numerous multimillion-dollar development projects/zoning changes** that were often initially met with resistance, skepticism, or roadblocks.
- **Performed in-depth market/risk/financial analysis** through due diligence for client merger/acquisition targets.
- **Achieved a 100% track record of favorable verdict outcomes** in 75+ litigated/arbitrated cases; never tried a losing case.
- Strategized and executed targeted marketing initiatives directly responsible for jump-starting revenues, resulting in millions of dollars in fees and an average **20% to 25% aggregate growth rate** during firm's first three years.

U.S. ARMY – Washington, D.C.

Director, Readiness Division (Rank: Lt. Colonel), 1991 – 1992
Mobilized for active duty during Gulf War, with high-profile assignment to ensure sustained operations during conflict and follow-on efforts. Traveled worldwide to identify and investigate systemic issues impacting USMC's wartime response capabilities. Interacted extensively with generals and senior officers (Army, Air Force, Navy) and directed staff in Washington, D.C. and in liaison offices at Army installations in the U.S., Asia, and Middle East.

BRADLEY JAMES JEFFERSON Resume, Page Two

U.S. ARMY – (continued) – *Key Accomplishments:*

- **Slashed division's travel expenditures by 50%** while simultaneously establishing a cohesive, homogeneous method of knowledge-sharing crucial information and policy interpretations.
- Drafted acted-upon recommendations to the commandant of the USMC, resulting in **global policy changes** related to the deployment and reconstitution of the Maritime Prepositioned Forces during combat.
- **Established mission-critical standards** for maintaining accountability that **enhanced levels of readiness and improved resource allocation** in volatile, conflict-prone areas of the world.

SOLUTECH, INC. – Bakersfield, OH – *Small manufacturer of high-speed communications computers*
CEO, 1992 – 1994
Led startup and expansion of profitable high-tech manufacturing operation, with accountability for daily operational oversight, P&L, strategic and financial planning, staff supervision (e.g., developers, technicians, sales reps), budget forecasting, product development/launch, sales/marketing, and quality assurance. *Key Accomplishments:*

- **Identified and seized early market opportunity** as one of the first manufacturers of high-speed computer modems capable of increasing bandwidth through a then state-of-the-art technology.
- **Rapidly built business from zero to seven-figure revenue mark within first 12 months.**
- **Delivered multimillion-dollar contract win** with division of the U.S. Marine Corps.

QUAMCO, INC. – Cooper, AZ – *Diversified metal manufacturer and assembler with 100 employees and international clientele*
CEO, 1983 – 1986
Recruited to turn around company's lagging performance, with challenges including a marked decline in the U.S. mining industry. Oversaw daily operations; developed financial plans, budgets, and project deliverable timelines; handled all government/commercial contracts; and led senior management team in identifying/bidding on project RFPs.
Key Accomplishments:

- **Right-sized production levels for a 40% improvement,** introduced efficiency enhancements that **slashed wasteful material handling 300%,** and **restructured subassembly line** for dramatic reduction in cycle time.
- Found buyers and structured the profitable sale of underperforming divisions for a **38% bottom-line improvement** within one year. Negotiated all financing packages with lenders and suppliers.
- **Positioned corporation for profitable growth, international expansion, and ultimate lucrative sell-off.** Won multimillion-dollar contracts, negotiated international letters-of-credit and export documents that paved the way for overseas sales in Europe and Asia, and structured sale of corporation to Brazilian-based operation.

U.S. ARMY/ U.S. ARMY RESERVE – Washington, D.C. – **Colonel,** 1973 – 2000
Demonstrated superior performance through repeated commendations and promotional advancements, culminating in rank of Colonel. Provided command/control to operations and exercises worldwide.

EDUCATION

ARIZONA STATE UNIVERSITY – Tempe, AZ – **Doctorate of Jurisprudence (JD),** 1980
KENT STATE UNIVERSITY – Kent, OH – **BA in Political Science / Minor in Economics,** 1973

CREDENTIALS & LICENSURE

- **Bar Admissions** – U.S. Supreme Court Bar – Washington, D.C. (1985); Ohio Supreme Court Bar – Cincinnati, OH (1981); District of Columbia Bar – Washington, D.C. (1993); U.S. Court of Federal Claims – Washington, D.C. (1984)
- **Top Secret Security Clearance** (Current)   ■ **Broker** – Ohio Department of Real Estate (1978)

Resume Strategy: *Bradley's impressive legal, corporate, and military career are summarized effectively in his resume's opening profile, showcasing his proven abilities in senior-level leadership positions. His "Executive Skills" section further summarizes his expertise, and he has selected accomplishments from his legal career that specifically relate to corporate and organizational achievements. Bradley's conservative, professional resume design further enhances his presentation for executive-level positions.*

JOHN J. JANOFF

9 Horsemans Lane ☐ Morristown, NJ 07960 ☐ 973-644-4444 ☐ john@resumepower.com

EXECUTIVE VICE PRESIDENT / COO / CMO

EXECUTIVE PROFILE

World-class executive accomplished at growing volume and profit by re-vitalizing businesses through brand/company repositioning and market-focused strategies. Recognized as a change-maker who drives companies toward a consumer and retail focus while improving business efficiencies that increase company value. Employ comprehensive new product development processes that integrate product/creative development, financial planning, and marketing and sales strategies to enhance success ratios. Backed by MBA.

AREAS OF EXPERTISE

- Volume and Profit Growth
- Pricing Strategy
- Strategic / Tactical Planning
- Fiscal Planning and Management
- Production Planning
- Integrated Marketing and Sales Programs
- Retail Operations Management
- Retail Site Development
- Catalog / Webstore Management
- Event Marketing

- New Brand / Product Development and Positioning
- Consumer Research
- Creative Development
- Media Planning
- Tradeshow Exhibit Development and Management
- Retail Merchandising
- Inventory Management
- Sales Planning and Volume Management

CAREER HIGHLIGHTS

ROBERT ASSOCIATES, LTD. — Fairfield, NJ
(*Midsize division of $8.5 billion international marketer/manufacturer of tobacco products.*)
VICE PRESIDENT, MARKETING, 1996 to 2001
Member of senior management team tasked with revitalizing organization and brands while rebuilding RBA into modern consumer/retail focused Consumer Goods Company. Directed strategic marketing vision and held tactical oversight of consumer and trade marketing activity within the United States.

Formulated and administered $2-million marketing budget utilized for event marketing, sponsorships, advertising, and creative and package development. Selected and managed outside agencies to support marketing and sales goals. Traveled to Europe to strengthen global brand positioning and develop quality products for U.S. market.

Key Accomplishments:

- Through collaborative team effort doubled volume and profits over four years in a flat category.
- Initiated pricing and selling strategies that led to an increase in net pricing by 75%, balanced trade flow between sales regions, increased investment in retail-distribution programs, and played instrumental role in key performance ratios.
- Revitalized two national brands repositioned as relevant lifestyle products through focused "big brand" print/radio/event/Internet marketing programs.
- Improved manufacturing efficiencies by 15% by leading effort to refurbish and modernize factory equipment and manufacturing facility.
- Eliminated poor-performing products and launched four new products that generated 100% incremental volume and profit.

JOHN J. JANOFF

CAREER HIGHLIGHTS

ROBERT ASSOCIATES, LTD. (*continued*)
□ Developed and managed high-impact customer interactive national tradeshow exhibits that generated quality retail chain buyer leads resulting in increased retail distribution vital for growing volume in a flat category.
□ Created multiyear new business development plans that involved volume forecasting, pricing, trade promotion, consumer marketing, new product development, and sales force expansion for new territories.

MATCH NORTH AMERICA — Richmond, VA
(*Marketer and manufacturer of consumer products, generating $200 million annually.*)
MARKETING MANAGER, 1992 to 1996
Led strategic and tactical marketing for three national and five regional brands. Managed $10 million marketing budget and reported to director of marketing. Directed consumer research and packaging, and developed volume and share forecasting to formulate new marketing strategies.

Key Accomplishments:

□ Instituted brand portfolio methodology on national and regional level that provided a structured and logical tool for allocating marketing resources.
□ Reviewed and redesigned packaging for all eight brands to create greater visual impact and perceived value.
□ Maintained category-leading share position by responding to unmet consumer demand and introducing new product concept that utilized innovated flavoring technology.
□ Launched consumer-driven special-event series that utilized database names and added value to category consumers as well as the trade.

TOBACCO, INC. — New York, NY
(*Market leading tobacco products company with $10 billion in domestic annual revenue.*)
BRAND ASSISTANT, NEW PRODUCTS, 1990 to 1992
Accountable for identifying new products, brand positioning, packaging graphics, consumer research, and media planning. Compiled financial projections, assessed future commitments, and managed $7.5 million budget.

Key Accomplishments:

□ Formalized new product development process along a business-building model, which focused on multiyear new product volume, share, and financial projections.
□ Strengthened position of new product by creating it as freestanding brand then applied to existing brand family. Project completed ahead of schedule while simultaneously undergoing parallel development with R&D, sales, and outside advertising agency.

EDUCATION

SOUTHERN METHODIST UNIVERSITY — Dallas, TX
MBA, 1985 (*accelerated 12-month program*)

INDIANA UNIVERSITY — Bloomington, IN
BS, PUBLIC POLICY, 1984

9 Horsemans Lane □ Morristown, NJ 07960 □ 973-644-4444 □ john@resumepower.com

Resume Strategy: *John uses an extensive "Areas of Expertise" section, powerful profile summary, and accomplishments-driven "Career Highlights" section to articulate how his executive skills are applicable to industries outside of tobacco manufacturing. Resume submitted by Judy Friedler.*

9

Sales/New Business Development

KEITH WAYNE

245 State Street
Philadelphia, PA 19143
Home Phone: 215-123-4567
Office Phone: 215-987-6543
E-mail: keith@resumepower.com

PROFILE SUMMARY:

AREAS OF EXPERTISE:

EXPERIENCE:

"Keith works as a substitute for me at the Health Fitness Center... reliable, prompt, and enthusiastic. [His] skills and knowledge combine to make him a valuable asset to my corporate-based wellness program. I very much appreciate his attitude and resourcefulness toward the members in my facility. Keith is comfortable in his role, exhibiting motivational techniques, good communication skills, and sensitivity toward each participant's individuality. I highly recommend Keith Wayne..."

– AT&T Corporate Wellness Program Director

Sales & Operations Management Professional

... Specializing in the health, fitness, and sports industries

Accomplished sales, management, and marketing professional with over seven years of success leading profitable operations. Exceptional same-day "closer" and repeat/referral business winner, with a proven track record of precedent-setting performance doubling average sales revenues. Persuasive communicator with fluency in Spanish. Passion for and in-depth knowledge of the health/fitness/sports industries. Reputation for creative problem solving, dedication, drive, and a customer-focused mind-set. Active community volunteer and fundraiser for the American Cancer Society and the Leukemia Society of America.

- □ B2C/B2B Solution-Centered Sales
- □ P&L Enhancement
- □ Public Speaking/Presentations
- □ Strategic Marketing/Media Buying
- □ Health/Fitness Expert
- □ Customer & Vendor Relations
- □ Strategic Marketing
- □ Startup Operations
- □ Leadership & Supervision
- □ Team Building & Training
- □ Budget Development & Administration

ADVANCED FITNESS CENTER – Philadelphia, PA
Owner/Manager, 1996 to Present
Wholly responsible for initial startup and daily operations of 20,000-sq.-ft. fitness center, including marketing, sales, development, and supervision of 14-member team, facility maintenance, fiscal management, accounts payable/receivable, policy/procedure development, customer relationship management, and fitness training. *Key Accomplishments:*

- □ **Directed all aspects of successful business franchise launch.**
  - □ Authored comprehensive business plan, incorporating cost projections, revenue forecasts, business environment indicators, competitive analysis, market research, and scenario comparisons.
  - □ Secured $35K in startup capital from private investor – closed the deal in less than 24 hours after initial presentation.
  - □ Developed and implemented presell strategy that set new standards for franchise – sold more than 300 "sight-unseen" memberships in three months (compared to the industry average of 50 memberships per month prior to opening). Generated over $10K before building construction was completed.

- □ **Developed, implemented, and continually refined strategic marketing plan and sales-training program** that has provided continued growth for the past four years despite aggressive competition.
  - □ Broke franchise sales records even during historically slow months – increased memberships 40% in November/December 2000, almost unheard of during the pre-New Year's holiday season when gym memberships typically decline.
  - □ Drafted marketing collateral and print/radio ads and managed all media buying.

KEITH WAYNE

EXPERIENCE:

ADVANCED FITNESS CENTER (*continued*)

☐ Launched successful, cost-effective marketing strategies for add-on profit centers, including tanning salon, pro-shop, café, and personal-training services. Secured funding from product suppliers that completely underwrote costs for direct-mail campaigns.

☐ **Built a winning sales team** whose individual monthly sales average is 50 memberships (higher than franchise average). Model and coach best practices as the top producer regionwide, averaging 75 memberships per month.

☐ **Created a positive, supportive work environment** with some of the lowest turnover rates franchisewide – a significant achievement with a minimum-wage staff.

A1 HEALTH AND FITNESS CONSULTING – Philadelphia, PA
Owner/Marketing & Sales Director, 1996 to 1999
Launched and directed successful 2,000-sq.-ft. lifestyle management/personal-training center and managed 16 trainers statewide. Networked with fitness centers and healthcare providers to grow operation and secure lucrative referral business. *Key Accomplishments:*

☐ **Built fiercely loyal client base of 100+ from the ground up,** including major- and minor-league ball players.

☐ **Won profitable and exclusive service provider status** with local gym to offer operation's first-ever customer orientation and professional personal-training services. Increased fitness center's sales by 30% the year service plan was implemented.

☐ **Developed relationships throughout the Philadelphia medical community** – a creative marketing approach that resulted in MD-referred personal-training clients.

PART-TIME EMPLOYMENT:
(*Concurrent with college enrollment*)

BALLY'S TOTAL FITNESS – Philadelphia, PA
Personal Trainer, 1994 to 1996
☐ **Repeatedly awarded** as top salesperson for personal training services.
☐ **Averaged approximately $5K in monthly sales.**

EDUCATION:

TEMPLE UNIVERSITY – Philadelphia, PA
Bachelor's Degree in General Studies (GPA: 3.0), 1996
Dual Concentrations in **Sales/Marketing** and **Exercise Science**

COMPUTER SKILLS:

☐ Microsoft Word
☐ Microsoft Excel
☐ Peachtree Accounting
☐ Windows 2000

CERTIFICATIONS:

AMERICAN COLLEGE OF SPORTS MEDICINE –
Exercise Leader, Health & Fitness Instructor

INTERNATIONAL FITNESS PROFESSIONAL ASSOCIATION –
Personal Fitness Trainer

Resume Strategy: *Keith's resume shows that his demonstrated management abilities contributed to his company's successful start-up and growth, and will be valuable to a company seeking strong sales and operations management leadership. His "Areas of Expertise" section includes keywords/key skills that would be important for managers at his level. Keith's experience section provides a bulleted list of accomplishments for each position held, showing that Keith is a results- and bottom-line-oriented manager.*

Tom Fields

15 Yonkers Rd.
Raleigh, NC 27603

Home: 919.555.5555
Cell: 919.555.5551

tom@resumepower.com
Available for Relocation/Travel

Career Goal: Pharmaceutical Sales Rep

Dynamic sales professional and expert closer, consistently ranked #1 in sales volume and account retention throughout sales career. Seeking entry-level pharmaceutical sales representative position to leverage track record of quota-surpassing performance across diverse industries. Polished, persuasive communicator, able to build lasting rapport and discuss benefits/value with conviction. Cultivator of key relationships and strategic partnerships, with demonstrated success building quality pipeline to drive multimillion-dollar sales increases.

Verifiable track record of top performance, including a 60% market-share increase and $2.8M in account growth despite fierce competition. Experienced leader of sizable teams (up to 150), skilled in coaching underperformers and instilling a customer-focused mind-set. Fearless cold-caller; effectively win over gatekeepers to close same-day sales with senior executives.

Proficiencies

- Channel Development
- B2B/B2C Sales
- Account Growth & Retention

- Relationship Management
- Sales Team Training & Supervision
- Product Knowledge & Skills Development

- Executive Presentations
- Market Penetration
- Plan of Action

Sales Achievement Highlights

- **Surpassed annual quotas by 200%+ every year of tenure** as company's first national account executive (1998–2000).

- Earned ranking as **top sales rep and #1 in account retention three years in a row** (1998–2000); closed **$2.8M in sales** and established **first-ever corporate presence in 16 major markets** (including Chicago, Miami, Philadelphia, Atlanta, Washington D.C., and New York) to increase DMA penetration 400%.

- **Closed Fortune 500 and other major accounts** including Wal-Mart, Allstate Insurance, Amazon.com, Hershey's, and Budweiser (1998–2000).

- **Positioned operation for lucrative expansion** by implementing major shift in account acquisition/target marketing strategy that resulted in **precedent-setting market penetration** (1998–2000).

- Opened largely untapped emerging markets as company's **Hispanic marketing specialist** (1998–2000).

- Conceptualized and jointly directed development of new company division that subsequently generated **$18M in annual sales** (1998–2000).

- Cold-called businesses and conducted creative sales presentations to close major accounts (e.g., Nabisco, Raleigh Hospital) that **skyrocketed sales of banquets/catering by 55% annually** (2001–present).

- Launched multitiered sales/target marketing/operational initiatives for investment group that **drove a 25% increase** in restaurant sales, **upped auto-dealership sales 50%** (an increase of $480K), **increased wholesale network more than three-fold, grew market share to 60%,** and **led company to record-breaking weekly sales of $50K+** (2001–present).

- Strategized and managed growth-enabling diversification and aggressive business expansion responsible for **increase of investment-group assets from $2M to $7M** (1993–present).

- Introduced systems automation that reversed prior history of lost sales (for a 15% margin improvement) and negotiated "buy-option" terms with multiple vendors for **$260K in annual savings** (2001–present).

Tom Fields

Page Two

Career History

BROTHERS HOLDING GROUP — Raleigh, NC
Sales Manager & Owner's Representative, 2001–present; **General Manager,** 1993–1997

FEDERAL EXPRESS — Raleigh, NC
Driver, 2000

PROMOTIONS, INC. — Birmingham, AL
National Account Executive, 1998–2000

THE UNIVERSITY OF ALABAMA — Tuscaloosa, AL
Special Events Coordinator, 1992–1993

Education

THE UNIVERSITY OF ALABAMA — Tuscaloosa, AL — **B.A. in International Business,** GPA: 3.1

- Who's Who Among College Students
- International Business Class President
- College All-Star Soccer Player
- UA Marketing Club and Diplomat

Awards & Recognition

- **Top National Sales Representative** — Promotions, Inc., 1998, 1999, 2000
- **Superior Innovation Award** — Promotional Advertising Association of America, 1999
- **Entrepreneur Award** — Small Business Association, 1997

Professional & Community Affiliations

- Member, North Carolina Media Association, 1998–2000
- Board Member, Raleigh Restaurant Association, 1995–present
- Board Member, Small Business Association (Raleigh Chapter), 1997–present
- Member, American Marketing Association, 1998–2000

Computer Skills

MS Office (Word, PowerPoint, Access, Excel); Adobe Photoshop; Windows 2000/98/95; PC/Macintosh Systems; UNIX; Linux; MS-DOS; TCP/IP; COBOL; JavaScript; C++; various databases

Testimonial

"Tom is a dynamic sales performer and individual. He has a unique ability to open doors. He understands and makes himself knowledgeable on his product and the marketplace. Tom also demonstrated a unique ability to bring in new business while effectively maintaining existing accounts..."

– Tyrone Wheaton, President & COO, Promotions, Inc. (505-555-5555, ext. 98)

Resume Strategy: *Tom's resume profile spells out his track record as a #1 sales leader. He uses a "Sales Achievement Highlights" section to list his selling accomplishments, with corresponding years that he achieved each feat in parenthesis. His "Career History" section lists all of his jobs, but he avoids wasting valuable resume space by not discussing in detail positions he has held that were unrelated to sales. He uses an attractive "RX" graphic to help reinforce his goal of breaking into pharmaceutical sales.*

John Foster

9245 Westview Drive ◆ Chandler, AZ 85248 ◆ Available for Relocation
home (480) 123-4567 ◆ cell (480) 987-6543 ◆ johnfoster@resumepower.com

Energetic, results-driven professional seeking to leverage strong healthcare knowledge base and excellent communication skills into entry-level position as a pharmaceutical sales representative.

PROFESSIONAL SUMMARY

Offer six-plus years of experience in the healthcare industry, demonstrating a track record of success and the capability of strong performance in a sales environment. Motivated, enthusiastic approach to client relationship development, goal achievement, and professional growth. Able to attain consistent "buy-in" from clients in adopting treatments and practices for improved well-being. Proven ability to build solid relationships with physicians, support staff, and other members of the healthcare community. PC literate.

Core Competencies:

➤ Public Speaking & Presentations	➤ Client Needs Assessment	➤ Case Management
➤ Client Relationship Selling	➤ Performance Improvement	➤ Strategic Partnerships
➤ Goal-Setting & Fulfillment	➤ Network Development	➤ Problem-Solving Strategies
➤ B2C Sales	➤ Team Building & Training	➤ Customer Retention

SKILL AREAS AND ACCOMPLISHMENTS

CLIENT RELATIONSHIP MANAGEMENT

➤ Developed and used strategic "selling" techniques with clients that reversed negative thought processes and influenced successful focus on personal strengths and positive approach.
➤ Implemented wide range of therapies and interventions to facilitate client progress and success.
➤ Established trusting relationships with clients, family members, and business partners.
➤ Initiated winning problem-solving tactics to manage crisis situations and overcome setbacks.
➤ Achieved "no-fault" findings on all mandatory state audits reviewing treatment plans.

SALES ACHIEVEMENT & PERFORMANCE REVIEWS

➤ Held position as Jewelry Sales Associate for Macy's in fall of 1997; earned position as #1 Sales Associate of the Quarter during Christmas season, despite having no formal sales training.
➤ Received positive evaluation from supervisor at ABC Child Guidance Center within first three months: "John has stepped into the position as outpatient counselor with enthusiasm and responsibility…now has about 30 cases…has done an excellent job in all areas."
➤ Earned numerous commendations from clients for personal influence on progress.

PUBLIC SPEAKING & PRESENTATIONS

➤ Delivered 45-minute "Genetics of Bipolar Disorder" presentation for colleagues assigned to Mood and Anxiety Program, receiving unanimous recognition for best performance among several presentations.
➤ Developed and presented public awareness projects to NASA Lewis Research Center staff.

HEALTHCARE BACKGROUND & PARTNERSHIPS

➤ Worked in tandem with physicians to secure necessary reports and evaluate cases involving hospitalization, providing information on symptoms requiring possible medication.
➤ Developed general knowledge of psychotropic medications used in mental health field.
➤ Collaborated with team members in departmental/agency meetings and committees.

John Foster

SKILL AREAS AND ACCOMPLISHMENTS *(continued)*

PROGRAM/CASE MANAGEMENT

➤ Held full responsibility for range of 40 to 95 cases in various positions throughout career, maintaining proper documentation/compliance and consistently meeting all deadlines.

➤ Managed entire cycle of program development, including admission, assessment, planning, research, implementation, and review; gained reputation for effective intervention and treatment.

➤ Built strong abilities in working successfully with individuals of all ages from diverse backgrounds.

EMPLOYMENT HISTORY

ABC CHILD GUIDANCE CENTER, Chicago, IL – Clinical Counselor   2001

DEF FAMILY SERVICES, Chicago, IL – Clinical Case Manager   2000

CHICAGO COUNSELING CENTER, Chicago, IL – Outpatient Therapist   1998 – 2000

MACY'S, Chicago, IL – Sales Associate, Jewelry Department   1997

EDUCATION & CERTIFICATIONS

Master of Education Degree, Chicago University, Chicago, IL (1997)
Bachelor of Arts Degree in Psychology, Temple University, Philadelphia, PA (1997)
Professional Clinical Counselor, State of Illinois Counselor and Social Worker Board (2000)

ENDORSEMENTS

"I consulted with John on many cases…[He] is knowledgeable in his field [and] is a competent and caring professional…relates well to colleagues and feedback from them is positive…eager and willing to learn…understands the art of persuasion. He has the drive to achieve and the type of personality necessary to relate well to others…able to speak clearly and present ideas and information well. I highly recommend him for a position in pharmaceutical sales."

– Kathy Strong, MD, Child Psychiatrist, ABC Child Guidance Center

"[John's] performance was of a consistently high standard…proved to be driven and goal-oriented…enthusiastic and energetic…He displayed excellent oral and written communications…John's interpersonal skills are critical to his accomplishments, both in his professional and personal relations…He would be an asset to any company who has the opportunity to hire him."

– Joy Smith, MSW, LSW, Outpatient Therapist, ABC Child Guidance Center

Resume Strategy: *John uses a bolded statement at the top of his resume to communicate his career-change goal, and emphasizes his healthcare background and prior sales experience in his "Professional Summary." He mentions his ability to gain client "buy-in" as a way to articulate his persuasive skills, and he uses a functional resume style to group his accomplishments under relevant skill categories. His resume concludes with powerful testimonials that directly speak to his ability to transition to pharmaceutical sales.*

Chris Wilde

North Oaks, MN 55127 — (651) 123-4567 — chris@resumepower.com

GOAL: PHARMACEUTICAL SALES

Profile

Energetic, self-motivated professional with a solid background in customer service, sales, and human resources environments. Comprehensive knowledge of medical/dental benefits and experience interfacing with pharmacies and medical professionals. Known for delivering impeccable service and follow-through. Comfortable delivering presentations to both small and large audiences. Computer literate (Microsoft Word, PowerPoint, Excel, Windows 2000/98, Repertoire, MS-DOS). **Supervisors' comments:**

"Moves willingly and easily from one assignment to another without disruption or delay...can prioritize and accomplish the most pressing task in the midst of many demands on her time."

"Her interaction with associates on the medical and prescription plans has improved the customer service level to our associates...Her follow-up is excellent in resolving problems."

Education

UNIVERSITY OF MINNESOTA — Twin Cities, MN
B.S. in Organizational Management, May 2000 (GPA: 3.70)
Related Courses: **Sales Force Management, Management, Finance, Marketing**

Professional Experience

XYZ COMPANY, INC. — Twin Cities, MN
Personnel Office Operator, Human Resources, 1997 to present

Coordinate several employee programs and serve as liaison between service providers, associates, and insurance companies. Orchestrate appeals processes for denied claims, and communicate with departmental managers regarding compensation issues. Maintain integrity of HR system and monitor all pertinent data for nonexempt employees, including employment status, personal information, salary and benefits history, and prior work experience. Contributions:

◊ Conducted new employee orientations, responded to inquiries, and counseled employees on benefits-plan options.
◊ Helped newly relocated employees find suitable housing, schools, and other local resources.
◊ Organized several special events, including service recognition dinner for 200, Easter event for 300, and Halloween program for over 800.
◊ Contributed to a 24% increase in perfect attendance by initiating employee-recognition luncheons, gift certificates, and increased vacation time rewarding excellent attendance.

Personnel Accounts Payable Servicer, 1990 to 1997

Investigated and resolved discrepancies with associates, vendors, and various computer systems to secure proper authorization. Assessed tax liability on invoices and performed payroll and cash-management functions. Contributions:

◊ Assisted with high-priority project that involved setting up an advanced shipping-notice program, resulting in considerable savings to company.
◊ Secured over $400,000 in cash discounts annually.

ABC CAR DEALERSHIP — Twin Cities, MN
Office Manager/Sales Support, 1986 to 1988
Provided sales and administrative support, generated month-end reports, and served as liaison between sales staff, manufacturer, and customers.

Resume Strategy: *Although Chris does not have any direct experience in sales, she highlights her experience working in sales and customer service environments in the first sentence of her resume profile. She also mentions her relevant background dealing with medical information and interacting with professionals from this field. The supervisors' comments she includes speak to her ability to solve problems and multitask. She lists sales-related coursework with her degree information in the "Education" section, and the bulleted "Contributions" she includes in her "Professional Experience" section show how she has consistently gone "above and beyond" in performing her duties.*

TITLE ABSTRACTOR TO SALES REPRESENTATIVE

P.O. Box 1414
Philadelphia, PA 19146

Tamara Gold

(215) 123-4567
tamara@resumepower.com

Ambitious, self-motivated professional with highly praised interpersonal, organizational, multitasking, and management skills, seeking to launch new career as a sales representative. Proven performer; awarded "Employee of the Year" in 2000 while balancing work with full-time college enrollment. Adept in the simultaneous management of multiple complex projects, with an analytical approach to problem solving gained from experience in the legal field. Personal and professional; effective in written/verbal communication and skilled in interacting with individuals from all organizational levels. Offer a background in front-line sales, eagerness to learn, and strong desire to succeed.

KEY KNOWLEDGE AREAS

- ➤ Customer Relationship Management
- ➤ Organization & Follow-through
- ➤ Creative Problem Solving

- ➤ Team Building & Training
- ➤ Diplomatic Complaint Resolution
- ➤ Project Management

- ➤ B2C Sales
- ➤ Research & Written Reports
- ➤ Supervision & Team Leadership

EDUCATION & TECHNICAL SKILLS

TEMPLE UNIVERSITY – Philadelphia, PA
BA in Paralegal Studies, 2001   (Concentration in **Business**)   GPA 3.5

Computer Skills: Word, Excel, PowerPoint, WordPerfect, Internet Research

EXPERIENCE

GREENE & FIRTH – Philadelphia, PA – *Law firm*
Title Abstractor, July 2001 to Present
Perform in-depth title research/abstraction for mineral, coal, and surface property and prepare reports on findings for partners/clients. Verify judgment liens, financing statements, wills, and land records in County Court House. ***Key Accomplishments:***

- ➤ Mastered the art of detailed, diligent, and persistent investigative research to uncover obscure records dating back to the 1800s. Meticulously reviewed hundreds of pages of often-handwritten records to determine precise chain of title needed to enable client purchase/lease of oil, gas, and coal rights.
- ➤ Became adept in Internet search strategy to locate information sources and reference material of arcane origins. Commended for preparation of accurate documentation and timely reports crucial to serving client interests.

COUNTRY GENERAL STORE – Buckingham, PA – *Bakery/restaurant/gift shop*
Bakery Manager (Concurrent with full-time college enrollment), October 1998 to February 2001
Supervised five-member team and managed daily operations of bakery, including product sales, employee scheduling, supply purchasing/sourcing, customer relations, daily/month-end financial reports, and order fulfillment. ***Key Accomplishments:***

- ➤ Awarded 2000 "Employee of the Year" for superior performance and management achievements.
- ➤ Contributed to bottom-line gains through sales of high-end specialty baked goods and daily items.
- ➤ Rapidly resolved customer complaints for win-win outcomes that built loyal clientele and referral business.

SEASONAL EMPLOYMENT / INTERNSHIPS

BUCKS COUNTY CIRCUIT COURT CLERK'S OFFICE – Buckingham, PA – **Assistant Clerk,** March 2001 to June 2001
- ➤ Completed general office work, including filing, answering phones, preparing court orders, and scanning documents.

PENNSYLVANIA YOUTH CENTER – New Hope, PA – **Camp Counselor,** Summer 1998
- ➤ Taught a youth craft class (ages 9–13) and served as EMT/camp nurse.

BUCKINGHAM HOUSING AUTHORITY – Buckingham, PA – **Summer Youth Worker,** Summer 1997
- ➤ Planned fun and educational activities for underprivileged children, building strong bonds that continue to present day.

Resume Strategy: *Tamara explains her career objective in her opening profile. Although she does not have extensive sales experience, as bakery manager she was involved in direct sales to customers, so she brings this out in the profile and in her description of this job. In her "Key Accomplishments," Tamara mentions achievements that would be valued in a sales representative, such as her ability to resolve complaints, conduct thorough research, and prepare written reports.*

KEISHA DUKE

1428 Wellington Drive
Atlanta, GA 30342
Home: (404) 123-4567
Cellular: (404) 456-7891
keisha@resumepower.com

AREAS OF EXPERTISE

PROFESSIONAL EXPERIENCE

EDUCATION

Goal: Career in Surgical Sales

Account Manager ■ *Field Representative* ■ *Sales Representative*

Top-producing salesperson seeking to leverage sales and business-development skills to benefit the bottom-line of a surgical supply/equipment company. Expert communicator with demonstrated ability to listen to customer needs, develop solutions to meet specific objectives, and build customers' trust and respect. Readily absorb technical information regarding complex products and services and persuade potential customers to realize the benefits.

- New Business Development
- Relationship Building
- Contract Negotiations
- Strategic Alliances/Partnerships
- International Expansion
- Territory Development
- Sales Training/Leadership
- Customer/Account Services
- Computers (Windows 2000, ACCPAC, Goldmine, TeleMagic)

ATLANTA SPORTS (*manufacturer of graphite golf shafts*) — Atlanta, GA
Sales/Supervisor of International Distribution, 4/1997 to present
Junior Sales Associate, 10/1995 to 8/1996
Recruited back to company to expand sales of 19-state territory and international distribution channels. Identify suitable distributors and negotiate terms. Train sales representatives and participate in worldwide tradeshows. **Sales Contributions:**

- Ranked as the company's top-performing sales representative. Achieved revenue of $1.1 million in 2002 and on-track for meeting $1.3 million projection for 2003.
- Expanded international sales by 40% in 2002. Evaluated international markets and assigned exclusive distributorships based on projected revenue.
- Established distributors in Germany, France, U.K., Sweden, Finland, Japan, South Africa, Malaysia, Australia, Singapore, and Thailand.
- Built relationship with Canadian distributorship that more than quadrupled sales from $30K to $122K.

GEORGIA CIRCUITS (*printed circuit board broker*) — Atlanta, GA
Sales Representative, 8/1996 to 4/1997
Hired to establish market presence in a previously undeveloped territory through outside sales of printed circuit boards. Identified and negotiated provisions with vendors in Hong Kong and Georgia. **Sales Contributions:**

- Accelerated territory growth and established customer database, growing annual sales from zero to $500K.
- Built 35+ major accounts that increased total company revenue by 15%.
- Worked with vendors to ensure on-time delivery and quality production.

ACE SPORTING GOODS (*sporting goods retail store*) — Atlanta, GA
Assistant Manager, 3/1994 to 5/1995
Sales Associate, 11/1993 to 3/1994
Promoted to assistant manager to enhance performance of retail sales reps.

GEORGIA STATE UNIVERSITY — Atlanta, GA
B.A. in Political Science, Minor in Business & French, 5/1993

Resume Strategy: *Keisha capitalizes on her solid track record in sales to position herself for a career shift to surgical sales. Her new industry objective is clearly indicated in the banner, which also helps her add the "surgical sales" keyword into her resume. Her professional experience focuses on her sales contributions, proving that Keisha is a top performer and would be an asset to her next employer.*

Wilber Dalton

245 Rosebud Way
Jacksonville, FL 32202

wilber@resumepower.com

Home: (904) 123-4567
Cellular: (904) 987-6543

CAREER OBJECTIVE: SALES & ACCOUNT MANAGEMENT

*Offering a Proven Track Record of Capturing Six-Figure Financing
and Heading Successful Organizational/Business Growth*

Self-motivated, resourceful operations leader with strong qualifications in articulate and persuasive communications, needs assessment, revenue generation, strategic business planning, and general management. Over 15 years of management experience in profit and nonprofit environments, with the ability to secure annual funding commitments of hundreds of thousands of dollars, build consensus among widely varying and politicized viewpoints, and drive productivity and profit improvements. Combine enthusiastic, results-driven approach with high level of ethics. *Cross-functional competencies include:*

Sales/Marketing Strategies ■ Persuasive Communications ■ Powerful Presentations (Print & In-Person) ■ Proposal Development
Relationship & Territory Management ■ Team Building & Leadership ■ Workflow Planning & Prioritization
Finance/Budget/Inventory Management ■ Customer Service ■ Public & Media Relations ■ Time & Resource Optimization

PROFESSIONAL EXPERIENCE

FLORIDA FOUNDATION — Jacksonville, FL   2001 – Present
DISTRICT SUPERVISOR
Oversee daily operations of district and satellite office of nonprofit agency aiming to eliminate crop-damaging vermin. Supervise 11 full-time employees and 70 seasonal workers. Hold full responsibility for staffing, inventory control, farmer relations, problem solving, and field operations for 250K-acre region. Maintain compliance with state regulations/laws.
Selected Accomplishments:

- Minimized objections from environmental groups and segments of farming community, convincing them of the benefits of crop spraying and building cooperative relationships to facilitate program funding and implementation goals.

- Addressed public concerns about environmental issues and generated favorable press through series of persuasive radio appearances and print submissions.

- Currently authoring procedures manual to address a full range of potential problems and standardize policy development.

- Built strong, loyal work team by implementing group training programs and reducing stress on new employees.

- Averted potential $400,000 staffing expenditure by assuming additional responsibilities and consolidating resources.

ABC FARM ORGANIZATION — Jacksonville, FL   1986 – Present
BUSINESS MANAGER
In charge of 1,200-acre farm operations, with direct supervision of four employees. Maintain business growth in highly volatile market characterized by frequent profit losses and subsequent foreclosures. Manage budget/finances, marketing, production/quality control, workforce training, and business development. **Selected Accomplishments:**

- Built business from zero to net worth of $500,000 in highly fluctuating market, holding top 75% status in open market/commodity projections through successful production contracts and hedging strategies.

- Sold banking institutions on solid foundation of business, winning repeated six-figure financing commitments every year of operation ($150K to $327K) through polished personal presentations and solid business plans (incorporating finance/yield projections and marketing strategy).

- Achieved continuous production improvements and controlled all aspects of business to ensure profitability.

EDUCATION & TRAINING

University of Florida — Gainesville, FL / Business Management Degree Program / Expected Completion: 5/2004
Leadership Training: AG Leadership Class & Leadership and Politics, 2000 – 2001

Resume Strategy: *Wilber's resume shows how his farming and nonprofit management background will help him to be successful in sales. He highlights his persuasive communication skills, giving repeated evidence of them in his "Selected Accomplishments," and includes key "Cross-functional Competencies" in his profile.*

ANDREW L. WEBER

179 Jane Street, Elizabeth Street ■ New York, NY 10012 ■ (212) 529-1744 ■ andreww@aol.com

PROFESSIONAL SUMMARY

Profit-driven service industry professional endeavoring to capitalize on extensive background in business consulting and transactions to break into sales profession. Excel in relationship building and negotiations with key decision makers. Skilled in presenting to groups and individuals. Demonstrate broad strengths in:

- **New Business Development**
- **Client Relationship Management**
- **Networking**
- **Solution Selling**
- **Management Consulting**
- **Consensus Building**

EXPERIENCE

Wilde, Stone, & Raines, PC (1994 – Present)

Smith & French, PC (1992 – 1993)

Brown, Arends, & Neiland, PC (1985 – 1991)

Associate

- Fifteen years of legal and business consulting experience providing leadership, business acumen, issues, and crisis management.
- Successfully initiate and expand client relationships, including acting as general counsel to a diverse group of corporate entities; render expertise and guidance on issues relating to real estate, due diligence, finance, taxation, fiduciary security agreements, trusts and estates, and contract negotiations.
- Edit and assemble condo and co-op plans drafted for sponsors and developers; review effective condo/co-op offering plans for individual clients to determine rights, obligations, and risk of purchase of residential apartments.
- Negotiate on behalf of buyers and sellers concerning contract terms of purchase and sale of condo/co-op apartments.
- Represent buyers and sellers at closings, with full authority to resolve issues arising at closing.
- Liaise with landlords, tenants, and lenders in drafting and administering contracts.
- Integrate financial information and prepare accountings reflecting receipts, gains, losses, expenses, distributions, and investments.
- Member of New York Bar (1985).

EDUCATION

Juris Doctor, BROOKLYN LAW SCHOOL, Brooklyn, NY

BA, Inter-Disciplinary Studies, NEW YORK UNIVERSITY, New York, NY

Resume Strategy: *Andrew's "Professional Summary" outlines his desire to break into a sales position and includes his main credentials for his career change goal. Sales-related keywords are included in his summary to show that he is highly qualified for his new objective. His "Experience" section focuses on sales-related accomplishments. Resume submitted by Marty Weitzman.*

10

Technology/Web/ Telecommunications

Shawn Cox
(818) 123-4567 ▪ shawn@resumepower.com ▪ 4 Springs Drive ▪ Pasadena, CA 91105

Objective SYSTEMS ANALYST ▪ TECHNICAL SUPPORT ▪ WEB DEVELOPER

Honors CIS student with highly regarded skills in programming (C/HTML/VB Script), networking, information systems, and Web site development. Seeking to leverage history of strong academic performance and expert analytical skills gained from prior chemist profession to launch IT career. Adept in technical troubleshooting and problem solving, with proven success engineering rapid solutions to complex issues. Undaunted by the prospect of initial entry-level assignment to prove technical acumen and commitment to furthering organizational objectives. Knowledge areas include:

TESTING / SCRIPTING / DOCUMENTATION ▪ TECHNICAL INFRASTRUCTURE ▪ CODE GENERATION
LANs / WANs ▪ WEB SITE DEVELOPMENT ▪ QA ▪ TROUBLESHOOTING & DEBUGGING

Education & Training

PASADENA CITY COLLEGE – Pasadena, CA – 2001–Present
Currently pursuing **BS in Computer Information Systems** (Concentration in **C Programming**)

- **Completed 60% of degree program requirements** (72/120 credits).
- **Earned current cumulative GPA of 4.0/4.0.**
- **Coursework highlights:** scored 98.75% in courses covering topics including processing/storage hardware, input/output hardware, system/applications software, communications technology and uses, IT systems analysis/design, programming languages, information management, and databases.
- **Co-authored group project** on the "Adoption and Deployment of Sabre Technologies at Northwest Airlines." Contributed research and personally wrote 70% of paper, which scored highest grade (earning 95%) among six group projects.

PASADENA INSTITUTE OF TECHNOLOGY – Pasadena, CA – 2001
Coursework in **Computer Information Systems**

- **Enrolled and excelled in C programming,** operating systems, statistics, and public speaking.
- **Achieved cumulative GPA of 3.5/4.0** to qualify for Dean's List honors.

ITC TECHNOLOGY INSTITUTE – Pasadena, CA – 1999
Coursework in **Applied Information Technology Program** (AIT), an accelerated, post-graduate diploma program for university graduates.

- **Completed intensive "Fundamentals of Network Computing" module,** covering Windows 98 OS, HTML, VB Script, FrontPage 98, Access 97, Visual Basic, and Web site development.
- **Project highlights:** served on six-member team charged with Web presence project for mock car rental agency. Successfully launched functioning site in eight weeks using FrontPage, HTML, VB Script, Access 97, and MS Word with minimal instructional help. Final Web site successfully processed car-reservation requests, incorporated numerous interactive features, and earned "A" grade.

UNIVERSITY OF CALIFORNIA – Berkeley, CA – **BS in Chemistry,** 1993

Technical Summary

Languages:	C, HTML, Visual Basic, Visual C++, VB Script, Turing
Systems:	Windows ME/98/95, MS-DOS, Macintosh OS
Networking:	LANs/WANs, Peer-to-Peer Networks
Software:	MS Office (Word, Excel, Access, PowerPoint, Outlook), MS Project, BVRP Phone Tools

Experience
* Detailed achievements on request

Product Development Chemist, R&D, 2000 – ABC COMPANY – Pasadena, CA

Emulsion/Jr. Emulsion Chemist, 1994–1997; 1988–1991 – DEF COMPANY – Pasadena, CA

Lab Technician, 1984–1985; **Quality Control Technician,** 1982–1983 – ABC PRODUCTS – Pasadena, CA

Resume Strategy: *Shawn's resume focuses primarily on his education and training, since this is more relevant to his career goal than his prior chemist career. He includes coursework/project highlights to show his IT expertise. His computer graphic reinforces his goal and helps to distinguish his resume from others.*

SALES REPRESENTATIVE TO COMPUTER/HELPDESK TECHNICIAN

ROBIN DOW

CAREER GOAL: Computer/Helpdesk Technician

24 Kettle Drive
Columbus, GA 31907
706-123-4567
robin@resumepower.com

Available for Relocation

A+ certified technician with hands-on experience and solid foundation in computer hardware troubleshooting, analysis, installation, maintenance, and support. Able to resolve functionality issues ranging from hardware to software and peripherals. Strong interest in technology with the ability to quickly learn, master, and apply new technical concepts. *Key knowledge areas include:*

- Hard/Floppy Drive Installation
- Memory/RAM
- System Boards/BIOS/Chipsets
- Software Applications
- Operating Systems
  (Win NT/2000/98/95/3.11)
- Computer Maintenance
  (Troubleshooting, Disaster
  Recovery, Backups)

- Supporting Input/Output Devices
- Expansion/SCSI Devices
- Multimedia Technology
- Electricity/Power Supplies
- Phone Line Communications
  (Cable Modems, DSL)
- Networking (Ethernet, Token Ring,
  NICs, Network Software)
- Customer Service/Tech Support

COMPUTER TRAINING

A+ certified, 8/2001

TECHNICAL INSTITUTE — Atlanta, GA
Certificate of Completion, Computer Repair Technician, 8/01
- Five-month intensive training program (classroom and computer lab work)

TECHNICAL EXPERIENCE

ABC PROGRAM — Atlanta, GA
Intern, Instructional Divisions, 7/01 to 2/02
Tested, evaluated, diagnosed, troubleshot, and upgraded computers for student use. Installed Windows 98 for approximately 100 end users as well as hardware and peripherals including CD-ROM/hard drives, RAM, printers, and scanners. Set up software such as Office 2000 and Outlook. *Accomplishments:*

- Diagnosed, configured, updated, reformatted, and repaired multiple computer systems. Achieved departmental goal to recycle a high number of parts and systems (e.g., hard/floppy drives, CMOS batteries, and faceplates).
- Analyzed and corrected numerous technical problems caused by outdated equipment, repairing systems to full functionality for use by 100 end users.
- Located drivers to install peripherals for 486/Pentiums, tested memory modules and components, and researched/resolved Windows problems.

DEF PHARMACY — Atlanta, GA
Sales Representative, 1/01 to Present; **Photo Lab Technician,** 1/01 to 1/02
Operate equipment to provide a full range of photo-processing services. Place uncompromising focus on customer satisfaction. *Accomplishments:*

- Readily learned how to use equipment and maintain photo lab.
- Generated repeat/referral business by providing courteous customer service.

EARLY CAREER

Prior to pursuing passion for technology, enjoyed a successful career as a social worker, customer service rep, and retail sales professional (1980 to 2000).

EDUCATION

MSW, New York University — New York, NY, 1979; ACSW certification, 1983
BA in Social Welfare, Brooklyn College — Brooklyn, 1977

Resume Strategy: *Robin repositions herself as a computer professional by highlighting her recent training and internship, placing the logo from her A+ certification at the top of the resume, and including a convincing array of "key knowledge areas." Her prior jobs in social work, customer service, and sales are only briefly mentioned on the resume since they bear little relevance to her goal.*

Chandra Winters

47 Mapleleaf Way Teaneck, NJ 07039	Home: 973-555-5555 Cellular: 973-555-5551	chandra@resumepower.com

CAREER GOAL

Software Engineer ▪ Computer Programmer

Seeking to specialize within the biotechnology or science arena

PROFILE

Upcoming honors graduate in software engineering with proven skills in application/database design and Internet, client/server, and object-oriented programming across multiple platforms. Demonstrated success delivering cost-effective and sophisticated technical solutions advancing major scientific project goals. Eager to combine state-of-the-art, hands-on computer degree with passion for and background in scientific research, biochemistry, and data analysis. Reputation for dedication, enthusiasm, creative problem solving, and results. Available for extended and irregular hours.

SUMMARY OF STRENGTHS

- Software Design & Engineering
- Object-Oriented Programming
- Client/Server Programming
- Internet Programming
- Database Design & Management
- System Security

- Detailed Project Management
- E-commerce Initiatives
- End-User Training
- Experiment Design & Analysis
- Scientific Research
- Data Collection, Analysis & Interpretation

EDUCATION

FAIRLEIGH DICKINSEN UNIVERSITY – Teaneck, NJ

MS in Software Engineering (All but thesis)   **GPA: 3.8**

<u>Coursework Highlights</u>:
Object-Oriented Software Development, Software Construction, C++ Programming (Data Structures, Algorithms and Advanced Language Features), Database Management Systems, Object-Oriented Analysis and Design, Software Engineering, Internet Programming, and Client/Server/Distributed Objects Programming

<u>Master's Degree Thesis Project</u>:
Currently designing a Linux-based application using Perl and PHP that will deliver online, user-friendly instruction of beginning C and Java programming on an Apache server.

NEW JERSEY CITY UNIVERSITY – Jersey City, NJ

BS in Biochemistry, 1992   **GPA: 3.0**

EXPERIENCE

NEW JERSEY CITY UNIVERSITY – Jersey City, NJ

Post-Graduate Researcher/Project Manager, Plant Pathology, 1992 to 1997

Selected for competitive research post studying plant/pathogen interactions to discover ways to avert U.S. crop disease, with the ultimate goal of assisting domestic growers in engineering a fungus-resistant, but good-tasting, commercially viable apple. Managed three laboratory assistants, conducted library and Internet research, directed experimental design, and performed/supervised experiments. Analyzed and interpreted data, troubleshot experimental protocols and methods, resolved research challenges, wrote in-depth reports, and collaborated with other scientists and apple breeders. Key Contributions:

- **Wrote complex computer program that resolved research dilemmas** presented when scope of research project expanded significantly – from analyzing a few hundred apples per season to multiple thousands of apple varieties every season.

  □ Innovated new ways to use existing software to overcome data-interpretation problems related to acid content and color/ripeness analysis and automate previously manual procedures, saving hundreds of hours in data-entry time.

Chandra Winters

Home: 973-555-5555	chandra@resumepower.com
Cellular: 973-555-5551	**Resume, Page Two**

EXPERIENCE

NEW JERSEY CITY UNIVERSITY (continued)

- □ Efforts enabled project to successfully meet its ambitious expansion goals at zero additional cost.
- ■ **Became self-taught expert on Visual Basic-based program,** and continued to modify/improve features, flexibility, and capacity.
- ■ **Trained graduate students and other scientists** in the use of scientific software.
- ■ **Worked closely with professor in making project decisions,** designing experiments and multiple variations, and interpreting results.
- ■ **Moved project forward** by achieving breakthrough identification of a phenolic acid in a resistant apple phenotype, which inhibits enzyme production in a fungal pathogen.
- ■ **Co-authored research results** in published article for respected scientific journal. (J.D. Wright, C.R.. Winters, F. Chen, H.L. Huff. 1999. Suppression of Monilinia fructicola Cutinase Production by Apple Fruit Surface Phenolic Acids. Physiological and Molecular Plant Pathology 54: 37-50.)

PROFESSIONAL DEVELOPMENT

NEW JERSEY CITY UNIVERSITY, Biotechnology Program — Jersey City, NJ

- ■ **Intermediate Bioinformatics,** 2001
- ■ **Introduction to Bioinformatics,** 2001

TECHNICAL SUMMARY

Languages:	C, C++, Java, XML (beginning), PHP, J2EE, Perl, Python, HTML
Systems:	UNIX, Linux, Windows
Software/DB:	Word, Excel, Access, VisioPro, Apache Web Server, Oracle, SQL

TESTIMONIAL

"... In my program, Chandra worked on several research projects of worldwide importance ... she displayed sharp intellect, and her analytical and organizational abilities exemplified throughout her work are certainly relevant, and transferable, to a technical position in software engineering and other areas of computing support ...

"Perhaps most relevant to her current career objectives are a series of programs she developed using Visual Basic and Excel for managing the large data sets obtained from our experiments. These sophisticated `macros' enabled us to reduce data-entry time by many days and man-hours. Chandra independently developed the programs with little consultation from other resources. Our department network administrator, who was familiar with her work, was very impressed by what she had accomplished ...

"On a personal level, Chandra is a superb colleague. She is bright, enthusiastic, cheerful, and spirited in her approach to work and her overall demeanor ... if we had a position available appropriate for her current career objectives, I would hire her in a minute."

– **James Wright** (973-555-5556/jwright@resumepower.com), **Professor/ Chair,** Department of Plant Pathology, New Jersey City University

Resume Strategy: Chandra effectively combines her past experience as a postgraduate scientific researcher with her upcoming MS in software engineering to position herself for a programming job within the biotechnology or science industry. Her resume's "Career Goal" relays this effectively, and her "Profile" and "Summary of Strengths" sections emphasize her IT expertise. Chandra uses a detailed "Education" section next to play up her upcoming technology degree, and she makes sure that the first "Key Contribution" she lists in her "Experience" section involves computer programming. The strong testimonial from her professor at the end of the resume further speaks to her software-engineering capabilities.

IMOGEN KAYE

15 Front Street, London, England (relocating to the U.S.) ■ U.S. Voicemail: (800) 123-4567
Home: 011-44-123-456-7891 ■ Email: imogen@resumepower.com

Career Goal: JUNIOR PROGRAMMER / ANALYST

Talented high-tech professional with versatile skills in computer programming, drafting, 3-D modeling, and AutoCAD, seeking to transition from mechanical design to computer-programming field following completion of pending computer-science degree. Qualified to analyze situations and develop computer systems/programs to solve challenging problems. Proven six-year track record designing cost-effective, value-added product solutions generating multimillion-dollar revenue. Demonstrated success delivering thoroughly tested designs enabling glitch-free production within tight time constraints. Bilingually fluent (English/Spanish). Relocating to the United States.

Relevant Knowledge Areas

- Computer Programming (Visual Basic/COBOL/C)
- Creative Problem Solving & Project Management
- Technical Manuals
- Test Reports
- Electromechanical Drafting & Design
- Detail Assembly Drawing (AutoCAD)
- Team Building & Leadership
- 3-D Modeling & Prototype Design/Testing

Education & Training

NEW JERSEY CENTER FOR DEGREE STUDIES – Newark, NJ
Associate's Degree in Applied Computer Science, expected in 2003

Relevant coursework: Computer Systems and Applications, Technical Writing, Advanced Programming (COBOL, BASIC, C), Fourth Generation Languages, Structured Systems Analysis, System Design, and MIS Operations.

COMPUTER LEARNING SYSTEM – Cranbury, NJ
Completed intensive training in AutoCAD, Visual Basic, Microsoft Office, SQL Server 2000, and Java, 1997, 2001

Professional Experience

LONDON ELECTRICS – London, England *(Electrical equipment manufacturer and distributor)*
Mechanical Designer, March 1995 to May 2001
Created detailed, technical drawings used to document equipment design, develop prototypes, and produce innovative new products. Prepared professional engineering drawings, planning sketches, technical manuals, parts lists, and test reports. Served as Visual Basic programming expert and managed accurate inventory tracking. ***Key Accomplishments:***

- **Played a crucial role in innovating groundbreaking product solutions and speeding them to market** through the timely completion of thoroughly documented production drawings in high volume, deadline-driven environment.
- **Earned a reputation for meticulous attention to detail** due to flawless final designs and thorough modeling in AutoCAD, facilitating problem-free manufacture.
- **Assisted lead engineer in all phases of design and project management of high-profile, six-figure assignment** – from conception through delivery. Completed project within tight, three-month time frame.
- **Shortened business cycle time and eliminated costly manufacturing delays** by delivering customized, computer-generated 3-D models using a variety of methods, which enabled customers to view finished product images and specify modifications before production phase.
- **Created automated, fully integrated accounting system,** increasing efficiency by at least 20%.

Technical Skills

Visual Basic ■ COBOL ■ C ■ Windows 2000/98 ■ Microsoft Office ■ AutoCAD

Resume Strategy: *Imogen's profile and "Knowledge Areas" sections explain her qualifications to enter the programming field. She highlights her pending computer-science degree and IT training prominently and chooses accomplishments related to her career goal in her "Experience" section.*

COPY CENTER ASSISTANT MANAGER TO NETWORK ENGINEER

ROBERT HALL, MCP

1267 Cliffside Circle ◆ Clifton, VA 20124 ◆ 703-555-5555 ◆ bobhall@resumepower.com

QUALIFIED AS: Network Engineer/Administrator ◆ LAN Manager

PROFILE

Technically skilled, quality-focused network engineering professional combining advanced MCSE training and A+ / MCP certifications with a track record of successful project performance in systems installation, configuration, troubleshooting, and maintenance. Creative, out-of-the-box thinker equipped to oversee network administration and devise solutions to address large-scale problems and drive performance improvement.

SKILLS

- Network & Systems Administration
- Disaster Recovery
- Hardware/Software/Server Integration
- Desktop Support
- LAN/WAN Setup & Optimization
- Technical User Support & Training

NETWORK TRAINING

NORFOLK TECHNICAL INSTITUTE, Norfolk, VA
Master's Certificate in Windows 2000 Administration/Desktop Support, 1/02 to 10/02
Enrolled in comprehensive, industry-focused program covering systems administration and support objectives in a hands-on, laboratory environment.
Overview of Assignments and Accomplishments:

- Installed, configured, and troubleshot numerous desktop components such as microprocessors, RAM, floppy/hard disk drives, as well as printers and portable PCs.
- Gained comprehensive background in compression utilities, disaster-recovery tools, antivirus utilities, drive-imaging software, hard-disk partitioning, and hardware diagnostics.
- Completed installation and configuration for systems and components:
  - Windows NT, 2000, Workstation, 2000 Professional, 98, and MS-DOS;
  - Client services and Gateway services for NetWare;
  - 2000 DNS for dynamic and secure updates.
- Planned, implemented, and managed a full spectrum of network components:
  - TCP/IP subnets and protocol suite in MS/intranet/extranet environments;
  - NT, 2000 DNS servers, MS Internet Information Server 5.0, MS Exchange Server, and 2000 Active Directory master servers.
- Created and managed Windows NT and 2000 user, computer, and group accounts.
- Addressed LAN/WAN domain planning and management issues.
- Managed user permission policies at the site, domain, and organizational levels.
- Pinpointed, analyzed, and troubleshot issues for TCP/IP network.

EDUCATION

- A+ Certification, 6/01
- Microsoft Certified Professional, 6/01

BACHELOR OF ARTS DEGREE, 6/87
Liberty University, Lynchburg, VA

TECHNICAL SKILLS

SOFTWARE: MS Office, Exchange, Internet Information Server; Visio
OPERATING SYSTEMS: Windows 98, NT, 2000 Professional and Server, Linux
NETWORKING: Novell NetWare, TCP/IP, NetBEUI, NWLink

ADDITIONAL EXPERIENCE

ASSISTANT MANAGER, Kinko's Copy Center – Norfolk, VA (8/98 to 12/01)
Supervised staff of 12 in copy-center activities and customer-service issues. Developed strengths in large-scale management of complex systems.

Resume Strategy: Robert devotes the most amount of space on his resume to a detailed summary of his technical training in network engineering. The certification logos at the top of the page reinforce his IT credentials and serve as colorful design elements.

Mohammed Farrar

456 West 23rd Ave. ■ Detroit, MI 48905
Phone: 420-555-5555 ■ mfarrar@resumepower.com

Systems Analyst ■ *Database Designer*

Accomplished systems analyst, database designer, and data analyst with seven years of high-tech and management experience, including four years as a Unisys Corp. senior consultant. Combine proficiency in information technology with business acumen to drive Fortune 500 technology projects to successful completion. Backed by an MBA in marketing, a BS in computer science, and a history of leading high-profile assignments and multidisciplinary project teams.

Areas of expertise include:

- Complex Database Design and Administration
- Systems Analysis
- Project Lifecycle Management
- IT Team Leadership

- Requirements Definition
- Software Testing/De-bugging
- Data Modeling and Analysis (Relational and Star Schema)
- Data Warehouse Technology

- Quality Assurance (QA)
- Marketing Strategies
- E-commerce Business Systems
- Programming/Analysis
- Developing Training Materials

Technical Summary

Languages: HTML, Java, SQL, PL/SQL, Visual Basic 6, COBOL, Natural

Systems: Windows 2000 Server/Workstation, Windows NT Server/Workstation, Windows 98, Novell 3.12

Databases: SQL Server 7 and 2000, Oracle 8i, DB2, Adabas, MS Access

Tools: Epiphany 4.0, Oracle Warehouse Builder, Lotus Notes, Rational's tools, Requisite Pro, Clear Case, ClearQuest, MS Visual Studio, MS FrontPage, Visio, MS Word, MS Excel

Professional Experience

UNISYS CORPORATION — Detroit, MI
Senior Consultant, May 1997 to June 2001
Managed multimillion-dollar consulting engagements – from business requirements analysis to project delivery – for Fortune 500/blue-chip clients. Accountable for project strategy, design, development, execution, and evaluation. Collaborated with cross-functional teams and provided technical and business strategies for implementation of large-scale network and e-commerce business systems. **Project Highlights:**

❖ **State Farm Insurance:** Served as analyst and QA team lead on a $60 million project for development of Web-based claims processing application. *Results:*

- Captured business requirements, prepared use cases and storyboards using RUP, and designed prototypes using HTML. Designed test cases, test scenarios, and automated test scripts using Rational's automated testing tools.
- Developed defect tracking and management procedures to ensure accurate identification and correction of defects. Completed quality-control audits to ensure accuracy, completeness, and proper usage of data in tables by creating complex SQL queries.

❖ **Nabisco:** Served as analyst on a $5 million data-warehouse project. *Results:*

- Defined and analyzed data warehouse requirements for Sales subject area using Unisys data-warehousing methodology. Designed the logical data model based on the requirements.
- Performed source systems and data-source analysis. Mapped source-data elements to attributes in the data model and developed conversion rules. Developed SQL extractors using Oracle Warehouse Builder. Prepared testing plans for data extracting, transforming, and loading into data warehouse.

Mohammed Farrar

Professional Experience

UNISYS CORPORATION (continued):

❖ **General Motors (North America):** Selected as lead implementer on a $2 million project for completion of a customer-centric data mart using Epiphany. *Results:*

♦ Analyzed source data and prepared data validation plans. Designed logical and physical data model using star schema. Performed database changes from development through testing on an SQL Server 7.

♦ Created facts and dimensions tables, attributes, topics, and Web pages. Developed SQL extractors to load data into Epiphany's data mart. Prepared end-user training materials.

❖ **Target:** Served as team lead on a $120 million Y2K conversion project. Led team of 21 consultants in the set-up of test environment for batch programs. *Results:*

♦ Identified and corrected noncompliant code in COBOL and Natural programs. Developed contingency plans and monthly communications. Prepared test results deliverables.

♦ Developed master repository in MS Access to catalogue entire inventory of mainframe applications (JCLs, Procs, Programs, etc.). Created Issue Management database in MS Access with a GUI interface using VBA for faster data entry and reporting.

❖ **Unisys (internal project):** Provided SQL Server 2000 administrative support to develop a Web-based self-service staffing application. *Results:*

♦ Extracted, transformed, and loaded dissimilar data elements into an SQL Server 2000 database using DTS. Designed database by creating tables, indices, and constraints.

♦ Provided database support by monitoring backups, investigating and correcting data issues, and assessing database performance.

UNITED WAY — Grand Rapids, MI
MIS Support Specialist, June 1994 to May 1997
Assisted with administration of four production SQL Server 6.5 databases. **Key Contributions:**

❖ Prepared ad-hoc queries and reports for end users using Transact-SQL.
❖ Provided day-to-day administration of a 250-user license Novell 3.12 network.
❖ Evaluated, purchased, installed, configured, and troubleshot PC hardware and software.

Education

UNIVERSITY OF MICHIGAN — Ann Arbor, MI
MBA in Marketing, June 1996

MICHIGAN STATE UNIVERSITY — East Lansing, MI
BS in Computer Information Systems, June 1993

Resume Strategy: *To facilitate his transition to systems analysis, Mohammed's resume needed to show his technical expertise and achievements. His resume leads with a tagline stating his current goal, followed by a summary that explains his top qualifications and a bulleted list of his expertise areas. Mohammed includes a "Technical Summary" on page one, giving hiring managers a snapshot of the systems, programs, and applications with which he is proficient. His experience section details highlights of technical project outcomes and results.*

Manny Winston

12 Mockingbird Way, Cranbury, NJ 08512 ■ Phone: 609-123-4567 ■ E-mail: manny@resumepower.com

PROFILE

INTERACTIVE MARKETER ■ WEB DESIGNER/DEVELOPER

Creative technologist with a passion for Web development. Combine graphic design skills with technical expertise to produce cutting-edge Internet/intranet sites. Highlights:

- **Web Site Design:** Skilled in HTML, JavaScript, Cascading Style Sheets, and Adobe/Macromedia development tools.
- **Web Development:** Write effective Web site content, design and develop Web sites and prototypes, and create extranet arms that add value for key customers.
- **Relationship Management:** Work with diverse clients around critical business issues. Currently support 700+ end users for troubleshooting, configuration, and training.
- **Applications and Systems Development:** Design/code purchase orders, product bundling, shared software and aging applications; design and integrate client/server networks; and physically relocate network infrastructures.
- **Technical and Web Design Training:** Possess a bachelor's degree in CIS and currently pursuing certificates in Web content development and graphic design.

KEY SKILLS

- Web Site Design & Development
- Creative Web-Based Strategies
- Targeted Customer Solutions
- Application Design & Development
- Extranet Value-Added Services

- Key Relationship Management
- Development Team Support
- End-User Technical Support
- Systems Integration
- Configuration Management

TECHNICAL SUMMARY

Web Applications & Programming Languages:

HTML, JavaScript, HomeSite, BBEdit, Active Server Pages, Cascading Style Sheets, Photoshop, ImageReady, Dreamweaver, Fireworks, C, C++, Visual Basic, Smalltalk, UML, UltraDev, MS SQL Server, MS Access

Office Programs and Systems:

MS Office 2000/97, Visio 2000, Exceed Hummingbird, WisdomWare, Windows NT/2000/98/95, Unix/Linux, Next, Macintosh OS, MS-DOS

EXPERIENCE

ABC SOFTWARE, INC. – Cranbury, NJ
Provides enterprise-class software and services to aid integration across applications, enterprises and e-business.

Senior Desktop Technician, Information Services, January 2000 to Present
Consultant, July 1998 to January 2000

Hired as a senior desktop technician after proving dedication and technical skills as a consultant. Provide hardware and software support, train employees, and maintain companywide desktop/laptop configurations. Oversee Information Services section of intranet site and company newsletter. *Contributions:*

- **Helped company bring Web work in-house through improved management of Web site archives.** Recommended and implemented method to easily move archived articles. Modified HTML to change site's navigational structure.
- **Initiated and currently author Information Services section of newsletter** "ABC-Ezine," which has enhanced internal communications regarding technology. Relay help desk Q&A/disaster-recovery plans to 700 staff nationwide.
- **Collaborate with Web development/application services team** on critical changes.
- **Successfully resolved software and hardware problems for 700 end users.** Troubleshot Windows NT 4.0 platform with Office 97 and department-specific programs such as SQL, WisdomWare for product documentation, Visual Cafe, SQL Server, Visio 2000, and Exceed Hummingbird suite for UNIX-to-Windows connectivity.

Manny Winston

EXPERIENCE

DEF TECHNOLOGIES, INC. – Princeton, NJ
System integrators for regional businesses.
Consultant, July 1998 to January 2000
Created Internet sites for the company and Web-based systems for clients.
Contributions:

- **Created prototypes for Web-based purchase-order systems.** Automated P.O. placement, viewing, and editing. Replaced a previously manual system that was inefficient and timeconsuming. Created user-friendly interface design and client demos.
- **Used shopping cart technology, Active Server Pages, HTML, and SQL Server databases** to prototype Internet P.O. management.
- **Developed extranet arm on company Web site.** Enabled customer to browse company's inventory and create menu choices for employee computer purchase plan. Established multiple password and security levels.

MAJOR TELECOM – Cranbury, NJ
Global innovator and provider of telecommunications solutions worldwide.
Software Engineer, May 1997 to July 1998

Helped company deliver EZComm project to support sales efforts. *Contributions:*

- **Assisted in the design of a product bundling and tracking system.** Used Smalltalk for development and unit testing, and worked with system analysts on specs.
- **Developed portion of object model that reused common software across multiple development teams.** Mapped how different objects worked in the system.

ABC DATA SYSTEMS – Princeton, NJ
Provides system design, manufacturing, installation, and support.
Network Support Engineer, February 1996 to May 1997

Worked with Teclab to investigate new technologies for integration clients. *Contributions:*

- **Created application to track procurement,** which replaced a manual system.
- **Developed network infrastructure for company relocation.** Used fiber-optic drops up to the desktop; trained users in NT 4.0.
- **Collaborated with network engineers on physical relocation of network infrastructure.** Helped with cable routing, router setup, and computer configurations.

XYZ CONSULTING – New York, NY
Global management and technology consulting firm with 65,000 employees in 47 countries.
Consultant, August 1994 to February 1996

- **Coded portion of application that recycled phone numbers via an aging process** for large telecommunications client. Increased efficiency of internal processes.
- **Worked with customer and software vendor to assess payroll system's compliance with federal regulations.** Analyzed/tested software and coded modifications.

EDUCATION

PRINCETON UNIVERSITY – Princeton, NJ
Bachelor of Business Administration, Major: **Computer Information Systems,** 1994

TECHNICAL UNIVERSITY OF NEW JERSEY – Cranbury, NJ
Web Content Development Certificate (in progress)

SESSIONS.EDU ONLINE SCHOOL OF DESIGN & MEDIA – New York, NY
Graphic Design Certificate (in progress)

Resume Strategy: Manny's resume uses a font that is common on the Internet, keeping in line with his career Web designer career goal. His "Profile" section includes his new goal and demonstrates how his technical and training background have prepared him for this career transition. The bulleted list of his key knowledge areas in his "Profile" section allows readers to easily scan through and digest his main qualifications. Manny focuses his job descriptions on his internal and client-based Web-related work. His "Education" section includes his two in-progress certificates related to his new goal.

KAY FORD

9 Tower St. • Washington, D.C. 20006 • 202-555-5555 • kay@resumepower.com

profile	**Web Site Developer**
	Web Design / Site Development / Creative Direction / Project Management / Content Development
	Web designer with formal training and practical experience in design, graphics, programming, and e-commerce business strategies. Seeking to leverage extensive business background, MBA degree, ten years of experience in the landscape-design field, and recent Web design training to positively impact on-line-marketing ventures. Applicable design skills include conceptual design, design development, and design presentation. Demonstrated ability to work in a collaborative team environment. Strong technical writing, research, and business-case development skills.
applications	• Training in HTML, CGI scripts, PERL, JavaScript, forms, FTP, AutoCAD, C++ • Experience using Macromedia Flash, Dreamweaver, Paint Shop Pro, HomeSite • Proficiency with Microsoft Excel, Word, PowerPoint, Access
education	GEORGE WASHINGTON UNIVERSITY — Washington, D.C. **MBA,** Major in Finance, 12/95 (GPA: 3.875) • **Beta Gamma Sigma** National Business Honor Society, 4/96 • **Certificate:** Institute of International Business, 4/96 TULANE UNIVERSITY — New Orleans, LA **BA,** Major in Landscape Design, 5/78
training	HOWARD UNIVERSITY — **Webmaster Skills Certification,** 8/02 • 90-hour program covering Web Page, Web Site, and Web Server skills • Designed, launched, and maintained **www.greengarden.com** IT ONLINE — Currently enrolled in **Web Site Design** certificate program J.D. EDWARDS & COMPANY — **Business Case Consultant Certification,** 9/99
experience	J.D. EDWARDS & COMPANY — Washington, D.C. **Associate Finance Manager,** Enterprise Software Division, 6/98 to present **Associate Finance Manager,** Consulting Division, 11/96 to 6/98 **Long-Term Contractor,** 10/94 to 11/96 NATIONAL WILDFIRE PREVENTION PROGRAM — Washington, D.C. **Hazard Mitigation Specialist,** 1/93 to 3/94 ABC LANDSCAPE DESIGN — Washington, D.C. **Landscape Designer,** 6/83 to 12/92

Resume Strategy: Kay leads her resume with a "Profile" that includes her new career goal and a description of her key qualifications for a Web developer position. She follows with Web applications with which she is familiar. Kay's "Training" section highlights recent coursework related to her objective. Her work experience is not given detailed descriptions as she is completely changing careers.

Carlos Robles

15 Sunshine Way • Boston, MA 02118 • Home: (617) 123-4567 • Cell: (617) 987-6543 • carlos@resumepower.com

Uniquely qualified for positions as...

Software Engineer • Systems Analyst • Systems Administrator

Award-winning IT professional with MCP and A+ certifications, solid knowledge of various software and operating systems, and successful high-tech industry experience. Skilled in a broad range of software engineering, systems analysis, and systems-administration functions. Technical expertise in hardware/software integration reinforced by proven ability to minimize downtime and anticipate problems before they occur.

Expert planner, leader, and strategist known for ability to master new concepts quickly, work independently or as part of a team, start or restructure departments, and develop business solutions that increase efficiency, productivity, and profitability. Excellent communication, presentation, interpersonal, and customer-service skills. Able to establish productive rapport with diverse individuals and staff levels, from computer operators to senior executives. Diligent, productive, and hard-working individual with special talent for end-user training and public speaking.

Certifications

• MCP (Microsoft Certified Professional)   • A+

Technical Summary

Software & Databases:	Microsoft Word XP, Microsoft Access XP, Microsoft Excel XP, Microsoft PowerPoint XP, Microsoft Office XP, Microsoft Office 2000, Adobe Photoshop, Gammadyne Mailer, Crystal Reports, Symantec, ACT!, Advanced Hardgoods Distribution, Advanced Web Commerce, Advanced Warehouse Manager, Advanced Warehouse Assistant, Advanced Remote Commerce
Systems:	Windows 3.x, 9x, 2000, XP, MS-DOS
Networking:	Proficient in TCP/IP, LANs/WANs, DNS, Servers/Cables

Professional Experience

ADVANCED SOFTWARE SYSTEMS – Boston, MA
Software manufacturer for the distribution industry

Inside Sales Manager, 2001 to 2002

Directed every operational aspect of Telemarketing Department, including personnel supervision, management of more than 20 databases ranging from 2,000 to 20,000 customer contacts, and responding to Requests for Proposals (RFPs). Developed, implemented, and monitored strategies to prospect for customers, develop new business, maximize opportunities with existing accounts, and minimize opportunities for the competition. Conducted software demonstrations at customer site and via Internet with WebEx.

Key Accomplishments:

- **Developed and implemented Telemarketing Department** where none had previously existed, performing comprehensive research to create prospect list; learning and teaching ACT!; recruiting, hiring, and training telemarketers; and providing leadership that enabled department to increase number of qualified leads by 150%.
- **Created cross-referenced databases** that successfully supported Sales Department, enhancing the department's ability to contact prospects and track sales.
- **Conducted software demonstration** that led to acquisition of $650,000 account.
- **Made formal presentations at Advanced Users' Conferences** for four consecutive years (1997 to 2000). Topics included consigned inventory, billing procedures, Web ordering, and AP/AR procedures.
- **Developed processes and training manual** to facilitate use of ACT! software by outside sales personnel.

Carlos Robles Page Two

Professional Experience (continued)

ADVANCED SOFTWARE SYSTEMS (continued)

Education Services Specialist, 1997 to 2001

Trained wholesale distribution customers in use of Advanced software. (Customers ranged from $3 million to $2.5 billion in annual revenue.) Maintained on-site presence during customer go-live. Assisted customer service representatives during periods of heavy volume.

Key Accomplishments:

- **Provided quality assurance on three new releases and seven modifications** during tenure.
- **Mastered new software and taught core classes** in first 90 days of employment.
- **Conducted technical training to more than 500 employees,** providing instruction in accounting, inventory, and order processing modules.
- **Maintained heaviest travel schedule** of any Advanced employee, generating $1,500 per day in billable hours.
- **Gained recognition as subject matter expert** on Advanced and non-Advanced software.

ACT COMPUTER SYSTEMS (ACS) – Boston, MA
Software manufacturer for automobile dealerships worldwide

Software Installation Specialist, 1993 to 1997

Performed on-site software installations at automobile dealerships, including ACS dealer solution and CD-ROM-based parts catalog. (Average cost was $1 million for dealer solution and $60,000 for CD-ROM-based catalog.) Planned and coordinated conversions from dealer software to ACS on UNIX and DX10 platforms. Provided consulting and training services and served as regional customer service representative for Massachusetts.

Key Accomplishments:

- **Earned three "Software Installer of the Month" awards.**
- **Installed 150 PC workstations at 85 dealerships** in ninety-day period without loss in efficiency.
- **Consistently handpicked to lead** or back up accounting software installations.
- **Created curriculum and conducted fifteen internal training classes** on dealership procedures.

Education

BOSTON COLLEGE – Boston, MA

Coursework in Microsoft 2000, Novell, and A+, 2000 to 2001

BOSTON UNIVERSITY – Boston, MA

Bachelor of Science in Criminal Justice, 1992

Specialized Training:

Advanced Automobile Dealership Business Practices, Act Computer Systems – Boston, MA, 1994

Reply To

Home: (617) 123-4567 • Cell: (617) 987-6543 • E-mail: carlos@resumepower.com

Resume Strategy: Carlos explains why he is uniquely qualified for software engineering and other IT positions in his opening profile. He places his "Certifications" and "Technical Summary" sections before his "Professional Experience" section since they are highly relevant to his career goal, and adds shading to the "Technical Summary" section to place further emphasis on it. In his "Experience" section, Carlos elaborates on all technical accomplishments from his background, using keyword phrases like "quality assurance" and "technical training" to help increase the number of "hits" his resume receives.

MARSHALL JONES

12 Meeting Way … Seattle, WA 98116 … (206) 123-4567 … marshall@resumepower.com

Professional Goal: Technical Installer □ Network Designer □ Help Desk Support
Specializing in the Telecommunications Industry

Skilled technical professional with substantial technical and customer-support experience within Fortune 500 companies. Excellent communication skills; able to break down complex information and offer step-by-step solutions to users at all levels. Frequently recognized by senior management for contributions towards organizational efficiency, improved customer relations, and cost reductions. Apply keen analytical and technical skills to identify and resolve challenging problems. Readily adapt to new environments and responsibilities. Establish and maintain positive relationships with high-profile accounts, managers, and colleagues.

AREAS OF STRENGTH

□ Technical Support	□ Customer Service	□ Warehouse Controls
□ Team Leadership	□ Administrative Support	□ 65+ WPM Typing, 10-Key
□ Dial-in Configuration Assistance	□ Report Preparation	Proficiency
□ Equipment Routing	□ Billing/Revenue Accounting	□ Quality Control

TECHNICAL SUMMARY

Protocols/Networking: LAN/WAN, routers, bridges, switches, hubs
Programming: C, C++, COBOL, Visual Basic
Operating Systems: Windows 2000/98, MS-DOS
Office Software: MS Office (Word, Excel, PowerPoint), Project, FrontPage, Lotus SmartSuite (Lotus 1-2-3), Visio, Freelance Graphics

PROFESSIONAL EXPERIENCE

WORLDCOM NETWORK SERVICES / ABC GLOBAL NETWORK SERVICES — Seattle, WA

Technical Customer Service / Back-Up Team Leader, 1997 to present
Retained by WorldCom after merger and assigned additional responsibilities as back-up team leader for team of five. Respond to queries on the MDNS (Managed Data Network Services) hardware help desk and resolve issues involving routers, modems, equipment routing, damaged equipment, delivery, and dial-in configuration problems. **Accomplishments:**

□ Initiated set-up of shared drive on LAN, freeing up PC hard-drive space and eliminating single points of failure that could jeopardize vital documentation.
□ Cited by management for maintaining high-level of database integrity, which has been key in successful audits and ISO 9000 recertification.
□ Researched and identified billing discrepancies within warehouse operations and consulted with management to resolve errors and reduce expenses.
□ Lauded by senior management for creating a financial report noting flaws within warehouse inventory, and clearly identifying valid inventory and necessary losses.
□ Currently preparing desk-level procedures to reflect departmental responsibilities and guidelines for full automation of functions.
□ Used Visio to create desk-level procedures and flowcharts for upper management within several departments.
□ Received award for providing excellent service to high-profile account.

MARSHALL JONES

Resume — Page Two

PROFESSIONAL EXPERIENCE

WORLDCOM NETWORK SERVICES / ABC GLOBAL NETWORK SERVICES (continued):

Senior Secretary Specialist, Managed Data Network Services (MDNS), 1996 to 1997
Secretary Specialist, Technology Assessment Organization, 1994 to 1996

Provided secretarial and administrative support to technology organization and backup support to president and COO. Coordinated schedules and travel arrangements, monitored supplies, and received and closed purchase orders. Sole contact person for ABC Company Fleet Maintenance regarding loss-prevention issues. **Accomplishments:**

☐ Reduced expenses by $50,000 by properly transferring ownership and legal fees of Fleet Maintenance back to ABC Company's main office.

☐ Received award for contributions and outstanding efforts during a period of reduced staffing.

ACTION COMPANY — Seattle, WA

Revenue Accountant, 1993 to 1994
Balanced billing statements and resolved billing errors.

U-HAUL — Seattle, WA

Secretary / Commercial Moves Project Coordinator, 1990 to 1993

EDUCATION & TRAINING

SEATTLE INSTITUTE OF TECHNOLOGY — Seattle, WA
Telecommunications Management major (Bachelor's degree expected December 2003)
GPA: **3.8/4.0**
☐ Epsilon Delta Pi Honor Society

RELATED COURSEWORK:

☐ Voice Communications	☐ PC Configuration and Management	☐ Financial Accounting
☐ WAN/LAN	☐ Network Operating Systems	☐ Project Management
☐ Computer Applications	☐ C/C++	☐ Legal Environment

IN-HOUSE TRAINING:
Workforce Diversity Training, 1998 and 2000

12 Meeting Way ... Seattle, WA 98116 ... (206) 123-4567 ... marshall@resumepower.com

Resume Strategy: *To facilitate Marshall's career change from technical customer service to an installer position, his resume includes a "Professional Goal" section that states his new goal and industry specialty. He then lists transferable skills that are important for an installer position in a career summary section. His bulleted "Areas of Strength" include relevant keywords for his new goal, while a "Technical Summary" on page one further positions him for a hands-on technical job.*

11

Education/Training

AARON BRADSHAW

14 Beach Drive ■ Delray Beach, FL 33444 ■ Home: 561.123.4567 ■ E-mail: aaron@resumepower.com

OBJECTIVE: Seeking entry-level higher education employment in administrative program/instructional support to leverage strong background in university teaching/corporate training, recruitment/retention, special event coordination, and operations management. Passion for continuous learning and academic environments.

CAREER PROFILE: Dedicated, dynamic manager with history of top-rated performance in both university and corporate settings. Experienced educator with proven success developing curricula and delivering quality, learner-focused, enrollment-driving training as an instructor for the University of Florida. Ranked among the university's top instructors campuswide. Well-honed skills managing people, programs, and operations; current responsibility for growth-enabling leadership of 100+ staff and daily activities (including all corporate training/event planning) for a $4.5 million restaurant. Known for articulate written/verbal communication (with intermediate bilingual fluency in Spanish), strong organizational skills, respected leadership, and ability to enhance service, efficiency, and profit margin. Credentials include an in-progress MA in information and learning technologies, MA/BA in religion, and PC proficiency.

EDUCATION

UNIVERSITY OF FLORIDA – Delray Beach, FL
MA in Information and Learning Technologies – Emphasis in Corporate Training/Instructional Technology (Currently enrolled/GPA: 4.0). Anticipated graduation: Summer 2003
MA in Religion (GPA: 3.43), 1999
Theta Alpha Kappa National Honor Society (1999)
DELRAY BEACH COLLEGE – Delray Beach, FL
BA in Religious Studies, Minor in **Philosophy** (GPA: 3.83), 1997
Graduated with Honors ■ Golden Key National Honor Society ■ Phi Kappa Phi National Honor Society (1997)

ACHIEVEMENT HIGHLIGHTS

INSTRUCTION & TRAINING

- **Earned repeated selection** (three consecutive semesters) for highly competitive graduate instructor/teaching assistant role for the University of Florida's Religious Studies Department.

- **Received "superior" ratings on student evaluations** for outstanding instruction; ranked in the top 5% campuswide among all teaching assistants. (*University of Florida*)

- **Developed a reputation for excellent classroom/lesson preparation,** enthusiastic instruction, and strong grasp of complex subject matter, compelling numerous nonmajors to enroll in a subsequent religion course. (*University of Florida*)

- **Revamped training manuals and developed comprehensive training programs** (across both hard- and soft-skill areas) for entire operations (100+ employees). Incorporated structured objectives, clear expectations, and measurable assessments into all programs, for marked improvements in productivity, accuracy, service, quality, and safety. (*ABC Company*)

- **Developed curriculum and led delivery** of management training in a number of business operations areas, including supply/inventory management, spreadsheet creation, waste tracking, product sourcing, loss control, and supervisory skills. Training efforts key in facilitating bottom-line gains. (*ABC Company*)

- **Innovated simple but effective job aid** that completely reversed operational inefficiencies and profit-margin loss. (*ABC Company*)

- **Rapidly became the "go-to" person for one-on-one computer training** and resolution of technical problems. Instructed management and staff on multiple applications/tools, including Excel and POS systems. (*ABC Company*)

- **Earned in-house credential as "Certified Trainer"** for kitchen operations and led team and one-on-one instruction in a number of F&B operational content areas. (*DEF Company*)

AARON BRADSHAW – Page Two

PROGRAM/OPERATIONS MANAGEMENT

- **Served as key member of startup management team** and currently direct $4.5 million restaurant operations catering to an average of 6,000 guests per week. Hold responsibility for recruiting, hiring, training, and supervising 100+ staff; coordinating bar, kitchen, and dining room functions; administering $300K budget; managing computer systems; overseeing daily, weekly, and month-end reporting; purchasing and sourcing; building strong vendor, customer, and employee relations; and orchestrating special events. (ABC Company)
- **Contributed to operation's strategic planning/marketing initiatives;** recognized by owner for role in growing operation from initial launch to a thriving business despite widespread market downturn within an industry marked by an average 60% failure rate within first two years. Operation presently preparing for two-state expansion. (ABC Company)
- **Became known as a cost-containment strategist,** launching multitiered program that slashed overhead well into the five-figures. Outcomes included reducing overtime by $32K+ annually. (ABC Company)

FACULTY/STUDENT/STAFF/CUSTOMER RELATIONS

- **Represented the university** in an exemplary fashion, interacting extensively with faculty, students, and staff in a professional, diplomatic manner. Praised for going "above and beyond" in performance of daily duties. (University of Florida)
- **Rapidly resolved complaints** to drive customer loyalty and negative experience turnaround. (ABC Company)
- **Conceptualized and executed well-received employee-recognition program** that included creative "Server Bucks" play-money incentive, reinforcing the concept of "catching" employees doing something right. (ABC Company)
- **Provide feedback and coaching to staff** to reward excellent performance and correct weaker areas. (ABC Company)

EMPLOYMENT HISTORY

ABC COMPANY – Delray Beach, FL – **Operations/Training Manager,** 10/1999 – Present (Concurrent with graduate enrollment)

THE UNIVERSITY OF FLORIDA – Gainesville, FL – **Instructor,** Religious Studies, 1/1998 – 5/1999

FALSTAFF COMPANY – Delray Beach, FL – **Certified Trainer,** 8/1997 – 8/1999 (Concurrent with graduate enrollment)

DEF COMPANY – Delray Beach, FL – **Certified Trainer,** 8/1995 – 8/1997 (Concurrent with undergraduate enrollment)

TECHNOLOGY SUMMARY

Proficient in: MS Office XP/2000/97 (Word, Excel, PowerPoint, Access), WordPerfect, Inspiration, Restaurant Magic, Outlook, Windows NT/2000/ME/98, Hard Drive Configuration, HTML, Dreamweaver, Fireworks, Freehand, Flash

ENDORSEMENTS

"Aaron…has exhibited a work ethic and commitment to excellence unsurpassed by anyone in our organization…successfully responsible for controllable budgets in excess of $25K per month. His employees and fellow managers have the utmost respect for him; his record for satisfying the 6,000 guests we serve a week is perfect."
– D. Crawford, **ABC Company Operating Partner**

"…not only an outstanding manager, but a great leader…has maturity and sense of responsibility that are not often found in people twice his age…liked by the entire staff…the best manager that I have ever worked with."
– K. Brochaus, **Falstaff Company**

Resume Strategy: *Aaron's career change goal from restaurant management to higher education administration/support is clearly spelled out in his objective and he articulates his most relevant qualifications up-front in his "Career Profile." Aaron moves his "Education" section to a prominent position on the resume to showcase his multiple degrees and in-progress MA in information and learning technologies. He uses a functional resume format, allowing him to group his most compelling achievements from diverse job positions under skill categories that are relevant to his career change goal (instruction/training, program/operations management, and faculty/student/staff/customer relations). He ends his resume with impressive, convincing testimonial excerpts.*

PATRICIA WEXLER

15 Grotto Drive ■ New City, NY 10956 ■ Home: (914) 123-4567 ■ Cell: (914) 987-6543 ■ E-mail: pat@resumepower.com

CAREER GOAL	**Senior Learning & Development Specialist ■ Diversity Manager**
PROFILE	Dynamic, learner-centered corporate trainer with 15 years of experience designing and delivering employee-development programs proven to produce results, including a more than tripled improvement in customer satisfaction and a 12% increase in annual revenue. Polished, persuasive communicator and expert presenter, with experience leading customized training programs across a wide range of content areas (including diversity, leadership, sales, change management, retail operations, communication, and customer service) for ABC Company and ABC Lenses.

EXPERTISE

- Corporate Training Program Development & Delivery
- Leadership Development
- Diversity Training
- Curriculum Design

- Profitability & Customer Service Improvement
- Adult Learning
- Strategic Alliance & Partnership Building
- Team Building & Supervision
- Community Service Program Management

EXPERIENCE

ABC LENSES – New City, NY
Mission Manager, Gift of Sight, June 2000–Present
General Manager, April 1998–June 2000; July 1995–October 1996
Corporate Trainer, November 1996–March 1998

Selected for increasingly responsible leadership roles, with each assignment including a heavy emphasis on training delivery/employee development. Currently accountable for all aspects of company's multimillion-dollar "Sight Improvement" program (an international philanthropic effort delivering eye exams and glasses to needy families).

Key Contributions (Mission Manager):

- **Built top-performing teams of individuals from diverse backgrounds and skill levels,** training mission/clinic volunteers and associates on both hard and soft skills including processes, accuracy, inventory management, cultural sensitivity, communication, and interpersonal relations.
- **Orchestrated and delivered companywide diversity-training program** for 150 ABC Lenses' associates from all organizational levels. Incorporated sensitivity training (cultural, racial, gender, AIDS, physical challenges) into well-received, eight-hour programs.
- **Facilitated improved sight for 95,000 people in need in underdeveloped nations** through administrative and on-site leadership of Site Improvement missions.
  - □ **Recruited and led 30-member volunteer medical teams** in Sight Improvement missions in Bolivia, Venezuela, Tunisia, Mexico, and Thailand.
  - □ **Heightened program visibility and garnered five-figure program donations** through public-speaking engagements worldwide.
  - □ **Surpassed goal of helping 73,000 people in underdeveloped nations by 124%.**
- **Planned and directed 100+ "Mobile Sight Van" clinics** for U.S. and Canadian children in cities including Chicago, New York, Philadelphia, Phoenix, Houston, Dallas, Baton Rouge, Portland, Toronto, Vancouver, and Cleveland.
  - □ **Coordinated all aspects of mobile eye exam units,** including team selection, training, and supervision; local publicity; fundraising; and transportation/program logistics.
  - □ **Raised $1.7 million in goods and services** by building alliances with charitable partners, enabling ABC Lenses to conduct over 8,500 eye exams and give hundreds of thousands of dollars in free glasses to children with little or no health care across North America.
- **Won the cooperation and support of government officials,** ministers of health, secretaries of state, school-board officials, and the media across North America and abroad.

PATRICIA WEXLER

Page Two

EXPERIENCE

ABC LENSES (continued)
Key Contributions (General Manager):

- **Drove sales increase from $2.1 million to over $3 million annually** (surpassing corporate targets by more than 5% each year), increased profitability from 18% to 34%, and delivered a 350% improvement in customer-satisfaction ratings through comprehensive associate-training program focused on team building, patient care, customer service, and employee satisfaction.
- **Trained and developed company leaders** (general managers, regional managers, lab managers, regional trainers) across the Northeast region.
- **Developed curriculum and conducted companywide training for associates** in various aspects of business such as sales, human resources, diversity, customer service, and quality.
- **Supervised 25 full- and part-time associates** on the retail floor, in the manufacturing laboratory, and in the doctor's office.

Key Contributions (Corporate Trainer):

- **Wrote and personally delivered training programs for 1,300 managers and front-line employees** to fulfill company's aggressive expansion goals of 100 new store openings in one year.
- **Pioneered new ground by introducing holistic training philosophy,** emphasizing the interdependence of various initiatives such as service, efficiency enhancement, and quality toward the fulfillment of corporate goals.
- **Balanced budgets to assure fiscal responsibility of $2 million development programs** in conjunction with creative training methods.

DATABASE DESIGNS – New City, NY
Account Executive, April 1998 to March 1999 (Concurrent with ABC Lenses GM position)
Closed sales with new and existing accounts, led teams in database projects, recruited new employees across multiple divisions (sales executives, software designers/testers, and project managers), contributed to corporate marketing efforts, and managed client relationships. Key Contributions:

- **Achieved 125% of sales goal, closing $1 million in sales in under one year.**
- **Set the stage for profitable expansion** for numerous clients by delivering business-growth-enabling systems to their operations.

ABC COMPANY – New City, NY
Store Manager, 1993 to 1995
Charged with daily management of $7 million entertainment retail operation, including training, development, and supervision of 70 full- and part-time associates. Key Contributions:

- **Delivered $7 million in annual revenue, nearly double the corporate sales target,** resulting in handpicked selection by company executives to launch sales/marketing programs companywide.
- **Selected to recruit, hire, and develop two new store teams** in the Vancouver, BC market.

EDUCATION

BROOKLYN COLLEGE – Brooklyn, NY
BA in Organizational & Industrial Psychology (Minor in **Business**), 1987

TRAINING

- Creative Transitions in Business Today, CREATIVE TRANSITIONS – New City, NY, 2001
- The Oz Principle, Civil Treatment, Diversity Training, Train the Trainer, ABC LENSES – New York, NY, 2000–2001

OF NOTE

- Delivered presentations to corporations and civic organizations including "Situational Leadership," "Five Steps of Leadership," "Diversity Training," and "Civil Treatment."
- Worldwide Ambassador, Lions Club International, 2000–2002

Resume Strategy: *Patricia capitalizes on the fact that corporate training has been a part of her work experience for many years. Her "Profile" outlines her key skills and experience for her new job target, while the "Experience" section concentrates on achievements related to training and development.*

Meet

YOLANDA PERCY

ENTREPRENEUR ◆ MOTIVATIONAL SPEAKER ◆ SALES FORCE ENERGIZER

Yolanda Percy wasn't necessarily envisioning a future of entrepreneurial success when she spent her days collecting soda bottles for pennies at age 5 – she was simply doing whatever she could to support her large family living in the inner-city of Chicago.

But from these humble beginnings and well-intentioned efforts that's exactly what she became – one of the nation's leading African-American women entrepreneurs.

From a very young age, Yolanda discovered that her success depended primarily on her own ability to "make it happen." She learned early how to discover a need and find a solution, how to transform "ambition into action," and how to give back more than you receive. That's what enabled her to overcome decades of prejudice when she was hired as the first African-American cashier at her local supermarket while still in high school. And that's what prompted her to return the scholarship she was awarded after painstakingly saving her minimum-wage earnings.

As an adult it was that same burning desire to succeed and help others that made her a success at one of the nation's largest financial institutions, Citibank. During her 16 years there she moved up the ranks quickly in positions including auditor, accounting supervisor, marketing manager, competitive analyst, strategic planner, and national corporate sales account manager. Yolanda's efforts netted $70+ million for the company – and that was the result of just one account.

While working for Citibank, Yolanda took an active role in the community, serving on the boards of many local and national organizations. She also joined Toastmaster's International, and when her first speech ("Pennies From Heaven") wowed audiences and earned her several prestigious awards, she soon began receiving invitations to speak from numerous organizations. For Yolanda, this was yet another way she could give back to her community and make a difference. Her motivational messages about the importance of having a vision for a better future and winning in

your business and personal life drew standing-room-only crowds.

This success got Yolanda thinking. If she could have such a positive impact on the lives of her fellow Chicagoans, why not expand her efforts to a nationwide scope?

In 1991 she left Citibank to pursue her life's dream of owning a business. Not only did Yolanda launch a successful motivational speaking practice (now in its tenth year), but she also began several lucrative businesses. As the president of Yolanda Percy, Inc., she was the first African-American to sell her distinct line of hats and handbags to Dillard's and Talbots, and she built a business development/acquisitions consulting company with an impressive Fortune 500 clientele including Ameritech, Exxon, Verizon, Aetna, IBM, and Walt Disney.

A sought-after public speaker, Yolanda has been the keynote presenter for many regional and national sales conventions as well as national organizations including the NAACP, the National Association of Female Executives, and the Black Women's Entrepreneur Network. She also has repeatedly appeared as a guest of internationally televised programs including Oprah, The Today Show, The View, Early Morning, and Live With Larry King. Recently, she was selected for the prestigious "Business Women on Tour" and invited as keynote speaker ("If You Can Dream It, You Can Become It") for the African-American Women's Foundation.

Yolanda was honored by recent nominations for two future awards to be presented later this year: the J. Walter "Sterling Award" and the Malvin Tellman "Phoenix Award." Both awards recognize those who have overcome major obstacles to become successful.

Yolanda's formal education includes an MBA from Harvard and a B.S. in business administration from George Washington University. Her motivational messages to corporate sales organizations have fueled record-setting product launches for Verizon ($280 million), IBM ($579 million), and Ameritech ($159 million), among many others. To schedule a speaking engagement, contact Yolanda Percy, Inc. at (800) 555-5555.

Resume Strategy: *Yolanda uses a biographical, brochure-style resume to market her motivational speaking services. Her compelling story explains her background, qualifications, and speaking results. Most resumes should not include a personal photo, but it's appropriate for fields like public speaking.*

QA CONSULTANT TO TECHNICAL/SOFTWARE TRAINING & DEVELOPMENT MANAGER

José R. Cantos	47 River Walk Dr. San Antonio, TX 79082	Home: 210-555-5555 Office: 210-555-5556	jose@resumepower.com

Career Goal
- Technical / Software Training & Development Manager
- Organizational Development Manager

Profile

Accomplished manager with extensive experience leading results-driven training, project management, business/systems analysis, organizational development, quality assurance, and Big 5 consulting engagement initiatives across diverse industries – from leading financial services to Fortune 500 retail operations. Impressive track record choreographing process and quality-improvement efforts resulting in measurable increases in efficiency, customer satisfaction, productivity, and bottom-line performance.

Proven ability to engineer enhanced workflow and standardize effective project management tools and systems. Respected leader, regarded as a key advisor and solution-finder by clients and executives, with demonstrated success guiding top-performing teams. Solidly credentialed – Columbia MBA/Education BS and certified quality analyst.

Expertise

- Continuous Quality/Process Improvement
- Curriculum Development & Training
- Strategic Planning
- Team Building & Leadership
- Project Management (Tools, Planning, Scheduling & Implementation)
- Quality Assurance (QA)
- Disaster Recovery

- Competency Models
- Efficiency & Productivity Enhancement
- Relationship Management (Customers/Vendors)
- Contract Negotiations
- Organizational Development
- Process Re-engineering
- Creative Problem Solving

Experience

THE BOEING COMPANY – San Antonio, TX

Quality Assurance Consultant, 2000 to present

Recruited to lead quality assurance efforts for high-profile project for the U.S. Air Force. Develop quality assurance strategy, coordinate the activities of five QA teams assigned to separate systems modules, identify and mitigate risks with potential to jeopardize successful outcomes, and analyze system and business requirements to ensure quality deliverables meeting all client expectations. *Key Accomplishments:*

- **Developed curriculum for companywide training program and instructed users** in quality assurance methods and systems, resulting in a shared, consistent vision of QA processes by other QA consultants and project managers.

- **Completed top-to-bottom analysis of system requirements and functionality for six different system applications** to build a comprehensive QA strategy for major integration effort of all systems into one complex, n-tiered system for client's operations.

- **Delivered client's first-ever detailed, systemwide strategy** addressing often conflicting requirements, business rules, and functionalities of each subsystem, enabling timely, high-quality delivery of final product.

- **Overcame tactical and operational obstacles to unite fractionalized departments,** further business goals, and satisfy competing and/or complex requirements involving legal agreements, policy systems, and all interfaces.

- **Facilitated delivery of new system,** scheduled for deployment in September 2003, which is expected to provide client with critical information to accurately track crucial equipment, missile, and aircraft functionality.

QA CONSULTANT TO TECHNICAL/SOFTWARE
TRAINING & DEVELOPMENT MANAGER (CONT.)

José R. Cantos	Home: 210-555-5555 Office: 210-555-5556	Resume	Page Two

Experience

KPMG CONSULTING, INC. – New York, NY

Program Manager (Testing Practice), 1998 to 2000

Supervised 12-member software quality assurance team, including two team leaders. Charged with project management of major initiatives to define software QA methodology requirements and implement competency model within testing practice. Participated in corporate knowledge-management initiative. *Key Accomplishments:*

- **Provided management support to testing team-leads** on team development, leadership, and solution-based project management. Outcomes included improved team member satisfaction, resource planning, and upward communication.
- **Instilled a deeper understanding of QA process implementation** and provided team with methods to encourage much earlier involvement in the development life cycle.
- **Implemented test-plan improvements** that resulted in more thorough and well-researched testing from early development stage to final delivery.

TECHNO SERVICES, INC. – New York, NY

Senior Client Consultant, 1997 to 1998; **Senior Business Analyst,** 1992 to 1997

Managed client projects and daily customer interaction. Configured software to conform to business rules and specialized needs for customized applications. *Key Accomplishments:*

- **Developed multiple workflow modules** for Fortune 500 retailer's new automated customer service call-center application. Realized five-figure cost savings for client.
- **Supported team members** in learning company processes and mastering technical and project-time-management tools.
- **Developed training courses and materials** and delivered well-received classroom and individualized software instruction to clients.
- **Reduced software defects 30%** through deployment of automated testing tools.

NEW YORK LIFE – New York, NY

Systems Officer / Trainer / Business Systems Analyst / Product Manager, 1988 to 1992

Managed training program development, workflow re-engineering efforts, user-acceptance testing, and data processing planning sessions. Developed curriculum and delivered highly rated software training classes for corporate users. **Key Accomplishments:**

- **Created and delivered new training program** for over 100 claims processing system users in three-month timeframe.
- **Integrally involved in design of new policy sales, syndication, and operations workflow processes** to maximize new system benefits.
- **Negotiated favorable service-level agreements,** enabling firm to compete in the marketplace through its ability to offer value-added claims-by-phone and online services.

Early Career

FIRST UNION BANK – New York, NY
Senior Systems Analyst, 1985 to 1987

ALLSTATE INSURANCE – New York, NY
Systems Analyst, 1981 to 1985

Education

COLUMBIA UNIVERSITY – New York, NY

MBA – Executive MBA Program – **Marketing Major, MIS Minor**

BS – Education, Concentration in Political Science and Economics

Resume Strategy: José's new career goal is printed as a large banner across the top of the page, immediately positioning him for a career change. His "Experience" section focuses on accomplishments that are related to education/training, demonstrating how he met the training needs of his previous employers in his capacity as QA manager.

Dina Kaye

14 Glendale Street
New Hyde Park, NY 11040

Phone: 516-123-4567
Cellular: 516-987-6543

dina@resumepower.com

CAREER GOAL: University Program Administrator

Profile

Dynamic administrator with over five years of university experience, including principal investigator for an 18-month research study and coordinator of a women's center. In-depth knowledge of violence against women and wellness issues. Strongly committed to team building, staff development, and community outreach. Experienced in research methods, grant funding, and workshop presentations. Demonstrated success mentoring college students and working collaboratively with staff, faculty, and administrators. **Expertise in:**

- Program Development and Management
- Project Management
- Team Building & Consensus Building
- Building Partnerships/Coalitions
- Budget/Grant Management
- Visionary Leadership
- Creative Problem Solving
- Public Speaking/Facilitation
- Persuasive Communication
- Strategic Planning

Education

HOFSTRA UNIVERSITY — Hempstead, NY
MA, Interdisciplinary Studies – Women's Studies & Sociology (GPA: 3.9), June 2000
- Thesis: Student Associations Making a Difference: A Guide for Peer Advocacy Programs

NEW YORK UNIVERSITY — New York, NY
BA, Psychology (Dean's List, 1996 to 1997), May 1997
- Assistant, Alcohol and Other Drug Abuse Prevention Program, January to December 1995

Experience

WOMEN'S COALITION INTERNATIONAL — Hempstead, NY
Project Administrator, August 2000 to May 2001

Streamlined and managed headquarters' office operations, including $100,000 office-operations grant and supervision of administrative staff, interns, and consultants. Developed and monitored project grant budgets totaling $150,000 and issued reports to funding authorities. Contributions:

- Collaborated with South Africa Program coordinator in creating strategy to accomplish goal of violence-against-women human rights program success.
- Contributed to long-range strategic plan, including board formation and development, diversifying funding sources and increasing international members' participation in newsletter.
- Networked with other human rights organizations and attended events.
- Handled financial affairs including international money transfers, bank accounts reconciliation, accounts receivables/payables, federal taxes, and payroll.

HOFSTRA UNIVERSITY — Hempstead, NY
Graduate Teaching Assistantship, September 1998 to June 2000

Served as interim coordinator of the Women's Center with full accountability for managing the center, overseeing programming and evaluating events, providing crisis intervention and referrals, and recruiting, hiring, and training interns/work-study students and volunteers. Contributions:

- Implemented a monthly educational program entitled "Women Who Dared," which enhanced community understanding of women's contributions throughout history.
- Created and implemented an evaluation procedure for the center's programs that increased attendance and recommendations for future events.
- Increased awareness of Women's Center services among Greek community while advising them on ways to improve their dating, health, alcohol, and sexual-assault programs.
- Advocated for financial and institutional support for four cultural centers through focused outreach and education.
- Conducted universitywide needs assessments regarding students' co-curricular involvement. Developed marketing plan that increased student participation rate by 40%.
- Represented department on campus' Diversity, Community Health, and Assessment Initiatives.

Dina Kaye

Experience
(continued)

LONG ISLAND UNIVERSITY (LIU) — Long Island, NY

Principal Investigator, January 1997 to July 1998

Served as lead investigator for 18-month research study entitled "Changing Student and Faculty Attitudes Toward Rape." Authored Institutional Review Board application and supervised ongoing compliance. Selected, trained, and coordinated a team of ten research assistants. Contributions:

- Led investigation that involved 1,300 randomly selected students according to study's protocols.
- Created a 15-minute video of popular movie segments to test hypothesis that men may be more visually oriented than female participants.
- Delivered presentations of findings to numerous venues, including professional conferences.
- Earned First Place in Social Sciences Category at Student Research Competition, 1998.
- Study published in LIU Academic Affairs Digest, LIU, September 1998.

Program Coordinator, Women's Resource Center, January 1996 to May 1997

Responsible for center's sexual assault prevention programming. Initiated presentations of "Living without Fear," a 28-minute theater piece about rape, with the Hempstead Repertory Company. Arranged and helped facilitate information sessions after the performances. Contributions:

- Identified and compiled database of community and university partners supportive of the center's sexual-assault prevention efforts; successfully advocated with university administration to avert budget decrease.
- Facilitated focus groups regarding safety precautions vis-à-vis sexual-assault incidents.
- Co-chaired Women's Studies Student Association and helped organize Women's Film Festival.
- Served on the President's Commission on the Status of Women Committee, 1996 to 1998.

HEMPSTEAD COUNTY HIGHWAY PATROL — Hempstead, NY

Plainclothes Auto Theft Investigator, September 1992 to April 1994
Felony Investigator, September 1991 to August 1992
State Traffic Officer, June 1988 to August 1991

Progressed through ranks of Highway Patrol based on superior performance and dedication. Performed investigative, service and enforcement functions to ensure public safety. Wrote numerous search warrants; served as liaison with district and city attorneys' offices.

Public Speaking

- Long Island University Women's Leadership Conference, speaker, April 2000
- Coalition for Cross-Cultural Outreach Conference, planning committee member, April 2000
- Violence Prevention Conference: Creating Safe Learning Environments, speaker, July 1999
- Traumatic Stress Studies Conference, participant, Hempstead, NY, November 1998
- Why Women Need Men to Join Violence Prevention Efforts, speaker, October 1998
- Running a Research Study, speaker, September 1998
- Women's Studies Association Conference, speaker, Hempstead, NY, April 1998
- "Living without Fear," LIU Women's Center, facilitator, March and November 1997
- "Why Mainstreaming Gender Issues is Important," LIU Women's Studies Student Association, facilitator, March 1996
- Presented several wellness workshops to Freshmen Orientation Classes, LIU, 1995
- "Alternatives to Drinking in a College Community," LIU, facilitator, October 1995

Phone: 516-123-4567 ▪ Cellular: 516-987-6543 ▪ dina@resumepower.com

Resume Strategy: *Dina's resume begins with her goal clearly announced in the title. Her profile emphasizes her background in university settings and includes a two-column list of her most relevant expertise for her job goal in university program administration. Because she is targeting the higher education sector, Dina places her "Education" section high on the resume to highlight her two degrees. Her "Experience" section showcases her ability to lead personnel, projects, and financials. Although her earlier career in law enforcement is impressive, Dina does not waste too much space describing this aspect of her professional background since it is less relevant to her career goal than her university experience. She ends the resume with an impressive list of her presentations at various university gatherings.*

12
Healthcare/Medical

REAL ESTATE AGENT TO HEALTH CARE—DRUG SAFETY, CASE MANAGEMENT, OR QUALITY CONTROL

Darla Fairfield, BSN, RN

Home: 732-721-8380 □ Cell: 850-555-5555
12 5th Ave. □ Pensacola, FL 32526 □ darla@resumepower.com

Objective

Seeking to leverage nursing training and experience in a drug-safety, case-management, or quality-control position.

Profile

Highly self-motivated, enthusiastic RN with strong organizational, case management, and quality improvement skills and a reputation for providing excellent patient care. Special ability to calm and relax patients, especially during stressful situations. Known as a patient advocate and team player; believe in empowering patients by listening carefully to their needs and rendering services to enhance quality of life. Versatile service provider, with training in various aspects of healthcare and ability to work in a fast-paced environment.

Dynamic interpersonal and communication skills – talent for building solid relationships with patients, family members, physicians, support staff, and other members of the healthcare community. Known for creative problem solving, team-player mentality, and goal-surpassing results. Internationally traveled, and culturally astute. Computer literate (WordPerfect, MS Word, and Internet programs).

Education & Credentials

BSN – Florida State University School of Nursing – Tallahassee, FL, 1996
BA in Political Science – Florida State University – Tallahassee, FL, 1989

Licensed Registered Professional Nurse, State of Florida, 1996
□ CPR, IV, and Phlebotomy Certified

RN Refresher Training

University of West Florida – Pensacola, FL, May to June 2002
□ *140 contact hours.* Review of pharmacology, dosages, and distribution.

Pensacola Regional Med Center – Pensacola, FL, August to December 2000
□ *390 clinical hours.* Assigned to Medical-Surgical and Special Oncology units. Provided direct patient care and developed physical-assessment skills.

Florida State University, Orange County Medical Center – Tallahassee, FL, May to June 1998
□ *140 contact hours.* Course topics included theoretical and clinical practices, physical assessment, common IV and drug therapy, and medical-surgical nursing. Delivered direct patient care, administered meds, and charted on GI/GU Unit.

Clinical Experience

"Darla is a positive asset to any staff and would be a loyal and dedicated employee, always willing to go the extra mile for her co-workers and patients."

– June Frank, BSN, RNC, Orange County Medical Center

ORANGE COUNTY MEDICAL CENTER – 334-bed hospital – Tallahassee, FL
Psychiatric Nurse Intern, Psychiatric Ward, 1996

Chosen for highly selective 21-week internship, with responsibility for providing one-on-one therapeutic communication with patients (up to 16 daily), promoting patients' interest and participation in reality, and fostering behavior contributing to integrated functioning. Interacted extensively with doctors, occupational therapists, and staff nurses as an active participant in daily staff meetings to discuss patient needs and ensure continuity and consistency of quality care. Held accountability for treatment of disorders ranging from anxiety to schizophrenia, substance abuse, and eating disorders. **Key Accomplishments:**

□ **Commended for tireless work ethic,** ability to manage a challenging and high-volume caseload, and uncompromising commitment to compassionate, quality care. Offered full-time position at conclusion of internship.

□ **Responded to numerous crises,** volatile situations, and violent outbreaks, earning the respect of physicians and co-workers for calm, levelheaded, and quick thinking to restore the safety and security of patients and staff.

□ **Leveraged expert communication skills** as a therapeutic tool to alleviate patient stress/anxiety and as a strategy for behavior change with clients.

Darla Fairfield, BSN, RN *Available for Relocation and Extensive Travel* **Page Two**

Clinical Experience (continued)	VISITING NURSE SERVICE OF FLORIDA – Home healthcare service – Tallahassee, FL

Clinical Experience (continued)

VISITING NURSE SERVICE OF FLORIDA – Home healthcare service – Tallahassee, FL

Nursing Assistant/Office Assistant, 1995

Aided home-care nurses by writing physical assessment reports based on clinical evaluations to facilitate continued client care and insurance coverage. **Key Accomplishments:**

- ☐ **Jointly resolved significant work backlog,** helping to bring department up to date on vast amounts of required paperwork and records.
- ☐ **Earned a reputation for "can-do" attitude** and creative problem-solving skills.

ADDITIONAL CLINICAL ASSIGNMENTS (Tallahassee, FL), 1994 to 1996

- ☐ County Hospital – Labor and Delivery
- ☐ University Hospital – Pediatric Oncology/Medical-Surgical
- ☐ Veteran's Administration Medical Center – Medical-Surgical Nursing
- ☐ Tallahassee Community Health Center – Home Health Care

Additional Experience

COLDWELL BANKER – Pensacola, FL; Melbourne, Australia
International residential and commercial real estate operation

Licensed Real Estate Agent, 1989 to Present (part-time)

Generate listings, show properties, and close residential home sales (from the low six figures to half a million dollars per transaction), representing both buyers and sellers. Research and pinpoint prime candidates for sales pitches/presentations and develop strategies to address buyer and seller needs (win-win approach). **Key Accomplishments:**

- ☐ **Consistently achieved peak sales production,** earning top three (out of 15) team sales volume rankings for seven consecutive years.
- ☐ **Recognized for superior performance; awarded "Top Sales Team Member of the Year"** in 1995 ($4M in sales), 1997 ($4.5M in sales), and 2000 ($6M in sales).
- ☐ **Regularly achieved the most leads, largest number of listings, and highest sales** of all part-time realtors in the office, averaging **$500K+ per month.**
- ☐ **Established a strong referral network and quality pipeline,** building annual sales to a peak level of **$6 million.**
- ☐ **Repeatedly demonstrated the ability to close tough sales.** Overcame obstacles presented by anxious first-time buyers and problematic inventory often deemed "unsellable."

"I was very impressed by Darla's clinical abilities...has excellent physical assessment skills, interacts well with the members of the healthcare team, and made sound clinical decisions."

– Renda White, RN, MS, CS, CCRN, Visiting Nurse Service of Florida

OFFICE RENTALS – *Office furniture rental firm serving small businesses* – Melbourne, Australia

Co-Owner/Office Manager/Bookkeeper, 1997 to 2000

Oversaw daily office operations (e.g., accounts payable/receivable, customer service, payroll, rental agreements/reservations), supervised 12-member staff, and held accountability for generating new and repeat business. **Key Accomplishments:**

- ☐ **Drove a $56K annual sales increase** through development of "thank-you pack" rewarding business referrals that catapulted monthly rentals by **150% to 500%.**
- ☐ **Developed strong relationships/rapport** with business owners through in-person visits and extensive telephone contact.

JOHNSON & McCART – *Product liability/personal injury law firm* – Tallahassee, FL

Paralegal to Managing Partners, 1989 to 1993

Verified validity of and opened new case files, conducted in-depth legal research, prepared preliminary proceedings, and assisted with trial preparation.

Resume Strategy: *Darla spells out her career goal at the top of her resume, and she devotes the entire first page to her nursing experience and training since they are most relevant to her professional goal of returning to the health care field. Although Darla is currently employed as a real estate agent, she de-emphasizes this by reordering her career history and moving all of her jobs unrelated to health care to the second page under an "Additional Experience" heading.*

Elizabeth Scruggs

15 Elm Road ■ Palm Springs, CA 92262 ■ (760) 123-4567 ■ elizabeth@resumepower.com

CAREER TARGET: CHILD LIFE SPECIALIST

Dedicated child development professional with diverse experience working with a wide range of youth populations. Deeply committed to enriching the lives of others; recognized for sensitivity to the needs of children and for ability to effectively balance professionalism with empathy. Work well under pressure and deadlines. Qualifications include excellent program leadership and public relations skills, administrative experience, and comprehensive knowledge of social services. Career history includes experience and record of success in community relations and public speaking endeavors. Deliver effective public presentations in both large and small group settings, serving as a highly visible organizational advocate.

SKILL AREAS

- Public Speaking & Presentations
- Behavior Modification Strategies
- Program Planning/Development
- Community Services & Resources

- Social & Emotional Development
- Community Outreach
- Youth Advocacy
- New Program Implementation
- Special Events/Activity Coordination

- Group Facilitation
- Crisis Intervention
- Child/Family-Centered Care
- Socioeconomic & Psychosocial Issues

PROFESSIONAL EXPERIENCE

PALM SPRINGS HOSPITAL; CALIFORNIA CHILDREN'S HOSPITAL – Palm Springs, CA   1999 – Present
Child Life Volunteer
Currently volunteer directly under a child life specialist at Palm Springs Hospital's regional referral center, educating the public about patients with extreme medical challenges. Work with pediatric patients between ages one and ten in coping with trauma of medical treatment through building positive psychosocial skills. Provide support to patients' families.

- Developed knowledge base in field of child life and understanding of inner workings within hospital environment.
- Completed 118 hours at California Children's Hospital's pediatric unit, assisting a child life specialist, providing comprehensive support, and showing compassion for patients and their families.

TABERNACLE CHURCH – Palm Springs, CA   2001 – Present
Children Liturgist / Second-Grade Faith Formation Teacher
Perform instructional duties in two concurrent volunteer positions. Approached staff with idea of implementing weekly religious program for children ages four to seven during mass on Sundays; received overwhelming endorsement to develop and conduct program as children's liturgist. As a teacher, prepare and present religious lessons to 15 second-grade students for 3.5 hours per week while also organizing special events and preparing students for major sacraments.

- Implemented and grew well-received Sunday program from 12 to an average of 20 children; instituted previously nonexistent discipline policy and in the process of finalizing and publishing accompanying discipline handbook.
- Maintained excellent classroom control with second-grade students and developed creative approach in illustrating significance of important religious events, including stage production of Christmas nativity.

PALM SPRINGS YOUTH ADVOCATE PROGRAM – Palm Springs, CA   1998 – 1999
Youth Advocate
Recruited to work in social service agency providing training and mentoring for disadvantaged and emotionally disturbed children, as well as support for their families. Emphasized one-on-one approach with children and focused on daily activities critical to future career success, including workplace punctuality, use of public transportation system, proper hygiene, importance of school achievement, and other work- and social-related issues. Challenged to "get through" to children (despite frequent absence of parental involvement) and balanced compassion with authority.

- Successfully reached students who had built up distrust for adult figures; helped one child graduate from high school and earned trust from another child classified as "extremely difficult."
- Earned reputation as an effective, dependable child advocate.

Elizabeth Scruggs – Page Two

PROFESSIONAL EXPERIENCE (continued)

ADVANCED INDUSTRIAL SYSTEMS – Palm Springs, CA   2001 – Present
Administrative Assistant, Accounting & Estimating
Promoted to provide administrative support to office manager and president of company in accounting and estimating functions, with full responsibility for ensuring smooth day-to-day operations and expediting resolution of problems.
- Initiated several new projects that succeeded in improving administrative processes and productivity.
- Earned two promotions following successful fulfillment of duties and recognition for effort and performance.

NATIONAL CENTER FOR MISSING CHILDREN – Palm Springs, CA   1999
Hotline Operator
ST. CHRISTOPHER'S SCHOOL – Palm Springs, CA   1998 – 1999
Fourth-Grade CCD Teacher
Served in two short-term positions requiring strong communication and problem-solving skills applied to uniquely different situations. As CCD teacher, taught fourth-grade students basic tenets and principles of religion; as hotline operator, answered national/international hotline, compiled in-depth information concerning family background and circumstances surrounding disappearances, and classified cases according to severity.
- Demonstrated ability to learn system rapidly and communicate effectively with highly emotional people (operator).
- Instituted uniform discipline policy that encouraged parental involvement and ensured classroom order (teacher).

PALM SPRINGS/COSTA MESA POLICE DEPARTMENTS – Costa Mesa/Palm Springs, CA   1996 – 1998
Police Dispatcher; 911 Dispatcher
Held concurrent positions for two local law enforcement agencies; received incoming emergency calls and dispatched police, rescue, and fire teams as needed in response to emergency situations. Communicated with public through emergency phone lines and gathered detailed information regarding each incident.
- Received letter of recognition from detective for outstanding performance during emergency situation.
- Earned Certificate of Appreciation for outstanding work within the community (1997).
- Maintained composure and employed calm, patient attitude to ease caller concerns and facilitate rapid responses.

EDUCATION & CREDENTIALS

PALM SPRINGS COLLEGE – Palm Springs, CA
BA in Criminal Justice, 1998

UNIVERSITY OF CALIFORNIA – Berkeley, CA
Graduate-Level Child Development Course, 2002

Professional Training Coursework:
- "Excel 2" – Apple Learning Center, Palm Springs, CA (2001)
- "Basic Communications Officer" – International Communications Academy, Palm Springs, CA (1997)
- "Basic Emergency Medical Dispatcher International" – ABC Institute, Palm Springs, CA (1997)

Affiliations: Associate Member, Child Life Council / Member, California Association of Child Life Professionals (CACLP)

Computers: MS Office Suite: Word, Excel, Access, PowerPoint

Language Skills: Basic fluency in American Sign Language (ASL)

Resume Strategy: *Because her volunteer experience is highly relevant to her career goal, Elizabeth treats these positions just as she would paid jobs, describing her duties and detailing her primary contributions. Elizabeth's opening profile communicates her solid background serving youth populations and her "Skill Areas" section lists expertise of value to employers in her targeted field.*

Catherine Hayes

Phone: (609) 123-4567 ▪ Pager: (609) 987-6543 ▪ 4848 Cider Lane ▪ Princeton, NJ 08850

HEALTHCARE INDUSTRY PROFESSIONAL

Dedicated healthcare professional with a reputation for providing excellent patient care. Special ability to calm and relax patients, especially during stressful situations. Versatile service provider, with training in various aspects of healthcare, including technical and direct care. Adept at working in a fast-paced environment and under pressure. Detail-oriented and a resourceful problem solver.

EDUCATION & TRAINING

PRINCETON UNIVERSITY, Princeton, NJ
Registered Nurse program, leading toward associate's degree, 1998 to present

- Courses completed: Nursing Process I and II, Pharmacology, Anatomy
- Completed ten hours a week in clinical training at GHI Medical Facility and Princeton Town Nursing Home

Certification: American Heart Association certified in Child CPR and Adult CPR, 5/99

Specialized Training:

- Administering medication (oral and injection)
- Taking blood pressure
- Positioning / moving immobile patients
- Reading and interpreting monitors

QUEENS COLLEGE, Flushing, NY
B.A. in Physician's Assistant program, 82 credits earned

ADVANCED TRAINING CENTER, Jackson Heights, NY
Nurse's Aide training program, Completed five-week intensive course, 1996

EMPLOYMENT

HOME DEPOT, Princeton, NJ   **Associate in Gardening,** 1999 to present
DPI CONTRACTORS, Princeton, NJ   **Laborer / Assistant,** 1995 to 1998
REHAB GERIATRIC CENTER, Princeton, NJ **Patient Aide / Dietary Aide,** 1996
BUG-AWAY, INC., Astoria, NY   **Exterminator,** 1992 to 1993

COMMUNITY SERVICE

CITY KIDS FOUNDATION, Princeton, NJ   **Volunteer,** 1989 to present
- Assist organization that shows city children the country life.

Resume Strategy: *Catherine's strongest credentials are her education and training, so she leads the resume with and devotes the most space to this section. Her earlier position in a geriatric center is also mentioned in the profile to help emphasize her experience working with patients.*

13
Skilled Trades

Kandar Aiden

P.O. Box 726
Kent, WA 98064
(253) 123 4567
kan@resumepower.com

Key Skills

- Interior & Commercial Design
- Floor Plans/Layout
- Space Planning
- Furnishing & Fabric Selection
- Color/Texture Theory
- Merchandising Strategies
- Fixture Design
- Product Assortment Planning

Training

- Licensed Aesthetician (1984)
- Interior Design Coursework (Fort Dodge, IA)
- Pending Real Estate License (anticipated completion: 8/02)

Of Note

Repeatedly retained by colleagues and friends to redesign residential living spaces.

Basic conversational Spanish skills.

CAREER OBJECTIVE:

INTERIOR DESIGNER / DESIGN CONSULTANT / MERCHANDISER

Talented designer/merchandiser with proven success creating beautiful, high-impact designs for residential, commercial, and retail spaces. Seeking to leverage strong skill set and hands-on experience in interior design, lighting, color, texture, floor-plan/store layout, traffic flow, and product sourcing/selection/mix to achieve career shift enabling full-time focus on these demonstrated strengths.

Adept in consulting with clients to create memorable, custom designs meeting divergent tastes/goals. Track record of fueling six-figure sales directly attributable to design/merchandising transformations. Expert customer service, sales, and interpersonal skills; able to build strong, sustainable client relationships and win lucrative repeat/referral business.

Accomplishment Highlights

- **Re-designed long-neglected retail nursery,** transforming five-acre operation to a Tuscan-style showplace within aggressive timeframe and restricted budget. **Results:** Outperformed revenue goals every month to achieve six-figure surge in profits (from $1.2M to **$1.5M**) within first year. Captured high-net-worth clientele, a completely new client base for 24-year-old operation. Expanded average duration of customer visits from ten minutes to over one hour – a major contributing factor to increased sales. (*Lakeside*)

- **Defined display areas, improved "shopability," and expanded product line** to include upscale gift items. **Results:** Built profitable new revenue stream, growing giftware/hard-goods sales from zero to **$90K** within six months. (*Lakeside*)

- **Innovated interior designs, showroom displays, and statuary presentations** for maximum visual and sales impact. **Results:** Adept merchandising and personalized client consultation drove a company record-setting **60% increase** in statuary sales (**$400K** – highest among all stores in chain). Hand-selected by owner to subsequently implement design/merchandising schemes across all 13 locations. (*Bountiful*)

- **Designed entire office for maximum efficiency, customer appeal/comfort, and ergonomics.** Additionally designed all corporate sales collateral. **Results:** Won rave reviews on commercial interior design that resounded effectively with upscale-area clientele. Extended corporate image through creation of professional, polished, printed materials. (*HPM*)

- **Engaged by individual clients from diverse backgrounds** to provide complete image makeovers. Additionally conducted well-attended seminars on color, makeup, and wardrobe coordination/selection. **Results:** Successfully completed hundreds of makeovers and appeared as local TV talk-show guest as subject-matter expert. (*Image Consultant*)

Career History

LAKESIDE NURSERY – Kent, WA – *Retail plant nursery*
Co-owner / Merchandise Designer, 2000 – 2002

BOUNTIFUL GARDEN CENTER – Kent, WA – *Corporate retail nursery with chain of 13 stores*
Buyer / Merchandiser, 1999 – 2000

COLONIAL MACHINE CORP. (CMC) – Kent, WA – *Computerized production machine shop*
Co-Owner / Interior Designer, 1985 – 1999

Image Consultant – Kent, WA – 1984 – 1990 – *Wardrobe/makeup/color consulting*

Resume Strategy: *Kandar uses a creative resume design, with a distinctive blue bar on the left and a gray margin containing key information, in keeping with his creative career goal. Although Kandar co-owns a nursery, his resume emphasizes design experience throughout. By listing his main qualifications in an "Accomplishments Highlights" section, Kandar draws out the relevant experiences from each of his positions. He uses an "Of Note" section to state that he is sought after to help with residential interior design projects.*

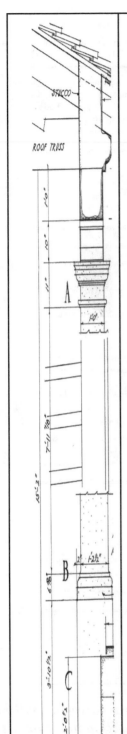

MINDY LONGO

15 Spring Ave. ◆ Newark, NJ 08512 ◆ 609.123.4567 ◆ mindy@resumepower.com

CAREER GOAL: ARCHITECTURAL INTERN / SET DESIGNER

Princeton University architecture graduate seeking entry-level/intern position to prove strong creative talents, architectural aptitude, and tireless work ethic. Offer experience as an intern architect and set designer, with demonstrated skills fusing project requirements, research, design concepts, and practical concerns (e.g., mobility, interchangeability, space/budget limitations) into imaginative yet realistic building and set designs. CAD proficient, fast learner, and dynamic communicator with reputation for quality work and innovative, cost-efficient solution delivery.

EDUCATION & TRAINING

PRINCETON UNIVERSITY – Princeton, NJ – **BA in Architecture/Ceramics Minor,** 1998 (GPA: 3.2)
Senior Thesis Project: Completed urban-renewal design project expanding French Quarter to encompass abandoned warehouse district. Incorporated European influences in a progressive, transformative waterfront renewal plan preserving architectural integrity/existing structures.

Coursework Highlights:

Architectural Design ◆ Structures ◆ Technology ◆ Design History & Theory ◆ Landscape & Urban Design ◆ Professional Concerns ◆ Visual Communication ◆ Preservation Studies

NJ COLLEGE OF ART – Cranbury, NJ – **Computer Graphics,** 1998 – 2000
Courses in Adobe Illustrator, Photoshop, After Effects, Macromedia Director, Flash, Dreamweaver

NEWARK COMMUNITY COLLEGE – Newark, NJ – **AutoCAD Training,** 1994

INTERNSHIPS

ABC PLAYHOUSE – Princeton, NJ – **Set Designer,** 1997
Designed, built, and painted creative, durable stage sets that maximized space and enhanced summer-theater productions/audience experience. Furnished sets, engineered pulley systems to execute special effects, and ensured cast members' safety through sound construction techniques.

◆ Met aggressive deadlines in the set design/construction/rendering for all productions.

◆ Collaborated extensively with director and cast to incorporate ideas into creative and functional design concepts. Overcame challenges presented by limited financial/physical resources through unique, multilevel designs that amplified small space while remaining within modest budgets.

◆ Recognized for superior set design in critical reviews published statewide.

NEW JERSEY PARK SERVICE – Princeton, NJ – **Intern Architect,** 1994
Selected by Park Service for highly competitive internship. Assisted senior architects/Park Service administrators in building-, space-, and landscape-design projects. Attended architectural board meetings and interfaced with designers from leading New Jersey-area firms.

◆ Reviewed and evaluated vignettes and architectural renderings for park welcome centers, amphitheaters, and snack shops, recommending best alternatives.

◆ Contributed to high-profile space- and landscape-design project for White House inaugural parade. Innovated design alternatives to accommodate project mandates of mobility and flexibility.

CURRENT EMPLOYMENT

NEW JERSEY ART CENTER – Princeton, NJ – **Account Executive,** 2000 – Present
Close sales of original art and educate customers about crafting traditions/processes.

Resume Strategy: *A distinctive architecture-related graphic along the left margin separates Mindy's resume from the crowd. She includes a clear career goal, followed by a summary of her main credentials. Her education is her strongest qualification, so "Education" precedes experience. She provides detail of her related internships in an "Internships" section, while her current employment is placed at the end of the resume.*

DISTRICT TRAINER, LOSS PREVENTION TO ENTRY-LEVEL ARCHITECT

Michael Scott

15 Flagstaff Way ■ Richmond, Virginia 23222
(804) 123-4567 ■ E-mail: michael@resumepower.com

Self-motivated professional seeking to build upon educational foundation and practical experience within the architectural field. Recognized for discipline, attention to detail, and outstanding problem-solving and follow-up skills. Team leader, able to prioritize, manage, and complete multiple projects within time and budget constraints. Demonstrated willingness to devote extra time to achieve the highest level of quality.

Architectural / Technical Skills

- ✓ **Drafting** (pencil & technical pens)
- ✓ **Freehand**
- ✓ **Color Rendering**
- ✓ **Model Building**
- ✓ **Spatial Planning**
- ✓ **Drawing Perspectives**
- ✓ **DataCAD** (working knowledge)
- ✓ **AutoCAD 14** (basic knowledge)
- ✓ **MS Word / MS Excel**
- ✓ **Windows NT / 2000**

Accomplishments

✓ As **draftsperson** for Action Research, manually drafted drawings for facilities/site planning, renovations, and topographic surveys of industrial and commercial use:
- Prepared all preliminary design sketches and perspectives for two (now completed) large-scale industrial/commercial buildings.
- Managed several projects (approximately 4-10 at one time); worked on plans, elevations, and structural details for heavy industrial equipment.

✓ Undergraduate projects:
- Worked with **Habitat for Humanity,** collaborating with architects in developing low-cost, low-maintenance, and energy-efficient dwellings for low-income individuals. Gained experience dealing with architects, other professionals, and residents.
- Piers in Manhattan: **"Living on the Edge."** Developed architectural/urban planning program; designed school to teach displaced homeless people how to build their homes on the pier.

✓ During tenure at ABC Retail Store, demonstrated initiative, leadership, and problem-solving skills:
- While managing **Top 20 Store,** achieved an average 23% sales increase annually for 3 years; reduced shrink between .16 and .26; and named **Manager of the Year** (1999) for the region.

Professional Experience

ABC RETAIL STORE, Richmond, Virginia   12/93 – Present

District Trainer, Loss Prevention (*10/98 – Present*)
Store Manager (*4/96 – 10/98*)
Sales Associate (*12/93 – 4/96*)

ACTION RESEARCH CORPORATION, Richmond, Virginia   Summer 1992, 1993

Draftsperson - Facilities Department (*co-op program*)

Education

RICHMOND INSTITUTE OF TECHNOLOGY, Richmond, Virginia

Bachelor of Architecture, 1995 (*Worked 20–30 hours a week while maintaining a full course load*)
Associate of Architectural Engineering Technology, 1992

Resume Strategy: *As Michael is looking to return to his architectural career, he outlines his goal and key qualifications in his summary section. He dedicates a section to his architectural and technical skills, while the following section includes his mostly architecture-related accomplishments. This functional style allows Michael to focus on his related experience and training, while downplaying his current unrelated position.*

14
Legal/Law Enforcement

Barbara Gooden

14 Eagle Cliff Way ◆ St. Cloud, MN 56377 ◆ Home: 320-123-4567 ◆ E-mail: barbara@resumepower.com

Objective
Profile

Paralegal

Accomplished professional seeking to leverage 16-year background in criminal investigation/research and administrative support into entry-level paralegal position. Backed by honor's degree in criminal justice and spotless career progression with ABC Company and its contracted security force. Polished, articulate communicator, known for flawlessly prepared, executive-level reports and ability to synthesize complex, ambiguous data into concise, persuasive material. Skilled researcher and "multitasker," able to perform meticulous review/analysis of print and video documents to support as many as 50 criminal investigations per month.

Readily master new technology and offer a solid foundation in MS Office, database management, and 90 WPM keyboarding speed. Expert interpersonal skills, able to network effectively with professionals from all levels. Proven leader – known for ability to quickly assess, respond to, and diffuse potential crises. Reputation for organization, dedication, discretion, and creative solution delivery.

Expertise

- Critical Report Writing
- Investigative Research & Analysis
- Database Management
- Leadership & Supervision
- Risk Management/Assessment
- Team Building & Training
- Project Management
- Criminal Justice & Legal Matters

Experience

ACE SECURITY (Contracted by ABC COMPANY) – St. Cloud, MN
Security Specialist, 12/99 to present
Provide a wide range of administrative support, office management, and investigative research for ABC Company's regional security headquarters. Create and maintain investigative database to track cases, losses, and recoveries; write and implement policies and procedures; draft executive-level security reports; prepare and track all security services purchase orders/invoices; and assist primary investigator with detailed background investigative work.
Key Accomplishments:

- **Introduced and currently maintain user-friendly database** to more effectively track high-visibility fraud and theft cases, transforming previous complicated and unprotected system into an easy-to-use, secure information management tool. Accurately monitor an average of 50 cases per month.

- **Interpret large volumes of paperwork from investigators to prepare concise yet thorough reports** on regional security activities, loss/recovery statistics, and status of in-progress cases for ABC Company senior executives.

- **Serve as investigative researcher** and perform meticulous review/analysis of files, records, financial statements, and videotape to assist lead investigators with case files.

- **Led regionwide effort to standardize security department policies/procedures** for high-level incidents. Delivered uniform, consistent set of detailed protocols and proper escalation processes to safely and rapidly respond to threats of violence, disgruntled employees, criminal/civil proceedings, etc. Commended by management for proactive, detailed approach and successful, first-ever regulation of policies across 15 sites.

- **Integrally involved in orchestrating reward program** to encourage employees to display identification badges while on company property. Increased voluntary badge use from 50% to 95% in one month.

- **Became corporate "go-to" person for resolving administrative issues** involving vendors, payroll/billing, client payments, and departmental purchase/credit records.

- **Earned a reputation as a team player** – voluntarily assumed expanded role during payroll administrator's absence, mastering new payroll system and providing back-up support.

Barbara Gooden Resume, Page Two

Experience

ACTION SECURITY (Contractor for ABC CO., acquired by ACE SECURITY) – St. Cloud, MN
Security Services Account Manger, 12/98 to 12/99

Managed seven-member site security department in a 24x7 environment. Administered payroll and budget, controlled overtime costs and overhead, and liaised with client to recommend, design, and implement risk-reducing programs. *Key Accomplishments:*

- **Implemented professional-development program/schedule** for site security officers and conducted training on report writing, systems, policies, and investigative procedures.
- **Insulated ABC Company from risk** by providing expert analysis of practices/procedures and recommending improvements to mitigate losses.

ABC COMPANY – St. Cloud, MN
Lead Security Officer, 6/91 to 12/98

Advised president's office on site security matters, provided off-site support to CEO regarding home security issues, coordinated security coverage for monthly board of directors' meetings, and supervised the work of 2 security officers and 3 receptionists. *Key Accomplishments:*

- **Established a professional, efficient daytime security workforce** who interacted well with tenants, leaving a lasting, positive impression of the security force. Repeatedly praised by employees/management for leadership of "the nicest, most professional force in the area."

ADVANCED TECHNOLOGY CORPORATION (Acquired by ABC COMPANY) – St. Cloud, MN
Lead Security Officer/Base Control Officer, 4/88 to 6/91; **Receptionist** (Security), 6/86 to 4/88

Education

ST. CLOUD STATE UNIVERSITY – St. Cloud, MN
BS in Criminal Justice, 1986   GPA: 3.3/4.0
Related Courses: Constitutional Law, Criminal Law, Economics, and Statistics

Training

ST. CLOUD POLYTECHNICAL INSTITUTE
MS Word, MS Excel, 1995; **Effective Presentations,** 1990

Of Note

"Barbara is currently an employee of ABC Security…but she may be affected by the broad downsizing that is anticipated as a result of a company merger. If that happens, a potential employer will have an incredible opportunity to hire an outstanding person…Barbara has always been the employee of choice to provide security, reception, and general support at monthly board meetings. Obviously, this speaks to her efficiency, but it also speaks to an attitude of cooperation and support that she displays constantly…I have relied on Barbara's quick thinking and diplomatic skills to handle countless sensitive situations…has a smile that is genuine, a concern that is obvious, and a business savvy that is always reliable…able to put customers in the right frame of mind…able to neutralize even the most difficult situations."
– **Roberto DeJesus, VP of Communications, ABC Security**

Reply To

Home: 320-123-4567 ◆ E-mail: barbara@resumepower.com

Resume Strategy: *Barbara's resume shows how her criminal investigation, research, and administrative support background make her uniquely suited for a paralegal position. Her "Profile" and "Expertise" sections emphasize her transferable skills for the paralegal profession, and her bulleted accomplishments focus on her achievements related to tasks similar to paralegal duties. She further emphasizes her strong familiarity with legal issues by highlighting law-related coursework from her BS in criminal justice. Barbara ends her resume with a favorable testament to her work performance in her "Of Note" section.*

Expertise

Public Safety & Administration

Emergency Planning

Investigations Management

Executive Leadership & Supervision

Law Enforcement

Tactical Field Operations

Multimillion-Dollar Budgeting

Project Scheduling & Management

Advanced Research & Analysis Tactics

Public Speaking & Presentations

Community Outreach

Public/Media/

Employee Relations

Workflow Planning, Scheduling & Prioritization

Regulatory & Legal Compliance

Counter-terrorism Strategies

David P. Smithers

14 College Way ■ Princeton, NJ 08542 ■ david@resumepower.com
Home: 609-123-4567 ■ **Cell:** 609-987-6543 ■ **Pager:** 609-123-4567

Goal: DIRECTOR OF CORPORATE SECURITY & SAFETY

Decorated law enforcement officer with extensive supervisory experience and 22-year track record in planning and managing investigations, security, intelligence, and police force activities. Career chronicled by meritorious promotions, outstanding performance reviews, and repeated awards (including New Jersey's "Police Officer of the Year" and 75 citations for bravery, meritorious service, and police duty excellence). Selected for executive core leadership as the current commanding officer of Princeton Police Department's 15th Precinct, with responsibility for the safety of 100,000 residents and direction of all daily operations and 300+ personnel.

Proven success in turnaround management of struggling or underperforming operations, with a history of delivering record-setting crime reduction, cost cuts, administrative improvements, and gains in productivity and morale. Strong qualifications in budgeting, personnel affairs, training, resource management, employee/public safety, and emergency response. Expert interpersonal skills; able to forge strong community and agency partnerships, win unprecedented support, diffuse volatile situations, and communicate effectively and honestly with supervisors and subordinates.

Career Progression

PRINCETON POLICE DEPARTMENT (PPD) – Princeton, NJ   1979 to Present

Inspector, 11/01 – Present; **Deputy Inspector,** 11/00 – 11/01; **Captain,** 12/97 – 11/00; **Lieutenant,** 9/92 – 12/97; **Sergeant,** 12/84 – 9/92 **Police Officer,** 11/79 – 12/84

Achieved series of career advancements and discretionary promotions culminating in current assignment as **Commander of the 15th Precinct,** three PPD boroughs, and 300+ subordinates (reporting directly to the PPD Chief of Police). Supervise two captains, seven lieutenants, 30 sergeants, 30 detectives, 250 police officers, and 40 civilian clerical staff in daily law enforcement, dispatch, and criminal investigation operations within an assigned district of approximately 100,000 residents. Challenged to reduce crime, strengthen community relations, and develop strategies to reduce costs while simultaneously improving service. Key Accomplishments:

■ **Improved police-community relations,** developing strong, sustainable, cohesive relationships with business, community, civic, and religious leaders.

  □ **Increased police department participation** in and sponsorship of a wide variety of community volunteer programs for win-win outcomes.

  □ **Personally directed startup and expansion** of programs including an after-school "Homework Club," "Computer Club," "Video/Photography Club," "Literacy/ Reading Program," and numerous sports leagues. Won enthusiastic, filled-to-capacity participation from children and adults and successfully staffed all initiatives with volunteer officers.

  □ **Formally recognized as the New Jersey Police Foundation's "Police Officer of the Year"** in 2000 (among 40,000 eligible candidates) largely due to exceptional community-relations efforts. Bridged gaps between predominantly African-American community and mainly Caucasian precinct by building close ties to resolve differences and unite community improvement efforts.

■ **Innovated crime reduction strategies** to drive a precedent-setting, **64% decrease** in every major crime category for four years in a row (1998 to present).

David P. Smithers – Page Two

PRINCETON POLICE DEPARTMENT (PPD) – continued

☐ **Launched full-scale crime information centers** specific to each platoon and sector to increase knowledge-sharing among police officers and pinpoint trends.

☐ **Cultivated cooperative partnerships** with other offices/agencies (e.g., Narcotics/Warrants Units, State Parole Office, District Attorney's Office) to effectively target, arrest, and prosecute "most-wanted" criminal contingents.

☐ **Benchmarked new "bests" in crime reduction,** reversing precinct's prior rating as one of the highest violent crime areas in the city.

■ **Procured six-figure funding for and oversaw** major physical renovations, equipment upgrades, and complete replacement of fleet of radio cars.

■ **Saved tens of thousands of dollars annually by decreasing overtime 30%** through improved personnel management, staff scheduling, and officer training programs. Efforts enabled precinct to survive drastic 40% budget cuts without compromising community safety, security, response times, or service.

■ **Awarded 75 citations** for bravery, meritorious service, and police duty excellence.

Education & Training

RUTGERS UNIVERSITY – Camden, NJ
BS in Business Administration, 1997 Graduated with high honors / GPA: 4.0

Licensure: Federal Counterterrorism Certificate – New York, NY, 1998

Coursework included hazardous materials (HAZMAT) handling, nuclear-threat response, and anti-terrorist tactics. Maintain certification through continual refresher courses.

Professional Development Highlights:

Counterterrorism, 1998 ■ Criminal Investigation Course (including forensics and crime scene analysis), 1982 ■ Auto Crime, 1982 ■ Advanced Management Training, 1998

Technology Skills:

MS Office (Word ■ Excel ■ Access ■ Outlook) ■ Windows 2000/98

Awards

■ **NJ Police Foundation "Police Officer of the Year,"** 2000
■ **Nine Commendations for Bravery,** 1979 – Present
■ **12 Meritorious Awards** (for acts of integrity or perseverance), 1979 – Present
■ **54 Citations for Creditable Crime Prevention Acts,** 1979 – Present

Of Note

Black Belt in Nanzen-kai (Japanese martial art) ■ Retained by various celebrities to provide personal protection services ■ Hold highest PPD security clearance ■ Featured speaker in PPD's cultural diversity training films ■ Director of Princeton Little League (1986 – 1997)

Resume Strategy: *David's resume is packed with evidence of his ability to manage law enforcement, security, and community safety efforts. His bulleted accomplishments play up not only his success in solving crimes, but also his strengths in managing people, organizations, and budgets—all highly relevant to the corporate world. He utilizes the left-hand, shaded column to list relevant expertise and recount excerpts from past performance reviews and published articles about him. Since he has won a series of prestigious awards, he groups these together in one section of the resume to call further attention to them. His "Of Note" section allows him to explain various additional aspects from his background that help to show his qualifications and well-roundedness.*

Roger Simpson, JD

14 Wells Road
Waco, TX 76705

Phone: (254) 123-4567
roger@resumepower.com

International Risk Analysis / Program Implementation / Project Management

Overview

Attorney with extensive experience working on Latin American economic development issues. International project manager with the ability to develop and implement legal and educational reform. Work extensively with foundations and government agencies to secure funding, technical assistance, and project support. Combine legal knowledge with business acumen; track record of establishing organizational systems, controls, policies, and procedures that support organizational goals. Comfortable working with people from diverse cultural and socioeconomic backgrounds. Proficient in Spanish with excellent written translation skills.

Expertise

- Grant and Proposal Development
- Project Management
- Country Risk Analysis
- Public Speaking and Teaching
- Marketing and Public Relations

- Negotiating and Closing the Deal
- Economics and Social Policy Issues
- Regulatory Compliance
- Anti-Corruption and Arbitration
- Contract Negotiations

Experience

GLOBAL STRATEGIES AGENCY – Waco, TX
[International organization that deals with Latin American and Caribbean development issues.]

Legal Officer, 1998 to present

Design and implement technical cooperation projects that enable Latin America and Caribbean countries to improve their legal systems. Monitor issues surrounding corruption, cyber-crime and arbitration. Oversee cooperation programs, including "Implementing the Criminal Measures Contained in the Inter-American Convention Against Corruption" and "Implementing the Preventive Measures Contained in the Inter-American Convention Against Corruption." Manage budget, conduct legal research, prepare reports, and deliver presentations.

Key Contributions:

- Prepared and assisted with proposal that led to $310,000 in funding in 2000 for anti-corruption and international arbitration projects. Introduced project ideas and drafted proposal and implementation plan.

- Wrote proposal, budget, and guidelines that helped secure an additional $220,000 for project to implement the Inter-American Convention Against Corruption. The implementation will focus on preventative measures of Convention in Central America.

- Developed international conference, "The Role of Legal Regulations in the Economic Development of the Americas" in conjunction with University of Houston Law Center. Conference was featured in a special edition of the Houston Journal of Law and Policy in International Business.

- Delivered closing address at joint OAS/OECD meeting on combating corruption, held in conjunction with the Government of Argentina in Buenos Aires.

- Edited and translated six documents and reports on departmental activities.

- Currently developing strategy to attract outside funding for FY2000; projected to generate an additional $500,000 to $600,000.

Roger Simpson, JD

Experience   UNIVERSITY OF HOUSTON LAW CENTER – Houston, TX

Director for Grants and Programs, 1993 to 1998

Promoted to newly created position to attract funding and manage grants and programs. Directed international programs that trained foreign lawyers and visits by foreign scholars and professors.

Key Contributions:

- Increased funding from $100,000 to $1.2 million during tenure. Ensured fundraising mechanisms were in place and informed faculty about funding opportunities. Developed a system for generating interest from outside funding sources and programs.

- Created annual conference series on the future of free trade in the Americas in conjunction with Toronto University, the National University of Mexico, and the University of Chile.

- Instituted exchange program that allowed lawyers from the U.S., Canada, and Mexico to experience foreign legal systems. Led consortium of nine law schools in developing the program.

- Helped manage foreign exchange programs with the City University of Hong Kong, the Central European University, and University of Paris. Ensured Hong Kong and Central European University participants were accommodated in the U.S.

Assistant to the Director, International Legal Studies, 1991 to 1993

Managed day-to-day operations of program for 150 lawyers representing more than 45 countries. Handled student issues, visas, applications, and academic advisement. Contributed to the admissions and scholarship awards processes and successfully marketed the program overseas.

Key Contributions:

- Helped elevate program to achieve international recognition, including top ten ranking by *U.S. News and World Report*.

- Developed Alumni Network comprised of 1,000 lawyers from more than 60 countries.

- Designed training programs for scholars in topics such as legal education, human rights, civil liberties, and development bank operations.

Director/Instructor, Legal Writing Program, 1991 to 1997
Instructor, 1991 to present

Co-developed introductory course on the U.S. legal system for foreign lawyers.

SCHULMAN AND GERARDI – Waco, TX

Law Clerk, 1990 to 1991

Education   UNIVERSITY OF HOUSTON LAW CENTER – Houston, TX
Juris Doctorate, 1991

TEXAS A&M UNIVERSITY – College Station, TX
Bachelor of Arts, Major in History, Minor in Political Science, 1988

Texas State Bar, 1993 to present

Resume Strategy: *Roger shows in his "Overview" how his combination of legal expertise and international business experience is a good match to a country risk analyst position. He includes relevant strengths and keywords in his "Expertise" section, and includes strong evidence of his success in global initiatives in his "Key Contributions."*

COMPLIANCE ANALYST TO DIRECTOR OF SECURITY

James W. Parkinson

15 Birch St., Chicago, IL 67094 ■ Home Phone: 620-555-5555 ■ Cell: 620-555-5553 ■ jimparkinson@resumepower.com

Profile	**DIRECTOR OF SECURITY / SAFETY**

Results-oriented security operations expert with experience protecting U.S. citizens, presidents, and United Nations/foreign government officials, as well as facilities and equipment. Hands-on and supervisory experience providing high-end security services in retail, healthcare, construction, and educational settings. Respected leader and trainer, praised for building morale, teaching departments to work in harmony, maintaining sound judgment under pressure, and motivating staff to excel. Extensive experience building effective working relationships with the public and law enforcement agencies. Advanced training with emotionally disturbed persons, surveillance, investigative, loss prevention, interviewing, and interrogation skills, with 12-year decorated service as a former Chicago police officer. Knowledge of OSHA guidelines as well as CVTV and other security systems.

Education

DEPAUL UNIVERSITY — Chicago, IL

- **Currently enrolled in M.A. in Security Management** program
- **B.A. in Psychology,** June 1981

Experience

STATE OF ILLINOIS DEPARTMENT OF DENTAL HEALTH — Chicago, IL

Compliance Analyst, 1/2000 to Present

Subpoena and review medical and insurance records; conduct investigations of alleged illegal and regulatory violations; interview complainants, respondents, and witnesses; document investigative findings; recommend corrective action; and testify at trials and hearings. Conduct undercover and site inspections at dentists' offices using specialized security equipment. *Key Results:*

- Successfully manage an average caseload of 60 concurrent investigations and consistently resolve cases within 180-day mandated timeframe.
- Launched formal program for CD site inspections, which enabled dentists to achieve regulatory compliance and reduced patient complaints.
- Currently serve as a consultant, training medical professionals in compliance guidelines/procedures.

COOK COUNTY SHERIFF — Chicago, IL

Security Officer, 1/1999 to Present

Provide security to county sheriff's office. Issue subpoenas, ex parte, and peace orders. Build and maintain strong community relations. *Key Results:*

- Drafted policies, revised security operations manual, and streamlined employee evaluation format.
- Assisted in the design of a CVTV system.

STATE OF ILLINOIS CONSTRUCTION BOARD — Chicago, IL

Site Investigator, 9/1997 to 1/2001

Investigated and evaluated complaints against construction project sites/companies across the state of Illinois. Conducted interviews with complainants and respondents; completed site inspections; prepared written documentation of allegations; and oversaw all phases of complaints processing. *Key Results:*

- Directed investigations for over 60 cases, including testifying before 50+ hearings and trials.
- Conceptualized, won Board approval for, and implemented OSHA site inspection procedures that reinforced OSHA/MOSHA regulations and reduced safety violations.
- Trained investigators in casework methods, OSHA regulations, and OSHA inspection procedures.

CHICAGO GENERAL HOSPITAL — Chicago, IL

Security Supervisor, 9/1995 to 9/1997

Ensured the security of 350-bed hospital facility located in a high-crime community and supervised 45 security-service employees in a 24/7 environment. Recruited and conducted thorough background checks for security workforce. Managed five-figure budget. Trained security and hospital staff in safety precautions, emergency procedures, and aggression management. *Key Results:*

- Strengthened relations between security and hospital staff through customer relations training and enhanced security procedures, reversing rampant animosity between the two departments.

COMPLIANCE ANALYST TO DIRECTOR OF SECURITY (CONT.)

James W. Parkinson

Experience

Security Supervisor, *Key Results* (continued):

- Held responsibility for security control room with up-to-date computerized control and fire command station; enforced regular security rounds/patrols and established strong security presence.
- Taught ongoing course in aggression management to healthcare professionals, earning commendations and praise for innovative three-day program.
- Forged strong alliance with numerous law enforcement officials.

CHICAGO POLICE DEPARTMENT — Chicago, IL

Police Officer, 1/1983 to 3/1995

Performed citywide patrol, investigations, and enforcement functions to ensure the safety of the public. Responded to calls for service and took appropriate action in accordance with the department's mission, policies, and procedures and federal, state, and local laws. Provided a sense of security for businesses and citizens within the Chicago community. Delivered safety lectures to the general public and maintained positive community-police relations. ***Key Results:***

- Successfully protected life and property, prevented crimes, apprehended criminals, maintained order, consistently demonstrated sound judgment, and received commendable evaluations.
- Chosen to work in two elite units – *Motorcycle and Emergency Service.*
- Provided security and loss prevention services to various retailers (Wal-Mart, Target) during off-duty hours.
- Achieved multiple awards for excellent service, including six police medals for excellent police duty, a medal for meritorious policy duty, multiple unit citations for excellence, as well as frequent letters of commendation.
- Received numerous awards (including 100+ life-saving crosses) from outside organizations for rescuing civilians from life-threatening situations.
- Performed Hurst Cross life-saving extrications for police and volunteer fire department.

CHICAGO UNIFIED SCHOOL DISTRICT — Chicago, IL

Security Supervisor (full-time), 1/1995 to 9/1995
Security Officer/Shift Supervisor (part-time), 6/1983 to 1/1995

Retained as security supervisor for 45 schools serving 5,000 students. ***Key Results:***

- Fostered an environment of increased student/staff safety and security.
- Led a number of undercover operations, including one that ended a string of burglaries. Apprehended and disarmed suspect and averted potential hostage situation.
- Built positive relations between school employees and security department.

Additional Training

Chicago General Hospital: Customer Relations, Aggression Management
FEMA: MOSHA-First Response, Disaster Assistance, Emergency Program Manager, Hazardous Materials
Cook County Fire Academy: Fire Exiting, Tools, SCBA-Breathing Apparatus, Ladders, Ventilation, Fire Inspection, Heavy Rescue, CPR
Chicago Police Department: Criminal and Accident Investigation, Firearms-Special Weapons, Arrest Procedures, Report Writing, Heavy Rescue, Building Collapses, Rapelling, Defensive and Advanced Driving, Motorcycle Operation, Escort Procedures, Drug and Alcohol Testing, Water Rescue, Vehicle Extraction, Traffic Enforcement, Testifying in Court, Use of Deadly Physical Force

Licenses

- State of Illinois Special Police Commission, 1996
- State of Illinois Security Clearance Card, 1996
- Hand Gun Permits – IL, IN
- CPR certified, 1999

Computers

- MS Office (Word, Excel PowerPoint), Corel WordPerfect, Windows 2000/98/95

Resume Strategy: *James begins his resume by selling his background in safety and security effectively in his "Profile" section. His "Education" section is placed next to highlight his in-progress graduate degree in security management. In his "Experience" section, James repeatedly brings out ways that he has strengthened workplace/employee/customer safety and loss prevention/crime reduction efforts. His "Additional Training" section further strengthens his candidacy for security/safety positions.*

VP SALES & MARKETING TO LAW SCHOOL APPLICANT

Tony Martin

82 Henderson Way ■ Salt Lake City, UT 84101 ■ Home: 801-123-4567 ■ Email: tony@resumepower.com

Upcoming BA graduate, driven achiever, and solid academic performer seeking law school admission to further professional career goals. Extensive experience in client relationship management, with proven ability to launch profitable start-up operations and secure VC funding/million-dollar grants. Offer additional financial expertise gained through successful track record in wholesale mortgage lending and brokering. Active community volunteer, computer literate (Windows, MS Office, C, C++, Access), internationally traveled, and bilingual (written and verbal fluency in Spanish).

Education

UNIVERSITY OF UTAH – Salt Lake City, UT
Currently completing Bachelor of Arts in Psychology. Anticipated graduation: April 2004 – Current GPA: 3.2/4.0
Extracurricular Activities:

- **Philanthropy Chair** – Sigma Chi Fraternity
  Active participation role orchestrating charitable events including blood drives, Habitat for Humanity builds, highway clean-ups, senior citizen holiday parties (Salt Lake City Nursing Home), toy drives for children with cancer (ABC Children's Hospital), and nonprofit fundraising ($6,000 raised during Charity Days).
- **Spanish/Math/Computer Tutor** (grades 6-8) – Utah Academy (Salt Lake City, UT), 2000 to 2002
- **Intensive four-week, 40-hour, full-immersion Spanish course** – Spanish Institute – Barcelona, Spain, 2002

Professional Experience
Concurrent with full-time enrollment

MEDICAL SOLUTIONS COMPANY – Salt Lake City, UT   **Vice-President of Sales and Marketing,** 2001

Strategized sales and marketing plan for startup operation, targeting both the human medical and equine veterinary fields. Developed contacts and sales leads and coordinated clinical trials with veterinary and other institutional partners.

- Secured exclusive, royalty-generating license for company's first product, the Automatic Ultrasonometer, setting the stage for a quarter-million dollars in clinical-trials funding.
- Co-developed business plan that won first place in advanced finance class and resulted in $8,000 in VC funding.
- Coordinated clinical trials with academic institutions and achieved technical validation from University of Utah Department of Engineering.
- Contributed to proposal that won $1 million in grant funding from the National Institute of Health.

ABC FINANCIAL CORPORATION – Salt Lake City, UT   **Loan Officer,** 2000 to 2001

Selected as the youngest member of sales force, charged with assisting borrowers in the mortgage application process. Matched client needs with lending packages, prepared loan files, and originated and processed loans. Innovated technical solutions that improved services through user-friendly spreadsheets utilized by lenders, brokers, and realtors.

DOUBLETREE CORPORATION – Salt Lake City, UT   **Intern, Sales and Operations,** 1999 to 2000

Sole intern out of 200 selected for continuing employment throughout school year following internship conclusion. Set up new-broker accounts, designed various loan submittal/underwriting software, and audited financials/licensing requirements.

Resume Strategy: *Tony's opening summary demonstrates that he is a proven achiever, with a track record of both business and academic successes. His summary highlights aspects of his background that would be important to law school admissions, including involvement in community affairs, international exposure, and bilingual fluency. He places education before experience and includes his extracurricular activities.*

FIELD SUPERVISOR/INSPECTOR TO RETAIL LOSS PREVENTION MANAGER

Pam Garrett	84 Worth Street Springfield, MO 65814	*Available for Relocation*	(417) 123-4567 pam@resumepower.com

GOAL: SECURITY & LOSS PREVENTION MANAGER

Career Summary

Dedicated and experienced manager of security operations and loss prevention programs for Fortune 500 retailers (e.g., Wal-Mart, Kmart, Sears, JCPenney, Esteé Lauder) and manufacturers/distributors (e.g., Pepsi, General Motors, 3M), with proven track record of minimizing losses and reducing shrink 22-fold. Adept in conducting comprehensive business needs analyses and security audits to uncover, correct, and/or augment asset protection, loss control, and workplace safety needs.

Strong background in legal issues, law enforcement, and criminal investigations gained from prior career as a deputy sheriff and police officer. Expert builder and trainer of highly motivated and cohesive security teams, with experience supervising guard forces of up to 100 in multisite operations. Certified law enforcement instructor, with extensive public speaking and teaching experience in diverse settings (elementary classrooms, sales floors, police academies, corporate boardrooms, courtrooms).

Expertise

- Security & Loss Prevention Management
- Criminal Investigations & Undercover Operations
- Workplace/Public Safety & Asset Protection
- Hazardous Materials (HAZMAT) Handling
- Public Speaking & Teaching
- Shrink Reduction & Loss Control
- Team Building, Training & Supervision
- Firearms Safety & Handling
- Legal Issues & Compliance
- Cultural Sensitivity

Experience

SPRINGFIELD SECURITY SYSTEMS – Springfield, MO

Field Supervisor / Inspector, 2001 to 2003 (March)

Held full accountability for management of 24x7 security operations within territory comprised of 35 Fortune 500/major client sites (e.g., Kmart, Pepsi Cola, 3M, General Motors, Esteé Lauder). Trained and supervised 70-100 guards; completed detailed investigative work on behalf of retail clients; responded to emergency situations; maintained comprehensive weekly logs of all activities; and observed workers in performance of duties to maximize effectiveness and coach/correct weaker areas. *Selected Accomplishments:*

- **Improved customer satisfaction/retention and salvaged the threatened loss of key accounts** (e.g., Pepsi) by initiating frequent, in-person meetings with client management.
- **Slashed costly employee turnover by 15% and wrestled out-of-control staff "no-shows" to nearly zero** while simultaneously strengthening employee morale, accountability, and productivity.
- **Conducted well-received on-site training** on topics including loss prevention/loss mitigation, security procedures, report writing, and inventorying processes.
- **Uncovered internal theft ring for Fortune 500 client** that halted losses of **$5,000–$6,000 every week.** Advised client of suspicions, instituted vehicle inspections, stopped criminal activity, and delivered a 22-fold shrink reduction for client distribution center.
- **Won accolades from newly acquired Kmart account** for proactive actions ensuring the security of receiving operations. Trained officers assigned to main gate on how to identify truck seal tampering and discrepancies on transit logs/documentation/records.

SPRINGFIELD SHERIFF'S OFFICE – Springfield, MO

Deputy Sheriff, Field Services Division, 1998 to 2001

Located, arrested, and returned fugitives and persons wanted for various criminal offenses and civil matters. Obtained necessary legal documents (warrants, extradition papers), maintained accurate records, managed high-volume caseload, and testified in court to present evidence. *Selected Accomplishments:*

- **Made well over 800 arrests** (400+ felony, 400+ misdemeanor) throughout tenure and received **frequent accolades** from supervisors and citizens for service, professionalism, and devotion to duty.
- **Apprehended theft suspects and initiated cases for prosecution** as a member of Sheriff's Office contracted security services team, working undercover to support loss prevention operations of major retailers (Sears, JC Penney's, Wal-Mart).
- **Regarded as a "favorite" expert or arresting officer witness by state attorney's office** due to proven strengths in verbal presentation and written documentation. Testified in approximately 50 court cases (ranging from theft, DUI, manslaughter, assault, and sexual battery).

> "...Deputy Garrett should be commended for the outstanding work she performed. Her immediate [action] was instrumental in the solving of several crimes in the Springfield area...[she] is an asset to our shift and our agency."
>
> – Letter of Commendation from Lt. Johnson, Springfield Sheriff's Office

Pam Garrett

(417) 123-4567　｜　pam@resumepower.com　｜　**Page Two**

Experience
(continued)

"...you were most certainly instrumental in effecting the arrests of the two suspects from the convenience store robbery... Clearly your tenacity in seeing this case to its fruition is highly commendable and your law enforcement techniques thorough thank you for your hard work"

– Sheriff Stolley, Springfield Sheriff's Office

SPRINGFIELD MISSOURI POLICE DEPARTMENT – Springfield, MO

Police Officer, 1995 to 1997

Conducted numerous investigative and surveillance operations with county, state, and federal agencies; responded to emergency situations; patrolled neighborhoods to ensure public safety; handled criminal investigations; processed crime scenes and collected/submitted evidence to crime lab; and testified extensively in courtroom trials. Frequently invited to conduct training programs for area retail stores and their employees on loss prevention tactics, strategies, and procedures. *Selected Accomplishments:*

- **Won the respect and trust of residents** in low-income, high-drug areas and decreased citizen complaints through relationship-building efforts. Demonstrated a commitment to protecting children, families, and property through high-visibility patrols and launched "Neighborhood Watch" programs.
- **Founded "Buddy Cop" program** to foster close ties between law enforcement and the community and augment child safety in largely "latchkey kid" neighborhood.
- **Assisted local small businesses in initiating monthly training** to better educate owners on loss prevention measures and maintaining the security and safety of their businesses and staff. Led group training sessions and in-person "security audits" to recommend corrective safety/theft prevention actions.

U.S. AIR FORCE – Based in London, England

Equipment Management Specialist, 1986 to 1990

Managed over 125 accounts, supervised two divisions (18 staff), and administered the auditable Delinquent Document Program. Researched and identified supply and equipment requirements and inventory control actions to ensure adequate support of Air Force operations. *Selected Accomplishments:*

- **Reduced delinquencies from 55% to zero** in three months.
- **Strengthened inventory control,** ensuring timely corrections of delinquencies and rapid investigation of losses through property accounting log.
- **Assisted in government investigations into internal theft,** resulting in multiple arrests.

Education & Credentials

SPRINGFIELD COMMUNITY COLLEGE – Springfield, MO

AA Degree in Paralegalism, 1992

COMMUNITY COLLAGE OF THE U.S. AIR FORCE – Virginia

Certificate in Logistics Management, 1987

Certifications & Training

- State Certified Law Enforcement Officer (State of Missouri), 1995
- State-Certified in HAZMAT Awareness and Emergency Management, 1994
- State-Certified Law Enforcement Instructor (Missouri Department of Law Enforcement), 2001
- State-Certified Field Training Officer (Advanced Training Certificate Program), 1999
- Certificate in Fraud Prevention (Visa Corporation), 1998
- Certificate in Interviewing and Interrogation (Missouri Department of Law Enforcement), 1995
- First Responder- and CPR-Certified – Infants and Adults (American Red Cross)
- "Hate Crimes Training" (Office of the Attorney General, State of Missouri), 2002

Speaking Highlights

Invited by Fortune 500 retailers, businesses, community groups, and schools to deliver presentations on loss prevention, workplace safety, criminal investigations, and violence prevention. *Highlights Include:*

- "Loss Prevention," Springfield Small Business Association, Springfield, MO – 2002
- "Preventing Violence in the Workplace," Wal-Mart Management, Springfield, MO – 2000
- "Human Diversity," Springfield Sheriff's Office – 2001
- "Criminal and Crime Scene Investigations," Springfield Community College – 2001

Resume Strategy: Pam clarifies her new career objective in a "Goal" section at the top of page one. Her summary emphasizes transferable skills and experience, followed by an "Expertise" section that proves she has the requisite skills for her career change. Testimonials in the left margin speak to Pam's work ethic and dedication to organizational goals.

Kevin Liss

210 West 28th St. ■ New York, NY 10010
212-999-0980 ■ Liss@email.com

CERTIFIED PARALEGAL

Recent graduate of New York University's prestigious Paralegal Certification Program. Recognized for ability to comprehend complex and intricate curriculum, achieving an A- average both semesters. Throughout professional career, recognized for discipline, excellent oral and written communication skills, and attention to detail. Skilled multitasker capable of handling and completing multiple projects simultaneously. Computer skills include MS Word, Excel, ACT!, and Westlaw.

EDUCATION

NEW YORK UNIVERSITY PARALEGAL CERTIFICATION PROGRAM — New York, NY
Paralegal Certification (ABA Approved), May 2002
Coursework:

- Intellectual Property
- Corporations
- Evidence
- Litigation
- Real Property
- Securities
- Trusts & Estates
- U.C.C.
- Taxation
- Torts
- Contracts
- Criminal / Civil
- Debtor/Creditor
- Ethics
- Matrimonial
- Research & Writing

NORTHERN ILLINOIS UNIVERSITY — Dekalb, IL
BACHELOR OF ARTS IN ENGLISH, 1985

CAREER HIGHLIGHTS

TEMPORARY STAFFING — New York, NY
BUSINESS DEVELOPMENT / SALES, March 2000 to present

- Interface extensively with representatives from small, medium, and large corporations to discuss and assess staffing needs.
- Prepare written and oral reports, contracts, weekly activity reports, and sales updates.
- Develop new account relationships while managing existing client base.
- Conduct extensive Internet research on specific companies and industries.

WESTERN MESSAGING COMMERCIAL SERVICES — New York, NY
EXECUTIVE ACCOUNT REPRESENTATIVE, September 1996 to January 2000

- Managed commercial accounts, generating over $125,000 in monthly revenue.
- Sold Commercial Messaging Services to high-volume prospects. Built account base via cold calling, referrals, and telemarketing.
- Conducted onsite presentations, consulted with clients, assessed needs, and provided ongoing access to ensure optimal satisfaction.
- Provided detailed feedback to sales manager of prospects, sales forecasts, and other activities.

JANUS MEDIA INFORMATION SERVICES — New York, NY and Chicago, IL
MEDIA/ADDRESSING DEPARTMENT MANAGER & CUSTOMER SERVICE (NEW YORK), 1994 to 1996
ADDRESSING DEPARTMENT MANAGER (CHICAGO), 1989 to 1994

- Opened New York office from ground up. Recruited, trained, and supervised production staff.
- Maintained hundreds of customer media lists and updated editorial information. Supervised staff of three, ensuring that workload was evenly distributed and tight deadlines were met.

PROSVETA NEWSPAPER, Chicago, IL
ASSISTANT EDITOR, 1986 to 1989

Resume Strategy: *Kevin recently completed training relevant to his career change, so he places "Education" before experience and emphasizes his training throughout his career summary section. Instead of simply listing his new paralegal certification, Kevin includes related courses so that hiring managers see the scope of his program and areas of knowledge. Resume submitted by Judy Friedler.*

15

Administrative Support

GLORIA FINE

15 Canal Place East
Southport, CT 06490

Objective: Administrative Assistant

Phone: 203-123-4567
E-mail: gloria@aol.com

Personable, technically skilled professional seeking to leverage strong background in office management, computer technology, bookkeeping processes, and customer service to obtain administrative support position. Strong computer literacy in a variety of PC/Mac applications and quick study of new technology. Former middle school English teacher with expert written and verbal communication skills; able to prepare accurate, effective documents ranging from professional correspondence to executive-level reports, marketing collateral, and Web site content.

Experienced in office and small business management, with hands-on familiarity in A/P and A/R, shipping/receiving, telephone reception, order processing, vendor selection, contract review, and supply management functions. Proven "multitasker," known for attention to detail, organization, high-quality timely deliverables, and impeccable service. **Key Skills:**

Organization & Follow-Through ■ *Contingency Planning* ■ *Written & Verbal Communication* ■ *Telephone Reception*
Professional Correspondence/Reports ■ *Special Event Coordination* ■ *Bookkeeping* ■ *Purchasing & Inventory Management*
Office Management & Team Supervision ■ *Relationship Management (Customers/Vendors)*

EDUCATION & TECHNICAL SKILLS

BA in English (GPA 3.4), 1990 – HARTFORD UNIVERSITY – Hartford, CT
Computer Skills: Word, PowerPoint, WordPerfect, Paint Shop Pro, FrontPage, QuarkXPress, QuickBooks, Excel (Basic), HTML (Basic), Windows ME/98/95, Macintosh OS

EXPERIENCE

A1 BUSINESS CORP. – Hartford, CT – *Manufacturer of business stamps and imprinted products.*
Consultant, Rubber Stamp Division, 7/01 – present
Retained following profitable sale of Gloria's Rubber Stamps to oversee smooth transition. Collaborate with freelance artists to develop new images, supervise illustrators in the creation of future lines, and collaborate on new Web site development.

■ **Delivered significant product line expansion,** working with six artists to develop over 160 new designs anticipated to drive additional revenue stream well into the five figures annually.

■ **Built customer contact database** to improve targeted marketing and coordinated all logistics for direct-mail campaigns.

■ **Planned tradeshow participation strategy,** determined inventory selection, and conceptualized visual layouts for shows.

GLORIA'S RUBBER STAMPS – Southport, CT – *Manufacturer/wholesaler of original art rubber stamp line.*
Office Manager/Owner, 7/97 – 6/01
Directed all aspects of ground-up small business and supervised three-member team in daily operations, including telephone reception, accounts payable/accounts receivable, order processing, supply/material sourcing and ordering, correspondence, catalog/flyer design, inventory control, tradeshow management, and customer service.

■ **Implemented marketing and operational plans** that rapidly expanded sales from zero to six-figure revenue mark.

■ **Collaborated with designer to create effective Web site** and wrote all Web content.

■ **Used computer skills and various tools to automate processes,** including order invoicing (QuickBooks), tradeshow booth inventory/layout (MS Works database), and magazine advertising design (Print Artist).

■ **Won repeat business and referrals through strong commitment to customer service,** expanding business from zero to 1,000+ retail and 100+ wholesale accounts. Efforts resulted in profitable buy-out offer by A1 Business Corp.

HARTFORD MIDDLE SCHOOL – Hartford, CT
English Teacher, 8/91 – 6/97
Taught English, language arts, and reading classes to students in grades 6-8. Accountable for classroom management, lesson planning, and curriculum writing. Repeatedly recognized for superior performance during annual reviews.

Resume Strategy: *Gloria brings out elements from her background that are most relevant to administrative support positions in every section of her resume. She effectively highlights accomplishments related to computer skills, event planning, revenue growth, and customer service. Compare this version to her alternate resume version targeting copywriting/marketing jobs in Chapter 18.*

SPECIAL EDUCATION TEACHER TO CLINICAL INFORMATION COORDINATOR TO EXECUTIVE ASSISTANT

Charles Whitler

14 Central Drive
San Francisco, CA 94117

(415) 123-4567
charles@resumepower.com

Career Target

Executive Administrative Assistant ◆ Office Manager

Qualifications Summary

Accomplished business professional seeking to apply 14 years of experience in office management, computer operations, report preparation, project management, data entry/analysis, and teaching/training to an executive administrative support role. Advanced user of technology, with solid background in MS Office Suite, database management, workstation/systems troubleshooting, and end-user training.

Expert communication skills, able to analyze and tabulate data to create insightful, comprehensive reports aiding senior management in strategic decision making. Interact and collaborate effectively with individuals from diverse backgrounds and levels, with reputation for patience and diplomacy.

Expertise

◆ Executive-Level Reports
◆ Data Input, Analysis & Interpretation
◆ Government Reporting
◆ Database Management
◆ Office Management & Supervision
◆ Business Process Improvement

◆ Team Building & Training
◆ Advanced Computer Skills
◆ Special Event Coordination & Fundraising
◆ Project Management
◆ Customer Relationship Management

Computer Skills

◆ Word
◆ Excel
◆ Outlook

◆ PowerPoint
◆ Access
◆ FrontPage

◆ Publisher
◆ WordPerfect
◆ Windows NT/2000/98

Experience

SAN FRANCISCO EXTENDED CARE FACILITY – San Francisco, CA   1998 to present
Long-term-care facility, nursing home, and rehabilitation center.
Clinical Information Coordinator, 9/00 to present
Analyze and interpret clinical data to create comprehensive, computer-generated reports on clinical standards and activity, thresholds, and final outcomes for department heads and senior administrators. Consult with continuing quality of care chairperson to jointly author patient-centered studies facilitating improvement initiatives and forward-thinking policy decisions. Supervise data entry personnel, oversee input process for all MDS (Minimum Data Set) information to ensure correct Medicare funding, and oversee timely online transmittal of all data to California State Department of Health. *Key Accomplishments:*

◆ **Created and implemented information-gathering processes and automated tools,** contributing to accurate and thorough reports on a wide range of mission-critical issues.
◆ **Developed, launched, and currently maintain clinical data repository** housing crucial nursing department information.
◆ **Prepared detailed reports for healthcare administrators,** providing up-to-the-minute, comprehensive overviews on patient status, treatment, and level of functioning. Reports have enhanced patient care and improved quality of services, which ultimately reduces incidents of infections, ulcers, accidents, wounds, and other medical conditions.
◆ **Earned a reputation for expert database management and troubleshooting skills;** serve as health provider network coordinator and liaise between facility and California State Department of Health computer security staff.
◆ **Designed user-friendly forms, logs, and instructional materials** to aid nursing department in delivering quality care to 380 residents.

Charles Whitler

Experience

SAN FRANCISCO EXTENDED CARE FACILITY (*continued*)

♦ **Enabled facility to receive maximum Medicaid reimbursement** by ensuring meticulous attention to detail, accuracy, and on-time completion of quarterly health department reports used to generate case-mix indexes.

MIS Coordinator, Finance Departments, 8/98 to 9/00

Input MDS data into medical records system, processed PRI (Patient Review Instrument) reports, and transmitted data to state health department. *Key Accomplishments:*

♦ **Improved tracking mechanisms and reduced report-writing time** by creating spreadsheets to efficiently monitor MDS flow status.

♦ **Conducted facilitywide computer training** for all department personnel on topics including medical records, progress notes, clinical assessments, and MDS/HCFA reports.

♦ **Served as technical resource person** for all computer systems.

♦ **Collaborated with all departments** to maintain proper MDS documentation.

CALIFORNIA ASSOCIATION FOR THE BLIND – San Francisco, CA   1990 to 1998

Nonprofit organization offering services for blind and visually impaired persons.

Special Education Teacher, Day Treatment Program

Improved the cognitive, daily living, and mobility skills of adults with multiple disabilities. Provided classroom instruction and developed/executed individual treatment/behavior modification plans, enabling clients to achieve a better quality of life. Completed documentation records for all residents, including daily statistics, progress notes, and behavior plans. *Key Accomplishments:*

♦ **Orchestrated operation's first-ever fully integrated music program,** generating enthusiastic participation from adults in all classroom levels. Efforts led to a fundamental change in entire program's class structure to emphasize individualized preferences.

♦ **Supervised and trained** teachers' aides and student interns on procedures, policies, and quality, compassionate care/instruction.

♦ **Coordinated department's first holiday concert** featuring solo, duet, and group musical performances. Secured community donations of food, invitation design/mailing costs, and participant attire, setting the stage for a festive, memorable event at near zero cost.

Early Career

CALIFORNIA MEMORIAL HOSPITAL – San Francisco, CA   1987 to 1990

Recreation Therapist

Education

UNIVERSITY OF SAN FRANCISCO – San Francisco, CA

B.A. in Psychology, Minor in Music, 1987

Reply To

(415) 123-4567 ♦ charles@resumepower.com

Resume Strategy: *To aid his transition to an executive assistant position, Charles outlines his new objective in a "Career Target" section. His "Qualifications Summary" shows the reader why he is qualified for his new goal by detailing his transferable skills. Charles's bulleted "Expertise" and "Computer Skills" sections illustrate that Charles has the requisite skills to succeed in an administrative support role. The "Experience" section demonstrates that Charles goes above and beyond his job duties to positively contribute to his employers' business operations.*

Bernice Johnson

489 Whispering Pines Rd.
Doylestown, PA 18901

bernice@resumepower.com
Cell: (215) 555-5554

Home: (215) 555-5555
Work: (215) 555-5551

EXECUTIVE/OFFICE ADMINISTRATIVE ASSISTANT

Performance-driven administrative professional with over 12 years of experience in facilitating support services and office management and additional background in marketing and sales. Demonstrated capabilities in development and execution of procedures for legal, operational, and financial activities, with history of entrepreneurial success. Strong organization, negotiation, and communication skills with the ability to independently plan and direct high-level business affairs. Core competencies include:

Confidential Legal Document Handling / Administrative Processes / Bookkeeping / Liaison Affairs
Public Relations / Workflow Planning & Prioritization / Records & Data Management
Corporate Recordkeeping / Sales & Marketing / Office Management / Client Services

—————————— PROFESSIONAL EXPERIENCE ——————————

BERNICE'S ANTIQUES – Doylestown, PA   1992 – Present

Shop Owner

Hold full responsibility for all operational activities and functions, including bookkeeping, payroll, staffing, marketing, sales, purchasing, budgeting, and customer service. Implement staff training and development programs to ensure fulfillment of customer service objectives and goals.
Selected Accomplishments:

- Tripled profits within first year of operations through establishing efficient administrative procedures, improving staff performance levels, and initiating creative marketing strategies.
- Boosted office productivity by incorporating systems automation and technology upgrades into business processes, with emphasis on use of Microsoft Office applications.
- Maintained 100% employee retention and loyal customer base throughout ten-year period.
- Piloted innovative marketing and promotional ideas that increased customer traffic.

GRADY, WHITESTONE, AND BERNSTEIN – Philadelphia, PA   1982 – 1988

Office Manager / Legal Administrative Assistant

In charge of all office administrative responsibilities for law firm, including file maintenance, document management and authoring, transcription, meeting arrangements, and client service activities. Coordinated busy schedule involving court cases, client appointments, and office management functions. **Selected Accomplishments:**

- Maintained proper, accurate filing and management of key court documents for easy access.
- Commended by partners for level of professionalism and efficiency in office administration.
- Upheld confidentiality in sensitive oral and written communications; honed skills in composition.

—————————— EDUCATION & TRAINING ——————————

Drexel University (Philadelphia, PA) Presently enrolled to complete **BA in General Studies**

Allentown Business School (Allentown, PA) – Completed 49 hours toward an AS Degree (1989 – 1990)

Legal Assistant Certificate - Graduated from **Business School** from the **Legal Assistant Program** at **Phoenix Institute** (Philadelphia, PA; 1982)

Advanced Word and Excel Certificate, Computer Training, Inc. (Philadelphia, PA; 1985)

Honors: Gregg Shorthand/Advanced Typing Award, Phoenix Institute ■ Dean's List, Allentown Business School

Computers: Microsoft Word, Excel, and PowerPoint

Resume Strategy: *Bernice's desire to return to her earlier administrative support career is communicated clearly in her resume title. Her opening profile highlights her background in office management, her computer skills, and her most relevant qualifications. She selects accomplishments from her background that show her capabilities in administrative support in her "Professional Experience" section and uses her "Education and Training" section to bring out her top credentials as an executive assistant professional.*

TEAM ASSOCIATE TO ADMINISTRATIVE ASSISTANT

Jessica Lederman

14 Turner Way
Palm Coast, FL 32164

Home: (386) 123-4567
E-mail: jessica@resumepower.com

Objective

ADMINISTRATIVE / EXECUTIVE ASSISTANT

Profile

Technically skilled business professional, seeking to leverage proven strengths in a variety of front- and back-office functions to achieve entry-level position as an administrative assistant. Offer diverse skill set encompassing cross-platform expertise (Windows/MS-DOS); advanced software proficiency (MS Office, spreadsheets, desktop publishing, database management); financial acumen (budgeting, general ledger accounting, purchasing); and customer service (switchboard, reception, complaint handling). Expert interpersonal skills – interact effectively with customers, vendors, and all levels of management/staff. Use tact and diplomacy to diffuse volatile situations and sensitively respond to the needs of special populations.

Strong qualifications and experience in maintaining impeccable organization and service levels within fast-paced, high-volume environments, with outstanding record of multitasking efficiently. Articulate communicator, skilled in the preparation of concise, accurate meeting minutes, C-level executive reports, financial statements, and professional correspondence. Adept in scheduling, coordinating, and facilitating all aspects of meetings and special events. Familiar with confidentiality rules/regulations and experienced handling very sensitive material and legal matters. Equally effective in both team and self-directed assignments.

Key Skills

- □ Project Planning & Scheduling
- □ A/P, A/R & Account Reconciliation
- □ Meeting & Event Planning
- □ Budgeting & Auditing
- □ Multi-Line Phone Systems/Reception
- □ Creative Problem Solving
- □ Complaint Handling

- □ PC-Based Administrative Word Processing
- □ Spreadsheets
- □ Relationship Management (Customers/Vendors)
- □ Financial & Executive-Level Reports
- □ Confidential Record Keeping
- □ Database Administration

Technology Summary

□ Word	□ Access (basic)	□ Paintbrush	□ CA$H
□ Excel	□ WordPerfect	□ Windows 2000/98	□ PHHORCE/GALAXY
□ Outlook	□ WordPad	□ MS-DOS	□ EDR/EDM
□ PowerPoint	□ Publisher	□ Right Fax	□ Mortgage Ware

Achievement Highlights

- □ **Successfully fulfilled a wide variety of administrative duties,** including accounts payable/accounts receivable, purchase order requisitions, front desk reception, switchboard operations (12-line system), filing, staff scheduling, meeting/event planning, correspondence/paperwork/chart preparation, collection referrals, and supply ordering. (*Team Associate; On-Call Office Assistant; Residential Counselor*)

- □ **Earned a reputation for meticulous attention to detail and flawless paperwork/report preparation.**

  - □ Reviewed and verified volumes of financial information to ensure "clean," complete loan packages as the primary support person for team of 12 mortgage loan counselors. (*Team Associate*)

  - □ Completed detailed, confidential intake assessments, prepared medication inventories, documented staff activities in government-mandated daily logs, and wrote patient evaluation summaries, behavior modification plans, and progress/incident reports for staff psychiatrists, PAs, and senior administrators. (*Residential Counselor*)

- □ **Proved the ability to rapidly master complex concepts, analyze financial data, and complete intricate calculations.** Performed loan-to-value computations, debt-to-income ratios, FICO score/credit reviews, compliance audits, and risk-based lending evaluations to discern key variables facilitating fair and informed lending decisions. (*Team Associate*)

- □ **Commended for flexibility and adaptability;** willingly volunteered for difficult or unpopular tasks such as temporary department reassignment to resolve work backlogs. (*Team Associate*)

- □ **Improved accuracy/efficiency, streamlined operations, and facilitated future-focused management decision making** by creating user-friendly spreadsheets, revamping documentation forms, and preparing a variety of ad-hoc reports. (*Team Associate*)

Jessica Lederman

Home: (386) 123-4567
E-mail: jessica@resumepower.com

Page Two

Achievement Highlights
(*Continued*)

☐ **Ensured 100% compliance with regulatory agency mandates** (e.g., FL Division of Developmental Disabilities, Division of Mental Health) by completing thorough medical chart audits. Efforts resulted in reversing prior history of underfunded applications, increasing referrals to agency, and obtaining provisional license. (*Residential Counselor*)

☐ **Demonstrated a strong service commitment,** with a more than five-year record of providing quality patient care to clients from diverse cultural and socioeconomic backgrounds suffering from various developmental, psychiatric, and substance abuse issues. Leveraged skills in sensitive, careful listening and critical decision making to correctly respond to crisis situations using empathy and discretion. (*Residential Counselor*)

☐ **Became adept in skillfully maneuvering through bureaucratic red tape to remove roadblocks for customers** without alienating key business partners. Assisted clients with HIV/AIDS in accessing community/government social services and health insurance services and won precertification of benefits for new clients through diligent communications with insurance carriers. (*Office Assistant; Residential Counselor*)

Work History

ABC MORTGAGE (Daytona Beach, FL)

Team Associate, 2/01 – Present

Provide central support to 12-member loan processing team. Verify customer credit information; assist in underwriting loan files; register and "drop" loans to CA$H system; distribute Compliance Packages to customers; and assign leads to sales staff. Respond to customer inquiries, managing switchboard to answer/route a large volume of external calls to appropriate business sources.

DEF HEALTH RESOURCES (Palm Coast, FL)

Office Assistant/Residential Counselor, 8/00 – Present

Provide on-call coverage to various residential units during times of staffing shortage. Fill in for absent or vacationing secretarial staff, update medical/billing information and charts, and refer delinquent accounts to collection agencies.

GHI PROFESSIONAL RESOURCES (Jacksonville, FL); JKL FOUNDATION (Palm Coast, FL); RESIDENCE INDEPENDENCE SERVICE (Orlando, FL)

Residential Counselor/Clinical Assistant, 6/96 – Present

Achieved "in-demand" status as a residential counselor/clinical assistant, recruited to fulfill various temporary, interim, or full-time vacancies for a number of mental health treatment centers. Conduct intake assessments for admitted clients; confer with medical/psychiatric staff to development and implement treatment plans; advise all patients on their rights and responsibilities; prepare medical charts, written evaluation summaries, daily logs, insurance forms, and various other paperwork; interact extensively with clients and insurance carriers; administer medications; and assist in various daily administrative tasks for treatment facilities.

Education & Credentials

UNIVERSITY OF FLORIDA – Gainesville, FL
Completed 51 credits toward a **BA in Psychology** while concurrently employed full time.

Professional Development: Crisis Intervention and Prevention ☐ Abuse/Neglect Training ☐ Managing Disruptive Behavior ☐ Task Analysis Behavior Support ☐ Consumer Rights/Confidentiality

Licensure: Notary Public of Florida ☐ First Aid & CPR Certified (American Red Cross)

Resume Strategy: *Jessica uses an "Achievement Highlights" strategy to enable her to group similar relevant accomplishments from various jobs she has held together. She explains where she was employed in parentheses next to each achievement. Her "Work History" section provides a career chronology, and she places her temporary positions under one heading to avoid the appearance of job hopping.*

16

Finance/Banking/Accounting/Insurance

9824 First Street
Delray Beach, Florida 33444

James Edwards
james@resumepower.com

Home: 561-123-4567
Cellular: 561-987-6543

JOB GOAL	**LOAN OFFICER ▪ BANK CUSTOMER ▪ CREDIT ANALYST**

PROFILE

Proven customer service performer with extensive experience in customer relationship/IT project management within the financial services industry. Transitioning from information technology focus to banking/finance operations in order to capitalize on passion for the industry and talent for serving its customers. Experienced in all aspects of customer service with a reputation for resourcefulness, tact, and win-win solutions.

Offer a customer-centered approach to front-office banking procedures, advanced problem/resolution skills, and demonstrated success in customer relationship management and team building. Polished, articulate communicator with ability to lead financial and IT professionals through complex problem resolution. Credentials include a BA in business (accounting major), computer programming diploma, three years' experience as a bank teller, and two years' experience as an accountant. Currently pursuing additional coursework to prepare for CPA exam.

KNOWLEDGE AREAS

- Banking/Teller Operations
- Customer Service
- Coaching & Training
- Bookkeeping/Analytical Skills
- High-Profile Technology Project Management
- Customer Relationship Management (CRM)
- Creative Problem Solving
- PC/Mainframe Technology

EXPERIENCE

ACT TECHNOLOGIES – Delray Beach, Florida
Technical Analyst/Client Liaison, 2000 to 2001
Provided cutting-edge solutions to bank, trading firm, and insurance company clients.
Selected Accomplishments:

- Hired as technical advisor, consultant, and client liaison to deliver mission-critical technology solutions furthering business goals, streamlining operations, and enhancing profitability. Also worked on internal projects to increase knowledge base.
- Handpicked as technical writer for key Fortune 500 account handling Web site documentation effort. Tested several hundred Web site links and produced 30-page report detailing functionality of the site, successfully positioning company for future change initiatives.
- Quickly mastered new technology – became self-taught on HTML, ColdFusion, Active Server Pages, JavaScript, Visual Basic, SQL Server, and MS Project in approximately six months.

ACT INSURANCE – Delray Beach, Florida
Programmer/Analyst/Customer Service Representative, 1997 to 2000
Provided information technology support to 500 HR professionals in a deadline-driven environment. Interacted with all levels of HR staff daily to investigate, troubleshoot, and resolve computer program and systems challenges and communicated corrective measures in easily understood terminology.
Selected Accomplishments:

- Initiated database improvements and one-on-one training sessions geared to individual skill levels that slashed data retrieval and information gathering time by 80%.
- Improved resolution turnaround time by creating computerized problem log in MS Access.
- Incorporated customer education into all service calls, dramatically enhancing efficiency by eliminating work slow-downs due to computer problems. Efforts resulted in reducing computer service calls from an average of 15 problems per day to nearly zero.

James Edwards

Resume, Page Two

EXPERIENCE	**ACT INSURANCE** (*continued*)

- Developed alternative ways to retrieve data that saved HR department thousands of dollars annually in new software licensing costs.
- Repeatedly praised by HR representatives: *"Thank you again for always being so helpful. You should get an 'A' in customer service!"* – Laura Lynn, HR Representative

Programmer/Analyst, Internal Audit Division, 1989 to 1996

Integral member of programming unit supporting auditors and corporate security. Consulted with auditors daily to assess and respond to their information needs; designed, wrote, and tested programs to produce required information; and trained users on report generation.

Selected Accomplishments:

- Improved internal audit quality by reducing the amount of time auditors spent trying to obtain crucial information.
- Automated reports using PC-based applications that eliminated time-consuming manual calculations to produce statistics.
- Voluntarily expanded role by taking the time to become familiar with hardware and software in order to troubleshoot minor problems encountered by auditors, which freed network support specialists to tackle more complex problems.

ABC CORPORATION / ADVANCED HEALTHCARE / ALLIED CO. – Delray Beach, Florida

Programmer, Information Systems, 1984 to 1989

- Received prestigious "Service Star" award for helping promote superior service and teamwork.

AMALGAMATED, INC. – West Palm Beach, Florida / BEST ELECTRIC – Delray Beach, Florida

Accountant, 1980 to 1982

FIRST FEDERAL BANK / PRIME SAVINGS / BANK OF COMMERCE – Delray Beach, Florida

Bank Teller, 1976 to 1979

EDUCATION	FLORIDA ATLANTIC UNIVERSITY – Boca Raton, Florida

B.A. in Business and Management, 1980

Major: **Accounting,** Minor: **Music**

COLLEGE OF TECHNOLOGY – Delray Beach, Florida

Computer Programming Diploma, 1984

COMPUTER SKILLS	■ Excel	■ Outlook	■ HTML
	■ Lotus 1-2-3	■ Windows 2000	■ JavaScript
	■ Word	■ IBM OS/MVS	■ COBOL
	■ Access	■ Visual Basic	■ JCL
	■ Project	■ SQL/ASP	■ Oracle Applications

Reply To – Home: 561-123-4567 ■ Cellular: 561-987-6543 ■ E-mail: james@resumepower.com

Resume Strategy: *James mentions his early career in banking/accounting in his opening resume profile since it is most relevant to what he now wants to do. He explains his goal of transitioning from IT to banking/financial services clearly, and provides ample evidence throughout the resume of relevant skills that would enable him to make this move smoothly. A detailed "Computer Skills" section is included at the end of the resume since these proficiencies are important to his career goal.*

Daniel Vanderbilt

1414 Louis Road
Louisville, KY 40202   Email: daniel@resumepower.com   Home: 502-123-4567
Office: 502-987-6543

Career Goal: **Entry-Level Financial/Accounting/Insurance Operations**

Successful business professional seeking to leverage strong background in fiscal and general operations management, expert relationship-building skills with vendors and affluent clients, and in-progress accounting BA to achieve career shift to a financial/accounting/insurance operations focus. Hands-on experience across diverse business functions including accounting, bookkeeping, payroll, systems automation, sales, marketing, purchasing, and inventory/loss control, with solid technology skills (Excel, Word, Access, Publisher, Windows).

Demonstrated success implementing sound management principles proven to: double efficiency and accuracy, grow sales from zero to multimillion-dollar levels, resolve billing and accounts payable backlogs, jump-start cash flow surges, and transform manual operations to fully integrated computerized systems. Offer a P&L mind-set, a track record of skyrocketing small business revenues 800% within 24 months, respected interpersonal skills, and multilingual fluency (Spanish/French).

Relevant Skills

- GAAP Standards & Compliance
- Bookkeeping/Payroll/Invoicing/Purchasing
- P&L Management ($3 Million)
- Systems Automation
- Accounts Payable/Accounts Receivable
- Account Reconciliation/General Ledger Accounting
- Startup & High-Growth Operations

- Relationship Management (Clients/Vendors)
- B2B/B2C Solution-Sales
- Financial & General Operations Management
- New Business Development/Account Growth
- Team Building/Training/Supervision
- Strategic Marketing & Promotions
- Cost Containment & Loss Control

Professional Experience

BOUNTIFUL NURSERY – Louisville, KY
Owner and General Manager, 1/01 to Present

Wholly accountable for financial and general operations of $1.5 million, five-acre retail nursery with 26-member staff. Provide expert advice to clients and oversee all aspects of accounts payable/accounts receivable, general bookkeeping, daily/month-end account reconciliation, product selection/sourcing/ brokering, management of $380K inventory, international importing, plant propagation, customer relations, and marketing/promotions. Ensure accuracy of financial statements, tax records, and payroll.

Key Accomplishments:

- **Modernized operations by establishing formerly nonexistent GAAP standards** and setting up fully automated accounting system. Implemented sound financial reporting, record keeping, and tracking systems that increased accuracy by 100% and reversed prior history of overdue accounts.
- **Directed complete redesign of nursery and its product inventory** to enhance appeal to high-net-worth clientele; efforts resulted in fundamental shift in operation's target demographic, enabling the capture of landscape and gardening business for multimillion-dollar homes/properties.
- **Recruited, hired, and trained top-performing staff of 26,** coaching best practices, a solution-sales approach, and an uncompromising focus on customer service – key to the rapid delivery of a six-figure lift in sales (from $1.2 million to $1.5 million) within first year.
- **Launched successful, multitiered marketing initiatives** including establishment of customer database; development of company Web site with e-commerce component; and creation of monthly, sales-driving newsletter distributed to 2,000 subscribers.
- **Expanded inventory** to include rare/unusual plants from across the globe by securing international import licenses. Additionally, **grew customer base** by winning interstate exporting approval.
- **Handled all purchase negotiations/contract review** for initial business procurement, negotiated all contracts with vendors/suppliers, and currently structuring deal for profitable sale of business.

Daniel Vanderbilt
Page Two

LOUISVILLE NURSERIES, INC., acquired by ABC GARDEN CENTER – Louisville, KY
Manager, 11/94 to 12/00

Retained by owners as a "key management asset" following acquisition of Louisville Nurseries, with P&L and management responsibility for the chain's largest, most profitable ($3 million/three-acre) operation. Supervised peak staff of 20, administered daily operations (including cash flow, banking, invoicing, A/P and A/R, and reconciliation functions), strategized marketing/advertising plans, and trained new managers and staff for subsequent satellite operations. ***Key Accomplishments:***

- **Built ground-up operation from zero sales to $3 million operation** within five years of business launch, setting the stage for successful corporate buyout by regional chain.
- **Designed and implemented all accounting and financial systems/procedures** and achieved successful integration with new corporate structure. Performed daily banking and reconciliation duties, and trained staff to investigate discrepancies to ensure complete accuracy.
- **Instituted purchasing programs and purchase order system** to enable efficient tracking/ verification of all orders, terms negotiated, and delivery schedules.
- Built strong, sustainable vendor relationships, negotiating win-win terms benefiting all parties.
- **Earned a reputation for expert financial, operational, and personnel leadership;** formally recognized as a "model" location and hand-selected by corporate headquarters to train new managers.

SOUTHERN NURSERIES – Cardiff, Wales
Owner, 3/92 to 8/94

Led staff of eight in a full spectrum of day-to-day operations (fiscal, general, and marketing/sales functions) of five-acre retail/wholesale propagation nursery, specializing in unique, native Cardiff plants as well as material from seed. ***Key Accomplishments:***

- **Catapulted revenue eight-fold** (from $100K to $800K) within two years of startup.
- **Architected all financial systems, procedures, and policies;** established routines for propagating stock to retail; and built significant B2B landscape trade sideline.

WELLINGTON NURSERIES – Cardiff, Wales
Leading Hand, 2/90 to 2/92

Education

UNIVERSITY OF KENTUCKY – Lexington, KY

- Currently enrolled in **BA in Accounting** degree program
- Completed **accounting and corporate finance** classes, 2002

Endorsements

"...Daniel handled all of his duties with the highest level of proficiency...proved [himself] invaluable to our operation...well organized and able to handle numerous tasks at the same time...Due in large part to Daniel's expertise, [we] grew to a multimillion-dollar business within five years...With his multiple skills, Daniel would be an asset to any organization." – **B. Kelly, President, Abbott Nurseries, Inc.**

"...hard-working, knowledgeable professional with integrity...his business acumen is very much appreciated...honest and very forthright." – **J. Cruise, Sales Manager, Tundrell Nurseries, Inc.**

Resume Strategy: *Daniel's resume emphasizes his talents in finance, accounting, and sales, repeatedly bringing out evidence of these skills in every section. He sells himself as a business professional instead of a nursery/plant expert by bringing out his background in fiscal and operations management and touting his successful record of maximizing sales and increasing efficiency. Since he's only just started his BA program, he leaves his education section toward the bottom of the resume, but he mentions his accounting major (relevant to his career goal) up-front in the profile. Daniel also includes important keywords to his career target in his "Relevant Skills" section.*

VICTOR ELLIS

14 Jaguar Drive
Chicago, IL 60643

victor@resumepower.com

Home: (773) 123-4567
Cellular: (773) 987-6543

Goal	**Entry-level Position in Finance — Financial Advisor / Securities Analyst**
Profile	• Hard-working professional with ten years of practical experience and a bachelor's degree in finance. • Top performer recognized for customer-relationship management and sales capabilities. Able to generate new business and maintain existing accounts by meeting customer requirements and offering service beyond expectations. • Team player with a commitment to working with colleagues to achieve corporate objectives. • International travel (Berlin, Amsterdam, Cairo, Johannesburg, and Abu Dhabi) has honed ability to interact with people from diverse backgrounds and cultures.
Education	UNIVERSITY OF CHICAGO — Chicago, IL **B.S. in Finance, Real Estate, and Law,** 2003 — Major in Finance, Minor in Business Law — Worked full-time while attending school full-time

Relevant Courses

• Corporate Finance	• Torts and Contracts	• Strategic Management
• Marketing Management	• Government Contracts	• Money and Banking
• Business Forecasting and Financial Planning	• Business Law	• Computer Information Systems
	• Macroeconomics	• Evaluation of Financial Policy
• Managerial Statistics	• Investment Analysis	• Financial Institutions/Markets

Experience	ABC DEPARTMENT STORE — Chicago, IL — **Sales Representative,** 1993 to present Fully accountable for maximizing sales in the Men's Shoes Department. Maintain customer database and deliver impeccable customer service. **Performance Highlights:** • Consistently outperformed sales goals for nine consecutive years. Ranked in the top three in department for sales volume and won over 50 sales contests. • Recognized for strong record of cross-selling merchandise and selected to train new employees. • Received numerous commendation letters from satisfied customers.
Activities	**Leadership:** President of Inter-Fraternity Council (1996 to 1997) — Elected to position to maintain strong relationships between 12 nationally based fraternities. Managed monthly budget and promoted philanthropy on and off campus. Nearly doubled membership within one year. **Memberships:** Finance Society (1996 to 1998), Society of Law and Contracts, (1997 to 1998), Sigma Chi (Rush Chairman/Historian/Secretary) **Teacher's Aide/Tutor:** Torts and Contracts Class (1997 to 1998) — Prof. Levine, J.D. states, "Victor was genuinely concerned for the students and quality of the course...excelled in his performance..."
Skills	**Computers:** Word, Excel, PowerPoint, Windows XP/2000/98 **Languages:** Written and conversational German; conversational Arabic

Resume Strategy: *Following his "Profile," Victor leads his resume with his "Education" section since his recent BS in finance is his most impressive credential to secure an entry-level finance position. This section is given extra detail with the bulleted list of "Relevant Courses," which helps to add in more keywords to the resume and shows the breadth of his academic background. He gives brief highlights of his sales job and uses an "Activities" section to showcase leadership skills and insert a testimonial from his professor.*

SHIFT SUPERVISOR (RESIDENTIAL TREATMENT PROGRAM) TO FINANCIAL SERVICES

Cindy Drew	55 State Street, Albany, NY 12223 ➤ (518) 123-4567 ➤ cindy@resumepower.com
Professional Goal	**FINANCIAL SERVICES INDUSTRY** **Financial Advisor / Funding Representative / Account Executive** Highly motivated professional pursuing a career in financial services. Offer excellent analytical, writing, research, communication, and computer skills. Regarded as a leader with an ability to develop cohesive and effective team environments. Comfortable delivering verbal presentations to small and large groups. Easily develop a positive rapport with people from diverse backgrounds and cultures.
Education **RELATED COURSES:**	SUNY AT ALBANY — Albany, NY **Bachelor of Arts in Political Science,** Minor in History, 5/02 Microeconomics, Macroeconomics, Modern Economic Principals, Computers, Public Administration, Statistics, Applied Ethics, Journalism, Public Speaking
Work Experience	NEW HORIZONS SCHOOL — Albany, NY (*Residential treatment facility for juveniles*) **Shift Supervisor,** 9/99 to present (part-time during school; full-time summers) **Staff Member,** 8/98 to 9/99 Promoted to shift supervisor position based on leadership skills and ability to provide quality services. Ensure smooth program operations and manage the schedules of students and employees. In charge of a team of seven youth advisors and crisis intervention counselors. Communicate with parents and keep them updated on treatment plans, progress, and issues. Intervene in crisis situations, such as deescalating students who are upset. Use sound judgment and common sense to quickly make decisions and resolve challenging problems. Coordinate details of special events. ➤ Recognized by administration for running a smooth program. ➤ Foster an environment of open communications between residents and staff. ➤ Develop positive relationships with staff members so that everyone works together toward common goals. ➤ Serve as a positive role model to students and encourage them to meet their potential. NEW-WAY DINER — Albany, NY **Prep Cook,** 8/95 to 5/98 UNITED STATES ARMY ROTC — Albany, NY **Cadet,** 6/95 to 8/95 Completed summer leadership courses and training. Served as executive officer of company, in charge of maintaining the schedule for 500 cadets for two weeks.
Computers	Windows 2000, PowerPoint, Word, Excel, Access, Project, WordPerfect, Mac OS
Community Activities	**Action Plus,** president (handled treasurer functions/special events), 8/98 to 5/02 **Student Environmental Action Coalition,** campus events director, 9/97 to 5/01 **Earth Day Network 2000,** campus organizer/charter member, 9/97 to 5/01

Resume Strategy: *Cindy explains her career change goal at the top of the resume and uses a brief paragraph to explain her most relevant, transferable skills for a job in financial services. In her "Education" section, she lists specific courses from her degree that hiring managers in the financial services sector would find appealing. In her "Work Experience" section, Cindy devotes the most space to positions she has held that involve management/leadership. She does not waste space detailing her job as a prep cook, since it is not relevant to her new career goal.*

8432 Logan Way
Doylestown, PA 18901

ANN COHEN

Home: 215-123-4567
E-mail: ann@resumepower.com

Financial & Insurance Services Professional

Career Goal: Entry-Level Underwriting / Claims Trainee ■ *Financial Consultant* ■ *Credit Analyst*

Series 7/66 licensed professional with additional certifications in life/health/long-term-care insurance, seeking to leverage these qualifications as well as experience in financial advising/analysis and risk assessment into entry-level claims, underwriting, financial consulting, or credit analyst position. Backed by strong educational credentials (in-progress CFP/MA; BA in criminal justice), with proven track record as a top performer throughout career. Expert interpersonal, presentation, and listening skills; able to build genuine rapport and diffuse stressful situations.

Solid financial analysis and budgeting skills with expertise in financial/retirement/tax/estate/cash-flow planning and in-depth understanding of a wide range of insurance and investment products (including variable universal life, variable/fixed annuities, mutual funds, wealth management services, term insurance, individual securities, CDs, Roth/traditional/SEP IRAs, and 529 college plans). Known for diplomacy and discretion; experienced dealing with sensitive and confidential information. Superior sales performer and record-setting revenue generator. Known for meticulous attention to detail, insightful analysis of complex data, and accurate report writing.

Licenses & Certifications

Series 7 (2000) ß Series 66 (2000) ■ PA Life & Health Insurance (2000) ■ Long-Term Care Sales Certification (2000)

Professional Experience

ABC FINANCIAL ADVISORS – Philadelphia, PA – **Financial Advisor,** 4/01 – Present

Sell financial plans and products and provide ongoing account management/portfolio reviews for company's No. 1 market group nationwide within high-volume office serving over 20,000 clients. Responsible for sales/marketing initiatives and new account acquisitions; delivery of knowledgeable, solution-centered advice customized to individual client needs and financial goals; and development of comprehensive financial plans and analyses. Perform asset allocation for assets ranging from $50K to $5 million. **Key Accomplishments:**

- **Built client base from zero to 90 loyal clients** with a broad equity mix, from high-net-worth individuals to beginning investors.

- Demonstrated exceptional follow-up, rapport-building, and relationship management skills, **resulting in a 50% success rate converting "be-backs" into clients – far above the 33% industry standard.**

- Set new company benchmarks for success; **outperformed appointment-setting averages by 700%, nearly doubled attendance ratios** (delivering an appointment "show" rate of one out of every 2.5 vs. the average one in four), **and achieved precedent-setting close ratios** (with a "buy" rate of one in three vs. one in four).

- **Delivered a higher than average gross dealer concession of $3,000 per client.**

- **Won lucrative referral business** through repeated word-of-mouth recommendations, with almost 17% of existing client base directly resulting from these referrals.

- **Passed the Series 7, Series 66, and Pennsylvania Life and Health Insurance exams** on first attempt.

- **Enhanced corporate visibility/sales as the selected representative/presenter** at international tradeshows.

COHEN COMMUNICATIONS CORPORATION – Doylestown, PA – **Office Manager,** 6/93 – 10/98

Accountable for on-time shipping/receiving operations, supervision of production line employees, quality assurance, training of all new-hires, data entry and order-taking, accounts payable/receivable, record keeping, year-end reports, and customer relationship management. Contributed to corporate marketing plans and traveled worldwide to represent company, expand clientele, and showcase products at major tradeshows and events. **Key Accomplishments:**

- **Personally responsible for a 20% increase in annual profits for five consecutive years** through innovation/implementation of results-driven marketing strategies and superior partnership-building initiatives.

- **Ensured optimal customer satisfaction and quality deliverables** by supervising full product assembly lifecycle, becoming self-taught expert on marine antennae and radio frequencies.

ANN COHEN

COHEN COMMUNICATIONS CORPORATION (*continued*)

- **Managed inventory of both product and parts/equipment** to guarantee smooth operations.
- **Contributed to a 35% productivity increase** through launch of company's first-ever employee incentive program.
- **Averted the loss of key accounts** through persuasive communication skills and talent for diffusing volatile situations.

U.S. CENSUS BUREAU – Philadelphia, PA – **Enumerator** (temporary position), 5/98 – 10/98

Updated maps and census data through review of town hall property tax records and in-person visits to assigned neighborhoods to interview residents and verify household information/street addresses. Prepared comprehensive reports for supervisor on all data collected. **Key Accomplishments:**

- **Doubled output expectations without compromising data integrity or thoroughness,** completing up to 12 interviews per hour compared to national average of 5.5 per hour.
- **Achieved a 100% accuracy assessment** on all submitted work.
- **Commended by supervisor** for compliments from survey respondents praising friendliness and professionalism.

BUCKS COUNTY ATTORNEY – Doylestown, PA – **Legal Intern,** Victim Witness Program, 9/97 – 12/97

Supported clients prior to trial, reviewed/updated case files, and prepared concise case summaries. Observed courtroom proceedings and gave feedback to attorneys and caseworkers.

Education

TEMPLE UNIVERSITY – Philadelphia, PA   GPA: 3.0

Currently pursuing **MA in Finance and Taxation and Certified Financial Planner (CFP)** credential. Anticipated completion: Fall 2003

UNIVERSITY OF LONDON LAW SCHOOL – London, England   GPA: 3.4

Graduate Diploma in Criminology (Graduate Coursework Certificate Program), 1999

Selected as Research Assistant for London Crime Commission.

BUCKS COLLEGE – Doylestown, PA – **BA in Criminal Justice,** 1998   GPA: 3.2

Training

- **Risk Management** – Philadelphia, PA, 2001
- **Disability Income Assessment** – New York, NY, 2001
- **Human Life Value Concept** – Philadelphia, PA, 2001
- **Financial Advisor Course** – Buckingham, PA, 2000
- **Tax Control Triangle** – Philadelphia, PA

Presentations

Financial Planning – *Delivered to 15 members of ABC Company* (New York, NY) – 2001
Retirement Planning for the Future – *Delivered to 21 staff* (Philadelphia, PA) – 2001
Stock Options – *Delivered to 25 ABC Fortune 500 Company staff* (Philadelphia, PA) – 2001

Technical Summary

MS Office Suite ■ Lotus Notes ■ Westlaw ■ Various financial advisory software and client data systems

---

Resume Strategy: *Ann is able to combine her dual career goals of either breaking into the insurance industry or achieving advancement in the financial services industry by showcasing her relevant strengths and credentials in each of these areas. She prominently highlights her key qualifications in the opening profile and in the "Licenses and Certifications" section and uses bulleted accomplishments with quantified numbers, percentages, and dollar amounts to prove her history as a top performer.*

Shanna Hart

15 Burns Road, Akron, OH 44310 ■ 330-123-4567 ■ shanna@resumepower.com

GOAL: INVESTMENT BANKING / MANAGEMENT CONSULTING

- **Business consultant** with a solid academic and practical foundation in global-business management, international finance, and business-process improvement within the financial-services sector.
- **Creative problem solver with the ability to apply analytical and quantitative skills** to evaluate business and client needs and formulate solutions that enhance operational processes and profitability. Recognized for strong project-management and team-leadership skills.
- **Keen understanding of the business implications of technology.** Keep up to date with changes in the high-tech sector through market research and strategic analyses.

AREAS OF KNOWLEDGE

- Advanced Corporate Finance
- Valuation Tools/Techniques (DCF, NPV, CAPM)
- Modeling/Sensitivity Analysis
- Capital Structure

- Financial Leverage and Risks
- Derivatives
- Mergers and Acquisitions
- Restructuring/Divestitures
- Project Management

- Strategic Behavior
- Investment Banking
- Financial Statement Analysis
- Money and Financial Markets
- Pricing Strategies/Negotiations

EDUCATION

UNIVERSITY OF AKRON — Akron, OH   **MBA, Management and Finance,** May 2002
UNIVERSITY OF LONDON — London, England   **Bachelor of Engineering, Computer Science,** 1993

PROFESSIONAL BACKGROUND

AKRON TECHNOLOGY GROUP — Akron, OH
Sr. Systems Analyst, July 1995 to present

Consult with Fortune 500 clients within financial-services sectors, including ABC Company, DEF Company, and GHI Company. Assess needs and design and implement an array of software systems, tools, and technology solutions to address client-management, legal, and reporting issues. **Key Accomplishments:**

- Currently coordinating systems between fixed income, commodity, and operations groups at ABC Company to optimize efficiency and minimize reporting errors.
- Developed legal systems at ABC Company to handle workflow management tools, trade agreements, commodity agreements, and intellectual property for all ABC Company entities.
- Served on team that simplified global management reporting system and reports for DEF Company.

FORTUNE 500 COMPANY — London, England
Sr. Programmer/Analyst, October 1994 to July 1995

Managed large-scale software development projects for international clientele. Led teams of up to 15, consulted with clients, defined project scope and schedule, and prioritized tasks. **Key Accomplishments:**

- Took over major project and guided it toward completion within proscribed time and budget constraints. Opened lines of communications and instituted measures to track project progress and deliverables.

SOFTWARE CONSULTING COMPANY— London, England
Software Engineer, February to September 1994

Resume Strategy: *A banner at the top of her resume positions Shanna for a career shift to investment banking. She continues to back up her qualifications by including a bulleted summary and "Areas of Knowledge" sections. Shanna emphasizes her exposure to finance-related industries throughout her experience section.*

17
Retail/Customer Service

Mike Black

14 Prospect Drive
Brooklyn, NY 11249
Home: (718) 123-4567
Cell: (718) 987-6543
mb@resumepower.com

Available for Extensive Travel

Expertise

- **Executive Leadership & Supervision**

- **Strategic Planning & Corporate Vision**

- **P&L Management**

- **Merchandising Strategies**

- **Purchasing Management**

- **Inventory Control**

- **Systems Automation**

- **Sales & Marketing**

- **Relationship Management**

- **Loss Prevention**

- **Team Building & Staff Training**

- **Turnaround Management**

- **Product Assortment Planning**

- **Market Trend Analysis**

- **Contract Negotiations**

Retail Operations Manager

Director of Operations ■ *Regional Manager* ■ *Purchasing Manager*

Accomplished executive, adept in all phases of retail management and corporate operations, with career chronicled by multiple awards, repeated promotional advancements, and goal-surpassing performance. Extensive experience across a full spectrum of retail functions (e.g., strategic planning, purchasing, inventory control, policy development, budgeting/forecasting, loss prevention, merchandising, marketing, staff development) at the store, regional, and corporate levels.

Turnaround management expert, with recurring success reversing underperforming locations to chainwide dominance in record time. Respected, dynamic leader of top-tier teams and proponent of service as the means to drive business. Enjoy training subordinates to deliver peak performance and contribute to the organization in greater positions of responsibility. Able to articulate a shared sense of purpose and win enthusiastic commitment to furthering corporate goals.

Professional Experience

ABC MUSIC AND VIDEO — Brooklyn, NY — 1983 – 2001
22-store music and video retail chain with annual sales of $50 million and per-store inventory ranging from $250K – $450K.

Purchasing Manager, 1994 – 2001

Progressed through company, with career marked by repeated promotional advancements culminating in senior management role with accountability for $10 million purchasing operations/strategy for chain's 24 locations. Met weekly with music distribution company executives to coordinate all purchasing, policies, and cooperative promotional strategies; supervised general operations and MIS department staff; negotiated all equipment leases and vendor contracts; directed operationwide pricing structures and inventory management; managed product database; and held responsibility for facility maintenance oversight companywide. Results:

- Architected strategic purchasing system and leveraged expert buying skills to enable **three complete inventory turns annually – double the industry standard** – for subsequent gross profit margin improvement of 28%. Created product priority code system and stock level differentials to standardize inventory, maximize sales, and optimize volume-driven product mix across diverse markets in five states.

- **Delivered $100K in annual savings** by slashing costly return penalties by an average of **60%**. Negotiated favorable profit incentives with 30+ distribution companies as well as record company giants.

- Formulated and executed buying plans that allowed company to reduce inventory levels by **10% to 15%** per store, for a chainwide inventory reduction of **$800K**.

- **Relocated corporate office** from a 40K-sq.-ft. center to a 5K-sq.-ft. facility, accomplished in eight days. Rapidly liquidated warehouse inventory, engineered creative storage solutions, and facilitated overhead reduction of **$120K annually**.

- **Captured $360K+** in co-op advertising annually and maximized dollars through strategic product selection and targeted marketing tied to regional trends and radio play.

- **Assisted in all aspects of new store openings and closings.** Supplied new stores with all opening orders, advised store managers on layout/merchandising strategy, helped regional managers with new employee hiring/training, set up POS systems, liquidated hundreds of thousands of dollars in inventory for closing stores, and minimized penalties from leasing contract disengagement.

- Solidified win-win agreement with five of the six major U.S. record companies that **secured recurring wholesaler discounts** despite company's retailer status.

Mike Black

Resume, Page Two

Home: (718) 123-4567
Cell: (718) 987-6543
mb@resumepower.com

Professional Experience (*continued*)

Regional Director, 1989 – 1994

Provided daily operational, financial, and policy oversight for 12-store, 200-employee, $20 million region encompassing three states. Held ultimate responsibility for regional P&L, inventory/operational control, loss prevention, sales forecasting, budgeting/payroll, staff development, and merchandising/promotional strategies. Approved all hiring, assessed problem areas and implemented corrective actions, and established product mix for each location. Results:

- Launched comprehensive internal loss prevention measures that **regained an estimated $40K within first year** of implementation and were subsequently adopted companywide. Cut shrink almost in half to achieve company-leading position, with a 1.25% shrink that **outperformed chainwide average by 100%.**

- Fostered the development and promotional advancement of multiple staff, with three store managers under personal supervision awarded **"Director of the Year."** (1989, 1992, 1993) Attained one of the highest management retention levels companywide.

- **Turned around underperforming locations,** transforming stores ranked in the bottom one-third companywide into top-five sales volume locations.

- **Maintained a visible presence regionwide.** Traveled extensively to win the confidence and trust of management team; created a supportive, customer-centered environment; significantly upped morale by regularly meeting with front-line staff, joining them "in the trenches," and encouraging upward communication.

- Modernized operation by introducing **chain's first fully integrated automated systems** for significant improvements to operational controls and efficiency.

- **Revamped company's personnel handbooks** and operational, policy, and procedures manuals to bring operation into full compliance with federal mandates and instill a shared vision across all levels of the organization.

- **Repeatedly honored with "Regional Director of The Year" award.** (1990, 1993)

- **Promoted to Purchasing Manager.**

Store Director (Staten Island, NY; Elmhurst, NY), 1983 – 1989

Challenged to right-size problem-riddled Staten Island location following superior performance managing Elmhurst store. Directed four managers and a 22-member team in all aspects of daily retail operations for 12K-sq.-ft., $2 million store, including strategic planning, staffing, budgeting, purchasing, loss prevention, and marketing/advertising. Results:

- **Reversed store's downward spiral** by overhauling systems, processes, and personnel. Addressed and corrected a myriad of issues including internal theft, lagging customer service, substandard store appearance, and poor morale.

- **Catapulted store's performance to a top-five location** chainwide within first year, skyrocketing sales over 40%. Surpassed projections by 15% following second year, to win subsequent top-three location rank companywide.

Training & Professional Development

Completed numerous retail management courses in customer service, inventory control, loss prevention, time management, leadership, and supervisory techniques.

Resume Strategy: *Mike capitalizes on his history of promotional advancements and management achievements to show that he is qualified for a shift to retail operations management from purchasing management. His new objective is stated in a large tagline at the top of his resume, followed by a narrative summary that explains his key qualifications. His resume also includes a list of his areas of expertise down the left margin. Mike's work history focuses on achievements related to improved performance of retail operations.*

ASSISTANT STORE MANAGER TO RETAIL DISTRICT MANAGER

BRETT CARTER

(718) 123-6543
brett@resumepower.com

15 East Street
Bronx, NY 10470

| Career Goal | **RETAIL DISTRICT MANAGER / STORE MANAGER** |

Executive Profile

Accomplished manager with exemplary 16-year career for Fortune 500 retailer marked by repeated promotions and awards. Well-rounded retail background, with experience managing all lines, big-box locations, workforces of up to 200, and a full complement of operational functions (e.g., P&L, receiving, sales floor, merchandising, purchasing, IT systems). History of maximizing sales, minimizing costs/shrink, and outperforming profit/service goals, as evidenced by achieving record revenues ($26 million), slashing overhead 17%, and earning #1 rankings in category sales and customer service benchmarks districtwide. Dynamic, high-energy leader and effective trainer, able to motivate and develop top-tier, customer-focused teams.

Expertise

- Profit Enhancement
- Market Share Increase
- Cost Containment
- Loss / Inventory Control
- POS / IT Systems
- Turnaround Management
- Marketing & Merchandising
- Team Building & Training
- Change Agent Leadership

Career Progression

ABC COMPANY – Various Locations   1986 to Present
Fortune 500 broad-line retailer with $41 billion in annual revenue.

Assistant Store Manager, Retail Central (Bronx, NY), 01/02 to Present
Merchant, Men's / Children's / Shoes (Princeton, NJ), 11/98 to 01/02
Department Manager, Home Improvement (Elmhurst, NY), 03/93 to 11/98
Operations Manager (Astoria, NY), 11/91 to 03/93
Manager of Receiving / General Office / Sporting Goods (Astoria, NY), 11/86 to 11/91

Advanced through series of promotions, with current joint accountability (with store manager) for overall financial performance of $26 million, 200-employee, big-box location in the Bronx. Provide simultaneous management of daily store operations (hard and soft lines) and 36-member department; execute and enforce corporate-driven programs, promotions, and policies; oversee sound merchandising and loss-control strategies; maintain national presentation/service standards; and ensure optimum customer satisfaction, associate morale, and attainment of P&L goals. Responsibilities in prior positions included inventory control, local purchasing program management, daily oversight of multiple departments, supervision/training/ scheduling/payroll for up to 60 associates, and direction of receiving/office functions. ***Selected Accomplishments:***

... as Assistant Store Manager *(2002 to Present):*

- **Jointly implemented strategic business planning,** associate training, and merchandising programs to outperform corporate revenue and profit goals by **+6%** and **+8%,** respectively.
- **Retained as one of only five managers** (out of 21 at location) during major corporate restructure, and subsequently provided effective change-agent leadership to hundreds of associates during significant shift in company mission, goals, and processes to reassure workforce, win across-the-board buy-in, and boost morale.
- **Functioned as store's computer/POS systems expert,** with responsibility for IT vendor negotiations/supervision and delivery of hands-on technical training to staff.
- **Developed many entry-level associates to leadership positions,** earning a reputation as a skilled coach and mentor.
- **Catapulted customer satisfaction levels 18%** (all-time high) by improving cooperation and cohesion between various departments. Engineered new "ride-along" program linking retail sales floor associates with Parts, Service, and Delivery department representatives to enhance teamwork and strengthen overall customer-focused mind-set.
- **Augmented corporate/store visibility,** strengthened community relations, promoted employee volunteerism, and raised thousands of dollars by coordinating numerous special events for charity (e.g., Big Brothers Big Sisters, Gilda's Club, Lifelong AIDS Alliance).

... as Merchant *(1998 to 2002):*

- **Earned #1 category ranking districtwide** (out of 15 locations), delivering a goal-surpassing 12% sales increase and **10%–12%** margin improvement across Men's, Children's, and Shoe departments in a single year (**$9 million** in sales).

BRETT CARTER

Career Progression

ABC COMPANY (*continued*)

- **Led the nation in licensed team apparel sales,** achieving new record of a **64%** revenue increase (**$1.5 million**) in this line over prior year.
- **Launched effective purchasing, merchandising, and customer care strategies** that resulted in store winning city award as "Best Place to Shop for Kids."

... as Home Improvement Department Manager (1993 to 1998):

- **Trained 60-member team on effective up-selling techniques,** generating goal-surpassing revenues in service contract and extended warranty sales.
- **Solidified #1 ranking in customer satisfaction** (out of 15 in district) for three consecutive years (1995–1998) through leadership of formal training and one-on-one coaching emphasizing service.
- **Surpassed revenue and profit goals,** bringing category from $7 million to **$10 million (42% increase)** during tenure through strategic initiatives that helped counteract arrival of major competitors (e.g., Home Depot) to local area.
- **Demonstrated talent for staff development,** fostering the promotional growth of eight hourly employees to department manager positions.
- **Managed $7 million store overhaul as remodel team leader,** guiding 50 team members across every department in all aspects of major initiative. Ensured on-time, on-budget project completion while simultaneously protecting sales and customer safety during each construction phase.
- **Directed product and department training for 15-store district,** conducting three sessions annually for hundreds of employees.

... as Operations Manager (1991 to 1993):

- **Delivered a 17% reduction in overhead** through outsourcing initiatives and a **26% upsurge in licensed business revenue** by expanding vendor programs during peak holiday season.
- **Oversaw storewide implementation and user training** of new register systems and established cross-training program for employees of discontinued catalog department.
- **Drove pace-setting sales of ABC Company credit cards** by innovating motivational incentive programs and contests.

... as Receiving / General Office / Sporting Goods Manager (1986 to 1991):

- **Outperformed revenue and profit goals consistently,** earning formal recognition and rapid promotional advancement.
- **Engineered improvements in receiving processes** to streamline operational efficiency.

Education & Training

HUNTER COLLEGE – New York, NY
Coursework toward a **BA in Business Administration**

Professional Development Highlights: Diversity (1999), Team Building (1998), P&L Management (1998), Store Simplification (1993), Customer Service (ongoing)

Resume Strategy: *Brett packs his resume with examples of how he has improved revenue, margins, and sales using numbers and percentages to back his claims. He emphasizes his diverse background in both hard- and soft-lines throughout various departments to help convince employers that he is ready for the next step in his career. He lists achievements for each of his positions held separately to help show how he has been an outstanding manager throughout his long-term tenure with his employer.*

JANET SHAW

(631) 123-4567 ◆ janet@resumepower.com ◆ 14 Courtyard Way ◆ Dix Hills, NY 11749

Sales Manager ◆ Retail Operations Manager

Accomplished sales and operations leader with a track record of advancement and accelerated growth in reaching district management level with Fortune 500 retailer. Strong decision maker, problem solver, and strategist with demonstrated ability to direct startup operations, develop effective business solutions, balance operational efficiency with customer service, and achieve optimal levels of profitability in complex, demanding environments. Reputation for integrity, innovation, and visionary leadership.

Special talent for new business development, referrals, and repeat business, resulting in dramatic revenue increases. Excellent communication, negotiation, and interpersonal skills. Able to establish a consensus, reconcile opposing objectives, and gain the cooperation of diverse individuals, including union and nonunion personnel. Bachelor's degree in management, reinforced by specialized training in sales and customer service. Skilled in process improvement, relationship building, cost containment/reduction, and multimillion-dollar budget administration. Proficient in Microsoft Office, IBM Mainframe, Lotus Notes, Environmental Research Systems Institute Routing Software, POS Systems, and Access.

Career Highlights

FORTUNE 500 COMPANY – Multiple Locations   1992 – Present
Full-line, Fortune 500 retailer with annual revenues of $40 billion.

District Route Manager – Brooklyn, NY, 2001 – Present
Progressed through company, with career marked by repeated promotional advancements culminating in accountability for $8.5 million payroll and manual routing of up to 2,000 repair/service calls per day from individual and corporate accounts in two-state, five-branch district. Responsible for 24 direct reports and more than 200 unionized, in-home service technicians. (Direct reports include technical managers, same-day route specialists, next-day route specialists, and message center specialists.)

Ensure compliance with union contracts, guidelines, and seniority mandates while preserving optimal levels of efficiency and customer satisfaction. Actively participate in collective bargaining and represent the company in grievance/arbitration hearings. Assume leadership role in forecasting, planning, implementation, and performance management. *Key Accomplishments:*

- **Provided the leadership** that enabled the company to service approximately 270,000 customers annually without a loss in efficiency, resulting in deeper market penetration.
- **Captured significant amount of paid labor dollars** by reducing amount of time necessary to dispatch technicians to customer locations.
- **Worked closely with lead union negotiator** to win needed concessions that resulted in total cost benefit of **$3 million.**
- **Reduced technical payroll by $1 million** by eliminating repair shops and farming merchandise out to centralized branch.
- **Increased service calls by 10%** in YTD 2002 through more efficient routing.
- **Slashed service call costs by $1.14 million.**
- **Increased customer satisfaction index 12 points,** the most significant increase in NE region.
- **Initiated weekly round-table conferences** to enhance management team communication.
- **Gained recognition for increasing level of teamwork** throughout district, management staff, and routing office.
- **Consolidated two operations into one** after organizational restructuring.
- **Developed spreadsheets to simplify decision making** and operational analysis.

Branch / Sales Manager – Elmhurst, NY, 1999 – 2000

Directed startup of highly successful sales, service, and repair operation with 6,800 square feet of selling space for hard lines merchandise (appliances, tools, hardware, and electronics). Maintained full P&L accountability. Designed plan-o-grams, merchandising strategies, and product mix. Hired, trained, scheduled, and supervised union personnel, including assistant manager, shippers, receivers, inventory control specialists, salespersons, and shop steward.

Expertise

Sales & Sales
Management

Operations
Management

Revenue
Production

New Business
Development

Customer
Relations

Relationship
Building

P&L/Budgeting

Cost
Containment

Decision Making

Routing/
Distribution

Training/Staff
Development

Collective
Bargaining

Process
Improvement

Labor
Relations

Merchandising
Strategies

JANET SHAW

FORTUNE 500 COMPANY – **Branch/Sales Manager** (*continued*) – *Key Accomplishments:*

- **Presided over opening of new facility and drove first-year sales to #2 ranking** in New York market, outperforming other Fortune 500 Company locations in operation for 30+ years.
- **Developed purchasing channels** that significantly increased sales and profit margins, acquiring appliances and parts as distressed goods for 25 cents on the dollar and reselling them. Also acquired return items from retail location, marked them down, and successfully resold them to homeowners, individual businesses, schools, institutions, and government agencies. These purchasing sources were later implemented districtwide.
- **Cultivated productive relationships** with all surrounding full-line retail locations and provided low-cost repair solutions, creating win-win situation.
- **Conceived of, wrote, and developed** 125-page employee manual on merchandising, sales, hiring, and staff development. This innovation went on to widespread use throughout district, enabling new merchants to add value to the company.
- **Hired, trained, and developed new front-line sales force,** a top-tier team that paid enormous bottom-line dividends.
- **Gained recognition as Fortune 500 Company's youngest district route manager.**

Technical Manager Trainee – Astoria, NY, 1999

Provided comprehensive support to technical managers, developing staffing forecasts using Access Payroll Planner, interpreting and communicating RMDS reports, and conducting meetings with technicians to resolve operational issues and enhance productivity. Completed ad-hoc projects in finance and accounting. *Key Accomplishments:*

- **Identified/eliminated numerous impediments,** including use of archaic laptop computers by technicians. Recommended enhancements and productivity tools that increased efficiency.
- **Conducted intensive business literacy training** for technicians, successfully imparting cost of doing business and need for high level of productivity. Technicians responded with improved performance in areas of cost control, revenue generation, and customer service.
- **Supplemented training effort with introduction of easy-to-read spreadsheets** that detailed key business factors.

Route Specialist – New York, NY, 1999

- **Devised cost-effective work routes,** enhanced levels of service to customers, controlled overtime expenses, and succeeded in eliminating work backlog and stabilizing branch.

Service Technician – Hempstead, NY, 1994 – 1999

- **Single-handedly resolved repair backlogs** at retail stores by monitoring repair orders more closely, serving as single point of contact, and making field visits.

Advanced through series of progressive, early-career promotions with Fortune 500 Company, holding positions of **Sales Clerk, Customer Service Representative, Surplus Inventory Returns Clerk,** and **Merchandized Inventory Control** Clerk (1992 – 1994).

Education & Training

HUNTER COLLEGE – New York, NY
Bachelor of Science in Management, 1999 / GPA in Major: 3.57

Attended seminars and training courses to enhance professional development, including:
Civil Treatment ◆ Managing an Organized Work Force ◆ Sales Management ◆ IT Management

Resume Strategy: *Janet uses her qualifications profile to point out her broad background in both sales and operations management as well as her track record of repeated promotional advancement. Janet's first choice is to return to a sales management position, so she places this first in her resume title and places "new business development" in bold and italics for emphasis in the profile. She also makes sure that her earlier position as branch/sales manager fits on the first page of the resume. Her bulleted accomplishments show her record of top performance leading both sales and business operations.*

Sarah Miller

(513) 123-4567
sarah@resumepower.com

15 Blossom Way
Cincinnati, Ohio 45227

TARGETING CUSTOMER SERVICE MANAGEMENT POSITIONS

Innovative, results-oriented manager / Respected team leader, motivator, and coach

Customer-oriented manager with ten years of experience providing high-impact solutions to global companies. Track record of delivering excellent customer service and training team members to strive for customer satisfaction. Accustomed to conducting business with people of diverse cultures and backgrounds. Bilingual in English and Spanish; able to read Portuguese. Dynamic trainer, comfortable speaking in front of small and large audiences. Solid understanding of global business issues, including tariffs and quotes, imports and exports, and monetary exchanges. Available for extensive travel. Advanced computer skills.

Professional Experience

Reliable Service Corporation - Cincinnati, Ohio   10/94 – present
Leading service provider to airline/travel agency reservation systems in the Caribbean and Latin America.

Quality Control Coordinator, 11/98 – Present

Challenged to improve the company's performance record and establish systems to maintain a high level of quality once achieved. Oversee delivery of services for two major customers, American Airlines (and its affiliated travel agencies) and Amadeus. Ensure that service calls are responded to and resolved on time and that contractual procedures are followed. Audit hundreds of calls daily and gather information on efficiency and quality. Monitor customer satisfaction and recommend procedures to enhance performance. Train and provide supervision to employees regarding policies and contracts. ***Key Accomplishments:***

- Increased quality-standard rate from approximately 55% to more than 90% within four months.
- Surpassed quality expectations through application of contract terms, implementation of audit procedures, and dissemination of regulations to all countries.
- Implemented internal performance reports to fuel healthy competition between country subsidiaries.
- Persuaded customers to allow fairness adjustments in the way they measure services, which in turn boosted company's service grades.
- Developed training manuals in English and Spanish to outline contract specifications. Country subsidiaries and Ohio dispatch have since adopted the ideas set forth in the manuals.

Dispatch Manager, 9/96 – 11/98

Oversaw an ever-growing, multifunction, international dispatch department. Handled staffing and scheduling decisions, training, motivating, and disciplining a large team of employees. Responded to upper management for the department, assisted customers, and collaborated with departments in the Ohio office and abroad. ***Key Accomplishments:***

- Instrumental in company's growth from a small enterprise with few employees to a dynamic, thriving business. As the company took on new business in Latin America, the Caribbean, and South America, team grew from three to over a dozen employees. Recruited skilled employees and attracted new contracts by presenting an image of quality and excellence.
- Boosted and maintained employee morale and consistently exceeded productivity standards, despite financial constraints and staff shortages.
- Created a cohesive, self-sufficient team environment by training staff to assume increased responsibility.

Management Assistant, 1/96 – 9/96

Managed auditing, inventory, invoicing, and billing for Galileo contract. Selected to resolve bookkeeping and accounting problems associated with Puerto Rican subsidiary. ***Key Accomplishments:***

- Rebuilt and reconciled bank records through careful research of poorly kept account records and canceled checks. Recovered unpaid employee advances by placing liens on offending parties.

Sarah Miller

Management Assistant (*continued*)

- Negotiated a deferred payment plan for a $5,000 balance to Puerto Rico Telephone Company following careful examination and reconciliation of charges.
- Renegotiated health-care contract for Puerto Rico office, which resulted in substantial cost savings.

Install Coordinator, 11/93 – 1/96

Oversaw Sabre-related installation activities, such as scheduling, dispatching, interfacing technicians with customers, and ensuring completion within contractual time frames. ***Key Accomplishments:***

- Effectively managed Sabre service contract for South/Central America and the Caribbean. Project expanded from 50 to 200 projects when service to Brazil started.
- Received numerous letters of commendation from customers, which led to promotion to administrative support and ultimately dispatch management.

Service Coordinator / Dispatcher, 10/94 – 11/93

Scheduled and dispatched service calls, responded to customer inquires, and secured technical support as needed. ***Key Accomplishments:***

- Established excellent rapport with technical staff, gaining respect for professionalism and expertise.
- Maintained immaculate records to minimize problems and financial loss.
- Regularly called upon to act as department head for every contract.

AVI Finance Company - Cincinnati, Ohio   5/89 – 10/94
Lending and financial institution, acquired by Ohio Bank and First Mutual Savings.

Financial Services Associate / Customer Service

Alternated between teller and customer service roles. ***Key Accomplishments:***

- Earned bonuses for several quarters in a row.
- Named "Employee of the Month," 3/93.

Education & Training

University of Cincinnati - Cincinnati, Ohio

MBA coursework, 1991 – 1992
Bachelor of Business Administration, International Business / Accounting, 1989

Professional Training:

- ISO 1900 Implementation, 1998, Certificate issued by QSI
- Excel Data Management, 2002, Executrain
- Excel Expert Topics, 2000, Executrain
- Excel Presenting Information, 1999, Executrain
- How to Supervise People, 1998, Fred Pryor Co.
- Coaching Skills for Managers and Supervisors, 1997, Fred Pryor Co.

Computers

- Word, Excel, PowerPoint, Access, Peachtree Accounting, Sabre, Windows 2000/98, COBOL, Fortran

Resume Strategy: *After stating her career goal, Sarah uses her "Profile" section to emphasize her key strengths in customer service, public speaking, and business processes, as well as her bilingual fluency. Her "Professional Experience" section highlights ways that she has strengthened team environments, quality standards, and business growth – achievements that are sure to be valued by employers looking for customer-oriented management professionals.*

Richard MacLeod

14 Elmpark Way ◆ Reno, NV 89509
Home: (775) 123-4567 ◆ Cellular: (775) 987-6543 ◆ E-mail: richard@resumepower.com

CUSTOMER SERVICE PROFESSIONAL

Seeking to Maximize Sales, Marketing, and Service Experience in a Customer Relations Position

Versatile, quality-driven customer service specialist with a proven track record of establishing and maintaining strong, sustainable relationships with customers leading to complete satisfaction and repeat/referral business. Place uncompromising focus on customer needs fulfillment while striving to meet and surpass corporate sales and performance goals. Excellent communicator, listener, and troubleshooter, with expert written and verbal fluency in Spanish and English. Able to manage multiple tasks in high-volume environments and relate to customers with a wide range of backgrounds, personality types, and experiences.

Core competencies include:

❑ Problem Resolution Strategies	❑ Customer Satisfaction/Retention	❑ Service Improvements
❑ Sales & Marketing Strategies	❑ Customer Relations	❑ Workflow Prioritization
❑ Staff Training & Mentoring	❑ Revenue & Performance Gains	❑ Quality Assurance Standards
❑ Event Planning & Coordination	❑ Cost Reduction & Avoidance	❑ Time/Resource Management

———— Professional Experience ————

ACE ASSOCIATES – Reno, NV (*Full-service real estate agency*)   2001

Independent Real Estate Agent

In charge of advertising, marketing, and buyer/seller relations as licensed agent for this high-profile firm. Used direct mail and cold calling to attract prospective buyers; built foundation for ten potential sales closings within first six months of employment.

❑ Through exhaustive efforts evaluating 40+ homes over three-month period, assisted couple in locating satisfactory property and negotiated price reduction of $43,000 off asking price.
❑ Gained experience in addressing customer-needs fulfillment within new industry.

ABC MOTOR INN – Reno, NV (*86-room hotel property*)   1997 – 1999

Overnight Front Desk Manager

Held full responsibility and decision-making accountability for operations, finance, sales, staff, customer service, and security management of high-volume location servicing local and out-of-town guests. Led crew of up to nine employees in achieving and surpassing guest satisfaction and quality assurance standards.

❑ Established and maintained outstanding customer service and satisfaction record throughout tenure; managed an average of 100 to 125 guest registries per shift.
❑ Streamlined registration processing from eight to 13 per hour by expediting turnaround from guest departure to new guest check-in, resulting in 62% revenue increase during peak periods.
❑ Resolved special needs situations on a weekly basis, including crime prevention/public safety incidents and extended stay arrangements for victims of residential fire damage.

EL FRITE / FREELANCE CHEF – Reno, NV (*Performed at bistros catering to upscale clientele*)   1994 – 1997

Executive Chef / Sous Chef (Emphasis on French cuisine)

Demonstrated excellent job performance and customer relations for two distinctly different dining establishments, overseeing inventory control, food preparation and preservation, staff training, event planning, and guest satisfaction issues. Reported directly to owner; put in charge of controlling costs for food and nonfood items, ordering from distributors and vendors, and instituting quality control measures.

❑ Coordinated series of special events introducing creative dining solutions and focusing on attentiveness to guest relations. Increased event calendar 14% and earned rave guest reviews.
❑ Revamped stock room and refrigeration areas to reduce food costs approximately 50% and maintain high ratings on quality assurance inspections.
❑ Earned promotion to executive chef based on innovative ideas and guest compliments.

Richard MacLeod

Professional Experience

RENO SUPPER CLUB – Reno, NV (*First-class destination restaurant with live entertainment*)   1990 – 1993

Assistant Manager

Key member of the management team for this exclusive food and entertainment establishment. Advanced from administrative position to management and led team of up to 24 employees in ensuring smooth operations and the achievement of customer service goals. Managed all operational aspects, including HR, training, cash management, inventory control, event coordination, sales/marketing, public relations, and liaison affairs. Assigned increasingly progressive responsibilities for guest satisfaction and profit initiatives.

- Created network of contacts with external business partners and frequent guests that built PR for establishment and led to successful negotiations and revenue flow.
- Ensured successful planning and execution of events for high-profile celebrities, including Mariah Carey, Bill Clinton, Liza Minelli, Whitney Houston, and Jack Nicholson.
- Accumulated high volume of guest thank-you notes and commendations for exceptional service and quality of food preparations.

Education & Training

Associate of Applied Science Degree in Hospitality Management

Reno Technical College, Reno, NV / G.P.A.: 3.4

Professional Development:

Home-Based Computer Training Course (2001)
Travel Agent, ABC Travel, Reno, NV (1983)
National Bartending Program, Reno, NV (1980)

Licenses:

Notary Public, State of Nevada (2001)
Real Estate Agent, State of Nevada (2000)

Affiliations:

National Association of Realtors, Member (2001)

Computer Skills

MS Word, Outlook, Excel; Intuit QuickBooks, Windows ME

Reply To

Home: (775) 123-4567 w Cellular: (775) 987-6543 ♦ E-mail: richard@resumepower.com

Resume Strategy: *Richard's resume title and qualifications profile bring focus to his document and provide a compelling overview of his background serving customers, driving loyal followings, and building relationships. For each of the diverse jobs he has held, Richard brings out how they contributed to his qualifications for customer service positions.*

18
Human Resources/Recruiting

Craig Starr

48 Western Lane ◆ Dallas, TX 75214 ◆ Home Phone: 214-123-4567 ◆ E-mail: craigstarr@resumepower.com

HUMAN RESOURCES PROFESSIONAL

Dedicated personnel administrator with solid background in all aspects of HR management including employee recruitment, training, benefits, discipline, and termination; salary surveys and administration; guidance of line supervisors in all labor relations activities; employment/labor law compliance and policy development; and dispute mediation. Backed by 16 years of additional experience as a workers' compensation, loss mitigation, and employee safety expert.

Superior communication/presentation skills with demonstrated success effectively diffusing highly charged situations in a professional and nonconfrontational manner. Formally recognized by repeated promotions. Skilled user of technology. Sensitive to cultural and diversity issues.

HIGHLIGHTS OF EXPERTISE

- HR/Personnel Management
- Employment/Labor Laws & Policies
- EEOC/FMLA/ADA/OSHA
- EPA Hazardous Waste Guidelines
- Benefits Administration/COBRA
- Unemployment Processes
- Expense Management

- Recruiting, Screening, Hiring & Training
- Disciplinary & Termination Procedures
- Salary/Wage Administration & Surveys
- Dispute Mediation
- Workers' Compensation
- Insurance Premium Review
- Supervisory Training

- Risk Insulation/Loss Mitigation
- Employee Safety
- Professional Presentations
- Budget Administration
- Leadership & Supervision
- Mentoring Programs
- Employee Morale
- Start-Up Operations

HUMAN RESOURCES ADMINISTRATION EXPERIENCE

AVANTE MANUFACTURING COMPANY – Dallas, TX
Personnel Administrator, Employee Relations Department, 10/84 to 10/89
Wholly responsible for all HR functions for the direct workforce of 200 including wage and salary administration, disciplinary review and oversight, safety, unemployment processes, benefits administration, and workers' compensation review and filing. Ensured compliance with ADA, COBRA, EEOC, OSHA, and EPA regulations and requirements. Maintained a nonunion environment in an industry where union membership is the standard. ***Key Accomplishments:***

- **Reduced turnover by 61%.**
  - ☐ Implemented company's first in-person, professional HR screening process and drug testing program, allowing for more selective hiring of quality associates.
  - ☐ Consulted with all levels of management to identify key core competencies, enabling more effective recruitment and selection of qualified candidates.
  - ☐ Instituted mandatory, thorough reference checks and DMV reviews.
  - ☐ Saved company an estimated $200K annually by reducing costly, frequent hiring, training, and productivity losses.

- **Cut absenteeism.**
  - ☐ Designed and launched supervisor training programs focused on effective listening, leadership, and cooperative team building skills.
  - ☐ Mediated employee/management disputes and earned reputation for fair and impartial resolutions.
  - ☐ Standardized disciplinary procedures and implemented new company policies regarding terminations, insulating company from legal risk of unfair termination charges.

- **Obtained workers' compensation experience modifier (mod.) of .66, slashing premiums by more than $47K.**
  - ☐ Implemented return-to-work light-duty programs, improved orientation programs, and safety education training to reduce mod. almost 40%.

- **Praised by CEO for improving employee morale and workplace atmosphere.**
  - ☐ Implemented first-ever mentoring program for new hires, assigning a "buddy" to all new employees.
  - ☐ Commended for helping new associates acclimate more quickly and offering "roving leadership" opportunities to front-line staff.

Craig Starr

CORPORATE LOSS MITIGATION & EMPLOYEE SAFETY EXPERIENCE

ACE INSURANCE SERVICES – Dallas, TX
Loss Control Manager, Loss Control Department, 9/97 to present
Manage loss control/mitigation efforts for over 4K corporate policyholders in a 55-county region. Supervise six loss control field consultants, manage $500K budget, and research and keep current on OSHA, ADA, EEOC, and numerous other employment and safety regulations/laws at both the state and federal level. Provide on-site assessment of prospective clients to ensure exposure and control standards are met. Review selected submissions prior to underwriting approval.
Key Accomplishments:

- **Promoted from senior loss control consultant to manager** after first few months.
- **Developed and implemented digitized/automated reporting methods and formats** for field consultants, transitioning region from outdated processes to a more efficient, modern, paperless operation.
- **Initiated value-added customer contacts for field consultants** by beginning program of customized letters to policyholders, prescheduled personal appointments, and detailed follow-up explanations and recommendations.
- **Successfully integrated differing state standards/laws/regulations** regarding workplace safety and drug testing into company procedures and ensured full legal compliance.
- **Created high-intensity service plan** for insured companies in jeopardy of losing coverage. Incorporated inspections, safety goals, and improvement timetables into plan.
- **Kept current on HR hiring and screening processes** to advise small business policyholders unable to afford a staff member dedicated solely to personnel management.

ABC INSURANCE, INC. – Dallas, TX, 10/89 to 7/97
Manager, Loss Prevention – Texas; **District Manager** – North Texas; **Sr. Loss Prevention Consultant** – North Texas
Developed customer service contact schedule and loss control programs, policies, and procedures for assigned territories. Supervised staff to ensure quality service to policyholders and swift resolution of claims and safety concerns. Conducted on-site property assessment for insurability. *Key Accomplishments:*

- **Managed start-up procedures for Texas and California operations,** including recruitment, training, and policy/procedure development and implementation.
- **Appointed to Dallas Chamber of Commerce "Drugs Don't Work" Advisory Board.**
- **Obtained ARM (Associate in Risk Management) Designation** to further credentials in exposure avoidance and risk financing, analysis, and assessment.
- **Oversaw more than 2K policyholders and $47 million in premiums.**

EDUCATION

THE UNIVERSITY OF TEXAS – Dallas, TX
B.S. Degree
Occupational Safety and Health Management, 2001

DALLAS COMMUNITY COLLEGE – Dallas, TX
A.A. Degree
Human Resource and Business Management, 1991

PROFESSIONAL AFFILIATIONS

Society for Human Resources Management (SHRM), present   Who's Who in Texas, 1993, 1994

Home Phone: 214-123-4567 ◆ E-mail: craigstarr@resumepower.com ◆ Available for Relocation

Resume Strategy: *Since Craig's earlier career experience is more relevant to his professional goal than his current position, he reorders his career chronology. Craig uses the heading "Human Resources Administration Experience" and places his older job as personnel administrator below it. This allows him to lead his "Experience" section with his most relevant position, even though it occurred earlier in his career. By placing the dates that he held this job right next to his job title (instead of off by itself, surrounded by white space), it helps to downplay the fact that this experience occurred more than a decade ago. For his current job, Craig emphasizes aspects that are related to HR management, working "Employee Safety Experience" into the heading and selecting accomplishments that are relevant to the human resources field.*

LYDIA TYLER WU

690 N.E. 53rd Ave.
Oklahoma City, OK 79487
Home: 405-555-5555 ◆ Cellular: 405-555-5555
E-mail: lydiawu@resumepower.com

JOB TARGET

HUMAN RESOURCES ASSISTANT ◆ *HUMAN RESOURCES COORDINATOR*

Dedicated, conscientious professional transitioning from social work to human resources to best utilize proven and relevant interviewing, counseling, program management, and documentation skills. Extensive experience interviewing clients from diverse socioeconomic and cultural backgrounds; maintaining in-depth, confidential personnel files; and providing sensitive counseling on a wide variety of issues including health, financial, and personal problems. Highly regarded interpersonal skills, known for diplomacy and discretion. Repeatedly praised for detail orientation and flawless preparation of crucial reports, court documents, and client files meeting all legal mandates and enabling fault-free government audits. Background in recruiting, interviewing, hiring, and training support-level staff.

AREAS OF KNOWLEDGE & SKILL

- Interviewing, Screening & Hiring
- Cultural Sensitivity
- Confidential Record Keeping
- Extensive Documentation
- Individual Counseling
- Audit Procedures
- Diplomacy & Discretion
- Personnel Files
- Team Building & Supervision
- Office Management
- Data Entry & Report Writing
- Excel, Word & Windows 2000

PROFESSIONAL EXPERIENCE

WOMEN'S RESOURCE CENTER—Oklahoma City, OK
Nonprofit organization providing counseling, job training, health support, and referral services to women in need, with approximately 100 employees.
Case Manager/Information and Referral Specialist, 2000 to 2001

Recruited for position following successful internship with center. Registered and conducted personal interview needs assessments for over 100 clients per month. Responded to daily inquiries on center services; consulted with clients and family members on confidential matters including health, financial, and personal issues; referred clients to appropriate community or government agencies; contacted agencies (such as Social Security, Welfare, Rape Crisis Center, and Job Corps) on behalf of clients; and conducted all necessary follow-up to resolve presented problems. Maintained and updated client personnel files and recorded the nature of each contact, problem, action taken, and outcome. ***Key Contributions:***

- Selected by supervisor to assume total responsibility for recruiting, interviewing, evaluating, hiring, and training all data entry clerks – sole case manager given this level of authority.
- Initiated vigorous community outreach efforts to enhance operation's visibility – a first for the center – by staffing open houses and coordinating visits to Welfare offices and shelters. Commended by director for proactive enrollment generation efforts.
- Earned a reputation as a sensitive interviewer and adept listener, able to uncover client needs not always verbalized.
- Repeatedly praised by family members of clients for providing quality, caring service to their loved ones.
- Recognized by entire data entry staff and immediate supervisor for voluntarily drafting much needed data entry training manual offering at-a-glance, concise instructions that greatly enhanced staff comprehension and efficiency.
- Coordinated all aspects of special events, guest speakers, and staff meetings.
- Adhered to strict guidelines in the preparation of client applications for government-sponsored programs. Meticulous attention to detail and thorough documentation resulted in three seamless government audits.

LYDIA TYLER WU

PROFESSIONAL EXPERIENCE (CONTINUED)

OKLAHOMA REGIONAL MEDICAL CENTER—Oklahoma City, OK
In-patient medical center providing psychiatric treatment/case management to dually diagnosed patients.
Social Work Intern, 1999 to 2000

Interviewed clients and wrote hundreds of psychosocial assessments incorporating psychiatric history, family history, and medical history to determine clients' mental health status and needs. Conducted individual and group therapy on a daily basis and completed extensive documentation on each client's progress. Coordinated efforts with community/housing resources, doctors, and family members to best meet individual client needs. ***Key Contributions:***

♦ Discharged noninsured clients under tight, 24-hour time constraints to prevent hospital revenue loss. Researched alternative placement solutions for these clients through tireless networking with directors and managers of nonprofit and healthcare organizations. Never failed to discharge a client within mandated time frame.

♦ Recognized for strong interpersonal skills with various authority levels, including doctors, nurses, social workers, directors, and lawyers, with the ability to discuss issues intelligently with each of these professionals.

♦ Asked to assume case management responsibilities as well as the supervision of other interns in supervisor's absence.

♦ Prepared court documents to prevent hospital liability under stressful, deadline-driven conditions. Authored detailed, multipage documents on all involuntarily admits within government-mandated 72-hour time frame.

WOMEN'S RESOURCE CENTER—Oklahoma City, OK
Data Entry Clerk (Part-time employment while enrolled in college), 1998 to 1999
Input data and prepared comprehensive weekly and monthly reports on active clients and services usage for seven departments. Trained four-member staff on data entry procedures. ***Key Contributions:***

♦ Facilitated maximum funding rates for multiple departments by preparing comprehensive reports detailing all services utilized by clients on a weekly and monthly basis. Reversed previous trend of underfunded departments due to "lost" activity from inaccurate or incomplete reporting.

♦ Researched and identified reporting discrepancies and implemented solutions to avoid unfavorable audit findings.

♦ Recognized for ability to multitask through additional case management and hiring responsibilities: interviewed clients when supervisor was unavailable and interviewed, evaluated, and hired three data entry clerks.

EDUCATION

OKLAHOMA CITY UNIVERSITY—
Oklahoma City, OK
Bachelor of Science in Social Work, 2000

TULSA COMMUNITY COLLEGE—
Tulsa, OK
Associate of Arts in Human Services, 1998

TESTIMONIALS

"[Lydia] has always proven to be dedicated to the organization and carried out her responsibilities with a great deal of efficiency…[maintained] a good rapport with all staff, clients, and volunteers, and they all had a great deal of respect for her…She will be sorely missed." – **Marion Sides, Director, Women's Resource Center**

"Excellent interviewing skills…dependable…warm and caring…organized…diplomatic…professional…learns quickly. I strongly recommend her!" – **Francis Hahn, LCSW, Oklahoma Regional Medical Center Social Work Director**

Resume Strategy: *Lydia places her job target at the top of the resume so that hiring managers don't immediately pigeonhole her into case management positions. Her summary outlines how her transferable skills from a case management career are applicable to her HR assistant goal. Her bulleted list of "Areas of Knowledge & Skill" continue to emphasize skills related to her new objective. Lydia's job descriptions are focused on accomplishments that are most related to HR.*

WEB DESIGN/HOSTING COMPANY DIRECTOR TO HR MANAGER

Doris Mott

15 Wayview Avenue ■ New York, NY 10014
212-123-4567 ■ doris@resumepower.com

CAREER GOAL *Human Resources Management*

OBJECTIVE	Accomplished operations administrator seeking to leverage extensive background in personnel management, recruiting/hiring/retention, employee relations, benefits administration, and professional development programs to secure a human resources position. Extremely motivated for career change goal and eager to contribute to a company's HR division.
PROFILE	■ **Offer versatile management background across diverse industries and challenging settings;** have led administration of large-scale healthcare operations within psychiatric hospitals and prison systems (supervising teams of up to 110), startup food service management, and joint direction of high-tech small business.
	■ **Knowledgeable in numerous HR-related matters,** including legal and compliance issues (FMLA, EEOC, ADA, workers' compensation); confidential record keeping, documentation, and personnel file management; policy development; disciplinary procedures; and sensitive, swift handling of complex personnel concerns (e.g., substance abuse, domestic violence, cultural sensitivity, sexual harassment, and inappropriate staff relationships with patients/inmates).
	■ **Skilled in fostering individual employee development** and able to resolve performance problems and employee conflicts by tailoring response to the individual and the situation.
	■ **Member of SHRM and NCHRA.**
CAREER HISTORY	DIRECTOR, 1998 to present **Web Solutions** (*Small Web design/hosting firm*) – New York, NY REGISTERED NURSE/UTILIZATION REVIEW SPECIALIST (Resource Pool), 1998 to 2001 **NYU Psychiatric Institute** (*Psychiatric hospital*) – New York, NY MANAGER/OWNER, 1996 to 1998 **Mott Coffee House** (*Coffee house/café*) – New York, NY DIRECTOR OF NURSING AND CLINICAL SERVICES, 1993 to 1995 **New York Health System** (*92-bed psychiatric hospital*) – New York, NY MEDICAL SERVICES ADMINISTRATOR, 1990 to 1993 **Avant Guard Medical Systems** (*Prison healthcare contractor*) – New York, NY QUALITY ASSURANCE COORDINATOR, 1985 to 1990 **City Hospital** (*300-bed hospital*) – New York, NY
ACHIEVEMENT HIGHLIGHTS	■ **Improved employee retention** through leadership of multitiered initiatives that enhanced staffing procedures, morale, individual accountability, and upward communication. Slashed costly annual turnover by 162% at New York Health System.
	■ **Became adept in a multitude of HR functions** as senior-level operations manager and/or de-facto on-site HR administrator for Avant Guard Medical Systems and New York Health System.
	☐ Administered hundreds of annual and probationary performance reviews.
	☐ Trained midlevel managers on a wide range of supervisory issues, including interviewing legalities and effective management skills.
	☐ Completed new-hire paperwork/orientation; maintained up-to-date, well-documented personnel files; and oversaw employee benefit program administration.
	☐ Wrote position announcements/job descriptions and interviewed, screened, hired, promoted, and terminated employees.
	■ **Rapidly mastered employment and payroll tax laws/procedures** as sole proprietor of café.
	■ **Counseled employees on numerous sensitive topics** throughout management career to turn around performance issues, ensure legal compliance, maintain a supportive environment, and reinforce adherence to company policies and procedures.
	■ **Revived employee recognition program** at Avant Guard Medical Systems.

Doris Mott

ACHIEVEMENT HIGHLIGHTS
(*continued*)

- **Developed curriculum and taught staff development programs** at Avant Guard Medical Systems and New York Health System on topics including sexual harassment, diversity training, stress management, employee safety/ergonomics, HIV/AIDS, and corporate policies/procedures.

- **Strategized staffing/cross-training initiatives** that introduced new cost-saving resource pool concept to Avant Guard Medical Systems (subsequently adopted nationwide at 100+ prisons), cut annual outsourcing expenditures **from $180K to zero,** and **reduced FTEs by 10%** without compromising service continuity or quality. Additionally developed hospital's first census- and acuity-based staffing levels for improved efficiency and patient care.

- **Honored as "Administrator of the Quarter"** in 1991 and 1992 by Avant Guard Medical Systems. Promoted to oversee inmate healthcare of largest prison facility in New York.

- **Managed operations and human resources within highly litigious, challenging prison system environment,** closely scrutinized by prison management and court-appointed attorney teams.
  - □ Achieved fault-free findings following unannounced inspections of healthcare operations at minimum-, medium-, and maximum-security sites.
  - □ Led comprehensive teambuilding and training initiatives to help staff cope with special morale issues presented by prison environment.

- **Proved the ability to update skills and acquire new proficiencies with minimal ramp-up time.**
  - □ Became self-taught expert in HTML coding, Internet design concepts/software, and Web hosting to successfully launch and direct expansion of Web Solutions.
  - □ Re-entered nursing field at NYU Psychiatric Institute with duties quickly expanded to include utilization review accountability (requiring rapid mastery of complex patient file documentation to maximize insurance reimbursement).

- **Repeatedly demonstrated financial/budgetary management acumen.**
  - □ Grew café from small startup to profitable concern requiring expansion to larger facility to accommodate out-the-door crowds.
  - □ Effectively administered seven-figure budgets throughout healthcare management career.

- **Voluntarily assumed expanded role** at NYU Psychiatric Institute to revamp medical documentation procedures for first-ever intra-departmental consistency.

EDUCATION & TRAINING

MBA, 1991 – New York University – New York, NY
BS in Healthcare Administration, 1986 – Wagner College – Staten Island, NY

Continuing Education: Completed numerous CEU courses on various management, nursing administration, and quality improvement topics.

Computers: MS Office (Word, Excel, Access, PowerPoint); Photoshop; HTML; Windows 2000

AFFILIATIONS

- Society for Human Resource Management (SHRM), 2001 to present
- National Council of Returned Peace Corps Volunteers, 1977 to present
- New York Human Resources Association (NYHRA), 2001 to present
- New York University Curriculum Development Committee, 1993 to 1996

Resume Strategy: *Doris has a varied management background that has included performing a broad range of human resources functions that she emphasizes in her "Objective," "Profile," and "Achievement Highlights" sections. The majority of Doris's HR-related achievements are from her positions in the health care sector, so to avoid an unbalanced resume presentation (with many achievements listed for some positions but only one or two for others), she groups them all together below her "Career History" section.*

DIANA SHARPE

Phone: (206) 123-4567 ❖ 1408 Hartsfield Road ❖ Seattle, WA 98195 ❖ di@resumepower.com

BENEFITS / PENSION ADMINISTRATOR / FUND MANAGER / CONSULTANT

Hands-on administrator recognized for skill in managing multitiered, multimillion-dollar union benefits program. Creative problem solver adept at identifying and resolving complex issues in an expeditious manner. Areas of expertise encompass:

- ❖ Compliance
- ❖ Operations
- ❖ Health & Welfare Funds
- ❖ Defined Contributions
- ❖ Defined Benefits
- ❖ Indemnity Plans
- ❖ COBRA
- ❖ Point of Service
- ❖ HMOs / PPOs

EDUCATION

UNIVERSITY OF WASHINGTON, Seattle, Washington

Currently pursuing **"Certified Employee Benefit Specialist"** designation (under the auspices of The International Foundation of Employee Benefit Plans and the University of Washington)

Completed Coursework: Employee Benefits Concepts, Design, and Administration; Retirement and Defined Contribution Plans; Asset Management; Accounting and Finance

PROFESSIONAL EXPERIENCE

INDUSTRIAL WORKERS' INTERNATIONAL ASSOCIATION, Local Union 54, Seattle, WA   1970–Present

Assistant Funds Manager

Through several administrations, have served as de-facto fund administrator for $3.5 million multiemployer health & welfare fund and $1 million defined-contribution plan for 500+ union members. Maintain oversight for day-to-day administration of funds and report directly to trustees, fund accountant, actuary, consultant, attorney, fund manager, and investment manager. Oversee the application of the provisions of various plans; interpret and apply regulations and laws governing them (ERISA, Department of Labor). Advise members on insurance and retirement options for defined benefit plan. Monitor accounts payable and receivable, encompassing premium collections and provider payments. Determine liquidity needs and confer with investment manager on available funds.

- ❖ Collaborated on the selection of new insurer; wrote portions of summary plan description and conducted orientation sessions on new plans.
- ❖ Determined eligibility for insured health benefits plan; managed claims processing of self-funded dental plan, vision plan, life insurance plan, prescription drug reimbursement plan, and hearing benefits. Collaborated with insurance vendors to resolve related claims problems and administer COBRA program.
- ❖ Maintain ongoing familiarity with indemnity plans, HMOs, PPOs, and defined contribution/benefit plans.
- ❖ Managed conversion of record-keeping processes, setting up automated systems for 11 funds.

AFFILIATIONS

- ❖ Abilities Club, Treasurer, 1990 to present
- ❖ International Foundation of Employee Benefit Plans, Member, 2000 to present

COMPUTERS

- ❖ Microsoft Word, Excel, PowerPoint, Windows 2000; Corel WordPerfect

Resume Strategy: *Although Diana's current job is primarily concerned with fund administration, she also holds responsibilities connected to benefits administration and she makes sure to highlight these prominently in her resume profile and "Professional Experience" sections. Her bulleted and bolded expertise items in the profile draw the eye to these relevant credentials and optimize keyword density. Her in-progress certification in employee benefits is relevant to her career goal, so Diana places her "Education" section first on the resume, right below the profile.*

SALES REPRESENTATIVE TO RECRUITER

Donna Grace

15 Mountain Way • Billings, MT 59105
406-123-4567 • donna@resumepower.com

PROFESSIONAL GOAL: RECRUITER

➤ Highly motivated sales/marketing professional with a strong interest in entering recruiting industry.
➤ Four years of experience as a top-performing salesperson.
➤ Excellent face-to-face and telephone presentation skills. Readily develop a positive rapport with people from diverse backgrounds and cultures.
➤ Demonstrated commitment to working with team members to achieve corporate objectives.
➤ Able to multitask, work in a fast-paced environment, meet deadlines, and produce high-quality work.
➤ Advanced computer user: Word, Excel, PowerPoint, WordPerfect, AutoCAD, and Windows 2000/98/95.

EDUCATION

Bachelor of Science, Marketing, 1996   THE UNIVERSITY OF MONTANA - Missoula, MT

PROFESSIONAL EXPERIENCE

Sales Representative, 1997 – Present   ABC CATALOGS – Billings, MT

Handle 80–100 inbound calls for leading computer catalog company. Serve customers from the United States, Europe, Asia, and Far East. Provide support and guidance for customers with technical questions. Participate in seminars and sales classes. Collaborate with corporate outbound sales reps on marketing, sales, and client relations. *Key Accomplishments:*

➤ Consistently achieved 110% of quota each month over the past year.
➤ Regarded among the top 10–15% (out of 200+ sales representatives) based on sales achievements.
➤ Frequently requested by customers to solely handle their accounts.
➤ Achieved gold membership in the Apple Learn and Earn Program by passing comprehensive exams.
➤ Recognized by Apple Computer as an "Apple Product Professional."

Research Assistant, 1993 – 1997   MEDICAL MARKETERS - Billings, MT

Assisted medical researchers in compiling medical data for pharmaceutical research firm. Processed raw data and designed charts, tables, and reports. Incorporated raw data into graphs using Excel and PowerPoint. Provided recommendations regarding presentation of research findings. Involved with more than 100 research studies. *Key Accomplishments:*

➤ Contributed to major medical research studies, including treatment of hypertension, diabetes, cardiovascular disease, photodamage, and HIV/AIDS.
➤ Acquired significant knowledge of medical terminology and conditions.
➤ Hired as a clerk and rapidly promoted to research assistant.

Sales Assistant, 1992 – 1993   FIDELITY INVESTMENTS - Billings, MT

Assisted broker with maintaining database of 500+ clients. Prepared charts, tables, slides, and documentation for sales presentations. Expanded client base by telemarketing and organizing seminars.

Resume Strategy: *Donna's strong sales and marketing skills are mentioned prominently in her opening profile since these are highly relevant to the recruiting profession. She uses six succinct bullet points to communicate the key strengths she brings to the table in her opening profile, and includes numbers and percentages in her "Professional Experience" section to demonstrate her history of top performance.*

MARKETING AND SALES INTERN TO EMPLOYEE RELATIONS SPECIALIST

CAREY P. SCHMIDT

888 Avenida de la Gloria
San Diego, CA 94538

E-mail: carey@resumepower.com
Fax: (510) 555-5555

Home: (510) 555-5553
Cell: (510) 555-5552

CAREER TARGET
EMPLOYEE RELATIONS ◆ HUMAN RESOURCES

HR-certified professional uniquely qualified to produce results for corporate employee- relations and human resources efforts. Offer proven track record of success developing and implementing recruitment, retention, and employee-satisfaction programs that reverse high turnover, facilitate upward communication, instill individual accountability, and increase teamwork, productivity, enthusiasm, and morale.

Extensive experience interviewing, screening, and hiring individuals from diverse socioeconomic and cultural backgrounds; maintaining in-depth, confidential personnel/client files; and providing sensitive counseling on a wide variety of issues including health, careers, and relationships. Demonstrated ability to orchestrate successful special events. Highly regarded interpersonal skills. Internationally traveled and culturally sensitive, with intermediate fluency in written/spoken Spanish. Backed by solid, relevant credentials – MA in counseling, in-progress MBA, and BS in psychology.

KNOWLEDGE AREAS

◆ Interviewing, Screening & Hiring
◆ Employee Relations & Accountability
◆ Project Management
◆ Confidential Record Keeping/Personnel Files
◆ Employee Retention & Satisfaction Programs
◆ Personality Assessment Tools

◆ Team Building & Supervision
◆ Marketing & Communications
◆ Employment Law
◆ Counseling & Problem Resolution
◆ Change Management & Six Sigma
◆ Special Event Coordination

PROFESSIONAL EXPERIENCE

EVENT PLANNERS, INC. – San Diego, CA
Regional Marketing & Sales Graduate Intern, 01/01 to Present
Assist in the direction, promotion, and coordination of special events for Fortune 500 clients. Develop and manage special event budget and network with marketing professionals and client company executives to develop strategic marketing and event plans. ***Key Accomplishments:***

◆ **Developed comprehensive special event strategy** and planning guidelines subsequently adopted companywide as the standard for conducting successful lead-generating, product demo events.
◆ **Conducted market research** to provide management with accurate, incisive data on target market demographics, competitor initiatives, and industry trends. Research used to generate measurable increases in response rates to direct mailings and enhanced segmentation of customer lists.
◆ **Quickly mastered new technology** to successfully communicate Event Planners's services to prospects.

L.A. COUNTY PROPERTIES, INC. – Los Angeles, CA
Assistant to the President/VP of Holdings (Functioning as HR Coordinator), 05/98 to 01/01
Recruited, screened, interviewed, hired, and supervised maintenance, cleaning, and restaurant personnel. Maintained personnel files, supervised purchasing and crew scheduling, oversaw property security, and assisted president and VP in a wide range of management and financial matters. ***Key Accomplishments:***

◆ **Reversed high turnover trend and low morale** by introducing multitiered recruiting, retention, and employee-relations initiatives.
  ◻ Initiated thorough reference checks, standardized interview questions, and instituted personality-assessment instrument during hiring process; developed first-ever job descriptions and detailed performance expectations and evaluations; and provided employees with "blueprint" for upward mobility.
  ◻ Improved morale and employee satisfaction, increasing individual accountability, instilling widespread teamwork mentality, and turning around costly replacement/training of staff. Upped average tenure from a low of six months to an average of three years.

CAREY P. SCHMIDT

L.A. COUNTY PROPERTIES, INC. (continued):

♦ **Organized English as a second language education program for Mexican restaurant employees.**
  □ Convinced president to fund badly needed program by detailing the potential for multiple benefits: enhanced restaurant productivity, reduced turnover, increased teamwork, and community relations.
  □ Partnered with Cultural Center staff to offer language instruction to employees.
  □ Achieved 100% participation from eligible employees and received positive feedback from students, restaurant management, and company president.
♦ **Transformed outdated, efficiency- and profitability-robbing manual processes.**
  □ Automated employee scheduling, slashing time spent from a full day to under two hours.
  □ Enhanced computer network by adding hubs/DSL line, saving $2,500 in annual computer line fees.

FAMILY THERAPEUTICAL INSTITUTE – Los Angeles, CA
Licensed Clinician, Mental Health Counselor, 09/95 to 05/98

Maintained weekly caseload of approximately 30 individuals, couples, and families. Provided counseling on a wide range of issues including marriage/family dynamics, overeating, smoking cessation, and stress reduction. Maintained detailed, confidential client/personnel files, completed and submitted in-depth insurance reports, established goals and treatment plans with all clients, consulted with psychiatrists to manage client medications, and directed discharge planning and appropriate placement. *Key Accomplishments:*

♦ **Made a positive difference in the lives of numerous clients,** providing them with tools and strategies to overcome challenges, build healthy relationships, and enjoy a more fulfilling quality of life.
♦ **Developed and presented educational programs to groups** of as many as 250 on various topics.
♦ **Cultivated a specialty area** to accelerate individuals' abilities to take control of their lives.
♦ **Conducted career counseling** to successfully set the stage for clients to re-enter the workforce.
♦ **Called upon as an "expert witness"** in court proceeding.

EDUCATION

UNIVERSITY OF SAN DIEGO – San Diego, CA
MBA Candidate – Evening/weekend degree in progress. Anticipated graduation date: 05/03

UNIVERSITY OF SOUTHERN CALIFORNIA – Los Angeles, CA
MA in Counseling with Honors, Dual Major in Mental Health & Marriage/Family Therapy, 05/96

UNIVERSITY OF THE PACIFIC – Stockton, CA
BS in Counseling & Psychology, 05/90

PROFESSIONAL EXPERIENCE

♦ Certification in Human Resources (University of Southern California), 1999
♦ National Certified Counselor, 1998 to present
♦ Licensed Mental Health Counselor, 1998 to present

PROFESSIONAL TRAINING HIGHLIGHTS

♦ Six Sigma
♦ Professional Management Program

♦ HR Employment Law
♦ Standards of Business Conduct

♦ Strategic Approach to International Customers
♦ E-Commerce Solutions

Resume Strategy: *Carey supports his goal of breaking into human resources by showing how his former position as assistant to the VP was heavily involved in HR functions. He also explains how his skills and credentials in mental health counseling are relevant to HR needs. Carey uses subbullets to explain accomplishments with multiple beneficial outcomes, a tactic that makes these achievements easy to quickly skim. He packs his resume with important keywords, and includes his most powerful qualifications up-front in his opening profile.*

SALES MANAGER TO HR SPECIALIST

14 Pike Road
Erie, PA 16507

Bill Forte

(814) 123-4567
bill@resumepower.com

GOAL: HUMAN RESOURCES SPECIALIST

Dynamic, performance-driven professional with a master's degree in labor studies, seeking an entry-level HR position with a large company. Extensive knowledge of labor laws and excellent negotiating skills. Recognized for strong leadership skills, project completions, and willingness to assume additional responsibilities. Self-motivated with a passion to achieve objectives through dedication, integrity, trust, and hard work.

Thrive on confronting challenges and developing and implementing effective solutions. Excellent public relations skills, writing/speaking ability, business acumen, interpersonal skills, and work ethic. Computer literate (Word, Excel, WordPerfect, Windows 2000/NT/98/95).

EDUCATION

TEMPLE UNIVERSITY   Philadelphia, PA

Master of Science, Labor Studies, 1997

- Internship: Operating Engineers — New Hope, PA, 1997
- **Related Courses:** Labor Arbitration, Composition of Labor Movements, Labor and Employment Law, Labor History, Labor Research Practicum, Collective Bargaining, Current Issues in Labor, Financial Analysis

QUEENS COLLEGE   Flushing, NY

Bachelor of Arts, Major in Sociology, 1993

PROFESSIONAL EXPERIENCE

ABC SPORTS COMPANY   Philadelphia, PA

Sales Manager, 1999 to present — Oversee daily operations and sales performance for sporting goods emporium. Interact with people of diverse backgrounds and provide impeccable customer service.

- Expanded company's product line and increased sales by 22% (2000 YTD) by targeting local market and initiating successful promotional campaigns.
- Added radio spots to advertising mix to increase sales and visibility in local arena. Promotions enhanced company's image and directly increased the number of shoppers.
- Built and established loyal customer base in local market, generating repeat business and referrals.

UNITED PARCEL SERVICE   Philadelphia, PA

Sorter / Unloader, 1998 to 1999 — Unloaded tractor-trailer trucks.

- Developed strategy for faster delivery and won approval to implement plan; promoted to sorter.

ACE ELECTRIC COMPANY   Astoria, NY

Machinist, 1992 to 1995 — Operated punch press and performed routine equipment maintenance.

- Participated in "High Involvement" program, serving as production representative and shop steward.
- Established credibility and trust with workers, which helped improve performance, productivity, and safety.
- Elevated employee morale by maintaining open communications, providing incentives, and organizing networking events. Employee relations strategies contributed to 15% increase in annual production.

Resume Strategy: *One of Bill's strongest qualifications supporting his career change to human resources is his master's degree in labor studies, so he mentions this in the opening line of his profile and also places his "Education" section before his "Professional Experience" section to give this credential maximum exposure. His willingness to take an entry-level HR position in order to get his foot in the door is also communicated well, as are his strengths in leadership and negotiations.*

Frank O'Conner

14 Raintree Path ■ Philadelphia, PA 19103 ■ 215-123-4567 ■ frank@resumepower.com

GOAL: HUMAN RESOURCE GENERALIST

Dedicated, top-performing team leader seeking an HR position that capitalizes on leadership skills, dedication to corporate objectives, and ability to communicate with staff at all organizational levels.

- Recognized by management for ability to tighten controls, improve quality and processes, and build cross-functional teams within manufacturing/production environments.
- Communicate with and support all levels of the organizational structure, including union/nonunion personnel and exempt/nonexempt employees.
- Fully experienced with reporting processes and summarizing production, quality, and staffing issues.
- Skilled at fostering a cohesive, productive, and motivated team environment. Work closely with colleagues to achieve and exceed corporate goals.
- Creative problem solver, adept at identifying and utilizing an array of resources to meet objectives.
- Continually strive to build upon existing knowledge base through ongoing training and education. Currently enrolled in accelerated MBA program.

AREAS OF EXPERTISE

■ Training and Development	■ Performance Evaluations	■ Administrative Reporting
■ Procedural Documentation	■ Quality Assurance	■ Cost Analysis/Control
■ Team Leadership/Motivation	■ Standards/Compliance	■ Maintenance Programs
■ Union and Nonunion Issues	■ Project Management	■ Process Control

EDUCATION

Temple University — Philadelphia, PA   **MBA, accelerated program,** expected May 2003

Pennsylvania State University — York, PA   **BS, Chemistry,** May 1992

CAREER HIGHLIGHTS

ABC COMPANY, LLC. — Philadelphia, PA
FACTORY CHEMIST, 1997 to 2002

Directed and trained a union shop of 30 chemists, lab benchmen, analysts, and sample carriers. Closely monitored performance for quality control, provided feedback to staff, completed employee evaluations, and presented recommendations for staff promotions. Forecasted annual inventory needs and monitored requisition processes. Collaborated with process engineers and production engineers on process control, compliance, production, and quality issues. Prepared daily administrative reports regarding inventory, production, and laboratory results.

Frank O'Conner

Resume - Page Two

CAREER HIGHLIGHTS

ABC COMPANY, LLC. (continued) — *Key Accomplishments:*

- Improved inventory order efficiency by 40% and reduced rush orders from 75% to 25% by creating inventory spreadsheet to calculate use of over 400 chemicals and supplies. Actions reduced shipping costs, enhanced project flow, and enhanced on-time project completion.
- Served as key member of quality analysis team that created routine calibration method, which reduced errors and improved accuracy by increasing calibration frequency.
- Created a motivated team environment and optimized performance by cross-training all staff.
- Carried out weekly quality-assurance checks to ensure adherence to quality and safety standards.

PRIME COMPANY, INC. — Doylestown, PA
LABORATORY TECHNICIAN, QUALITY ASSURANCE, 1995 to 1997

Accountable for conducting daily qualitative production analyses and determining quality of quarry samples for use in production. Filed daily quality reports with central laboratory, maintained historical database, and monitored inventory levels. *Key Accomplishments:*

- Instituted routine inspection and replacement program, extending life of air-quality motors by 300%.
- Created confirmation process that expedited timely reporting and supported company audits.
- Minimized downtime, reduced costs, and ensured compliance to EPA standards through the development and implementation of formal maintenance program for air-quality motors.

COMMUNITY ACTIVITIES

- State of Pennsylvania **Coach License** (Soccer), 1998
- State of Pennsylvania Youth Module **Coach License** (Soccer), 1997

SPECIALIZED SKILLS

Computers:	Windows NT/2000/98/95/3.X, Word, Excel, WordPerfect, Lotus 1-2-3, Quattro Pro, MS-DOS
Foreign Language:	German (working knowledge)

14 Raintree Path ■ Philadelphia, PA 19103 ■ 215-123-4567 ■ frank@resumepower.com

Resume Strategy: *Frank's opening profile shows employers how his experience is relevant to human resources functions and he pulls out relevant skills from his background to place in his "Areas of Expertise" section. He knows that an MBA is highly valued in his targeted field, so he mentions this in-progress credential twice: in the profile and in his "Education" section. Even though there is little similarity between his current job as a chemist and his stated objective of human resources, Frank makes sure that he shows how he has contributed to improved operations in his bulleted accomplishments in his "Career Highlights" section.*

SMALL BUSINESS OWNER/CONSULTANT TO COPYWRITER/MARKETING ASSISTANT

Gloria Fine

| | 15 Canal Place East Southport, CT 06490 | Phone: 203-123-4567 E-mail: gloria@aol.com |

OBJECTIVE: COPYWRITER / MARKETING ASSISTANT

Resourceful, entrepreneurial professional seeking to leverage proven creative talents, strong writing skills (former English/creative writing teacher), demonstrated marketing acumen, and project management abilities to obtain entry-level writing or marketing position. Career background includes creating a successful small business startup and architecting marketing activities (print/Web/special event/direct marketing) to grow it to rapid six-figure sales success and eventual lucrative sell-off. Thrive in deadline-driven, multitasking environments and undaunted by the prospect of an initial entry-level assignment to gain "foot in the door." Polished, persuasive, and articulate communicator, able to innovate winning, "out-of-the-box" approaches.

KEY SKILLS

Promotional Writing (Print & Web Delivery)

Marketing Support

New Product Launch

Tradeshow Management

Collateral Development

High-Impact Communications

COMPUTER SUMMARY

WordPerfect

Word

Paint Shop Pro

FrontPage

QuarkXPress

PowerPoint

QuickBooks

Windows ME/98/95

HTML (Basic)

Excel (Basic)

OF NOTE

Portfolio on Request

PROFESSIONAL EXPERIENCE

A1 BUSINESS CORP. – Hartford, CT – *Manufacturer of business stamps and imprinted products.*
Consultant, Rubber Stamp Division, 7/01 – present
Retained following profitable sale of small business to oversee smooth transition. Collaborate with freelance artists to develop new images; utilize design tools to prepare artwork for manufacture; supervise illustrators in the creation of future lines; and collaborate on new Web site development. *Key Accomplishments:*

- **Delivered significant product-line expansion,** working with six artists to develop over 160 new designs anticipated to drive additional revenue stream well into the five figures annually.
- **Leveraged strong research skills and keen "eye" for artistic talent** to identify, locate, and sign new illustrative talent.
- **Integrally involved in development (writing/design) of marketing collateral,** magazine ads, and 155-page catalog targeting commercial/direct retail and wholesale channels.
- **Built customer contact database** to improve targeted marketing efforts.
- **Planned tradeshow participation strategy,** determining inventory to be featured and conceptualizing visual layouts for all shows.

GLORIA'S RUBBER STAMPS – Southport, CT – *Manufacturer/wholesaler of original art rubber stamp line.*
Owner, 7/97 – 6/01
Directed all aspects of ground-up small business and implemented strategic marketing initiatives to spur high growth and eventual lucrative sell-off to A1 Business Corp. Supervised team in daily operations, including advertising/PR, product development, catalog design, and tradeshow management. *Key Accomplishments:*

- **Transformed "hobby" into successful startup,** implementing growth-enabling marketing and operational plans that rapidly **expanded sales from zero to six-figure revenue mark.**
- **Orchestrated a full spectrum of marcom activities,** including participation in ten consumer tradeshows and retail conventions, design of magazine ads targeting end users, development and launch of direct marketing campaigns (print and e-mail), and Web content development/launch.

HARTFORD MIDDLE SCHOOL – Hartford, CT
English Teacher, 8/91 – 6/97
Taught English, language arts, and reading classes to students in grades 6–8. Accountable for classroom management, lesson planning, and curriculum writing. *Key Accomplishments:*

- **Augmented English instruction** by adding creative writing workshop component.
- **Repeatedly recognized for superior performance** during annual reviews.

EDUCATION & CREDENTIALS

HARTFORD UNIVERSITY – Hartford, CT
BA in English (GPA 3.4), 1990 ■ **Secondary English Education License** (CT), 1991
Completed 22/33 credits toward **MA in English Education** (GPA: 4.0), 1990 – 1991

Resume Strategy: *Since Gloria has two very different career goals, she effectively develops two different versions of her resume bringing out her most relevant qualifications for each. (Compare Gloria's "Administrative Support" resume version in Chapter 15.) For this resume version, Gloria emphasizes her skills and accomplishments related to marketing, writing, and design.*

19
Consulting/Contractors

Lynn D. Brush

14 Clove Lakes Park   Staten Island, NY 10309   Phone: 718-123-4567   E-mail: lynn@resumepower.com

Career Target – Management Consulting ◆ Accounting ◆ Auditing

Recent New York University MLA graduate with ten years of experience in budget and financial management/analysis, accounting, and inventory/cost control. Proven success initiating programs and practices that increase cash flow by hundreds of thousands of dollars, generate new multimillion-dollar sources of revenue, bring financial operations into full compliance, cut purchasing expenses four-fold, and reduce business cycle time. Demonstrated ability to lead top-performing teams and facilitate compromise between union/nonunion employees. Highly regarded interpersonal skills, with a reputation for impeccable service, astute listening, and tactful persuasion. Multilingual and culturally sensitive. Sitting for CPA exam in November 2003.

Skills

◆ Financial Analysis	◆ Leadership & Supervision	◆ Audit Strategy
◆ Managerial & Payroll Accounting	◆ Vendor & Customer Relationship Management	◆ Inventory Control
◆ GAAP	◆ Process Improvement & Cycle Time Reduction	◆ Budgeting
◆ Supply Chain Management	◆ Economic Value-Added Analysis (EVA)	◆ Grant Proposals
◆ Activity-Based Costing (ABC)	◆ Nonprofit Management	◆ Crisis Management
◆ Balanced Scorecard & Break-Even Analysis		◆ Labor Relations
		◆ Team Building & Training
		◆ Advanced Computer Skills

Education

NEW YORK UNIVERSITY – New York, NY
Master of Liberal Arts, May 2002   GPA: **3.25/4.0**
Certification: **Accounting and Business**   Certification: **Spanish-American Studies**
NYU Academic Support Program, Mentor, 1996 to present
NYU Graduate Association of Spanish-American Students, Officer, 1999 to 2001

PACE UNIVERSITY – New York, NY
Bachelor of Science in Business Administration, May 1991
Major: **Accounting**   GPA: **3.34/4.0**
Beta Alpha Accounting Honor Society, 1987 to 1991
Who's Who in the American Universities, Academic & Service Award, 1991

Experience

NEW YORK UNIVERSITY – New York, NY

Business Office Administrative Assistant (Functioning as Budget Analyst/Office Manager/Payroll Accountant), June 1996 to present

Concurrent with post-baccalaureate and graduate school studies.

Promoted from administrative assistant to business office administrative assistant to direct accounting and business affairs for three university departments: Law Library, IT Services, and Media Technology Center. Manage accounts receivable, cash receipts, inventory control, payroll, budgeting, and purchasing. Research, formulate, and prepare budgeted and actual year-end financial statements. Prepare and analyze daily, quarterly, and annual statistics and reports; hire, train, and supervise new library employees; and prepare and submit in-depth grant proposals. Entrusted to handle confidential information and resolve disputes and complaints.

◆ **Reduced supply purchasing expenses 50% and equipment purchasing costs almost 400%** by designing centralized inventory-control system for multiple departments. Automated purchase-request procedures, enhanced inventory security, secured "bulk" purchasing discounts, and initiated tracking log to maintain cost controls and eliminate duplicate and/or unnecessary supply ordering.

Lynn D. Brush — Page Two

NEW YORK UNIVERSITY (continued), *Accomplishments:*

- **Brought departments into full compliance with university regulations and financial reporting standards,** while simultaneously streamlining processes.
- **Integrally involved in planning, implementation, and transition of new NYUCard conversion** using "Smart Chip" technology. Worked closely with NYU management and vendors including PNC Bank, Xerox, and AT&T to ensure seamless conversion to new system.
- **Introduced first repair/renovation work request log** to aid building administrator in cost-reduction initiatives. Ability to track requests key in design of a preventative-maintenance schedule that saved University thousands of dollars and reduced work requests – from 100 per year to 13 or less.

NEW YORK UNIVERSITY (Alumni and Development Office) – New York, NY

Research Assistant, November 1994 to June 1996
Researched, analyzed, and prepared complex grant proposals for individuals, corporations, and foundations. Prepared and managed million-dollar budget, developed financial statements, and oversaw payroll and inventory. Supervised support staff and student workers. *Accomplishments:*

- **Facilitated hundreds of thousands of dollars in increased income** by upping the number of grant proposals submitted. Expert ability to research, compile, and write comprehensive grant proposals resulted in reducing average turn-around time from several months to two weeks per grant, allowing one hundred grants to be submitted in 1995 and 1996.
- **Reconciled three-month backlog of grant awards** for all 12 schools within the university to bring institution up to date and in full compliance with each individual grant's guidelines.

A1 MANUFACTURING INCORPORATED (Accounting Department) – Staten Island, NY

Credit Assistant Manager, February 1992 to November 1994
Recruited for management position in accounting department of $14 million building materials manufacturing company. Reviewed, analyzed, and approved credit for new customers and set account limits. Reconciled account balances and bank statements and collected on past-due and delinquent accounts. Managed accounts payable, accounts receivable, budgeting, cash receipts, inventory, payroll, and purchasing. Hired, trained, and supervised staff accountants. *Accomplishments:*

- **Increased inventory turnover 30%,** leading to a multimillion-dollar profit increase.
- **Eliminated a six-month backlog of nonreconciled monthly statements,** with many accounts more than 120 days in arrears. Called customers personally to speed collection process and prevent further daily losses of thousands of dollars. Efforts resulted in a cash flow increase of six figures.
- **Initiated and facilitated an inventory-control team** to correct discrepancies and speed "wasted" inventory to market. Efforts resulted in performance award and promotion.

Professional Development Highlights

NEW YORK UNIVERSITY:
- BEN Reports (Business Enterprise Network – Oracle Web-Base Reporting)
- Grant Reports & Writing
- FINMIS Reports (Financial Management Information System – Oracle Character Base Reporting)

DUN & BRADSTREET:
- Credit & Collections

ADP:
- Payroll Reporting

***Resume Strategy:** Lynn has been functioning as an office administrative assistant while completing her graduate studies, and is looking to transition to management consulting in the accounting/auditing field. Her resume places education before experience so that she may emphasize her master's degree and business certifications. A gray box called "Skills" provides a bulleted list of her accounting and management skills. Her diverse work history spotlights business-related accomplishments that have given her employers a competitive edge, showing excellent qualifications for a management consulting position.*

Matthew Tobias, M.D.

5600 West Silver Ridge Rd. ■ Boston, MA 02127
Home: (555) 555-5551 ■ mt_md@resumepower.com

Career Target — **Medical Administration & Consulting**

Profile

- **Respected M.D. and accomplished medical director** seeking to leverage 11-year clinical and operations management background into administrative/consulting specialty.
- **Proven success building top-performing, patient-oriented teams** and leading operations within teaching clinic and medical practice settings. Liaise effectively between physicians, staff, medical/insurance community, and corporate management.
- **Strong understanding of financial management and budgeting,** with hospital medical executive committee experience and a track record of improving P&L performance.
- **Assistant professor of medicine** serving as teacher and role model to medical students and residents, with extensive instructional background in a university program. Committed to a preventive, holistic approach to medicine and the pursuit of lifelong learning demonstrated by exceeding continuing education requirements.
- **Expert interpersonal skills,** known for approachable, inclusive management style and commitment to compassionate patient care. Skilled negotiator and relationship-builder, with demonstrated ability to facilitate cross-departmental and HMO cooperation, ultimately benefiting patients through value-added services, continuous quality improvement, and timely, informed response.
- **Bilingually fluent** (Spanish), **computer proficient, and solidly credentialed** – board-certified in internal medicine, multistate medical licensure, and in-progress MBA.

Medical Administration Expertise

- Patient Care Administration
- Private Practice & Clinical Operations Management
- Strategic Planning/P&L Enhancement
- Supervision & Leadership
- Team Building & Training
- Resident & Medical Student Instruction

- Relationship Management (Patients/Vendors/HMOs/Physicians)
- Chart Management
- Continuity of Care
- Budgeting & Fiscal Management
- Continuous Quality Improvement
- Internal & Preventive Medicine

Professional Experience

BOSTON MEDICAL CENTER – Boston, MA
Medical Director/Clinical Internist/Assistant Professor of Medicine, May 1992 to present
Direct daily operations of medical practice, including coordination of physician's office, hospital, and on-call schedules; supervision of nurses/office manager/staff; policy/procedure development and implementation; fiscal management/budgeting; billing review; and patient relationship management. Liaise with HMO, insurance companies, and physicians/staff to ensure optimal patient treatment with a preventive healthcare focus. Selected Contributions:

- **Achieved a standard of excellence in inpatient/outpatient medical care,** with a weekly patient load average of 100. Stress preventive care during patient interactions, and encourage open communication to facilitate correct diagnosis/treatment and avoid misunderstandings.
- **Generated five-figure improvement in HMO incentive payment reimbursement.** Implemented thorough documentation procedures of all preventive medical screening and patient counseling efforts. Educated physicians on HMO requirements and correct documentation procedures and created new patient encounter and clinical evaluation chart forms. Maximized incentive reimbursement and improved practice net income by $115K.
- **Instilled a patient-focused approach among resident teams and medical students.** Provide instruction on the art of medicine through clinical service, with an emphasis on compassionate, quality care.
- **Convinced corporate ownership to fund badly needed office remodeling** and oversaw all facility improvements.
- **Led negotiations and managed transition of medical practice** during ownership transfer.

Matthew Tobias, M.D.

Professional Experience

BOSTON MEDICAL CENTER – *(continued)*

- **Built cohesive, empowered office staff** and initiated team-oriented approach to TQM. Introduced morale-building initiatives, such as first-ever employee reward program, and actively sought input from all staff to improve office policies and procedures.
- **Forged relationships with hospital administrators, healthcare providers, and insurance companies** to provide quality care and value-added services.

MASSACHUSETTS HOSPITAL – Boston, MA
ABC Medical Director/Attending Physician, June 1990 to June 1992
Medical Resident, June 1987 to June 1990
Recruited as medical director for the ABC Medical Clinic, with ultimate responsibility for the optimal healthcare of all clinic patients. Worked with ABC's manager to ensure smooth operational leadership, supervised 30-member medical staff, reviewed patient charts and ensured appropriate follow-up, and provided outpatient clinical care. Selected Contributions:

- **Conducted individualized and classroom instruction** to residents on quality, cost-effective, and compassionate patient care.
- **Devised and instituted cross-departmental initiatives resulting in measurable improvements** in the coordination of care between clinic and various ancillary services. Decreased medical report turn-around time to more rapidly respond to patient needs.

PRIVATE MEDICAL PRACTICE
Clinical Internist, June 1990 to June 1992 (*Concurrent with ABC Medical Directorship*)
Opened private internal medicine practice, managed all aspects of operational start-up, and provided quality inpatient and outpatient care. Selected Contributions:

- **Launched private practice from the ground up,** including HMO contract negotiation, advertising, fiscal management, facility lease, office setup, malpractice coverage, staff recruitment/hiring/supervision, and benefits administration.
- **Achieved break-even operation in less than two years,** building a successful practice.

Education

BOSTON UNIVERSITY – Boston, MA
MBA candidate; completed first year of program. Anticipated graduation: June 2003

LONDON SCHOOL OF MEDICINE – London, England
M.D., May 1987

BOSTON COLLEGE – Boston, MA
B.A., Biology and Classical Civilization, May 1982

Licensure & Certifications

Fellow of the American College of Medical Practice Management (ACMPM), 2001
Certified by the American Board of Internal Medicine (ABIM), 1992
Licensed to practice medicine in Massachusetts (1988), Florida (1997), and Georgia (1997)

Affiliations

- American Medical Association, 1990 to present
- Massachusetts Medical Society/Florida Medical Society, 1990 to present
- American Board of Internal Medicine, 1992 to present
- American College of Physicians, 1990 to present
- American College of Physician Executives, 2000 to present
- American College of Medical Practice Management, 2000 to present
- Boston General Medical Staff, 1992 to present

Resume Strategy: *Matthew's resume leads with his new goal to pursue medical administration and consulting assignments. His related qualifications are outlined in his "Profile" section, and his "Experience" section demonstrates his success in the management and development of successful medical operations.*

Joe R. Smythe

4695 Watson Dr. ■ Doylestown, PA 18901
(215) 794-9527 ■ js@resumepower.com

TECHNOLOGY CONSULTANT

- FULL LIFECYCLE PROJECT MANAGEMENT
- WORKFORCE DEVELOPMENT & TRAINING
- STRATEGIC/TACTICAL BUSINESS PLANNING

Offering Expertise in...

- **Systems Design & Implementation**
- **LAN / WAN Design, Setup & Optimization**
- **Strategic Visioning Sessions**
- **Development & Programming Management**
- **Large-Scale Project / Process Management**
- **Cost-Effective Technology Solutions**
- **Senior-Level Consulting**
- **Business Development & Strategic Planning**
- **Business Unit Management**
- **Technical Training (End Users, Sales / IT Team)**
- **Web Site Development**
- **Ebusiness / Ecommerce Strategy**
- **Object-Oriented Analysis & Design**

About Joe...

With 15 years of diverse technology experience, seven industry certifications, and advanced computer/project management skills, Joe is a proven developer and deliverer of state-of-the-art solutions. His background encompasses large-scale systems, network, and application design across multiple platforms (e.g., Windows/UNIX/Linux/Macintosh) and programming languages. A sophisticated project manager, Joe has extensive experience leading all phases of high-profile projects, from business requirements definition, planning, and testing/documentation to execution. He has repeatedly innovated customer-focused technology solutions on time and on budget, with advanced expertise across a wide range of hardware, software, tools and data/voice technologies.

Commended as an effective manager and trainer by both clients and employers, Joe bears a solid track record of building and leading cross-functional teams to enhance profitability and customer satisfaction. He is a proven relationship builder, adept in cultivating solid, value-added affiliations with major vendors and creating long-term, mutually beneficial business alliances. Dynamic, enthusiastic, and results-driven, he is able to liaise effectively between business and technical areas and clearly convey information to professionals at all levels of technical expertise.

About Pioneer Consulting LLC...

Joe launched Pioneer Consulting LLC in 1999, and has successfully architected winning strategic plans, conducted well-received technical training programs (from beginning to advanced) and led high-profile projects for clients across diverse industries. Joe begins by analyzing clients' technology and business issues, finding the "need behind the need" to ensure long-term, total solutions instead of temporary, "band-aid fixes." Joe has been engaged to provide:

- Overall IT Strategies
- Network Architecture/Management
- Software Development Lifecycle Planning
- Large System Design
- System Migrations
- Distributed Infrastructure Management (Desktop & Server)
- E-commerce Web Site Development
- Voice/Video Technology Solutions
- Call Center Management
- Technology Goals/Issues Definition
- Infrastructure Plans
- Visioning Sessions
- Focus Group Presentations
- Change Management Consulting
- Business Development Consulting

Credentials...

CompTia IT Project+ Certified	Microsoft Certified System Engineer (MCSE)	Microsoft Certified (NT)	Novell Certified Network Engineer
CA Unicenter Certified	Who's Who in IT, 1995	Sun Solaris Certified	Advisory Board, "People Do Matter"
Duquesne University Accelerated Program for Professional Studies (1991–1993)	Computer Systems Institute; 4.0 GPA in Computer Programming Language Studies (1989)	Miller Heiman Sales Operating System (2001)	Advanced C++, OOA, OOD (1991)

Joe R. Smythe

Technology Summary...

Systems:
Windows 95/98/ME/
NT/XP, Linux Redhat,
UNIX (Solaris, AIX,
HP/UX, SCO),
Macintosh, BSD
Freeware

Networking:
LANs/WANs,
Windows NT,
Windows NT RAS,
Novell NetWare, NFS
TCP/IP, IPX/SPX,
AppleTalk

Hardware Platforms:
PCs, RAID systems,
RS/6000, Sun Ultra line

Languages:
C++, C, Perl, SQL,
UNIX Shell languages

Software:
MS Office, MS Project,
Visio, ACT!, Goldmine,
CA Unicenter, CA
Advanced Help Desk,
Dreamweaver, Appgen
Accounting,
QuickBooks, Real
Work Accounting

Databases:
Oracle, Sybase, MS
Access, Unify, MS SQL
Server

(215) 555-5555
js@resumepower.com

Project Results...

- **Grew startup unit to exceed $4.5 million** annual revenues within two years.
- **Planned and participated in highly efficient system migration** from Novell/NT mixed environment to Windows 2000/Citrix metaframe backbone for major U.S. legal firm.
- **Coordinated conversion of hybrid computerized/paper-based accounting system to fully integrated Web-enabled system.** Strategically designed network and systems, planned migration, managed project, and coordinated third-party vendors and subcontractors. Trained client in optimum use of upgraded system.
- **Increased annual corporate revenue 33%** ($250K increase) by introducing new service lines.
- **Originated company's first partnership plan,** forging relationships with Microsoft, Sun, Novell, and Computer Associates. Improved competitive edge by establishing company as a VAR, capturing large clients.
- **Decreased system shutdowns** in 150-user Novell system by migrating to a Windows system.
- **Supported technology integration for internal portals** of overseas-based company.
- **Implemented new Windows 2000 system** for 250 U.S. users within global user group.
- **Trained clients in UNIX/NT operations,** project management methodology, and helpdesk.
- **Ensured on-target operations** by directly managing critical network/application implementation and software development projects, employing Unicenter, AHD, CA Opal, CA Jasmine, Visual Basic, and Java.
- **Enabled effective support and management of "road warrior" technical consultants** by instituting Internet-based virtual-office infrastructure.
- **Improved quality of service** by leading client focus group and visioning sessions.
- **Oversaw IT teams and vendors to ensure 100% client-oriented performance** during setup, maintenance, and troubleshooting of all offerings.

Career Highlights...

PIONEER CONSULTING — Pittsburgh, PA — **President / Managing Director,** 1999–Present
Provide technology, business management, project management, and change management consulting as well as strategic planning and teambuilding solutions for diverse industry clients. Build and direct technical teams to precisely design client-specific solutions.

ABC SYSTEMS, INC. — Pittsburgh, PA — **Senior Account Executive,** 2001–Present
Innovate technology solutions to address clients' business challenges, utilizing Microsoft-centric technology infrastructure and ebusiness/ecommerce Web site development. Contribute to IT project team for major mixed environment system migration. Ensure on-time/on-budget project completions including system migrations, Internet portals, and Web-based projects. Develop business and manage all projects/engagements within vertical markets.

PARADIGM, INC. — Pittsburgh, PA — **Practice Manager,** 1994–1999
Designed, directed, and managed startup of new business unit providing broad-spectrum services including database migration, application/database design and development, enterprise network management, and helpdesk/call center integration solutions. Utilized Web integration, database modification, middleware, etc., to incorporate solutions into existing environments. Supervised 50-member team of technical consultants/trainers and administrative, marketing, and sales staff.

XYZ TECHNOLOGY — Pittsburgh, PA — **Manager,** 1992–1994
Provided LAN/WAN network design and architecture assistance for 500-user systems in Novell, NT, and Sun SCO environments. Managed all network, server, and desktop implementations.

GEMINI SYSTEMS — Pittsburgh, PA — **Programmer/Analyst,** 1988–1992

Resume Strategy: *Joe's presentation-style resume is appropriate for his career goal of launching his private consulting business. The original resume, done in full color, provided client prospects with an appealing summary of Joe's technical expertise and proven results, broken out into strategic sections on both pages.*

JOSEPH O'CONNER

390 Magnolia Dr. □ Columbus, GA 31907
Phone: (706) 565-5555 □ Cellular: (706) 555-5551

MANAGEMENT CONSULTANT
Specializing in Organizational Development & Employee Training & Development

Dynamic manager with cross-functional expertise in strategic planning, human resource development, customer-driven service, team building, and change management. Proven ability to implement strategies that drive organizations to maximize profitability, improve operations, and elevate corporate image. Highly motivational, with the ability to boost morale and motivate employees to peak performance. Public speaker, comfortable delivering presentations to small and large audiences. Generate mission statements that give organizations the competitive edge. Manage multiple projects while maintaining the highest emphasis on quality.

EDUCATION

UNIVERSITY OF GEORGIA – Athens, GA
Master of Science in Training and Development, 1999 □ GPA: 3.98
Thesis: "Using Sensory Training Modules and Self-Directed Learning in High Performance Organizations"

VALDOSTA STATE UNIVERSITY – Valdosta, GA
Bachelor of Arts in Business Administration, Minor in Marketing, 1994 □ GPA: 3.59

PROFESSIONAL EXPERIENCE

CHARTER LEARNING ACADEMY – Columbus, GA   1998 to present
Chief Pastor / CEO / Chairman of the Board

Aggressively recruited for senior management position to streamline core operations, gain strong market position, improve public relations, administer budget, and increase operating revenue. Oversee full-time teaching/office staff and volunteers serving customer base of 140. Highlights of achievements:

➤ **Strategic Planning:** Wrote business plan, incorporating mission statement, six-month goals, and long-term objectives. Created departments and developed organizational chart, which resulted in clear understanding of roles and increased accountability. Researched, planned, and implemented capital improvement project involving the complete redesign and enhancement of 3,000-square-foot facility. Assembled team of 30 that achieved radical transformation of space, at 50% below budget, completed within three months.

➤ **Team Leadership:** Developed curriculum for personnel training and development. Brought leadership and cohesion to operation, which improved communications and employee morale. Effectively delegated tasks, empowering individuals to take on more responsibilities.

➤ **Financial:** Cultivated relationships with local businesses, including Wal-Mart and Kraft Foods, and organized joint ventures that helped quadruple regular income within months of assuming position. Introduced debt reduction strategy, which created a $4,000 monthly surplus. Established and chair bimonthly board meetings.

➤ **Marketing & Advertising:** Identified target market and initiated promotional campaign that focused on elevating the organization's image. Coordinated special events, including a first-of-its-kind black-tie affair that received rave reviews. Modernized organization's image by hiring a designer to update logos and brochures. Performed outreach to business community and media, resulting in media coverage and enrollment increase.

➤ **Customer Service:** Built and established loyal customer base, more than doubling enrollment to 140.

JOSEPH O'CONNER

Resume □ Page 2
Phone: (706) 565-5555 □ Cellular: (706) 555-5551

PREMIER CLEANERS – Atlanta, GA   1994 to 1998
Founder / Owner

Launched new business, providing dry cleaning services throughout metro Atlanta in a highly competitive marketplace. Developed business development initiatives and long-term growth strategies. Highlights of achievements:

➤ **Human Resources:** Devised systems for payroll, benefits, and compensation. Developed job descriptions and personnel training programs which greatly improved services and employee productivity.

➤ **Business Development:** Secured financing and transformed run-down buildings into desirable locations for business. Selected product lines and developed strategic plans. Developed entire operation from ground floor, and built the company into a thriving business, with seven locations.

➤ **Sales & Marketing:** Developed marketing strategies by identifying consumer trends and creating high-impact promotional materials. Successfully penetrated market, exceeding sales expectations and building a loyal customer base. Increased visibility through planning and orchestrating special promotions, sales, trade show exhibits, store displays, radio advertisements, and newsletters.

➤ **Customer Service:** Ensured delivery of impeccable customer service, earning the company a reputation for quality and service.

GEORGIA BANK & TRUST – Atlanta, GA   1990 to 1993
Assistant Corporate Manager

Recruited to manage corporate office tellers and customer service representatives. Handled schedules, placement, interviews, and evaluation. Highlights of achievements:

➤ **Training & Development:** Selected by senior management to prescreen and train employees both in-house and for other branch locations.

➤ **Organizational Processes:** Organized teller windows to maximize efficiency and productivity. Recognized by senior management for consistently balancing accounts to the penny.

➤ **Customer Service:** Created a loyal client base in excess of 300 through outstanding service delivery. Received award for outstanding performance for two consecutive years.

O'CONNER MANUFACTURING – Thomasville, GA   1984 to 1990
Assistant / Administrator

Employed at family-owned equipment manufacturing business. Assisted with growing the business.

COMPUTERS

Windows 2000/98/95, Macintosh OS, Microsoft Word, PowerPoint, Excel, Access, Oracle

Resume Strategy: *Joseph's resume shows how he led a religious organization as if he were running a corporation, making him a strong candidate for a management consulting position. Joseph leads his resume with a tagline that includes his new career goal along with his top two areas of specialization. His education is placed before experience because his new MBA is related to his management consulting objective. His position descriptions include subtopics that emphasize business and management achievements throughout his career.*

20
Advertising/Marketing/PR

PHARMACIST/WAITER TO ADVERTISING TRAFFIC COORDINATOR, PHARMACEUTICALS

Whitney Reed

757 Rosewood Dr.
Los Angeles, CA 90284

Home: 555-555-5555
Cell: 555-555-5550

whitney@resumepower.com

CAREER GOAL: Traffic Coordinator (Pharmaceutical Advertising)

Profile

Licensed pharmacist with exceptional interpersonal, organizational, project management, and customer service skills, seeking career change to pharmaceutical advertising. Adept in building collaborative partnerships with professionals from all organizational levels, with proven success right-sizing stalled or complex processes, projects, service issues, and inefficiencies.

Superior performance repeatedly recognized through fast-track promotions. Proven "multitasker" with diverse skill set; currently employed as both a pharmacist and waiter. Willingly volunteer for challenging or unpopular tasks, with reputation for positive work ethic, contagious enthusiasm, and respected team leadership. Bilingually fluent (Spanish), culturally sensitive, and computer literate.

Expertise

- Workflow Planning & Prioritization
- Project Management
- Organization & Follow-Through
- Team Building & Consensus Building
- Customer Relationship Management
- Creative Problem Solving
- Persuasive Communication
- Pharmaceutical Operations

Achievement Highlights

PROBLEM SOLVING & ORGANIZATION:

- **Redesigned workflow** for mail order pharmacy operations to right-size customer service issues and reverse prior history of lost/misplaced prescriptions. (Direct RX)

- **Leveraged strong relationships with physicians** to convince initially reluctant MDs to embrace hospital's new "nonformulary" pharmacy project, resulting in a five-figure annual reduction in medication costs. (LA County Hospital)

- **Managed a high volume of patient accounts;** interacted with physicians and patients daily to fill prescriptions, review side effects, discuss drug interactions, and resolve medication delivery problems. (Direct RX)

- **Solved shipping, delivery, and organizational problems** by overhauling pharmacy procedures and introducing improved labeling system. Outcomes included improved efficiency and thousands of dollars in cost savings without compromising service or quality. (Direct RX)

- **Helped facilitate improved intradepartmental communication,** cooperation, and workflow as member of hospital's pharmacy-nursing liaison committee. (LA County Hospital)

- **Salvaged key accounts** (hospitals/MDs) by restructuring department; assigned pharmacists to each customer for dramatic improvements in customer satisfaction. (Direct RX)

- **Coordinated all aspects of third-party billing** and resolved discrepancies for improved cash flow. (Direct RX)

- **Drove improvements** to drug-inventory management that reduced waste and back-orders. (Leo's)

- **Innovated automatic-prescription-refill strategy** to attract elderly clients. (Leo's)

- **Repeatedly commended for ability to proactively address and resolve** numerous customer issues. (Direct RX/Leo's/Olive Garden)

- **Enhanced controlled-substance record keeping** through automated solution and jointly prepared drug-use evaluation reports to resolve process problems. (LA County Hospital)

LEADERSHIP & SUPERVISION:

- **Managed HIV department** and supervised two pharmacy techs to ensure efficient and economic operations of mail order component. (Direct RX)

- **Asked to assume role of store operations manager** in his absence. (Leo's)

- **Recognized for encouraging teamwork and improving morale** of co-workers by rewarding good work and using humor to diffuse stress. (Direct RX, Olive Garden)

PHARMACIST/WAITER TO ADVERTISING TRAFFIC COORDINATOR, PHARMACEUTICALS (CONT.)

Whitney Reed

Achievement Highlights	**CUSTOMER SERVICE & SALES** ■ **Turned around disgruntled/dissatisfied clientele** through deep commitment to providing optimal customer service. Used patient listening, prompt response, and a calm and caring demeanor to repeatedly win over guests. (Olive Garden) ■ **Built excellent relationships** with customers/patients from all walks of life. Sought ways to reduce waiting time and deliver value-added service. (Leo's, Direct RX, LA County Hospital) ■ **Cultivated a strong network** of physicians that was directly responsible for generating an average of 108 new patients per month. (Direct RX)
Career History	LEO'S PHARMACY – Orange, CA – Independently owned retail pharmacy. **Pharmacist,** 2000–present (part-time) OLIVE GARDEN – Los Angeles, CA – Nationwide restaurant chain. **Waiter,** 2001–present (part-time) DIRECT RX – Los Angeles, CA – Mail order pharmacy for HIV/transplant patients. **Manager of HIV Department,** 1997–1998 **Regional Sales Representative,** 1997 **Staff Pharmacist,** 1996–1997 LA COUNTY HOSPITAL – Los Angeles, CA – Hospital with full-service pharmacy. **Staff Pharmacist,** 1992–1996
Education & Training	UNIVERSITY OF SOUTHERN CALIFORNIA – Los Angeles, CA – **BS in Pharmacy,** 1994 (GPA: 3.4) UNIVERSITY OF SAN DIEGO – San Diego, CA – **BA in Natural Science/Biology,** 1991 (GPA: 3.6) UC-IRVINE – Irvine, CA – **MS Office Software Training Program,** 2000 UNIVERSITY OF SAN DIEGO – San Diego, CA – **Six-month Computer Program,** 1999 (GPA: 3.8)
Computers	MS Office (Word, Excel, PowerPoint, Access), MS FrontPage, Macromedia Dreamweaver, Adobe Photoshop, Cute FTP, Windows XP/98, HTML 4.0, Visual Basic 6.0, C++
Of Note	**PUBLIC SPEAKING HIGHLIGHTS:** ■ Repeatedly invited by day treatment centers, nonprofit organizations, and social worker groups to speak on HIV/transplant medications and drug interactions. ■ Developed curriculum and conducted numerous drug-therapy seminars in English and Spanish for healthcare workers and HIV/transplant patients. **CERTIFICATION & LICENSURE:** ■ CA-Licensed Pharmacist – 1994–present ■ HIV/AIDS-Certified Pharmacist – 1996
Endorsement	"Whitney is bright, intelligent, and personable...able to assess a job and determine a creative way to produce a quality product...known to take projects home...a person of high moral character who is well liked by colleagues...brings both a high level of enthusiasm, an unfailing sense of humor, and an attention to detail to all assignments...I recommend her without reservation." **– B. Littleton, former Pharmacy Director, LA County Hospital**

Resume Strategy: _Whitney's functional resume format allows her to group achievements from diverse jobs as a waiter, pharmacist, and bartender into skill categories relevant to her career goal of becoming an advertising traffic coordinator for pharmaceutical advertising. She discusses her top qualifications in her "Profile" and includes a work chronology in her "Career History" section._

37 Berkestone Ave. ■ New Haven, CT 02567
555-555-5555 ■ serena@resumepower.com

SERENA KEMPER

Account/Project/Event Management □ Public Relations

Proven talents managing projects and PR and a passion for the high-tech/new-media industry.

Dynamic, creative, results-oriented professional adept in leading effective campaigns, projects, and events — from conception through delivery — on time and under budget. Award-winning public speaker with expert PowerPoint skills. Experienced researching, analyzing, and communicating complex data.

Comfortable and experienced delivering polished presentations to White House staff, senior FBI and CIA officials, university presidents, and Fortune 500 executives. Thrive in fast-paced environments with little supervision. Grasp software programs/technology quickly and easily.

Highlights of Qualifications

□ Public Relations
□ Marketing/Sales
□ Project Management
□ Copywriting/Editing

□ Research/Analysis
□ Media/Publicity
□ Presentations/Events
□ Volunteer Motivation

□ Computer Technology
□ Creative Problem Solving
□ Member: American Institute of Graphic Arts

"[Serena] is bright, creative, and highlighy motivated ... exceptionally articulate in both her oral presentations and written work ... ranks among the top two percent of students [whom] I have taught ..." (University Professor)

"Serena continues to demonstrate an exceptional ability to work with others under often difficult and stressful circumstances." (Govcorp Supervisor)

Education

YALE UNIVERSITY — New Haven, CT
Enrolled in **MA in Technology** program (evenings)
Awarded $75K Graduate Scholarship in Leadership/Excellence

CONNECTICUT INSTITUTE OF ART FOR GRAPHIC DESIGN — New Haven, CT
Enrolled in **Certificate Program** (weekends)

ARCADIA UNIVERSITY — Glenside, PA
BA in Mass Communication, 1995

Experience

GOVCORP — Washington, D.C.

Analyst (Project Manager), 1998 to 2001

Researched and analyzed data and prepared technical reports, programs, publications, and presentations for senior FBI, CIA, and U.S. government officials. *Key Contributions:*

□ Credited with enhancing critical partnerships and relationships between Federal Drug Administration and White House staff, physicians, and government officials.

□ Handled sensitive and confidential material for the FBI, DEA, and CIA.

□ Coordinated interagency program review meetings for experts in fighting illegal drug use.
  □ Designed and edited policy papers, technical presentations, and major publications such as National Drug Research and Development Blueprint Updates.
  □ Hosted academicians, industry executives, and senior government personnel.
  □ Managed conference logistics for attendees.

□ Overhauled computerized indexing system, increasing productivity by 20%.

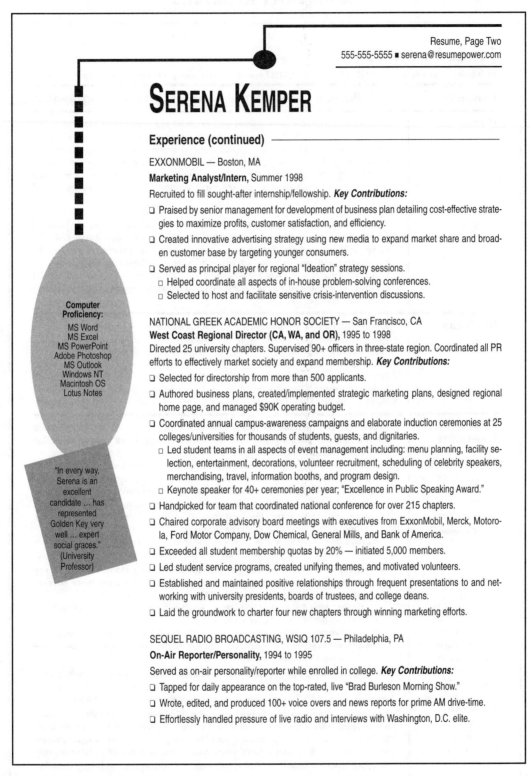

SERENA KEMPER

Experience (continued)

EXXONMOBIL — Boston, MA
Marketing Analyst/Intern, Summer 1998
Recruited to fill sought-after internship/fellowship. *Key Contributions:*

❑ Praised by senior management for development of business plan detailing cost-effective strategies to maximize profits, customer satisfaction, and efficiency.

❑ Created innovative advertising strategy using new media to expand market share and broaden customer base by targeting younger consumers.

❑ Served as principal player for regional "Ideation" strategy sessions.
  ▫ Helped coordinate all aspects of in-house problem-solving conferences.
  ▫ Selected to host and facilitate sensitive crisis-intervention discussions.

NATIONAL GREEK ACADEMIC HONOR SOCIETY — San Francisco, CA
West Coast Regional Director (CA, WA, and OR), 1995 to 1998
Directed 25 university chapters. Supervised 90+ officers in three-state region. Coordinated all PR efforts to effectively market society and expand membership. *Key Contributions:*

❑ Selected for directorship from more than 500 applicants.

❑ Authored business plans, created/implemented strategic marketing plans, designed regional home page, and managed $90K operating budget.

❑ Coordinated annual campus-awareness campaigns and elaborate induction ceremonies at 25 colleges/universities for thousands of students, guests, and dignitaries.
  ▫ Led student teams in all aspects of event management including: menu planning, facility selection, entertainment, decorations, volunteer recruitment, scheduling of celebrity speakers, merchandising, travel, information booths, and program design.
  ▫ Keynote speaker for 40+ ceremonies per year; "Excellence in Public Speaking Award."

❑ Handpicked for team that coordinated national conference for over 215 chapters.

❑ Chaired corporate advisory board meetings with executives from ExxonMobil, Merck, Motorola, Ford Motor Company, Dow Chemical, General Mills, and Bank of America.

❑ Exceeded all student membership quotas by 20% — initiated 5,000 members.

❑ Led student service programs, created unifying themes, and motivated volunteers.

❑ Established and maintained positive relationships through frequent presentations to and networking with university presidents, boards of trustees, and college deans.

❑ Laid the groundwork to charter four new chapters through winning marketing efforts.

SEQUEL RADIO BROADCASTING, WSIQ 107.5 — Philadelphia, PA
On-Air Reporter/Personality, 1994 to 1995
Served as on-air personality/reporter while enrolled in college. *Key Contributions:*

❑ Tapped for daily appearance on the top-rated, live "Brad Burleson Morning Show."

❑ Wrote, edited, and produced 100+ voice overs and news reports for prime AM drive-time.

❑ Effortlessly handled pressure of live radio and interviews with Washington, D.C. elite.

Computer Proficiency:

MS Word
MS Excel
MS PowerPoint
Adobe Photoshop
MS Outlook
Windows NT
Macintosh OS
Lotus Notes

"In every way, Serena is an excellent candidate ... has represented Golden Key very well ... expert social graces." (University Professor)

Resume Strategy: *Serena's bold resume design (in bright, primary colors on the original resume) creates an energetic and dynamic presentation that is appropriate to her career goal of breaking into a creative field. She brings out her most relevant qualifications/accomplishments throughout the resume.*

Janet Fuentes

14 Dupont Avenue • Boston, MA 02126 • Phone: 617-123-4567 • janetfuentes@resumepower.com • Available for Relocation

CAREER GOAL	***EVENT PLANNER • COMMUNITY RELATIONS • OUTREACH COORDINATOR***

PROFILE

- **Experienced marcom professional** with expertise in event planning, event marketing, and community relations. Proven success coordinating all aspects of capacity-crowd special events, including sports competitions/championships, professional meetings, national conferences/symposiums, training programs/classes, speakers' bureaus, athlete appearances, contests, and network media weekends. Expert in detailed logistical planning encompassing travel, facility, venue, agenda, entertainment, menu, sponsorship, volunteer coordination, and security arrangements.

- **Demonstrated ability to architect results-driven marketing plans** and powerful print/broadcast promotions benchmarking new "bests" in ticket sales and attendance (including a 21-fold increase). Polished, persuasive communicator; builder of partnerships and alliances; and award-winning public speaker/presenter. Backed by solid credentials: BBA (with honors) in marketing management and advanced technology skills (Certified MS Office User Specialist, Adobe PageMaker, Lotus Notes, Designer's Edge, MS Outlook, MS Project, Paintshop Pro, Visio).

KEY SKILLS

- Special Event Planning & Management
- Volunteer Coordination & Supervision
- High-Impact Presentations
- Large-Scale Project Management
- Vendor Evaluation & Selection
- Strategic Marketing & Promotions
- Media/Community/Client Relations

- Communication/PR Strategy
- Organization/Planning
- Focus Group Facilitation
- Newsletters
- Collateral Development (Writing & Design)
- Team Building & Training
- Contract Review

ACHIEVEMENT HIGHLIGHTS

"Every detail was handled with perfection and [Janet] made me look like a hero in my client's eyes."

— ABC Executive

"Everything was wonderful, from the food, my room, the facilitators, to the program. The overall environment really added to the program's effectiveness. Thanks for making everything look like it was effortless..."

— Three-Day Training Program Participant

- **Repeatedly commended by senior management, presenters, and participants for the detailed planning and seamless orchestration of all aspects of major events and classes.** (*ABC and Company LLP*)
  ○ Handled session logistics, event marketing, site selection, vendor/supplier/facility contract negotiations and review, menu planning, agenda planning, a/v support, course materials design (print and Web), collaboration with sales/catering staff, and entertainment coordination.
  ○ Planned a full spectrum of events including one-day internal classes (10–60 participants), one-day client conferences (25–90 participants), multiday classes (20–60 participants), and national symposiums (up to 200 participants).
  ○ Provided on-site hosting and management during events to ensure smooth operations, rapid response to last-minute requests/challenges, and successful outcomes.
- **Strategized and implemented cost-effective marketing plans for ten varsity sports programs, with outcomes including history-making attendance records surpassing season averages by over 2,000%.** (*Boston College Athletics*)
  ○ Created and placed on-campus and community advertising, oversaw sponsor solicitation and contract fulfillment, and directed game-day event management.
  ○ Innovated results-driven promotions that consistently outperformed prior average season attendance, including new record for the highest single-game attendance ever (drew 6,800+ compared to season average of 300).
- **Choreographed high-profile ABC Sports/college football weekend.** Organized entire weekend of activities and served as primary media liaison and weekend escort to handle last-minute requests of ABC Sports executives and their guests. (*Boston College Athletics*)
- **Recognized with prestigious honors for outstanding presentation, public speaking, and training skills** as the twice-awarded "Distinguished Instructor" in 1999 and 1998. Taught 90+ classes in a four-year period for hundreds of business professionals across topics including team building, train-the-trainer, personal effectiveness, and technology. (*ABC and Company LLP*)
- **Directed Speakers' Bureau,** coordinating/supervising all athlete public appearances and ensuring full compliance with NCAA requirements and reporting regulations. (*Boston College Athletics*)
- **Revamped marketing scheme** for "Sports Gold" card, the college's all-sports pass, by developing sport-specific and football-weekend passes as two new offerings. The addition of these new enticements was key to achieving record-setting sales. (*Boston College Athletics*)

Janet Fuentes

ACHIEVEMENT HIGHLIGHTS

"…thank you for hosting this outstanding affair. This was a success from the moment the participants arrived until we put them on the plane home. Our guests left with a first-class impression of our firm."
— ABC Partner

"Janet, you came through again for us. You are truly an excellent resource, efficient, and committed to doing a quality job."
— ABC Manager

- **Provided game-day management at football, men's basketball, and other varsity sports,** with sole accountability for scripting and timing of pregame flag presentations, arranging half-time ceremonies and contests, and coordinating other special presentations with college officials and special guests. (*Boston College Athletics*)

- **Recruited, trained, and supervised 20-member student volunteer team,** administered department budget, and managed special project assignments to further community goodwill (e.g., multi-school-district ticket-drawing contests, cheerleading-tryout judging, and representation of university at various community and campus meetings/events). (*Boston College Athletics*)

- **Assisted with development of promotional plan and sponsor packages** for NCAA Division I Women's Tennis Championships. (*Boston College Athletics*)

- **Initiated, wrote, designed, and managed department newsletter** for two years, creating an internal publication that successfully communicated key message points, drove increased participation in company programs/training initiatives, and quickly became an in-demand, key business reference companywide. (*ABC and Company LLP*)

- **Leveraged expert interviewing and interpersonal skills to conduct in-depth needs analysis** with internal client groups (from business-unit, value-unit, and individual levels). Dug beneath initially expressed "surface needs" to uncover underlying issues, facilitating the delivery of total training solutions. (*ABC and Company LLP*)

CAREER HISTORY

"I just received my packet for the symposium and wanted to let you know how impressed I was with a) the organization and completeness of the material and b) 'The News For You.' This last piece was well written and fun. And it makes it look like we have our 'act together.' Great job and keep up the good work."
— ABC Client

ABC & COMPANY LLP, Boston, MA — 1996 to Present — *Accounting/consulting firm*
Manager — Instructional Design (2000 to Present)
Instructional Designer — Educational Services (1998 to 2000)
Client Conference Coordinator (1996 to 1998)

Recognized for superior performance through series of promotions. Currently hold accountability for the design, development, coordination, and delivery of employee-centered training classes and programs. Prior responsibilities included coordination of marketing/logistics for all educational conferences and special events and design/production of all course materials and conference collateral.

ACE CASES INCORPORATED, Boston, MA — 1995 to 1996 — *Custom-case manufacturer*
Sales Service Coordinator

Provided support to customers and sales representatives worldwide, maintaining two in-house customer accounts with annual orders totaling over $3 million.

BOSTON COLLEGE ATHLETICS, Boston, MA — 1993 to 1995 — *Big East Conference*
Sports Marketing Assistant (1994 to 1995); **Sports Marketing Intern** (1993 to 1994)
Hand-selected as first full-time marketing assistant for department after successful culmination of internship. Oversaw game management, event coordination/promotions, budget reconciliation, student athlete speaking engagements, and other special projects for ten varsity programs.

SOFTWARE INNOVATIONS COMPANY, Boston, MA — Summer 1990 — *Software solutions provider*
Marketing/Communications Intern

Chosen for highly competitive internship, with responsibility for media utilization tracking, redesigning product brochure layouts, coordinating trade shows, and creating/distributing monthly KPI reports (e.g., sales, new clients, press hits) for Board of Directors and other international stakeholders.

EDUCATION

Boston College, Boston, MA — **B.B.A. with honors, Marketing Management** (1993)

Resume Strategy: *Janet's resume highlights her experience in event planning and outreach initiatives, even though she's been out of the field since 1998. Her "Profile" and "Key Skills" sections communicate her main strengths and the "Achievement Highlights" section allows her to place her accomplishments in any order that she chooses, regardless of when they occurred in her career.*

Dipti Shabda

15 Orange Grove Ave.
Cambridge, MA 02139

dipti@resumepower.com

Home: (617) 555-5555
Cellular: (617) 555-5556

GOAL: MARKETING / CORPORATE COMMUNICATIONS / POLICY ANALYSIS

Seeking to use solid communication, decision-making, analytical, international, and business skills in a position within a globally oriented corporate environment

Multifaceted professional with the ability to research, analyze, and synthesize information into sound economic, marketing, and development plans. Ten years of international exposure has fostered cultural sensitivity and adaptability to diverse global-business practices. Valued team member and team leader, able to build a harmonious work environment.

Strong knowledge of international and Indian affairs, as illustrated by appearances on issue-oriented television programming, receipt of a fellowship to the Institute of Indian Studies at Harvard University, and participation in a number of policy forums. Multilingual (English, Portuguese, French, three Hindi dialects, and working Spanish).

Proficiency Areas

- **Quantitative Analysis**
- **Country Risk Assessment**
- **Economic Forecasting**
- **Market Research**
- **Feasibility Studies**
- **Internet Marketing**
- **Proposal Development**
- **Program Management**
- **Public/Press Relations**
- **Television Production**
- **Internal/External Communications**

Education

HARVARD UNIVERSITY, SCHOOL OF INTERNATIONAL & PUBLIC AFFAIRS – Cambridge, MA

Master of International Affairs, May 1999

Concentrations: **Economic and Political Development, Policy Analysis, and Indian Studies**

BOSTON UNIVERSITY – Boston, MA

Bachelor of Arts in English, *Minors:* **French and Portuguese,** May 1988
- Certificate for Teaching English as a Second Language (ESL)

Career Highlights

- As **information officer** for U.N. Peacekeeping Operations in India, created public awareness programs that enhanced U.N.'s image and created a sense of trust. Awarded promotion to next grade level for reducing operational costs of information unit by 30%.
- Integrated analytical skills and in-depth knowledge of Indian affairs to conduct a **political analysis** of Bombay for UnitedPartners International.
- **Increased Web site traffic** for Sanskrit.com by 40% within four months by improving search engine placements after analyzing and restructuring keyword strategies. Uncovered and pursued leads that became major accounts; increased number of business-to-business sites by 20%.
- Member of **portfolio management** team that managed a $500,000 emerging markets portfolio, as part of class project at Harvard University's School of International & Public Affairs. Demonstrated investment savvy and use of analytic tools/strategies to maximize returns. Increased portfolio's value by 40% in a four-month period, outpacing the S&P Index by 6% during same period.
- Awarded **fellowship** to the Institute of Indian Studies, Harvard University. Selected from among 200 candidates in recognition of previous professional experience and academic excellence.

Dipti Shabda

Resume - Page Two

Professional Experience

UNITEDPARTNERS INTERNATIONAL, LLC – Boston, MA
(Organization promoting and facilitating U.S. investments in India, Asia, and the Caribbean.)
Consultant, June 1999 to present

Conduct research and provide economic and political analysis of current and past trends. Prepare country risk assessment for use in lobbying efforts.

INSTITUTE OF INDIAN STUDIES, HARVARD UNIVERSITY – Cambridge, MA
(Major U.S. resource center for information on India.)
Program Assistant, 1998 to 1999

Organized weekly seminars and several major conferences relating to Indian social, economic, and religious topics. Maintained oversight for public-relations efforts and administrative matters. Interacted with student population and provided curriculum and program guidance.

SANSKRIT.COM – Boston, MA
(Internet business designed to promote investment and tourism in India.)
Marketing Consultant, Spring 1998

Assessed feasibility of initial business plan, conducted market research on e-commerce industry, and developed marketing strategies to meet goals of growing business.

WORLD DEVELOPMENT PROGRAM – Providence, RI; Bombay, India
(Provides policy instruments, experts, and advice to government officials of developing countries.)
Intern - India Bureau, Policy Unit, Summer 1998

Assessed policy documents and provided feedback on areas for improvement. Attended and summarized several World Development lectures and a four-day workshop on Social Assessment. Researched and wrote 30-page paper on India's policy environment to assess postconflict improvements for rural women.

Information Officer, 1992 to 1997

Stationed in Bombay, India to serve as press liaison and wrote daily press bulletins apprising World Development headquarters of ground developments. Supervised television crew; created public awareness campaigns; and oversaw production, budgeting, archiving, and programming processes.

Affiliations ■ Publications ■ Presentations

- Member, Women in International and Public Affairs
- Managing Editor, Newsletter of the Institute of Indian Studies, Harvard University, 1998 to 1999
- Panelist on Indian Affairs, *NBC International Forum,* June 22, 1998
- Presenter, Indian Economic Forum, Harvard University, Spring 1999

Willing to Relocate and Travel Internationally

Resume Strategy: After stating her career goal and value proposition ("Seeking to use solid communication..."), Dipti summarizes her key strengths for positions in marketing, corporate communications, or policy analysis in her profile. She includes an easy-to-skim "Proficiency Areas" section, followed by her impressive master's degree from Harvard University in the "Education" section. The use of a "Career Highlights" section allows Dipti to bring out accomplishments that are most relevant to her career goals despite the fact that she achieved these several years earlier. She follows this with a brief run-down of the positions she has held throughout her career in her "Professional Experience" section.

Julie Barnes

15 Bay Street ■ Staten Island, NY 10312
Home: 718-123-4567 ■ Pager: 917-123-5678
julie@resumepower.com ■ Cellular: 917-987-6543

Communications Professional

Technical & Creative Writing ■ Instructional Design ■ Corporate Training
Digital Video Production ■ Web Site Development ■ Project Management

Profile

- **Communications specialist with diverse industry experience and multifaceted talents.** Experienced writing highly praised, results-driven materials including radio/video scripts, press releases, marketing collateral, training manuals, Web pages, RFPs, statements of work, position papers, and interactive instructional programs.

- **In-demand corporate trainer,** skilled in classroom, CBT, and WBT curriculum development and instructional design/delivery for computer users and sales professionals.

- **Advanced user of technology,** including desktop publishing using Adobe PageMaker, Microsoft Publisher, and Microsoft FrontPage. Solid IT credentials – Certified Network Administrator (CNA) and Certified Network Engineer (CNE).

- **Skilled in video production/editing.** Hands-on experience drafting storyboards, operating camera and audio equipment, supervising production crews, directing studio and field shoots, and editing raw footage.

- **Multimillion-dollar project manager with P&L mindset** – repeated success in turnaround management of stalled, lagging, or overbudget projects. Proven ability to slash costs, generate revenue, streamline operations, and increase customer satisfaction.

Education

NEW YORK UNIVERSITY – New York, NY

Master of Science, 1985   Major: **Communication**   Minor: **Political Science**
Bachelor of Science, 1983   Major: **Broadcast Journalism**   Minor: **Political Science**

Work History

ABC WIRELESS, INC. – Staten Island, NY
Project Manager – Training Department, 2000 to Present ■ **Business Analyst,** 1999 to 2000

ACTION INFORMATION SERVICES – New York, NY
Senior Project Analyst – National Project Support Center, 1998 to 1999 ■ **Team Leader/Technical Support Specialist – Solution Line** (Help Desk Services), 1996 to 1998

INDEPENDENT CONTRACTOR – Staten Island, NY
Communication Consultant/Technical Writer, 1994 to 1995

COMPUTER CENTER – New York, NY
Sales Associate, 1992 to 1994

ABC INSURANCE GROUP – New York, NY
Sales Training Specialist, 1989 to 1992 ■ **Procedure Analyst,** 1987 to 1989

Julie Barnes

Resume, Page Two

Communications Experience

ABC WIRELESS, INC. – Staten Island, NY
Project Manager –Training Department, 2000 to Present
Develop and deliver Web-based training courses for approximately one-third of company's workforce. Conduct training needs analysis and prioritize instructional program development, incorporate measurable outcomes into curriculum design, author/design scripts and storyboards for classes, and consult with subject-matter experts to develop and fine-tune course content.

- **Coordinated major billing system rollout/consolidation by introducing time- and cost-saving computer-based and Web-based training solutions.**
  - □ Enabled small, eight-member training department to meet aggressive six-month system rollout schedule for 48 states by introducing company's first CBT/WBT programs.
  - □ Designed two mock CBT modules using PowerPoint and convinced senior management to field-test high-tech programs for customer service representatives.
  - □ Achieved overwhelmingly positive test results, which led to enthusiastic endorsement of new WBT program and saved $80K in program costs.
- **Slashed course development time from six months to ten weeks** by initiating company's first-ever online training database.
  - □ Worked closely with IT team to identify network capabilities and restrictions. Screened and selected vendor to develop program code and proprietary database with the versatility to create interactive, online training in-house for virtually any subject.
  - □ Incorporated streaming video system, audio narration, and live digital-video capabilities into training database, addressing the needs of different learning styles.
- **Authored and distributed comprehensive but concise WBT guide** for trainers and managers which enhanced cooperative understanding of how to transform concepts into effective online realities.

INDEPENDENT CONTRACTOR – Staten Island, NY
Communication Consultant/Technical Writer, 1994 to 1995
Hired to develop strategic communication plans, write technical and/or marketing copy, and develop comprehensive software/hardware training plans for a wide range of private- and public-sector clients including ABC Company, DEF Company, and GHI Company.

ABC INSURANCE GROUP – New York, NY
Sales Training Specialist, 1989 to 1992; **Procedure Analyst,** 1987 to 1989
Identified training needs and conducted on-site product/service instruction for new and existing insurance agents within ten-state territory.

- **Proposed company's first Sales Training Department** and became a ground-floor member of the team.
- **Reduced insurance agent turnover 28%** through development of customized, modular-based training materials and curriculum.

Computer Skills

Systems:	Novell NetWare 4.X / 3.x, UNIX, Windows 3.1/95/98/NT/2000/ME, Windows for Workgroups, MS-DOS 5.0/6.0
Software:	Project, Word, Excel, Access, FrontPage, Publisher, PageMaker, Macromedia Authorware, Visio, Camtasia (video capture software), VirtualDub (video editing software), Premiere

Resume Strategy: *Even though Julie's career is mainly in project management, sales, and training, her resume clearly shows her qualifications for her communications specialist objective. Her resume leads with a large banner that positions her for communications jobs and follows with a profile of her related experiences. Julie provides a complete work chronology on page one to satisfy hiring managers who would like to see a full work history, but then omits her unrelated positions in her "Communications Experience" section.*

Susan Smith

15 Randall Street
Martinsville, VA 24112
Home: 540-123-4567
Cell: 540-987-6543
susan@resumepower.com

Available for Relocation

❖ ❖ ❖ ❖

KEY SKILLS

Copywriting & Collateral
Development (Print/Web/
Video)

Media & Public Relations

Communication Strategy

High-Impact Presentations

Public Speaking

Large-Scale Program &
Project Management

Special Event Planning

Press Releases

Communication Tools

Advertising Campaigns

Community Outreach

Article Research &
Authorship

Controversial & Complex
Subject Matter

Consensus Building

Mediation & Negotiation

Strategic Alliances &
Partnerships

Team Building & Training

PUBLIC RELATIONS & MARKETING SPECIALIST

Dynamic public relations practitioner and marcom professional, with outstanding communication, public speaking, and interpersonal skills. Effective strategist of media and communication plans; adept in persuasive and articulate message development/delivery addressing complex or controversial subject matter. Polished presenter, able to sway public opinion, build consensus, and gain crucial support.

Experienced in print and Web collateral development, marketing/advertising campaign management, special event coordination, and employee training program development (classroom/video). Demonstrated ability to anticipate problems; design innovative, cost-effective solutions; and balance multiple high-priority projects with competing deadlines. Effective in self-managed and team environments. Strong technical knowledge base and research/analytical skills gained from 17-year career in environmental safety.

❖ ❖ ❖ ❖

RELEVANT EXPERIENCE

XYZ ENGINEERING GROUP – Martinsville, VA
Community Relations Writer, June 2001 to Present
Environmental Safety and Health Specialist II, March 1999 to June 2001
Rapidly advanced to key community relations role, serving as public and media liaison for the U.S. Department of Energy's $1 billion Revitalization Site Action Project (RSAP), a 15-year, DOE-directed radioactive depository cleanup initiative. Research, write, edit, and disseminate a variety of collateral (e.g., press releases, media advisories, public information documents, community newsletters, advertisements, brochures, Web pages) to fulfill communication objectives of frequency, honesty, and accuracy.

Jointly coordinate public forums, meetings, special events, and conference presentations; conduct site briefings and tours for visiting dignitaries and the general public; and ensure timely and strategic response to information requests from the public, news media, and special interest groups on often controversial issues. *Selected Contributions:*

- **Commended by site manager** for quickly taking over a number of key, ongoing community relations projects with minimal training or ramp-up time.
- **Hand-selected for expanded, concurrent role** as interim community relations and training department manager during two-month search for permanent replacement, with supervisory responsibility for all PR/communication activities.
- **Adeptly handled a myriad of community concerns and controversial matters** as DOE media liaison and public spokesperson. Strategized message points and ensured accurate and prompt response to time-sensitive information requests from the public and news media, as well as protests by special interest groups.
- **Praised by local government officials, school teachers/administrators, and parents** for direction of "Partners in Education" program aimed at encouraging students to pursue science/industry careers.
  - ☐ Prepared and delivered numerous well-received school and on-site presentations, customized for age appropriateness, on topics including radiation, soil conservation, and geology.
  - ☐ Wrote and designed all supporting materials, including brochures, pamphlets, and PowerPoint slide presentations.
- **Authored and co-edited** "KEY FACTS," a community newsletter distributed to 25,000+ households.

Susan Smith

Home: 540-123-4567
Cell: 540-987-6543
susan@resumepower.com

Page Two

❖ ❖ ❖ ❖

EARLY CAREER

BFI MICROMEDICS
SYSTEMS – Nyack, NY

**Technical Service
Representative,**
1987 to 1989

ELMHURST HOSPITAL –
Queens, NY

**Nuclear Medicine
Technologist,**
1984 to 1987

❖ ❖ ❖ ❖

**EDUCATION &
CREDENTIALS**

BROOKLYN COLLEGE –
Brooklyn, NY

BA in Sociology

Training:
Completed 40-hr. program
in Hazardous Waste
Operations & Emergency
Response

Computer Skills:
MS Windows, MS Office
(Word, Excel, PowerPoint,
Outlook)

Professional Memberships:
Physics Society –
Martinsville, VA
(1996 to 1998)

Laser Institute of
America –
Martinsville, VA
(1997 to 1998)

XYZ ENGINEERING GROUP (*continued*)

◆ **Orchestrated all aspects** (logistics, advertising, media, speakers, food, presentations, agenda) of successful special events (e.g., public opinion meetings, open houses, press conferences).

◆ **Researched, co-wrote,** and obtained DOE approval of all copy/captions for displays, kiosks, and flipbooks for center's museum. Provided a visually powerful and easy-to-understand chronology of site's cleanup that generated strong community interest and school participation.

◆ **Hosted visiting dignitaries,** conducting site briefings and tours for officials including Congressman Bill Simms.

◆ **Liaised between display design contractors and DOE administrators** as primary point of contact, overcoming numerous logistical hurdles (e.g., aggressive timeframes, cost constraints, fabrication/design challenges) to deliver completion of Interpretive Center on time and on budget.

◆ **Scripted "This Is RSAP" slide presentation,** an information tool used extensively to educate the public on DOE remediation efforts.

◆ **Cut labor-intensive physical inventory of 1,000 items in half** by revamping department's $1 million computerized system.

ACTION PHARMACEUTICALS – Martinsville, VA
Worldwide research and pharmaceutical company that discovers, develops, manufactures, and markets human and animal health products and services.

Health Physics Specialist / Staff Health Physicist, July 1989 to October 1998
Managed the Radioactive Waste Program (24,000-sq.-ft. waste depository), with full accountability for employee safety communications as manager of the Radiation Safety Training Program serving all research/ancillary/student co-op personnel. Designed Web-based, video, CBT, and in-person training programs to achieve 100% regulatory compliance for the security, control, shipping, and inventory maintenance of radioactive hazardous materials (HAZMAT). *Selected Contributions:*

◆ **Initiated, wrote script for, directed, and produced 25-minute training video** on radiation safety lauded by management for its thoroughness. Video program enabled new-hires to meet training requirements for same-day assignment start, reversing prior trend of costly, three-week start-date delays.

◆ **Identified department training needs/knowledge gaps,** developed curricula, wrote training manuals/assessments, set training schedules, and conducted learner-focused classroom presentations. Developed computer-based training (CBT) modules to expand accessibility of learner options.

◆ **Spearheaded improved internal communications** through Web-based development of a radioactive "expert" program on department's intranet. Selected Web site content/visuals and oversaw launch, with results including measurable decreases in processing errors and a crucial reduction in regulatory vulnerability.

◆ **Actively participated in management cross-training program,** fulfilling rotating, six-month role as laboratory services supervisor over unionized workforce of 15 in five research facilities. Interpreted union guidelines, resolved staff conflicts, motivated team, and conducted disciplinary and grievance interviews.

❖ ❖ ❖ ❖

Resume Strategy: *Susan emphasizes her top selling points for a career change to marketing/PR in her profile section and "Key Skills" listed in the left-hand margin. Her "Selected Contributions" in her "Relevant Experience" section focus on achievements relevant to marcom positions, such as community/media relations, public speaking, and writing/design. Her less relevant jobs are relegated to an "Early Career" section in the margin on page two of the resume.*

Rashem Abid

15 Barrow Street, New York, NY 10028 ◆ (212) 123-4567 ◆ Cell: (917) 123-8765 ◆ rashem@resumepower.com

Goal	**MUSIC PROMOTIONS / TALENT BOOKING / NEW MEDIA ASSISTANT**
Profile	**Results-oriented promotions/marketing assistant** with an educational foundation in journalism, excellent internship experience, and a passion to excel in a music-industry career. Thrive in deadline-driven environments and provide uncompromising attention to detail and rapid problem resolution. Skilled interviewer and relationship builder, with the ability to network with Fortune 500 accounts, educational leaders, and international experts across diverse industries. Known for tireless work ethic, eagerness to learn, and emphasis on quality. Proficient in Spanish (written and verbal).
Education	PACE UNIVERSITY — New York, NY **Bachelor of Arts in Journalism,** Minor in Psychology, 5/01 (GPA: 3.8) ◆ *Honors:* Dean's List (1998 to 2000), Writing Award (2001); Sisk Scholarship (study abroad, 1999) ◆ *Activities:* Journalism Society, Resident Assistant, Program Board, Freshman Register
Experience	E-COMMERCE.COM — New York, NY **E-Commerce Intern,** 7/00 to 8/01; **Global Affairs Department Intern,** 10/99 to 1/00 ◆ Assisted with scheduling and moderating dozens of online chats and message boards hosted by high-profile e-commerce experts. ◆ Contributed to the success of Youth Day 2002, an online event linking youth with working professionals to give them an up-close look at the world of work. ◆ Trained corporate clients on the use of online career fairs to ensure they took advantage of advanced features to attract suitable job candidates. ◆ Elevated the quality and appropriateness of 30+ message boards by regularly monitoring content. ◆ Reviewed and edited hundreds of pages of content for accuracy and consistency. ◆ Edited Community Handbook that standardized guidelines for chat/message board moderators. STYLE MAGAZINE (UK) — London, England **Intern,** Editorial Department, 2/00 to 5/00 ◆ Researched, edited, and wrote for "Monthly Style Bits" column. ◆ Conducted in-depth interview with Chris Isaak for Q&A section. ◆ Interviewed managers of London clubs to compile information for a London nightlife guide. HIP MAGAZINE — New York, NY **Intern,** Editorial Department, 10/99 to 1/00 ◆ Fact-checked and proofread articles and conducted research for magazine features.
Computers	Word, Excel, WorldMerge, PowerPoint, Dreamweaver, QuarkXPress, Photoshop, FileMaker Pro
Testimonials	*"I was always impressed with Rashem's ability to complete all assignments on time, if not before they were due…his interaction with clients was always professional."* — Harriet Fischer, Program Director *"Rashem has excellent presentation and organizational skills…he has demonstrated leadership capabilities by guiding co-workers and managing relationships with ease."* — Stu Adler, Sales Director *"Rashem will serve your organization with devotion, intelligence, and experience."* — Sidney Cohen, Content Producer

Resume Strategy: *Rashem's profile emphasizes his marketing/promotions internship experience and articulates his eagerness to break into the music industry. He gives bulleted highlights of his internships, being sure to mention his experience dealing with musicians and club managers. His "Testimonials" offer further proof of his qualifications.*

21
Writing/Editing

Laura Chen

15 Forest Street, Staten Island, NY 10314 / 718-987-6543 / laurachen@resumepower.com

---

WRITER ... EDITOR ... RESEARCHER
Travelogues, Promotional Copy, Research, Copy Editing, Proofreading

---

Talented writer seeking an entry-level or internship position in a corporate environment. Possess a passion for travel-related writing and an insatiable curiosity for a wide range of subjects. Have written about travel experiences in Hawaii, Indonesia, California, Washington, and Oregon. Additional qualifications:

➢ Experience writing promotional copy for start-up business that led to phenomenal corporate growth.

➢ Academic foundation in psychology and journalism; diverse background has strengthened research, time management, organizational, interpersonal/team building, and business skills.

➢ Commitment to excellence in all endeavors and maintain the highest standard of integrity.

➢ Computer literate (Microsoft Word, Windows 2000, Internet research). Conversational French.

Education

PACE UNIVERSITY – New York, NY
MA, Clinical Psychology, 1996; **BA, Journalism**, 1994

Project Highlights

➢ Designed A+ Bakery's marketing materials, including presentation sheet, logo, catalogs, labels, and packaging.

➢ Collaborated with president of A+ Bakery on Web site concept and design. Developed content and conducted extensive field research to promote the nationwide marketing of a gourmet cookie product.

➢ Wrote optional master's thesis; research centered on a psychological study of adolescent female sexual desire, on file in the Pace University Library.

➢ Developed writing portfolio with 25 short stories, poetry, nonfiction, and travelogues.

➢ Managed a research, design, and editing service at Pace University. Tutored students on proper editorial and writing techniques. Designed logos for small businesses throughout New York.

➢ Member of Knights of the Round Table (1998 to 2002), an Internet-based short story writing group.

Professional Experience

A+ Bakery – Staten Island, NY   **Marketing Consultant**, 1998 to present
➢ Coordinate marketing and PR efforts for launch of baked goods product into national market.

Master's Program Internships – New York, NY   **Counselor,** 1995 to 1998

➢ Provided crisis intervention and individual, group, and family counseling at several mental health and community intervention programs throughout New York City.

➢ Designed program and all collateral materials for an innovative grief/loss therapy group for at-risk youth.

➢ Coordinated "Free 4 the Weekend," a citywide celebration for Pace University students who contract to remain drug and alcohol free, as part of the NY Council on Alcoholism and Drug Abuse program.

Writing Samples Available on Request

Resume Strategy: *Although Laura's educational background prepared her for a career in clinical psychology and her current position is marketing-related, Laura decided to follow her dream of being a writer. This career-change resume helped her secure an excellent position with a national magazine. She uses a tagline at the top to draw attention to her new goal, while emphasizing her related writing experiences in her summary and "Project Highlights" sections.*

Dean R. Nunzio

Current: P.O Box 68974. Springfield, MO 14532 • (417) 555-5555 • dino@resumepower.com
After May 1, 2003: 787 E. College Ave., Howard Hall • St. Joseph, MO 14587

RESEARCH PROFESSIONAL
Analysis • Reporting • Administration • Education • Public Relations

Dedicated MBA with extensive experience in information collection, analysis, and dissemination. Strong background in education, urban, social, and ecological planning.

- Talented researcher with expertise in administration of nonprofit educational institution.
- Published author, excellent verbal and visual communicator, and comfortable working independently or collaborating with team members.
- Proficient in management planning, implementation, and evaluation.
- Media contact and frequent guest speaker for universities, seminars, civic/social groups, health organizations, and Internet chats.

PROFESSIONAL EXPERIENCE

DIABETES FOUNDATION — Springfield, MO   1989 to Present
[Nonprofit charitable organization with 50–75 employees and volunteers dedicated to research and fundraising toward the treatment and eventual cure of diabetes.]

Assistant to the President (1990 to Present)

- Write and edit correspondence, papers, and presentations.
- Design and deliver lectures and slide shows for organization that presents to 450,000 people per year. Developed and regularly deliver 180-slide presentation that has been well received by audiences.
- Initiated computerization for improved production and editing of physician notes and papers.
- Secured initial media coverage and was featured in two television reports that generated inquiries for the treatment and prevention of diabetes.
- Established office staff procedures, job roles, responsibilities, and office manual.
- Created 36-page master bibliography for use as organizational reference.
- Edit monthly workshop brochure; wrote all captions and assisted with developing text for illustrated flyer.
- Collaborate on design, composition, review, and revisions to publications such as exhibit at New York Disease Prevention Center and workshop materials for "Insulin-Free Diabetes Treatment."

Research Associate (1989)

- Invited by Dr. Tallwort, co-founder of the foundation, to join him in performing a comprehensive analysis of current research. Planned project research, objectives, data collection, and analysis methodologies.
- Issued two major reports on research project and developed bibliographies for the study.
- Analyzed and summarized research objectives and results.

Consultant, Books Division (1981 to 1984)

- Co-authored book with Dr. Tallwort; researched, composed, and edited text.
- Selected illustrative slides and composed bibliography, captions, and index.
- Wrote patient reference manual and pamphlet distributed to hospitals and healthcare organizations nationwide.

Dean R. Nunzio

Resume • Page Two

PROFESSIONAL EXPERIENCE

RENTAL CENTER — Springfield, MO   1986 to 1989
[Nationwide furniture/appliance rental store.]

Senior Credit Analyst/Credit Authorizer

- Supervised up to 20 credit authorizers engaged in credit history analysis and credit extension; responsible for detecting credit fraud; accessed credit bureau consumer reports.

- Promoted to senior credit analyst in second year; trained 25 people.

- Established and maintained order during corporate merger and computer system upgrade.

- Received two awards for outstanding customer service.

EDUCATION

SOUTHWEST MISSOURI STATE UNIVERSITY — Springfield, MO (1986)
Master of Business Administration (MBA)

- Dean's List and Award for Outstanding Achievement

COLLEGE OF SANTA FE — Santa Fe, NM (1978)
Bachelor of Arts (Major: Sociology, Minor: Urban Planning)

- Dean's List; Frank Lloyd Wright Scholarship, 1978

PUBLICATIONS

- "Current Findings in Diabetes Research," *American Health Journal*, 1989

- "The Treatment of Juvenile Onset Diabetes," *Disease Prevention Digest*, 1986

- "Controlling Type II Adult Diabetes," *Disease Prevention Digest*, 1984

PRESENTATIONS & SPEAKING ENGAGEMENTS

- Diabetes Treatment and Prevention – numerous community/civic group education programs (1989 to Present)

- Featured Guest - America Online Conference on Diabetes (1991 to 1994)

- Invited Speaker at Southwest Missouri State, Auburn University, and College of Santa Fe (1986 to 1989)

COMPUTERS

Macintosh OS, Microsoft Word, FileMaker Pro, Outlook, Windows 2000

Resume Strategy: *Dean's desire to specialize in research is communicated clearly in his resume title and backed by an effective, concise summary highlighting his relevant experience. For each of the jobs he has held for the Diabetes Foundation, he brings out all assignments related to research, writing, and reporting. Other relevant qualifications he brings to the table, including his published writings and public speaking engagements, are included on page two of the resume.*

Quincy Rivers

7909 East Lansing Blvd., Kearney, NE 68847 • Phone: (308) 555-5555 • E-mail: quincy@resumepower.com

ENTRY-LEVEL WEB CONTENT WRITER / EDITORIAL ASSISTANT

Talented and creative writer seeking to write and edit content for a dot-com or brick-and-mortar company. Possess a solid knowledge of Web standards, persuasive writing skills, attention to detail, and commitment to quality. Offer more than five years of experience using the Web for information, research, and source material. Solid understanding of how Web content should enhance the user's experience. Prolific writer with flexibility in writing copy in a variety of styles and voices. Dedicated to working with team members to achieve corporate objectives. Computer literate—MS Word/Excel, ACT!, Windows, and Mac OS.

KEY SKILLS PROFILE

▪ Creative Writing	▪ Research Abilities	▪ Event Planning
▪ Internet Savvy	▪ Conceptual Thinking	▪ Fundraising
▪ Communication Skills	▪ Sales and Marketing	▪ Decision Making
▪ Project Management	▪ Problem Solving	▪ Negotiating Skills

EDUCATION

UNIVERSITY OF NEBRASKA – LINCOLN — Lincoln, NE
B.A. in English, Creative Writing emphasis, 5/00

ACTIVITIES:

▪ Nebraska Native American Society — Co-President, 9/97 to 12/98; Public Relations Director, 1/96 to 6/97
▪ Residential Advisor, 9/96 to 12/97

RECENT WRITING:

▪ **Nonfiction:**   "Views on EEO/Affirmative Action," "Leaving the Reservation"
▪ **Fiction:**   "Smoke Signals"
▪ **Poetry:**   "Infinity," "Praise," "Paradigm Shift," "Jack the Dripper"

EXPERIENCE

MEDIA PARTNERS and THE MAIZE FOUNDATION — Lincoln, NE
Administrative Assistant / Fundraising Assistant for The Maize Foundation, 9/99 to 12/99

▪ Collaborated with Media Partners president on coordinating major events and industry tradeshows.
▪ Researched and located media firms and Web sites, negotiated contracts with media outlets, and scouted locations for press conferences.
▪ Organized special events that enabled companies to attract TV, print, and Web media "hits."
▪ Secured major sponsorships for The Maize Foundation, including Kraft Foods and IBM.
▪ Recognized for efforts in raising $50,000 for the foundation.

TWIN BLUFFS — Lincoln, NE (Employed by five-star dining operation to finance education.)
Host/Waiter, 3/98 to 5/98 and 8/98 to 12/98

WRITING SAMPLES AVAILABLE ON REQUEST

Resume Strategy: *Quincy emphasizes his career change goal by including a banner at the top of the page followed by a summary and key skills profile that lists his main credentials. He includes "recent writing" in his "Education" section to further emphasize his passion for writing. Minimal space is dedicated to work experience unrelated to his goal.*

22

Hospitality/Tourism/Travel

Marlane Hoffman

Seeking to leverage proven project management, communications, promotion, and sales skills gained from 11 years in successful international event management into a marketing/PR position within the travel/tourism industry.

Profile

Dynamic professional with 11-year track record of project management success, including copywriting, marketing collateral development, public relations, event management, and sales. Proven ability to promote event destinations in over 60 U.S. locations, four European countries, the Caribbean, South America, and southeast Asia. Polished and persuasive communicator, effective and articulate verbally and in writing.

Comfortable and experienced in visible roles interacting with Fortune 500 and nonprofit senior executives and department heads. Able to lead paid and volunteer staffs in furthering company goals and orchestrating successful events that maximize profits and generate strong brand identity. Flexible and versatile – selected to manage a wide range of multimillion-dollar projects throughout diverse industries. Reputation for meticulous attention to detail, diplomacy, professionalism, and integrity. Passion for international travel and cultural diversity.

Areas of Expertise

- Project Management
- Destination Promotions
- Copywriting
- Marketing-Collateral Development
- Customer & Vendor Relationship Management
- Contract Negotiations
- Budgeting/Cost Containment
- Global Event Management
- B2B/B2C Sales Presentations
- Team Building & Leadership
- Strategic Planning & Research

Professional Experience

INDEPENDENT CONTRACTOR — Detroit, MI
Provide international conference/event management and operations/logistics management for Fortune 500 companies, nonprofit organizations, and meeting-management companies.

<u>Conference/Event Management Consultant; Travel Director,</u> July 1993 to Present
Oversee conferences/events/fundraisers – some from conception through delivery – for Fortune 500 and nonprofit clients. Provide travel-management services and on-site destination promotion in locations throughout the continental U.S., Hawaii, Canada, the Caribbean, South America, France, England, Switzerland, Ireland, and Singapore. Work with executives on multimillion-dollar projects, with responsibilities for event and conference planning, destination promotions, and public relations. Coordinate volunteer and staff training and supervise up to 15 staff per event.

Outcomes:

- Launched successful consulting practice and won contracts with and repeat business from impressive client base to orchestrate filled-to-capacity events.

- Executed 200 programs and events within a wide variety of corporate/nonprofit cultures and industries, including pharmaceutical, high-tech, consumer products, and financial services. Managed a diverse assortment of activities including corporate advisory-board meetings, national sales conferences, product launches, corporate incentive sales programs, trade shows, fundraisers, training seminars, association meetings, and satellite-video conferences.

- Adeptly handled unanticipated crises and incidents, including overbooked hotels, last-minute banquet relocations, medical emergencies, and attendance numbers significantly surpassing reservations for RSVP-required events. Expert behind-the-scenes management abilities allowed for virtually transparent crisis resolution with minimal disruption.

P.O. Box 6809 • Detroit, MI 25678
Home Phone: 555-555-5555 • E-mail: marlane@resumepower.com • Cell Phone: 555-555-5999

Resume   Page Two

Marlane Hoffman

INDEPENDENT CONTRACTOR (continued), Sample Events:

• Hired as on-site logistical manager for a Fortune 500 company to run front-of-the-house operations throughout six-week event in Aruba. Oversaw registration/welcome center activities for 4,000 attendees. Praised by senior management for superior organization and seamless traffic flow, accommodating 300 to 400 guests every five days.

• Selected for highly visible, prestigious post as one of the on-site coordinators of a Worldwide Sponsor Hospitality Program at the 1996 Centennial Olympic Games in Atlanta. Managed logistics at various venues, supervised eight support staff, and accommodated the needs of four waves of 2,500 people from opening ceremony to closing events.

• Led all aspects of first-ever nonprofit organization awards dinner and silent auction for 200 at New York's Plaza Hotel. Wrote all copy for promotion catalog, trained ten volunteers, set up displays, coordinated meal service with hotel banquet staff, and directed gift distribution following event. Overwhelmingly positive response from board of directors and participants led to repeat sponsorships from multiple corporations.

BERKWHYTE, INC. — Detroit, MI
Corporate meeting planning, management, and travel services firm.

Project Coordinator, Meeting and Incentive Division, January 1990 to July 1993
Planned corporate meetings and conferences for Fortune 500 leaders and liaised with numerous departments including data management, air travel, creative services, and accounting to facilitate project management. Created promotional materials and attendee program correspondence, negotiated contracts with vendors, managed on-site event operations, and ensured all profitability goals were met through scrupulous budget administration.

Outcomes:

• Researched and authored "A through Z – Things to Do in Florida," mailed to 9,700 people.

• Planned and implemented five consecutive sales incentive programs, each averaging 300 attendees, in an unheard of six-week timeframe. Tireless efforts to deliver quality programs within time constraint won high praise from client.

• Executed over 50 corporate meetings and conferences throughout the continental U.S, Caribbean, and Hawaii.

Education & Training

THE UNIVERSITY OF MICHIGAN — Ann Arbor, MI   Bachelor of Science in Business Administration, 1987
• George Montgomery Memorial Scholarship, 1986 to 1987

MARYGROVE COLLEGE — Detroit, MI   Event Management Certificate, 1999
• Courses in event coordination, event marketing, risk management, sponsorship, and sports event management.

DETROIT NEWS SERVICE, INC. — Detroit, MI   Completed 160-hour practicum, June to September 1998
• Helped organize the Detroit Monitor's "News in the New Millennium Conference," their first large-scale conference with 1,900 in attendance.

Activities

• Business Volunteers for the Arts, Greater Detroit Chapter, 2000 to present
• Courses in Chinese (advanced beginner), Marygrove College, 2000 to present
• Active student of jazz and modern dance, 1993 to present

Resume Strategy: *Marlane's resume spells out her transferable skills for a marketing/PR position by including an italicized blurb under her name on page one. Her "Profile" demonstrates how her excellent management and communication skills, combined with marketing-related experience and in-depth knowledge of the travel industry, qualifies her for her career change goal. Each of Marlane's positions includes an "Outcomes" section to show that she is*

Via Dei Mar
Steffisburg, Switzerland CH-3612

HELEN BENDER

Phone: 0041-91-554433
helen@resumepower.com

TOUR LEADER . . . TRAVEL CONSULTANT

Widely traveled, multilingual professional with an excellent educational foundation in travel and tourism, and practical experience within service-oriented and public administration positions. Personable and outgoing, comfortable communicating with people from all walks of life, cultures, and ethnic backgrounds. Offer hands-on experience in coordinating international meetings and conferences, securing travel arrangements for participants and speakers, and arranging all ancillary matters, such as banqueting, equipment, and meeting space. Thrive on challenges and adapt quickly to new environments. Available to relocate internationally.

Training

ABILITY INSTITUTE — Brisbane, Queensland, Australia — **Diploma of Travel and Tourism,** 2000

Selected Coursework:

- International Travel Industry
- Galileo Computer Reservations System
- Travel Agency Operations
- Retail Travel Administration
- Wholesale Operations
- Fares and Ticketing
- Supervision/Management
- The Law and the Travel Agent
- Travel Promotions
- Sales and Marketing
- Workplace/Team Effectiveness

Travel History

Traveled extensively across several continents:

- Canada
- Italy
- England
- Australia (lived)
- USA (lived)
- France
- Madagascar
- Spain
- Japan (lived)
- Morocco
- India
- Greece
- Maurice Island
- Germany
- Nepal
- Tunisia

Languages / Computers

Languages: Italian, English, French, familiar with Japanese and German

Computers: Galileo, MS Word, Outlook, FileMaker, Excel, PowerPoint, Internet applications

Professional Experience

STATE OF SWITZERLAND — Lugano, Switzerland — **Secretary,** 1994 to present
AMALAGMATED COMPANIES SA — Bellinzona, Switzerland — **Junior Clerk,** 1981 to 1984

Provide administrative support to director and professional staff of up to 20. Respond to public inquiries with regard to environmental and land issues and coordinate appointment and meeting schedules. **Highlights:**

- Handle special assignments, including secretary for high-profile commission.
- Serve as member of a special military group that responds to emergency situations. Assigned to information center, disseminating information to the public, managing flow of information, and ensuring task forces are kept abreast of most recent developments.
- Coordinate meetings, prepare agenda, book space, arrange banqueting, and ensure proper facility setup.

Resume Strategy: *Helen's resume starts with a clear title and convincing profile, which she follows with her impressive "Professional Training" section to emphasize her highly relevant studies. Next comes her "Travel History" section, which gives readers an at-a-glance picture of the 16 different nations where she has either visited or lived. Her foreign language and computer literacy is a plus to her career aspirations, so she includes these in a stand-alone section. Finally, her "Professional Experience" section brings out accomplishments that bear relevance to her job goal.*

Peter Campano

15 Dai Mansion   Home: +9872-65-4321
Tokyo, Japan 164-0011   peter@resumepower.com

GOAL: TRAVEL & TOURISM POSITION IN THE U.S.

Bilingual Japanese-English / Committed to excellence in customer service and public relations

Internationally traveled educator specializing in Japanese culture, language, society, traditions, and business practices after residing in Japan for 15 years. Currently pursuing travel-related position in the United States; available for immediate relocation. Personable and outgoing, comfortable communicating with people from all cultures and ethnic backgrounds. Thrive on challenges and adapt quickly to new environments and responsibilities. Experience as a freelance Japanese-English translator. Natural public speaker, with experience presenting to diverse audiences within educational environments. Articulate teacher, communicator, manager, and motivator.

PROFICIENCIES

- Japanese Language/Culture
- Translation
- Event Coordination
- Public Relations
- Leadership/Motivation

- Conflict Resolution
- Staffing/Training
- Program Development and Marketing
- Computer Literacy

- Crisis Management
- Administration
- Individual/Group Tutoring
- Community Outreach
- Teaching

EXPERIENCE

GLOBAL REACH SCHOOL — Tokyo, Japan   1990 – Present
[Private pre-K school providing English as a Second Language instruction. Staff includes 18 Japanese and foreign instructors.]

Supervising Instructor

Develop school curriculum and teach classes with 18 to 36 students. Train and orient newly hired, multinational staff. Coordinate and interpret information between teachers and parents to facilitate open communications. Work collaboratively with colleagues in the pursuit of common educational goals. Foster strong rapport with students, supervisors, and co-workers. Design and implement student activities that stimulate learning. Organize student events such as summer camps and cultural exchanges between school and nearby American military base.

Highlights:

- Helped increase student enrollment from 30 to 150 within eight years of initial startup. Hired, trained, and motivated new staff to maintain the highest teaching standards. Dedicated extra hours to assist with special events that resulted in exposure for the school.

- Continued building school's reputation through dedication to academic excellence, effective marketing, and management of community exposure.

- Created a classroom atmosphere that is adaptive to the varied needs of students. Incorporated learning-style preferences into instructional methods, encouraging interest in course materials, and creating an enjoyable learning experience for students.

- Recognized as a key team member in elevating and preserving the school's positive community image.

Peter Campano - Page Two

EXPERIENCE

TOKYO COMMUNICATIONS SYSTEMS — Tokyo, Japan   1990 – 1993
[Provides English teachers for schools, after-school programs, and private or group tutoring sessions.]

Teacher

Taught English as a second language in one-on-one and group settings with as many as 30 students. Developed curriculum for younger students.

Highlights:

- Increased student enrollment and number of classes, which justified and secured funding for an additional teaching position.

INTERNATIONAL ENGLISH ACADEMY — Tokyo, Japan   1988 – 1990
[With more than 100 employees and multiple locations, company provides teachers to organizations throughout Japan.]

Teacher / Assistant to Head Teacher

Taught English as a second language to children and adults. Served as English translator as needed.

Highlights:

- Successfully developed a series of three children's workbooks that are still in use at the Academy.

- Assisted head teacher with supervisory and administrative functions.

- Presented oration on educating children and helping them reach their potential at Japan Music School.

PROFESSIONAL PROFILE

JAPAN UNIVERSITY — Tokyo, Japan
Courses in economics, business management, and anthropology, 1988 – 1989

BUCKS COUNTY HIGH SCHOOL — Doylestown, PA, Graduated 1985

JAPANESE LANGUAGE PROFICIENCY EXAM — Highest Level, 1993
Administered by the Association of International Education and the Japan Foundation

LANGUAGES: Fluent in English and Japanese (speak, read, and write at an advanced level)

HOBBIES: Shorinji Kempo (Japanese martial art) — Black Belt

COMPUTERS:
Systems: Macintosh OS, Windows 2000/98 (English and Japanese versions)
Software: Word, Excel, ClarisWorks, PageMaker, Photoshop, Illustrator, Nisus Writer

Relocating back to the United States

Home: +9872-65-4321 ■ E-mail: peter@resumepower.com

Resume Strategy: *Peter is changing careers and looking to relocate internationally, so his resume spells out his interest in both. His strategy includes leading with a tagline that explains his career goal, following with a summary that lists his key credentials for a travel and tourism position, and adding a "Proficiencies" section to show that he has the required skills to succeed in his new career goal.*

23

Real Estate/Property Management

Marissa Hart

15 Cottage Way
Lancaster, PA 17603

marissa@resumepower.com

Home: (717) 123-4567
Cellular: (717) 987-6543

CAREER GOAL: **PROPERTY MANAGER**

Accomplished professional uniquely qualified for property management career; able to leverage proven and relevant skills gained through 18 years' experience as a property rental assistant, home construction remodeler, and claim representative/independent adjuster. Advanced understanding of commercial/residential construction, maintenance, and repair, with ands-on experience across virtually all aspects (plumbing, roofing, electrical, carpentry, masonry, and tile work).

Expert interpersonal skills; adept in negotiating favorable terms with vendors and contractors, experienced insurance and legal liaison, and comfortable interacting with individuals from all backgrounds. Persuasive and articulate communicator, able to build consensus, translate complex issues into easily understood terms, and secure win-win outcomes during times of stress. Trusted by the nation's leading insurers to make financial decisions independently, with successful track record of handling over 5,000 property claims since 1993. Reputation for superior customer service, rapid mastery of new technology, and positive results. Internationally traveled and multilingual (intermediate Spanish/basic Italian).

PROFESSIONAL EXPERIENCE

Independent Insurance Adjuster – Lancaster, PA, 3/98 – present *(Self-employed)*

Travel throughout the U.S. to handle everyday and catastrophic insurance claims on behalf of the country's leading insurers, including Allstate, State Farm, Nationwide, Travelers, and others. Inspect property damage caused by flood, fire, hurricane, tornado, wind, hail, or vandalism; interpret complex insurance policy language/provisions from dozens of different companies to determine applicability of claim to coverage; write detailed estimates using various computer estimating programs; include comprehensive justifications for all estimate reports; and settle or close claims through payment or denial based upon company, policy, and state guidelines. Interact extensively with policyholders, building/remodeling contractors, vendors, public adjusters, insurance company representatives, and attorneys. **Key Accomplishments:**

- ☐ **Quickly mastered the three most popular computer estimating programs** to maximize field effectiveness and win repeat business from all of the nation's leading insurance companies.

- ☐ **Earned a reputation for sensitivity, sincerity, fairness, and rapid response.** Eased the emotional stress of policyholders who often had suffered devastating property losses by demonstrating thorough knowledge of property damage estimatics and patiently explaining settlement procedures and payment to insureds.

- ☐ **Earned XYZ National Catastrophe** (an independent insurance adjuster brokerage) **over $32K in less than six months** by closing hundreds of claims.

- ☐ **Demonstrated the ability to quickly and competently close claims** (with a daily close-rate double the national average), resulting in enhanced customer satisfaction, fortified company reputation, and fewer settlement disputes.

- ☐ Innovated property estimating tool that **significantly enhanced accuracy and thoroughness of estimatic reports** and ensured complete damage reimbursement for victims of a loss.

- ☐ Developed the capacity to **build genuine rapport with individuals from diverse cultural, ethnic, and socioeconomic backgrounds.** Settled claims in all regions of the U.S. for homeowners with property values ranging from $25K to over $5M.

Marissa Hart

ACTION CONSTRUCTION – Lancaster, PA *(Residential construction and remodeling firm)*
Remodeler, 12/96 – 3/98
Performed carpentry, roofing, plumbing, masonry, and tile work for residential clients. Estimated material/labor costs and delivered optimal customer service. **Key Accomplishments:**

☐ **Gained practical hands-on knowledge of all aspects of home construction.**

☐ Developed broad-based skills and **assisted in the completion of projects varying in scope from simple fixture installations to doubling the square footage of a home.**

STATE FARM INSURANCE CO. – Philadelphia, PA *(Nation's largest home, auto, and life insurer)*
Claim Representative, 8/93 – 12/96
Inspected residential and commercial property damage to prepare complete repair estimates and quickly and fairly settle claims. Supervised all two-story property damage claims within Philadelphia area. **Key Accomplishments:**

☐ **Saved company $125K** by uncovering fraudulent commercial roofing claim following in-depth investigation and multiple interviews with all parties involved.

☐ **Commended by policyholders and managers** for courteous, professional claim handling.

☐ **Selected for catastrophe duty,** an elite team of claim representatives specially trained to respond to major natural disasters throughout the U.S. on a moment's notice.

☐ **Appointed "Action Network Captain"** for unit due to organizational and team-building skills, and orchestrated numerous morale-enhancing activities and functions.

RENTAL SERVICES INC. – Lancaster, PA *(Residential apartment rental operation)*
Rental Assistant, 1/82 - 3/98
Assisted in the property management, rental, upkeep, and maintenance of a dozen homes with multiple apartment units. Placed ads to fill vacancies, set appointments to show properties, interviewed prospective tenants, performed background checks on prospects, collected rent, served eviction notices when necessary, and maintained units. **Key Accomplishments:**

☐ **Learned the fundamentals of real estate rental operations:** performed plumbing, electrical, and carpentry repairs; painted/cleaned vacant units to prepare for rapid turnover; and became adept in screening applicants.

☐ **Minimized profitability-robbing downtime** by renting vacancies in less than one week.

☐ **Mediated tenant disputes,** diffused volatile situations, and resolved tenant complaints.

EDUCATION & TRAINING

PENN STATE – York, PA	TEMPLE UNIVERSITY – Philadelphia, PA
MBA, 2001 GPA: 3.5	**BS in Marketing,** 1989

Professional Development: Effective Speaking and Human Relations - Dale Carnegie Institute, 1989; Property Estimatics Training – ABC Institute, 1994

Licensure: Pennsylvania State Property Adjusters License, 1998

Computer Skills: Word, Excel, PowerPoint, Outlook ☐ Xactimate, DDS, Simsol ☐ Windows 2000

Resume Strategy: *Marissa positions herself for her new property management objective by including a clear career goal, a gray box that includes her top qualifications, and an experience section that draws out her transferable skills and achievements.*

Gerald Foster

(617) 123-4567 ▣ gerald@resumepower.com
15 Cartwright Avenue ▣ Boston, MA 02118

PROFESSIONAL GOAL: Assistant Property Manager
Bilingual English / Spanish

Dynamic professional seeking a career opportunity in the real estate management industry. Offer diverse experience with a real estate financial lending institution and skills in finance/mathematics, research, marketing, customer service, and relationship building. Currently pursuing a bachelor's degree in real estate. Able to manage multiple projects simultaneously and meet deadlines. Computer literate with proficiency in Word, Excel, PowerPoint, Contour-Loan Handler, and Byte-Qualifier Series. Key skills encompass:

▣ **Sales / Marketing**	▣ **Presentations / Negotiations**	▣ **Customer Relationship**
▣ **New Business Development**	▣ **Staff Supervision / Team**	**Management**
▣ **Residential / Commercial**	**Building**	▣ **Market Research**
Real Estate	▣ **Finance / Accounting**	▣ **Collections**
▣ **Public Relations**	▣ **Data Management**	▣ **Contracts**

Professional Experience

ACE FINANCIAL SERVICES, INC. - Boston, MA – 1998 to Present

Real Estate Mortgage Processor

Coordinate the processing of residential mortgages and ensure applications are processed smoothly and efficiently. Collaborate extensively with bank representatives, managing agents, underwriters, attorneys, brokers, and clients to facilitate the process. Request and follow-up with obtaining necessary documentation. Monitor the status of files and ensure the timely processing of bank clearance. Guide clients through the mortgage finance process and provide exceptional customer service. *Key Achievements:*

- ▣ Earned a reputation for excellent follow-through based on a track record of smooth mortgage closings.
- ▣ Recognized for efficiently processing 40–60 loans per month.
- ▣ Promoted from Assistant after two months based on dedication and excellent job performance.

FINANCIAL NEWS CORPORATION - Boston, MA – 1996 to 1998

Marketing Coordinator

Developed and implemented strategic marketing plans. Handled domestic and foreign third-party marketing agreements. Fostered strong relationships with U.S. and foreign contacts. Coordinated direct mail campaigns, promotions, and conferences. *Key Achievements:*

- ▣ Implemented strategies that contributed to 7% increase in subscription sales within one year.
- ▣ Consistently met deadlines for six newsletters, covering topics such as compliance, global money management, global funds, real estate, and emerging markets.
- ▣ Led the marketing team and took over supervisor's responsibilities in her absence.
- ▣ Trained and oriented new coordinators; assisted colleagues with special projects as needed.

Education

B.S. in Real Estate program, BOSTON COLLEGE - Boston, MA – 2001 to Present

---

Resume Strategy: *Gerald highlights his career goal prominently, as well as his bilingual fluency in Spanish, a sought-after skill in the field of property management. His profile explains the relevance of his real estate background to property management, and his "Key Achievements" show his history of promotions and revenue-building success.*

Anna Hyang

15 Race Street	anna@resumepower.com	Home: 718-123-4567
Bronx, NY 10451	Fax: 718-234-5678	Office: 718-987-6543

AWARD-WINNING CONSTRUCTION PROJECT MANAGER

Specializing in premium-quality, luxury residential construction and land development for single- and multifamily dwellings

Accomplished and experienced construction project manager offering a 12-year background in field construction supervision, highly developed business sense, and proven success leading all phases of construction projects for on-time, on-budget, and award-winning completion (including one luxury condominium project honored as The National Association of Homebuilder's "Community of the Year"). Expert relationship builder and negotiator; able to rapidly win government approvals, permits, concessions, and exemptions; secure favorable contractual terms and cost-savings from vendors and suppliers; and architect win-win solutions benefiting all parties concerned. Adept in a full spectrum of construction project management functions (bidding, planning, staffing, workflow scheduling, prioritization, time/resource management, budgeting, quality assurance, and code/safety compliance). Respected leader of sizable teams, able to instill a strong sense of urgency without compromising quality, safety, or customer satisfaction.

EXPERTISE

- Quality Assurance/Quality Control
- Multimillion-Dollar Project Management (All Construction Phases)
- Budgeting/Forecasting/Cost Control
- Sourcing & Bidding (All Trades)
- Complex Negotiations
- Regulatory Compliance (OSHA, UBC)
- Workflow Planning & Prioritizing
- Crew Supervision & Leadership
- Government/Community Relations
- Creative Problem Solving
- Logistical & Contingency Planning

CAREER HISTORY

President – INTELLIGENT TRADING, INC. (Bronx, NY) – 1996 to Present

Construction Planning Project Manager – ABC DEVELOPMENT COMPANY (Staten Island, NY) – 1995 to 1996

Construction Project Manager – DREAMBUILDERS / JAKOBS & STERN (Princeton, NJ) – 1994 to 1995

Construction Project Manager – JLT PROPERTIES / MARSH CONTRACTORS (Cranbury, NJ) – 1991 to 1994

Project Manager – XYZ ARCHITECTURAL COMPANY (Princeton, NJ) – 1990 to 1991

Construction Manager / Superintendent – TRIDENT CONSTRUCTION (New Brunswick, NJ) – 1985 to 1990

CONSTRUCTION PROJECT HIGHLIGHTS

- **Recruited to "rescue" stalled construction proposal for $28 million, 100,000-sq.-ft., luxury condominium project** and coordinated all aspects of project planning, including oversight of approval, permit, budgeting, bidding, and contract-negotiation processes. *(ABC Development Company)*

  - **Averted six-figure losses and threatened yearlong project delay** through skillful negotiations with City of New York officials under looming expiration deadline of less than four weeks. Commended by owners for winning approvals from every city department (e.g., zoning, land use, parks, sewer, etc.), obtaining all construction permits one week ahead of schedule in one of New York's most challenging cities for developers due to code/space restrictions.

  - **Developed and finalized project budget,** key to bank approval and final project funding.

  - **Established bidding process, reviewed 80+ bids, and negotiated/awarded contracts across all major trades** (e.g., site clearance, temporary power, waste management, temporary construction facilities, demolition, tree removal and maintenance, excavation and grading, waterproofing, plumbing, electrical, HVAC, concrete, masonry, and framing).

  - **Obtained rare exception from strict city ordinance** to win approval for the removal from project site of 25 mature, protected oak, maple, and palm trees (weighing five tons a piece) that were ultimately reintroduced as part of project landscape design or replanted at other mutually agreed upon locations.

  - **Negotiated with City of New York Transit Authority** to successfully secure agreement relocating a bus stop which otherwise would have posed a safety hazard to waiting passengers as well as significant impediments to jobsite access.

- **Finalized building plans with owners and architects** and managed construction for opulent, multimillion-dollar, 7,500-sq.-ft. two-story estate, featuring six-car garage, swimming pool, and lush fountains/landscaping. *(Dreambuilders / Jakobs & Stern)*

Anna Hyang

CONSTRUCTION PROJECT HIGHLIGHTS (continued)

- ☐ **Created construction budget and workflow schedule,** secured owner and city approvals/building permits (City of New York), bid out all trades, and negotiated/structured/awarded all contracts and change orders.

- ☐ **Field-supervised all phases of construction,** ensuring quality/cost control, safety adherence, timeline fulfillment, and code/community standards compliance throughout.

- ☐ **Demonstrated flexibility and strong service commitment,** maintaining responsiveness to and accommodation of frequent client change-order requests without compromising budget parameters to ensure owner satisfaction from beginning through Certificate of Occupancy. Efforts resulted in timely project completion, thrilled homeowners, and subsequent multimillion-dollar referral business wins.

- ■ **Selected as construction project manager for $18 million luxury condo endeavor** (130,000 sq. ft.) that was subsequently honored with the **1996 National Association of Homebuilder's** Community of the Year Award. Served as developer's representative and liaison to architects, designers, and government agencies and supervised/scheduled all on-site construction and land development for on-time, on-budget completion. *(JLT Properties / Marsh Contractors)*

- ☐ **Cultivated excellent relations** with neighboring property owners and the New York Department of Building and Safety, which proved crucial in keeping construction on a disciplined timeline and facilitated the expeditious, economical, and win-win resolution of complex street- and land-development issues.

- ☐ **Integrally involved in sales/marketing campaign** following Certificate of Occupancy, with all units sold in 14 months.

- ■ **Managed, supervised, and scheduled all on-site construction and land development for 10,000-sq.-ft. luxury estate.** Authorized progress payments; represented developer in all negotiation, design, and building phases; and inspected all work for 100% fulfillment of plans, specifications, and codes. *(XYZ Architectural Company)*

- ■ **Drove on-time, on-budget completion of nine major multifamily condo/apartment complexes and two large commercial projects** (multistory, subterranean concrete/block garages). Supervised projects from start to finish, ensuring timely bidding, accomplishment of construction milestones, and certificates of occupancy for all projects. *(Trident Construction)*

ADDITIONAL EXPERIENCE

- ■ **Demonstrated financial and investment acumen** as president of an investment corporation, fueling an average 15% revenue growth for three consecutive years and a 150% ROI in operation's fourth year. Innovated intricate analysis process and computer-based trading system to drive consistent profits despite market fluctuations. *(Intelligent-Trading, Inc.)*

EDUCATION & EXPERIENCE

Certifications:	**New York State Contractor's License**
Education:	NYC SCHOOL OF ENGINEERING – New York, NY – **Construction Management Program**
	NEW YORK UNIVERSITY – New York, NY – **BA in Sociology**
Public Speaking Higlights:	**Construction Coordination** – Numerous presentations to subcontractor groups, 1984 to 1996
	Project Safety – Numerous presentations to subcontractor groups, 1984 to 1996
	Project Scheduling & Progress – Numerous presentations to owners/architects/construction managers/ staff, 1984 to 1996
	Budgeting & Planning – Numerous presentations to owners/architects/designers/staff, 1984 to 1996
	Concept & Design – Numerous presentations to owners/architects/designers, 1984 to 1996
Computer Skills:	Word, Excel, Primavera, MS Exchange, Lotus 1-2-3, SureTrak, Expedition, Outlook, PDAs, Modems, Windows 2000 Pro/XP Pro/98, Wireless Networking, LANs, WANs, OLAP

HOME: 718-123-4567 ■ OFFICE: 718-987-6543 ■ FAX: 718-234-5678 ■ ANNA@RESUMEPOWER.COM

Resume Strategy: *Anna's resume title ("Award-Winning Construction Project Manager") explains her career goal and shows her impressive track record in this field. She downplays her current position as president of an investment corporation and focuses the resume instead on her impressive accomplishments within the construction industry. Anna provides key details of the various projects she has managed, leaving no doubt in readers' minds about her ability to return to this career.*

MARISOL DIZON

5000 North Shore Road
Chicago, IL 60657

mdizon@isp.com

Cell: 773.818.5555
Home: 773.525.7777

CIVIL AND STRUCTURAL ENGINEER

EXECUTIVE SUMMARY

Results-driven, hands-on business administrator with a proven track record of more than 20 years of entrepreneurial leadership in the start-up, turnaround and successful growth of two highly regarded construction and fabrication enterprises and a telecommunications firm. Consistently deliver superior quality full-site commercial construction, capital improvements, renovation, and preventative maintenance services on time and within budget. Sold companies to Worldwide Construction, Inc.

Combine cross-functional, cross-technology expertise in strategic planning, financial management, business systems, processes, and organizational infrastructures with engineering, contract administration, and client management. Achieve annual increases in productivity, operating efficiency, sustainable cost reductions, and net earnings while continuing to support critical operations within a highly competitive industry. Earned bachelor's degree in civil engineering and State of Illinois Civil Engineering Certification in 2002. Seeking position of civil engineer.

Areas of expertise and strength encompass:

- Business Operations Management
- Contract Administration
- Review Competitive Bid Packages
- Project Budgeting / Cost Containment
- Full Life-Cycle Project Management
- Master Project Schedule Documentation
- Workflow Planning / Coordination
- Quality Control / Site Supervision
- Regulatory Compliance
- Capital Equipment Acquisition
- Financial Planning / Analysis / Management

- Purchasing / Materials Managemen
- Budgeting (Capital & Operations)
- P&L Administration
- Accounting / Reporting / Disbursements
- Equity & Debt Financing
- New Business / Market Development
- Business / Service Contract Negotiation
- Vendor / Subcontractor Partnerships
- Customer / Government Relations
- Multilingual: English / Spanish / Portuguese / Italian / Tagalog / Llonggo / Visaya

SAN MIGUEL FABRICATION. INC. – Philippines

Vice President, COO, Corporate Secretary / Treasurer, Purchasing Manager, Project Manager   1991 – 2000

Senior administrative director responsible for strategic planning, financial affairs, budgeting, all business infrastructures, accounting, HR, management information systems, purchasing, and inventory management. Managed business development, customer relations, contract negotiations, contract compliance, government affairs, regulatory compliance, and project oversight. Employed 8–10 engineers, 5–6 accounting/support staff, and 20–100 skilled workers (per project) with an average weekly payroll of 300,000 pesos.

Representative Accomplishments

- Grew company from a category D with capitalization of 100,000 Philippine pesos to category B with a maximum of 10 million pesos in projects.
- Increased monthly contracts by more than 100%.
- Constructed 3 full-service bank-branch facilities from ground breaking to opening in 60 days.
- Averaged 90-day maturation for bank-facility construction.
- Expanded client base for structural maintenance from 30 to more than 100 firms.
- Secured the primary maintenance contract for the largest banks in the country.
- Negotiated initial credit line of 200,000 Philippine pesos and increased to 1.5 million pesos.
- Improved cash flow by negotiating final construction payouts from 15 days to 1 day from project completion.
- Spearheaded financial operations; initiated accounting, internal audit, payroll and payable/receivable systems.
- Conducted legal and financial negotiations with the government and private companies.
- Developed HR policies and procedures and authored job descriptions and functionalities for staff members.

MARISOL DIZON
Page Two

WORLD COMMERCIAL GLASS & ALUMINUM – Manila, Philippines
Sole Proprietor
1990 – 2000

Established electrical component trading and supply company. Expanded the business to distribute a full range of construction supplies from small equipment to heavy materials. Launched the glass and aluminum fabrication enterprise to capture an untapped share in both site construction and structural maintenance niche markets. Managed all business operations. Employed 2 engineers, 4–15 fabricators, and 1 office manager.

Representative Accomplishments

- Secured $200,000 in start-up capital.
- Improved capitalization by 1,000% to $2 million pesos in receivables.
- Awarded $1.6 million contract for Shell Oil of the Philippines.
- Selected as Prime Contractor for Far East Bank and Trust Company and Primary Subcontractor for KBC, Martinez Engineering, and San Miguel construction companies.
- Averaged 3–5 concurrent onsite fabrication projects nationwide.
- Opened storefront–warehouse to serve growing public market and generate additional revenue streams.

PHILIPPINES LONG DISTANCE TELEPHONE COMPANY – Bacolod City and Sampaloc, Manila, Philippines
Vice-President of Customer Service Operations
1981 – 1990

Recruited to reengineer nationwide customer service operations.

Representative Accomplishments

- Directed $8 million peso technology migration and integration project to support customer service operations.
- Reduced installation and repair completion times from two weeks to 48 hours in first year.

PROFESSIONAL PROFILE

EDUCATION	PROFESSIONAL CONTINUING EDUCATION	CERTIFICATIONS
NORTHWESTERN UNIVERSITY Evanston, Illinois *Bachelor of Science in Civil Engineering – 2002* UNIVERSITY OF THE PHILIPINNES Manila, Philippines *Master of Business Administration – 1995* SAINT AUGUSTINE COLLEGE Bacalod City, Philippines *Bachelor of Science in Commerce – 1990*	PACIFIC MANAGEMENT FORUM *Project Management* *How to Organize and Tighten* *Accounting Controls and Procedures* *Supervisory Management* TECHNOLOGY & LIVELIHOOD RESOURCE CENTER *Entrepreneurship* *Accounting & Record keeping* UNIVERSITY OF THE PHILIPPINES *Financial Management for Small Business*	STATE OF ILLINOIS *Civil Engineer No. 12345678* **INFORMATION TECHNOLOGY** *Proprietary Construction and Engineering Software* *Windows 2000/98* *Word & Excel* *QuickBooks* *Project Management*

Representative Site Construction and Maintenance Projects
Available on Request

Resume Strategy: *Marisol possesses 20+ years of successful senior management experience, but she only recently completed training for her new career goal of civil engineer. Her resume includes a tagline that clearly states her objective, while her summary shows how her entrepreneurial track record combined with her new credentials (B.S. degree in civil engineering and state certification) make her well qualified for her new goal. Resume submitted by Murray Mann and Julene Elliott.*

24

Nonprofit/Social Services/ Government

SMALL BUSINESS OWNER TO COMMUNITY RELATIONS/ CASEWORK MANAGEMENT

NEIL ELLIOTT

1414 Court Street
Raleigh, NC 27603

neil@resumepower.com

Home: 919-123-4567
Cellular: 919-987-6543

SEEKING CAREER IN COMMUNITY RELATIONS / CASEWORK MANAGEMENT

Dedicated casework manager, client advocate, and community-/government-relations professional with ten years' experience facilitating needed assistance and resolving a wide range of issues for individuals from diverse cultural, socioeconomic, and disadvantaged backgrounds. Knowledgeable in the inner workings of government agencies (e.g., Social Services, VA, Immigration/Naturalization, State Department), with unique ability to combine tact with tenacity to expedite proceedings on behalf of clients, speeding problem resolution, and win-win outcomes without alienating crucial partners.

Skilled collaborator, liaison, and coalition/consensus builder, able to garner support and cooperation from elected officials, government offices, community groups, and business leaders. Offer versatile government and private-sector background, with considerable program/casework/event-management experience. Reputation for expert interpersonal, organizational, and problem-solving skills.

EXPERTISE

- Casework Management
- Client Advocacy
- Community Outreach
- Government Agencies

- Community/Government Relations
- Diverse Populations
- Event & Program Management
- Volunteer Coordination & Motivation

- Coalition & Consensus Building
- Leadership & Supervision
- Creative Problem Solving

ACHIEVEMENT HIGHLIGHTS

As **Constituent Liaison / Case Worker** for *DISTRICT OFFICE OF CONGRESSMAN BILL JONES...*

- **Managed casework and community-outreach initiatives,** with accountability for resolution of a wide variety of constituent issues involving immigration/naturalization, veterans' affairs, Social Services, and the State Department.

- **Removed bureaucratic red tape/roadblocks for hundreds of constituents from all walks of life** (e.g., foreign nationals, disadvantaged/indigent populations, veterans), successfully resolving issues of varying complexities. Tactfully maneuvered throughout multiple government agencies to expedite issue resolution within high-volume environment, typically managing an average of 50 cases monthly.

- **Organized outreach initiatives** and orchestrated well-received town hall meetings, researched issues and briefed congressman on specific topics of concern, and represented the congressman at numerous community meetings/events and neighborhood associations.

- **Achieved outstanding record of solving assigned cases,** obtaining necessary referrals, assistance, cooperation, and successful issue closure for people in need.

- **Provided expeditious, diplomatic, and sensitive handling of cases** involving special populations such as the mentally ill.

As **Assistant Community Relations Director** for *ABC MEDICAL CENTER...*

- **Conducted community outreach programs,** including medical center's food-pantry operation serving both patients and community members in need.

- **Built key coalitions with elected officials and numerous community groups** to garner support for hospital programs and local healthcare initiatives. Facilitated open dialogues to help improve public perception of the drug-treatment programs/residential facilities on the medical center campus.

- **Integrally involved in outreach campaign** during medical center's expansion. Jointly facilitated community board meetings, contributed to collateral message development, presented progress updates at community/civic group meetings, and coordinated/conducted community tours.

256

Neil Elliott

ACHIEVEMENT HIGHLIGHTS, *ABC MEDICAL CENTER (continued...)*

- **Represented hospital** at all health/community fairs. Set up and staffed booths, coordinated hospital volunteers, and conducted health-related activities for children and adults.
- **Promoted camaraderie and teamwork** by staging various events/fundraisers throughout the year.

As ***Clinical Assistant*** for *RALEIGH WOMEN'S AND CHILDREN'S FOOD PROGRAM...*

- **Administered successful WIC program** with over 1,000 participants throughout 12 clinics. Assisted women, infants, and children with demonstrated nutrition, health, and economic needs.
- **Coordinated outreach programs** targeting participating grocery stores (ensuring proper use of program food voucher and adequate stock levels of approved brands) and eligible participants (setting up displays in health centers and churches featuring menus cooked with WIC ingredients).
- **Launched legislation tracking initiative** for more proactive response to proposals with potential to impact WIC program and its participants.
- **Improved voucher delivery system** to ensure program compliance and optimum participation levels.

As ***Volunteer Coordinator*** for *BILL JONES FOR CONGRESS CAMPAIGN...*

- **Choreographed the activities of 500+ volunteers** across a multitude of senatorial, congressional, and presidential election campaign endeavors. Matched strengths/skills/interests of diverse volunteer group with tasks at hand and trained, motivated, and supervised volunteer workforce.
- **Introduced volunteer tracking system** to better utilize talent pool and avoid duplication of efforts.
- **Motivated volunteers to work independently** for maximum productivity on projects including rallies, phone banks, mailings, and assisting candidates on the campaign trail.
- **Organized many events** throughout campaign cycle, with winning election outcomes for all candidates.

As ***Vice President*** of *ADVANCED STUDIOS, INC...*

- **Jointly directed startup and expansion** (from zero to $1.4 million) of profitable small business, providing strategic financial/operational planning that drove a steady stream of business.
- **Led product/services repositioning** that enabled proactive response to marketplace changes and captured diverse industry corporate accounts (e.g., advertising, biotechnology, allied health services).
- **Lowered labor costs 25%** without compromising service or quality deliverables.

CAREER HISTORY

ADVANCED STUDIOS, INC. – Raleigh, NC – **Vice President,** 3/94–present

ABC MEDICAL CENTER – Raleigh, NC – **Assistant Director of Community Relations,** 3/93–1/95

BILL JONES FOR CONGRESS – Raleigh, NC – **Volunteer Coordinator,** 10/91–3/93

DISTRICT OFFICE OF CONGRESSMAN BILL JONES – Raleigh, NC – **Constituent Liaison,** 3/86–9/90

U.S. SENATOR ABBY WINTHROP – Raleigh, NC – **Case Worker** – 7/84–3/86

RALEIGH WOMEN'S AND CHILDREN'S FOOD PROGRAM – Raleigh, NC – **Clinical Assistant,** Health Department, 8/81–7/84

EDUCATION

THE UNIVERSITY OF NORTH CAROLINA – Chapel Hill, NC

BA in Government & Politics (Concentration in ***Issues of Aging***), 1980

Resume Strategy: *After owning his own business for nearly ten years, Neil is returning to a former career in community relations/casework. His functional-style resume allows him to concentrate on his related experience while downplaying his work chronology. His strategy includes leading with a career goal and summary that explains his new direction and related credentials, adding an "Expertise" section that lists keywords related to his goal, and creating an "Achievement Highlights" section that allows him to reorder his work history to draw out his most related accomplishments.*

John B. Lawrence

45 Snake Hill Road
Staten Island, NY 10309
SSN: 444-44-4444
Citizenship: U.S.
Announcement: Special Agent

john@resumepower.com
Cellular: 718-123-4567

Veteran's Preference: 5 Points
Reinstatement Eligibility: N/A

Evening: 718-456-7891
Day: 718-987-1234
Grade: E-6 (U.S. Marine; tour ends 10/2003)
Highest Fed. Civilian Grade: N/A

Grade Applying For: GS-7

CAREER TARGET: CRIMINAL INVESTIGATOR

Seeking to continue dedicated service to U.S. interests by securing entry-level position with the U.S. Secret Service

Driven, self-motivated achiever with nine-year decorated military career chronicled by "superior" rated performance, meritorious promotional advancement, academic success, and high-profile assignments including providing security for traveling heads of state and safeguarding Top-Secret classified material and millions of dollars of government equipment/assets. Eager to continue service to country by leveraging proven and relevant strengths:

- **Hold current Top Secret security clearance.**

- **Firearms proficient,** with "expert" marksman status on the M-16A2 Service rifle, Beretta M9 pistol, Smith and Wesson .357 revolver, and M870 Shotgun. Diligent in adherence to safety measures with solid understanding of considerations associated with carrying concealed weapons.

- **Exemplary academic achievement,** with consistent record of top 10% or above performance in all military and civilian schools (including 3.82 GPA for BS degree while concurrently on active duty).

- **Worldwide deployable** and internationally traveled (Russia, UK, Pacific Rim, Middle East, Cuba, Europe, Asia). Accustomed to traveling, working, and living abroad and adept in accomplishing important objectives in foreign (and sometimes volatile) regions of the world.

- **Respected, trustworthy leader,** skilled in directing diverse teams in the seamless orchestration of complex assignments protecting U.S. Missions, classified material, and American lives. Known for team-player mentality, discipline, tireless work ethic, and enthusiastic embrace of new challenges and difficult assignments.

- **Articulate and effective communicator** with expert interpersonal skills and "Master Instructor" certification.

PROFESSIONAL EXPERIENCE

UNITED STATES MARINE CORPS
Supervisor: William Strong – Supervisor's Phone: 718-222-2222 (You may contact)
Weekly Hours: 40+ – Salary: $27,912

Instructor, 6/1999 to Present (Active duty to conclude 10/2003)

Charged with curriculum development and execution of course modules comprising in-depth, six-month electronics repair training program for hundreds of entry-level Marines, officers/NCOs, Army soldiers, and allied country (Turkey, Greece, Taiwan) military officers. Provide instruction on efficient troubleshooting, repair, and maintenance of anti-tank/armor missile systems, laser rangefinders/designators, fire-control systems, electronics equipment, thermal imaging devices, and passive/active night-vision devices. **Key Contributions:**

- **Achieved "Master Instructor" status** as one of 34 Master Instructors out of over 600 military and civilian instructors and the sole **Marine Master Instructor certified in 2002.** Completed 1,250 hours of classes, earned "outstanding" evaluations by other Master Instructors and student participants, and completed 40-page white paper on distance-learning innovations (Video/CBT) to attain certification.

- **Fostered the development of instructor colleagues,** providing constructive critiques of instructional techniques and curriculum to advance program quality. **Helped fellow instructor achieve Master Instructor credential,** and currently mentoring two other colleagues in pursuit of same.

- Enhanced learner experience, retention, and comprehension through **first-ever introduction of high-tech, multimedia presentations,** subsequently adopted locationwide by all instructors.

- **Streamlined and standardized instruction** through major design overhaul of Basic Knowledge and Skills (BK&S) course by consolidating seven military occupational specialties (MOS's) for multiple beneficial outcomes: **cut instructor manpower requirements** 200%, **eliminated redundant/outdated instruction,** centralized BK&S school, slashed student downtime by **3,000 hours annually,** and reduced course duration by half while improving quality of instruction.

- Innovated learner-centered curriculum improvements that **catapulted pass-rate from 91% to 98%.**

John B. Lawrence

SSN: 444-44-4444

Resume, Page Two

UNITED STATES MARINE CORPS (continued)

- Researched, designed, and implemented new ordnance course for SNCOs that **filled knowledge gaps** to enhance safety, reduce wasteful repair spending, shorten repair-cycle times, improve inspection rates, and better utilize key resources (e.g., digitized publications and online tools).

- Initiated crucial upgrade of computer-based training (CBT) to resolve system crashes and negotiated favorable terms for new equipment acquisition that **saved the Marines over $100,000.**

- **Commended for fulfillment of mentorship role to 20 Marines** under personal charge. Enrolled Marines in military correspondence courses to strengthen their promotional opportunities, organized outings to benefit local community, and provided individualized coaching on steps to attaining a successful military career.

UNITED STATES MARINE CORPS
Supervisor: Richard Foster – Supervisor's Phone: 718-444-4444 – Weekly Hours: 40+ – Salary: $25,404

Staff Noncommissioned Officer in Charge (SNCOIC), 4/1998 to 4/1999

Oversaw $2.5 million in test equipment and assets for Electronics Control maintenance shop. Managed 50 Marines, produced and reviewed daily maintenance reports for commanding officer, briefed CO on repair status of all mission-critical equipment and systems, served as quality-control inspector for millions of dollars of weapon systems and equipment, and directed troubleshooting and detailed repair/maintenance of electronics equipment within high-volume, fast-paced environment (requiring repairs of varying complexities of an average of 50 components daily). **Key Contributions:**

- Upgraded unit's mission-capable status from **80% to 95% within two months** (despite officer and senior staff shortage) through large-scale restructure of processes and infrastructure to reverse prior history of steady decline. Efforts enabled unit to support more missions, ensuring moment's notice deployment of field fire-control repair teams.

- **Strengthened unit cohesion/morale** by emphasizing individual accountability, engineering unit-wide missions requiring interdependent teamwork, and recognizing/rewarding exemplary performance.

- Implemented successful substance-abuse-control program that stringently complied with military court-mandated testing procedures, resulting in **increasing conviction rate of individuals testing positive to 100%.**

- Increased repair turnaround and accuracy **10% to 15%** by introducing quantifiable proficiency-measurement standards for all equipment/systems.

UNITED STATES MARINE CORPS/UNITED STATES DEPARTMENT OF STATE – American Consulate; London, England
Supervisor: Jonathan Hart – Supervisor's Phone: 444-444-4440 – Weekly Hours: 40+ – Salary: $23,436

Marine Security Guard/Assistant Detachment Commander, 2/1997 to 3/1998

Accountable for guarding the largest American consulate in the world. Provided security services at diplomatic and consular facilities to prevent compromise of classified material and equipment. Protected U.S. citizens and property within Mission's principal building and maintained continual readiness to execute plans for protection of foreign service post and its personnel. Scheduled watch-standers for duty, coordinated security drills, authored official correspondence, and supervised nine detachment Marines. **Key Contributions:**

- **Meritoriously promoted** to the rank of Staff Sergeant 1/1998 and achieved **one of six meritorious promotions awarded to the 1,600 embassy duty-deployed Marines that year.**

- **Rebuilt key relationship** between detachment Marines and Detachment Commander. Leveraged strong interpersonal and leadership skills to augment operational security mindset of ten-man detachment that won the respect of Detachment Commander, proved mission-readiness, and repaired relationship.

- **Selected by CO to augment security for presidential visit to Moscow.** Security detail assignment included guarding classified White House material and assisting in the physical security of the vice president. Interacted with Secret Service agents, White House personnel, and diplomats in a highly professional manner, and performed mission without incident.

- **Redesigned security reaction response to terrorist threats** for 100% compliance with policies. Developed realistic, challenging training that delivered much-improved operational proficiencies and security reaction abilities.

- **Enhanced relationships between Marines, consulate, and British community** by creating well-received "Adopt a Marine for the Holidays" program and "Toys for Tots" campaign. Overcame initial resistance and skepticism, delivered goal-surpassing results, and created immeasurable goodwill between American and British citizens.

- **Modernized detachment's incident reporting (IR) procedures** by designing user-friendly database for significant incident-response-time improvement, expanded reporting detail, and widened information access.

John B. Lawrence   SSN: 444-44-4444   Resume, Page Three

UNITED STATES MARINE CORPS/UNITED STATES DEPARTMENT OF STATE – American Embassy; Amsterdam
Supervisor: George Williams – Supervisor's Phone: 777-777-7777 – Weekly Hours: 40+ – Salary: $21,936

Marine Security Guard, 9/1995 to 2/1997

Responsible for security services at diplomatic and consular facilities to protect classified material and equipment of national security interest to the U.S. Guarded U.S. citizens and property within principal building and demonstrated readiness to rapidly respond to emergency situations. **Key Contributions:**

- **Commended by CO** for professional demeanor, attention to detail, and leadership capacity. Personally requested to transfer to American Consulate in Amsterdam to improve operational proficiencies/security reaction abilities.

UNITED STATES MARINE CORPS/UNITED STATES DEPARTMENT OF STATE – Marine Security Guard School
Marine Security Guard/Student, 7/1995 to 9/1995

UNITED STATES MARINE CORPS
Electronics Repairer, 11/1993 to 7/1995; **Electronics Repair Student,** Schools Company, 1/1993 to 10/1993
United States Marine/Combat Skills Student, 12/1992 to 1/1993; **United States Marine/Recruit,** 9/1992 to 12/1992

EDUCATION

NEW YORK UNIVERSITY – New York, NY 11204 – **Bachelor of Science in Business Management (BSBM),** 2001
Total Credits Earned: 45 (Semester schedule)   GPA: 3.82

STATEN ISLAND COMMUNITY COLLEGE – Staten Island, NY 10314 – Major: **Business Management**
Total Credits Earned: 18 (Semester schedule)   GPA: 3.5

RICHMOND COLLEGE – Staten Island, NY 10314 – Major: **Business Management**
Total Credits Earned: 28 (Semester schedule)   GPA: 3.5

PORT RICHMOND HIGH SCHOOL – Staten Island, NY 10314 – **High School Diploma,** 1992

TRAINING

Completed numerous military school training and correspondence courses including war fighting skills (1999), expeditionary operations (1999), military justice (1997), tactical communications (1997), leadership (1997), administrative plans/policies/ procedures/programs (1995), physical training management (1995), combat intelligence (1998), and terrorism counteraction (1995).

CERTIFICATIONS & LICENSURE

- Tan Belt in the Marine Corps Martial Arts Program (2001)
- Master Instructor Certified (2001)
- Rifle Expert (M16A2) in the Marine Corps Marksmanship Program (1999)
- Pistol Expert (M9 Beretta) 2nd Award, in the Marine Corps Marksmanship Program (1999)
- Firing Range Safety Officer (1999)
- Combat Water Survival Qualified in the Marine Corps Combat Water Survival Program (1998)
- Department of State (DOS) Pistol (357 Smith and Wesson) Qualified (1995)
- Department of State (DOS) Shotgun (M870) Qualified (1995)
- Valid Driver's License (New York)

AWARDS

Recipient of numerous ribbons (below), awards, and commendations, including Navy Marine Corps Achievement Medal, Memorandums of Commendation, Meritorious Mast, and Perfect (300/300) Physical Fitness Certificate.

Resume Strategy: *John's federal-style resume is detailed and lengthy, but the information it includes is appropriate and expected for government jobs. His resume profile shows his record of outstanding performance, and his "Professional Experience" section is packed with achievements.*

ANALYST INTERN TO PUBLIC POLICY/BUDGET RESEARCH & ANALYSIS

Glen Lee

14 Richmond Circle ◆ Staten Island, NY 10314 ◆ home: (718) 123-4567 ◆ e-mail: glen@resumepower.com

---

CAREER GOAL: PUBLIC POLICY RESEARCH & ANALYSIS / BUDGET ANALYSIS

- **Research and analysis specialist** with strong educational background in geopolitical studies, international events, cultural protocols and issues, global economics, human services, and other public affairs.
- **Skilled Internet researcher;** consolidate findings into high-impact reports and presentations.
- Able to **manage multiple tasks** and responsibilities in demanding work environments and project settings.
- Experience in **large-scale program/project/event management;** skilled organizer and problem solver.
- Expertise in **Chinese-English** translations and interpretation; effective communication abilities.

EDUCATION & SKILLS

Master of Public Affairs Degree Pending, Expected Graduation in May 2003 / GPA: 3.9, NYU, New York, NY

- *Relevant Coursework:* Statistics, Financial Management, Management Science, Business Competitive Intelligence, Micro/Macroeconomics, Public Administration, Public Policy & the Internet
- *Honors:* Steinway Fellowship, High Academic Achievements (2002), High Performance in Statistics (2001)

BA in English, East China Normal University, Beijing, China, 1998 / GPA: 3.6

Foreign Languages: Fluent in Chinese and English, intermediate in Japanese
Computer Skills: Lexis-Nexis, Dialog, Internet research, Access, MS Office Suite, PC/Mac, FTP

PROFESSIONAL EXPERIENCE

ACTION STRATEGIES, New York, NY – **Analyst Intern**   2001 – Present

Selected among large pool of applicants to fulfill internship objectives for private provider of global intelligence to top business leaders and government officials. Conduct research for analysts on international affairs, compile daily reports on geopolitical developments, and monitor information sources to track specific events. Participate in daily analyst meetings to discuss ongoing developments and issues. **Key Contributions:**

- Improved research skills and **exceeded analysts' expectations** regarding quality and quantity of data.
- Recognized as key source of information and insight on world events, with **emphasis on affairs in China.**

ABC RESEARCH & DEVELOPMENT CENTER, Beijing, China – **Program Coordinator**   1997 – 2000

Planned and coordinated international research projects for high-level think tank providing wide range of consultancy services to China's State Board and partnering with other foundations and corporations. Organized international seminars and conferences, arranged academic research activities in conjunction with government agencies and companies, and translated research papers in meetings with distinguished foreign officials. Traveled extensively across Europe to liaise with agencies and foundations. **Key Contributions:**

- Oversaw **five successful joint economic research projects** sponsored by international organizations. Served as primary representative for projects, wrote winning proposals that secured finalization of deals, and implemented budget and research-planning functions for all endeavors. Key projects included:
    - *$1 million Urban Poverty Research Project*   - *$.8 million State-Owned Enterprise Reform in China*
    - *$.2 million Rural Development Research Project*
- Coordinated **14 international conferences and seminars** throughout China, maintaining smooth flow for all events and troubleshooting emergency situations to achieve successful presentations.
- Won **$2 million bid** from Asian Development Bank for research proposal based on urban poverty in China.

Resume Strategy: *Glen's effective profile and "Key Contributions" leave no doubt as to his readiness to advance to the next career step. His résumé is filled with high-impact details and still fits on one page.*

Rachel Miner

5789 West Cactus Court	*Available for Relocation &*	Residence: 480-555-5555
Scottsdale, AZ 85250	*Extensive Domestic / International Travel*	E-mail: rachel@resumepower.com

CAREER GOAL: CHRISTIAN CHILDREN'S FUND DEVELOPMENT DIRECTOR

Visionary, dedicated, and well-respected pastor with exemplary record of leading congregants, laity, and diverse community groups in church-life activities and grassroots efforts to affect positive change. Proven success strategizing multitiered initiatives to catapult church participation; revitalize stagnant programs; solicit and generate funding support; and build strong, sustainable, interfaith bonds and community partnerships.

Dynamic public speaker and motivator, skilled in developing and conducting persuasive presentations. Able to unite fractionalized groups, instill a shared sense of purpose, win enthusiastic support, and bridge gaps by making immediate human connections. Sensitive to issues of importance to diverse cultural, socioeconomic, and religious groups. First-hand knowledge of domestic and Third-World poverty and hunger issues, with passion for making a positive difference and deep concern for social justice issues. Solidly credentialed: DMin/MDIV/BA in Biblical studies/psychology.

AREAS OF EXPERTISE

- ❑ Fundraising & Fiscal Management
- ❑ Community Outreach & Leadership
- ❑ Public Speaking/Professional Presentations
- ❑ Congregation-Based Community Initiatives
- ❑ Cultural Sensitivity

- ❑ Special Event & Program Planning
- ❑ Advocacy
- ❑ Relationship Building & Consensus Building
- ❑ Strategic Partnerships & Alliances
- ❑ Tact & Diplomacy

PROFESSIONAL EXPERIENCE

WEST SCOTTSDALE PRESBYTERIAN CHURCH — Scottsdale, AZ
Minister, July 1993 to Present
Selected for congregant-appointed church leadership role within United Presbyterian system, with ultimate responsibility for preparation and leadership of weekly worship services, staff supervision, administration and fostering of church life, and the care and nurturing of 132-member congregation. Provide spiritual guidance and leadership through group and individual interaction and oversee the work and functioning of church boards/committees (e.g., church-governing administrative council, finance board, trustees committee, and staff/pastor/parish relations committee). Represent church in community of 170,000+, collaborating extensively with conference and community organizations to build partnerships, alliances, and enthusiastic support toward humanitarian efforts, volunteerism, and positive change. Selected Contributions:

- ❑ **Enjoyed repeated success leveraging talent for lifting parishioners out of complacent, indifferent, or apathetic "ruts"** through gentle persuasion and "infectious" enthusiasm.

- ❑ **Revitalized dwindling programs** (e.g., Bible study groups), **launched new initiatives** (e.g., Bread for the Hungry program), and **reenergized lagging enthusiasm** by encouraging/rewarding new ideas; interacting continuously with congregants, boards, Sunday school teachers, staff, and committees; and regularly incorporating visual aids, drama, and/or interaction into weekly services.

- ❑ **Contributed to a membership resurgence in numerous church-life activities** and programs and **a 200% increase** in regular church attendance.

- ❑ **Strengthened church's financial health** through improved management of financial resources/investments and orchestration of all aspects of on-target or goal-surpassing fundraising drives.

- ❑ **Initiated outreach to individuals without a church home** through local implementation of Phoenix program, a worldwide initiative encompassing videos and dinner discussions on a wide range of spiritual and religious topics.

- ❑ **Cultivated strong, interfaith bonds throughout community.** Furthered the growth of the church by ministering to people outside of its membership through hospital visits, casual conversation, and active participation in community programs and events.

Rachel Miner   480-555-5555 ▪ rachel@resumepower.com   Page Two

WEST SCOTTSDALE PRESBYTERIAN CHURCH — *(continued)*

❑ **Responded to national tragedies** (Columbine, 9/11) by uniting grieving residents from all age groups and all walks of life in prayer services.

❑ **Helped ease the depression of the holiday season** experienced by those mourning the death of a loved one through the development of an annual Holiday Memorial Service. Received extremely positive feedback from participants grateful for an avenue in which they could openly express their grief in a supportive and understanding environment.

❑ **Augmented connectional relationship between the church and the Western Conference** by winning greater involvement of the laity in church and conference activities.

FIRST UNITED PRESBYTERIAN CHURCH — Phoenix, AZ
Interim Associate Minister, June 1991 to February 1992

Recruited by Staff-Pastor-Parish Relations Committee to jointly fulfill (as part of two-person pastoral team) church leadership role during appointed pastor's sabbatical leave. Primary duties included visitation of church members, shut-ins, hospital patients, and newcomers and a shared role in worship and chapel-services leadership. Selected Contributions:

❑ **Eased period of transition for congregation,** helping to keep church on track spiritually and financially through worship, committee work, and planning for the future.

❑ **Helped orient visitors** to the church and incorporated new members into daily church life.

BREAD FOR THE WORLD INTERNATIONAL *(Nondenominational Faith Mission)* — Argentina/Peru/Bolivia
Missionary / Area Hostess, 1977 to 1985

Planned and coordinated efforts to house and feed visiting work teams from the U.S. Wrote articles and letters for mission board describing work and detailing needs to supporters. In charge of supplies purchasing/inventory, meal preparation, and development/execution of presentations outlining the work of churches in the U.S. Selected Contributions:

❑ **Utilized strengths in persuasive written communications** to advocate for and successfully secure badly needed fund increases from U.S./Canadian supporters, used to improve student nutrition, kitchen equipment, and dorm facilities.

❑ **Demonstrated unwavering commitment** to Bread for the World goals, overcoming risk to personal safety and severe logistical challenges while traveling to purchase supplies in highly volatile, remote, mountainous areas.

EDUCATION & CREDENTIALS

PHOENIX THEOLOGICAL SEMINARY – Phoenix, AZ – **Doctor of Ministry,** 2000
Dissertation: "Spiritual Growth through Volunteerism and Community Service"

ARIZONA STATE UNIVERSITY SCHOOL OF THEOLOGY – Tempe, AZ – **Master of Divinity,** 1993
Merit Scholarship Award Recipient (for academic achievement), 1990 to 1993

CENTRAL AZ COLLEGE – Coolridge, AZ – **Bachelor of Arts in Biblical Studies,** Dual Major in **Psychology,** 1989

Licensure: Ordained Elder in the United Presbyterian Church (1997)

Professional Development: Basic Spanish (Instituto de Leñgua Española – Buenos Aires), Facilitator Training (Phoenix, AZ)

CONTACT

480-555-5555 ▪ rachel@resumepower.com

Resume Strategy: *Rachel has a very specific organization she is targeting with her resume, so she mentions the agency name right in her resume's "Career Goal" title. Her profile and "Areas of Expertise" sections communicate her top qualifications and relevant experience, which are further detailed in her "Professional Experience" section. Rachel ends the resume with a strong "Education & Credentials" section.*

Lulu Walker

12 Boardwalk Ave
Reno, NV 89509

Phone: (775) 123-4567
lulu@resumepower.com

PROGRAM DIRECTOR
Specialized experience within recreational, social, educational, and cross-cultural settings

Inspirational and results-oriented manager, recognized for outstanding performance within team-oriented, sales, and academic environments. Consistently meet and surpass organizational goals and motivate team members by providing guidance, training, mentoring, and support. Recruited to several positions for ability to build productive teams, resolve conflicts, and enhance program's image. Adept at assessing problems and instituting long-lasting solutions. Designed and implemented programs that have improved operational efficiencies, profit margins, employee morale, and sales revenues.

AREAS OF ACCOMPLISHMENT

- Team Building / Leadership
- Project Management
- Budget Planning / Cost Control
- Motivational Strategies
- Conflict Resolution
- Problem Resolution
- Training and Development
- Sales and Marketing
- Public / Community Relations
- Fundraising / Sponsorships

EDUCATION

RENO COLLEGE — Reno, NV

MBA, Business, July 2002 (GPA: 4.0)
BA, Physical Education and German, 1983

CAREER HIGHLIGHTS

RENO YMCA — Reno, NV

Senior Director, Swim Team, 1994 to present

Member of senior management team, with full oversight for swim-team operations. Recruited to build team, train coaches and swimmers, resolve fiscal and administrative problems, and elevate awareness of swimming sports in a traditionally ball-oriented community. *Key Accomplishments:*

- **Expanded team membership from 28 to 120,** with members representing diverse cultural and socioeconomic backgrounds.

- **Eliminated $30,000 deficit** and created completely self-supporting program.

- **Developed and currently oversee finance committee** that administers scholarship funds, endowments for new programs, and promotional programs with local business to attract potential donors.

- **Designed comprehensive parent handbook,** which encourages parental involvement and provides behavioral and performance guidelines. The handbook is used as the model for other teams.

- **Created an environment that fosters athletic, academic, and social consciousness,** achieving 100% college-acceptance rate on swimming and/or academic scholarships.

- **Built winning team,** with members achieving recognition at YMCA national and state championships.

- Voted **Reno Swim Association Coach of the Year** (1999) out of 20 coaches.

Lulu Walker

Resume — Page Two

CAREER HIGHLIGHTS (continued)

TRAVELPROS — Reno, NV

Travel Consultant, 1991 to 1994

Provided travel services to a diverse, international clientele. Promoted destinations with in the Caribbean, and utilized online booking system to develop itineraries and manage accounts. *Key Accomplishments:*

- **Achieved highest sales volume** out of all consultants.
- **Built account portfolio** contributing to a 20% increase in annual sales.

CARIBBEAN TOURIST OFFICE — Reno, NV

Senior Sales Representative, 1987 to 1991

Created promotional and marketing strategies, supported other consultants, and received training on database and account management systems. *Key Accomplishments:*

- **Designed and instituted seminar** to teach agents on territory management and expansion.
- **Developed several innovative and well-received promotions,** including "It's Time for the Caribbean" which appeared in travel and information shows and tied in with baseball season.
- **Featured on television shows,** including "Islands in the Sun" (public television network).
- **Personally appeared on several radio shows** at national stations, including KISS-FM.
- **Named Salesperson of the Year** (1990) out of 500 representatives.

PROFESSIONAL DEVELOPMENT

- Reno College: **Head Swim Coach** - Built a nationally recognized swimming program, integrating academics, athletics, and community involvement into core of program, 1994 to 2000
- American Swim Coaches Association: **Leadership and Administration, Time Management, Foundations of Coaching, Physiology of Coaching,** 1994 to present
- YMCA: **Group Work,** 2002; **Volunteerism,** 2002
- Dun and Bradstreet: **Customers Relations Skills,** 2000

AFFILIATIONS

- Police Crime Control Plan Group
- Reno Chiefs Club
- Special Olympics
- Invest in Youth (YMCA)

- American Swim Coaches Association
- College Swim Coaches Association
- Kappa Delta Phi
- Phi Kappa Phi

SPECIALIZED SKILLS

Foreign Languages: Fluent in Dutch, German, and English; basic French and Spanish

Computers: MS Word, Business Manager, Team Manager, Workout Manager, TransLink Translation Software, WordPerfect, Windows 2000

Resume Strategy: *Lulu's resume needed to show her business savvy to help her transition from swim team director to a general program director position. Lulu's summary touts her dedication to organizational goals and leadership achievements. Her work history downplays sports achievements, while emphasizing business-related accomplishments such as expanded membership, cost reduction, and board involvement.*

25
Internships/Apprenticeships

ENGINEERING ADVISOR TO MANAGEMENT CONSULTING—
SEEKING INTERNSHIP WITH MBA PROGRAM

Georgia Rush

12 Highlander Way
Washington, D.C. 20006

(202) 123-4567
georgia@resumepower.com

Management Consulting / Business & Financial Analysis / Venture Capitalism

Highly motivated business professional with experience in technical project management and academic foundation in business management. Continually recognized by senior management for contributions to organization, ability to improve procedures, and skill at revitalizing lagging operations. Effective communicator, comfortable interacting with and delivering presentations to staff at all levels. In acknowledgment of solid judgment, analytical, and research skills, selected as an internal auditor, a position usually offered to those with far more seniority.

Areas of expertise encompass:

- **Project Management**
- **Team Building/ Leadership**

- **Training & Development**
- **Quality Control & Auditing**

- **Operational Procedures - Design & Implementation**
- **Research & Analysis**

Education

THE GEORGE WASHINGTON UNIVERSITY SCHOOL OF BUSINESS – Washington, D.C.

MBA program, degree anticipated in August 2001

- Major: **Finance/Management**
- GPA: **3.925/4.000**

NEW YORK UNIVERSITY – New York, NY

Bachelor of Engineering, Major in Mechanical Engineering, May 1986

- Merit Scholarship (full tuition)

Career Highlights

XYZ INTERNATIONAL – Washington, D.C.
Engineering Advisor – Pressure Technology Codes and Standards, 1995 to 2000

Led the implementation of new and updated codes and standards, with oversight for all phases of project lifecycle development. Gathered resources and input from experts and conducted due diligence regarding antitrust and tort liability, protection of organizational marks, and infringement on copyright and patent rights. Coordinated multiple projects simultaneously and monitored for productivity and effectiveness. Trained and oriented new personnel. **Key Contributions:**

- Assigned to oversee high priority major codes and standards projects. Refocused teams and encouraged production of standards that could command higher fees, continuing department's position as lead revenue generator.

- Revived inactive codes and standards committees. Drove effort to update archaic codes and standards, which improved overall industry safety and reinforced organization's leading position.

- Selected to serve as internal auditor on several major projects. Audited Accreditation and Certification committees and programs, including ISO 9000.

- Requested to deliver presentations to senior staff within and outside of organization. Consistently the most organized and skilled at creating a cohesive and effective presentation.

Georgia Rush

Resume - Page Two

XYZ INTERNATIONAL (continued...)
Senior Engineering Administrator – Pressure Technology Codes and Standards, 1992 to 1995
Engineering Administrator – Pressure Technology Codes and Standards, 1989 to 1992

Promoted to senior engineering administrator to develop and publish engineering codes and standards. Served as liaison between industry and code developers, international standards organizations, and governmental agencies with regard to compliance issues. **Key Contributions:**

- Led the development of over 40 codes and standards, from inception through revision, interpretation, and publication.

- Involved in successful appeal to international standards organization against a European firm, which attempted to impose requirements that would be detrimental to American companies conducting business abroad. Compiled research and provided technical expertise in preparation of arguments.

ENGINEERING ASSOCIATES – New York, NY
Mechanical Engineer – Heating, Ventilation and Air Conditioning (HVAC), 1987 to 1988

Conducted energy and cost-analysis studies. Created and implemented engineering software for load calculations and energy studies. Assisted in the design of HVAC systems, using groundbreaking Computer Aided Design (CAD) system.

Licenses ▪ Affiliations ▪ Presentations

- Certified Internal Auditor, Washington, D.C., 1994
- Certified Intern Engineer, New York State, 1986
- Member, American Society of Mechanical Engineers, 1985 to Present
- Presenter, "International Standardization," National Institute of Building Standards (NIBS), 1994
- Presenter, "International Standardization," National Conference, 1994

Skills

Computers
Office Software: Microsoft Word, Excel, and PowerPoint; WordPerfect; Lotus 1-2-3
Programming: Fortran; CAD; BASIC

Foreign Languages
Hebrew: Conversational (basic)
Spanish: Conversational (basic)

(202) 123-4567 ▪ georgia@resumepower.com

Resume Strategy: *Following Georgia's resume title and profile, where she articulates her career goal and major strengths, an "Areas of Expertise" section allows hiring managers to quickly glean the key competencies she offers. One of Georgia's strongest credentials is her upcoming MBA, so she places "Education" before "Career Highlights." She lists her most relevant certification in internal auditing first in the "Licenses/Affiliations/Presentations" section, and groups computer and foreign language skills together to finish the resume.*

WAITER (POSITION NOT INCLUDED ON RESUME)
TO ART MUSEUM CONSERVATION INTERNSHIP

Abdul Ahmid

2216 Princeton Ave. ■ St. Cloud, MN 56377
Phone: (320) 555-5555 ■ abdul@resumepower.com

GOAL: ART MUSEUM CONSERVATION INTERNSHIP

Meticulous and talented artist seeking an internship in an art conservation center or museum. Offer a passion for conservationism, deep appreciation for the arts and history, experience as an art director and film/TV production designer, and a formal education in fine arts, art history, and science. Fine manual dexterity demonstrated during such endeavors as painting, drawing, sculpture, and photography.

Recognized for tenacity in achieving objectives when performing detail-oriented, art-related construction projects. Utilize natural interpersonal and communication skills while networking effectively with all levels of staff and clients. Able to make sound judgment calls and accurately assess daily priorities within overall organizational vision. Fluent in Farsi, good Spanish comprehension, and knowledge of Latin. Have traveled extensively throughout Europe and the Middle East.

ARTISTIC TALENTS

Painting:	Acrylic and Oil on Canvas and Wood
Drawing:	Pencil, Charcoal, Pastel, Ink
Printmaking:	Etchings, Mono Prints, Linoleum Cuts
Sculpture:	Clay, Limestone, Sheet Metal, Glass
Photography:	Black & White Development and Printing

PRODUCTION EXPERIENCE

Clerks (Feature Film – Comedy) 2001   **Production Designer**

- Successful in translating director's vision of film atmosphere and mood into actual production life. Completed project well within time and budget constraints.
- Utilized available resources to achieve envisioned ambiance. Secured and arranged furniture and decorative fixtures while strategically applying appropriate paints to reinforce context.
- Oversaw production design team through all phases of project, from concept to implementation.
- Clearly conveyed vision of artistic endeavors to all department heads.

The Cars: You're Just What I Needed (Music Video) 2001   **Art Director**

- Successfully preserved atmosphere of film site's historical location (the French Quarter in New Orleans) while incorporating existing architectural and decorative features.
- Implemented director's vision for theme change by painting several murals and backdrops throughout various stages of video.

The Bully (Television Movie – Aired on ABC's "After-School Specials") 2001   **Art Director**

- Offered valuable assistance to production designer in all areas of project implementation and set design. Met production objectives and stayed within budget constraints.
- Researched strategies for production design.
- Directed construction crew in the arrangement of set scenery.

Abdul Ahmid

Dark Avenger (CD-ROM) 2000   **On Set Dresser**
- Maintained logical continuity of set by accurately documenting each shoot with photographs and notes.
- Constructed sci-fi gadgetry for actors to use during filming.
- Created atmosphere that supported film's overall theme as well as special effect/game elements necessary for creation of CD-ROM.

Samurai Dragon (Feature Film - Martial Arts) 2000   **On Set Dresser**
- Replicated battle swords to correspond with historical context in which story occurred.
- Ensured backdrops and props were continually painted and prepared for set.

The Little Match Girl (Feature Film) 1999   **On Set Dresser**
- Assisted efforts for set construction utilizing a variety of materials to include aluminum sheets, wood, tile, and glass to enable smooth integration with building's architectural style.
- Ensured arrangement of interior and exterior scenery corresponded with position changes of cameras, maintaining logical continuity of changing camera angels.

Lizzie Borden (Television Movie) 1998   **Assistant Art Dept. Coordinator**
- Organized and catalogued photographic visuals relating to objects and locations of the 1890s, facilitating access to Art Department's visual resources.

Donaldson Ltd. 1996 – 1997   **Retail Sales Assistant**
- Sold antiques while maintaining upscale international merchandise.
- Gained familiarity with antiques inventory and met decorators' requests.

EDUCATION & AFFILIATIONS

Concordia College, St. Paul, MN, 1996
Bachelor of Arts in Fine Arts (Dean's List, Spring 1996)

Minnesota Historical Society, 2000 – Present
Preserve and protect natural sites and buildings of historical significance and collect materials pertaining to local history.

COMPUTERS

MS Word and Windows 2000

PORTFOLIO AVAILABLE ON REQUEST

Available to Relocate Internationally for Internship Opportunity
Phone: (320) 555-5555 ▪ E-mail: abdul@resumepower.com

Resume Strategy: *Abdul's television and film production art background is leveraged to maximum benefit on his resume and his profile explains its relevance to his goal of a museum internship. He prominently highlights his artistic abilities and does not mention his current job as a waiter since he has only held this position for a few weeks and it is not relevant to his career goal.*

BRUCE LEVINE

689 Mission Hills Dr., Apt. 5 ▪ Astoria, NY 11105
blevine@resumepower.com ▪ Home: (631) 555-5555 ▪ Cell: (631) 555-5551

Experienced business professional seeking graduate school admittance to further career-change goals and fulfill passion for international politics, economics, and information management/research. Backed by BS in physical science and extensive, hands-on experience in quantitative/qualitative research, large-scale project management, and cross-functional team leadership. Strong analytical foundation, with reputation for insightful market/competitor analysis, advanced organizational abilities, and articulate communication skills. Internationally traveled, knowledgeable in foreign business protocols, and technologically fluent.

PROFESSIONAL EXPERIENCE

ACE. CORP. – *Technology consulting firm, software reseller, and solutions provider* – New York, NY 1999 to present

Senior Product Manager, Engineering Operations, 6/99 to present

Direct all OEM partner-support programs and initiatives with industry giants (Dell, Sun Microsystems) to sustain and strengthen Ace market share. Perform revenue, market penetration, and competitive research/analysis to provide senior executives with key information contributing to future-focused decisions. Lead product enhancements through authorship of marketing requirement documents and product roadmaps for software engineering team.

Key Accomplishments:

▪ **Founded and managed Ace Alliance Partner Program (AAPP).** Equipped developers and integrators with the essential tools, information, and support needed to test and promote partner products with Ace software; enabled Ace to offer business-generating discounts; and added strategic partners to Ace's arsenal that facilitated market penetration.

▪ **Completed meticulous, two-year analysis** of OEM revenues received through Dell partnership, subsequently used as the basis for new market segmentation strategy.

▪ **Achieved co-synchronous (Dell/Ace) product release,** a win-win outcome that completely resolved four-to-six week development lag times and saved Dell over $180K annually in manufacturing costs.

▪ Proposed promotional package using Sun Microsystems hardware and Ace software that **netted over $2 million in royalties for Ace after one year** (surpassing target by more than 50%).

▪ **Recognized for "Outstanding Partner Management"** (2000 & 2001) and launch of new marketing Web site.

DELL COMPUTER CORP. – *Premier computer systems company with $32 billion in revenue* – Austin, TX 1996 to 1999

Senior Project Manager, Customer Support, 9/97 to 6/99; **Project Manager,** Customer Support, 5/96 to 9/97

Rapidly promoted to oversee large-scale customer-support projects, with accountability for product lifecycle management. Performed in-depth phase reviews and determined "go/no-go" status throughout each stage of product development and launch, guiding cross-functional teams across engineering, operations, and support.

Key Accomplishments:

▪ **Co-authored in-depth research/recommendations report** to facilitate global product support strategy improvements. Traveled extensively to evaluate support operations and glean insights from call center and logistics staff based in Australia, Asia, Latin America, and Mexico.

▪ **Played a key role in establishing new Vendor Integration Program (VIP) partners.** Initiated, secured, and managed agreement with partner that provided cooperative handling of technical-support issues.

▪ **Strategized complex, worldwide, 24x7 support-system infrastructure** for multiple products, ensuring multilingual call center support (English, French, Spanish, German, Chinese, Japanese, Korean).

EDUCATION & TRAINING

BS in Information Technology, 1996 – TEXAS CHRISTIAN UNIVERSITY – Fort Worth, TX

Recent Training: Business Communications within Asia/Pac; Market-Focused Organizations; Project Management

Available for travel and relocation ▪ Technical resume/skills on request

Resume Strategy: *Bruce proves his worthiness for graduate school admission in international politics by emphasizing his background in global project management and international business. His profile articulates his objective and he supports his admission candidacy by providing evidence of his leadership, research, and academic achievements.*

MARKETING INTERN TO HR INTERN

Lauralee Wilkenson

14 Elmira Way ■ Palm Coast, Florida 32164
(386) 123-4567 ■ lauralee@resumepower.com

JOB TARGET	HUMAN RESOURCES INTERNSHIP ■ HR ASSISTANT
PROFILE	**Recent business graduate** eager to begin career as a human resources professional. Proven track record of excellent performance for part-time employers while concurrently enrolled in college. Experienced developing rapport with individuals from diverse cultural and socioeconomic backgrounds. Well-regarded interpersonal skills – skilled in diffusing highly charged situations by using articulate, tactful persuasion. Known for organization, follow-through, and enthusiastic teamwork. Willingly volunteer for weekend/evening projects to get the job done. Readily learn and master new technology.
EDUCATION	UNIVERSITY OF FLORIDA – Gainesville, Florida **Bachelor of Science in Business**, 5/2002 ■ Dean's List: Fall 1998, Fall 2000
SKILLS	■ Confidential Record Keeping ■ Relationship Management (Customers/Vendors/Colleagues) ■ Cultural Sensitivity ■ Diplomacy & Discretion ■ Professional Correspondence ■ Technically Savvy: Word/Excel/PowerPoint/Outlook/Windows 2000 ■ Team Building & Training ■ Data Entry & Database Operations ■ Critical Thinking ■ Front Desk Reception
HR ACTIVITIES	**Member,** SOCIETY FOR HUMAN RESOURCE MANAGEMENT (SHRM), 2001 – Present **Currently enrolled** in Daytona Beach Community College's HUMAN RESOURCES DEVELOPMENT (HRD) PROGRAM (evening classes).
EXPERIENCE (Concurrent with full-time college enrollment)	ACTION FITNESS CENTER – Palm Coast, Florida **Marketing Intern,** 1/2002 – 5/2002 Selected for sought-after marketing internship from numerous applicants. Assisted in promoting individual memberships and corporate fitness/wellness programs. Key Accomplishments: ■ Created and distributed promotional letter targeting 200+ area physicians. Efforts resulted in penetrating new market and winning doctor-referred clientele. ■ Developed user-friendly automated tool in Excel to provide center with first-ever quick and easy reference of hundreds of businesses for future targeted marketing campaigns. ■ Cold-called local businesses and achieved an 80% success rate securing requests for fitness program information. YMCA PALM COAST – Palm Coast, Florida **Front Desk Attendant,** 8/2000 – 4/2001 [Part-Time Employment] Assisted over 3,000 YMCA members, answered phones, sold memberships, handled cash transactions, maintained confidential client files, and monitored payments. Coordinated workout schedules and special events. Ensured smooth, on-time operations for all classes. Key Accomplishments: ■ Volunteered many evening hours beyond scheduled work time to help ensure timely completion of major facility renovation. Recognized by management for going "above and beyond" job duties. ■ Adeptly handled emergency situations and confrontations between members. WAL-MART – Palm Coast, Florida **Sales Floor Associate,** 9/1997 – 5/1999 [Part-Time Employment]

Resume Strategy: : *Lauralee includes her HR job/internship target and then backs up her key qualifications in a "Profile" section. Inclusion of a bulleted "Skills" section draws attention to skills Lauralee developed through part-time work experiences. Her dedication to a career in HR is further demonstrated by an "HR Activities" section that includes industry training and membership in a professional HR organization.*

Appendix A:
Online Resources for
Career Changers

Please note: Due to the constantly changing nature of the Internet, some of these Web site links might have changed since publication.

America's Job Bank: www.ajb.dni.us—Department of Labor's job site where users can search for jobs and submit their resumes. Site allows registered users to conduct customized job searches.

Best Jobs in the U.S. Today—www.bestjobsusa.com—An employment search engine. Search job openings in the United States, read employment news, and peruse a career guide.

CareerBuilder.com—www.careerbuilder.com—Provides jobs, career advice, columns, and tips to get ahead in today's workplace. Job seekers may search newspaper listings by state and job openings with leading employers.

CareerCast—www.careercast.com—Fill out a brief form to submit your resume, then search their database for available jobs. Search by employer Web sites or Usenet jobs.

CareerShop—www.careershop.com—Internet site for the computer generation. Learn about job opportunities, training, and career management.

CareerSite—www.careersite.com—Create a profile and then conduct a confidential job search.

Department of Labor—For help with job descriptions, the Department of Labor's *Dictionary of Occupational Titles (DOT)—http://www.oalj.dol.gov/libdot.htm, Occupational Outlook Handbook (OOH)—http://www.bls.gov/oco,* and *O*NET—http://online.onetcenter.org* are searchable online. Also visit the *Bureau of Labor Statistics—http://stats.bls.gov* to research data, the economy, surveys and programs, publications, regional information, and jobs.

FlipDog—www.flipdog.com—Offers job seekers comprehensive resources for finding a job online.

GO Jobs—www.gojobs.com—Search the job database by region, occupation, and employment type. Post your resume to their database.

HotJobs—www.hotjobs.com—Find a job by location, job type, or company, and browse their library of company profiles. Site also offers message boards and job seeker resources.

JobBank USA—www.jobbankusa.com—Job seekers may visit a comprehensive directory of Internet employment resources, including a Job Metasearch page that accesses a large employment database.

Job-Center.com—www.job-center.com—Job seekers may post resumes and search openings.

Monster—www.monster.com—The world's top online career resource, matching job seekers with employers, providing a wealth of career advice and resources, and offering a top-notch career networking community.

Monster Career Changers—http://content.monster.com/careerchangers—Comprehensive content and interactive tools designed for career changers.

Net-Temps—www.americasemployers.com—Resources for a comprehensive job search, including job search tips, a resume bank, advertised positions, a company database, networking, and online chat.

ProHire—www.prohire.com—Job board, resume bank, and career center for job seekers.

Salary.com—www.salary.com—Generate a personalized salary report and learn your market value.

SearchBug—http://searchbug.com/jobs—Search for jobs at top sites, including Monster, Yahoo!, America's Job Bank, Dice, Net-Temps, CareerBuilder, Hot Jobs, Computerwork.com, and Best Jobs USA.

TrueCareers—www.truecareers.com—Job seekers may post resumes, search jobs, learn about job fairs, and research companies. Contains career-related articles and newsletter.

Vault—www.vaultreports.com—Job seekers may browse jobs and sign up to receive e-mail notification of matching jobs. Provides an excellent resource for researching companies (history, goals, how to get hired) and a water-cooler/gossip message board to get the inside scoop from current or former employees.

Yahoo! Careers—http://careers.yahoo.com—Comprehensive employment site, where job seekers can search for jobs, research companies, and post their resumes.

RESUME DISTRBIUTION SERVICES

Executive Agent—*www.executiveagent.com*—Kennedy Information's resume distribution service that targets executive recruiters in your field.

Pro/File Research—*www.profileresearch.com*—Direct mail, e-mail, and fax campaigns to companies and recruiters.

ResumeRabbit—*www.resumerabbit.com*—Posts your resume on 75 career sites.

ResumeZapper—*www.resumezapper.com*—Sends your resume to thousands of recruiters.

ResumeBlaster—*www.resumeblaster.com*—Sends your resume to thousands of recruiters.

ResumeBroadcaster—*www.resumebroadcaster.com*—Submits your resume to recruiters.

Your Missing Link—*www.yourmissinglink.com*—E-mail your resume to companies, executive recruiters, and venture-capital firms.

Appendix B:
Resume Writers/Contributors, Resume Associations, and Career Coaches Web Sites

PROFESSIONAL RESUME WRITERS/BOOK CONTRIBUTORS

Karen Hofferber, M.Ed., CPRW
Advanced Career Systems, Inc.
McKinney, TX 75070
Phone: 800-203-0551
Email: Karen@ResumePower.com
URL: *www.ResumPower.com*

Kim Isaacs, NCRW, CPRW
Advanced Career Systems, Inc.
Doylestown, PA 18901
Phone: (800) 203-0551
Email: Kim@ResumePower.com
URL: *www.ResumePower.com*

Judy Friedler, NCRW, CPRW, JCTC, CCM
CareerPro International
Buffalo, NY 14216

Phone: (866) 433-6033

Email: info@rezcoach.com

URL: *www.rezcoach.com*

Resumes appear in Chapters 8 and 14

Murray Mann and Jolene Elliott

Global Career Strategies

Newport Beach, CA 92659

Phone: (949) 548-5520

Email: *info@resumecompass.com*

URL: *www.resumecompass.com*

Resume appears in Chapter 23

Marty Weitzman, NCRW, CPRW, JCTC

Gilbert Career Resumes Ltd.

New York, NY 10016

Phone: (212) 661-6878

Email: *gilcareer@aol.com*

URL: *www.resumepro.com*

Resume appears in Chapter 9

RESUME WRITING ASSOCIATIONS

National Resume Writers' Association (NRWA)—*www.nrwa.com*

Professional Association of Resume Writers and Career Coaches (PARWCC)—*www.parw.com*

Professional Resume Writing and Research Association (PRWRA)—*www.prwra.com*

CAREER COUNSELORS AND COACHES

Association of Job Search Trainers (AJST)—*www.ajst.org*

Career Masters Institute (CMI)—*www.cminstitute.com*

International Association of Career Management Professionals (IACMP)—*www.iacmp.org*

International Coach Federation (ICF)—*www.coachfederation.org*

National Board for Certified Counselors (NBCC)—*http://www.nbcc.org*

Index

About the Authors

Kim Isaacs, CPRW, NCRW, is Monster's resume expert and director of ResumePower.com, a resume writing company serving job changers across the globe.

Karen Hofferber, CPRW, is senior resume writer for ResumePower.com. She has also served as Monster's resume advisor, where she wrote articles on resume writing and provided advice to thousands of job seekers.